THE ANTHOLOGY OF BABEL

Before you start to read this book, take this moment to think about making a donation to punctum books, an independent non-profit press,

@ https://punctumbooks.com/support/

If you're reading the e-book, you can click on the image below to go directly to our donations site. Any amount, no matter the size, is appreciated and will help us to keep our ship of fools afloat. Contributions from dedicated readers will also help us to keep our commons open and to cultivate new work that can't find a welcoming port elsewhere. Our adventure is not possible without your support.

Vive la Open Access.

Fig. 1. Hieronymus Bosch, *Ship of Fools* (1490–1500)

THE ANTHOLOGY OF BABEL. Copyright © 2020 by the editor and authors. This work carries a Creative Commons BY-NC-SA 4.0 International license, which means that you are free to copy and redistribute the material in any medium or format, and you may also remix, transform and build upon the material, as long as you clearly attribute the work to the authors (but not in a way that suggests the authors or punctum books endorses you and your work), you do not use this work for commercial gain in any form whatsoever, and that for any remixing and transformation, you distribute your rebuild under the same license. http://creativecommons.org/licenses/by-nc-sa/4.0/

First published in 2020 by dead letter office, BABEL Working Group, an imprint of punctum books, Earth, Milky Way.
https://punctumbooks.com

The BABEL Working Group is a collective and desiring-assemblage of scholar–gypsies with no leaders or followers, no top and no bottom, and only a middle. BABEL roams and stalks the ruins of the post-historical university as a multiplicity, a pack, looking for other roaming packs with which to cohabit and build temporary shelters for intellectual vagabonds. We also take in strays.

ISBN-13: 978-1-950192-47-2 (print)
ISBN-13: 978-1-950192-48-9 (ePDF)

DOI: 10.21983/P3.0254.1.00

LCCN: 2019951803
Library of Congress Cataloging Data is available from the Library of Congress

Book Design: Vincent W.J. van Gerven Oei
Cover Image: Gustave Doré, "The Confusion of Tongues" (1865)

HIC SVNT MONSTRA

The Anthology of Babel

Edited by Ed Simon

Contents

Labyrinths of Imagined Literature
ED SIMON
15

The Body-Loving Philosophers
STEPHEN DAVID ENGEL
27

Encounters with the Unknown and Manifestations of Fear:
Discerning the Purpose of the *Great Darkness Text*
SETH LIGO
49

The *Romance of the Minotaur* Reconsidered
KATHERINE MCLOONE
73

"The Very Globe Came Undone": Ontological Negation in
Enoch Campion's *The Tragedy of Dracule*
ED SIMON
91

"All My Heroines Must Like Him":
Circumscribing the Spouse in Jane Austen's *Plan of a Husband*
TOM ZILLE
101

Linus Withold and the Birth of the Rhizomatic Text
ERIC D. LEHMAN
119

Eighth Draft of "First-Order Variables & Repression:
Oedipal Relations in 'The Sandwich' by Rubiard Whimp" by
James Lichtenstein
AUSTIN SARFAN
139

Under Imaginary Skies:
Scholarly Variations on *The Rainberg Variations*
REED JOHNSON
157

Pedro Somar, traductor de Ramned, autor del Quijote
DAVID BEN-MERRE & RAUL NEIRA
173

El fin del mundo:
Uncharted Territory of Ernest Hemingway's Fiction
MARIA-JOSEE MENDEZ
197

The Unfinished and Lost Texts of Richard A. Conlan: An Examination of an Obsession, by Mark Conlan, Ph.D.
INTRODUCED AND ANNOTATED BY JAMES SPEESE, PH.D.
215

Stirring the Sentient Dust: Marie-Rose Souci's *The Grey Moth*
CLAIRE DAIGLE
235

Traduttore, Traditore:
Authorial Inconsistencies in the Works of Redondo Panza
JULIA COURSEY
251

The Purists: Cooperative Fundamentalism
and Aesthetic Dogmatics
MATTHEW NEWCOMB
261

From Paratext to Text, Scholar to Ragpicker: Inverted Criticism
and the "Heidi B. Morton Papers and Library"
RYAN MARNANE
279

"What Else Was There To Do?": Fat Futurity and the Limits of
Narrative Imagination in *Desolation*
EM K. FALK
305

"All My Life My Writing Is":
The Auto-Bio-Graph of Smalloysius F.: Being Told by Itself
STEPHEN HOCK
323

The Gravity of the Situation
BRUCE KRAJEWSKI
345

Darkness Made Visible: Eamonn Peters on Imagined Literature
ED SIMON
365

Acknowledgments

My gratitude to the organizers of the 48th annual Northeastern Modern Language Association for their support of my panel that was the germinating seed for this project, as well as to all of our presenters in Baltimore. Additional thanks must be given to publishers Vincent W.J. van Gerven Oei and Eileen A. Fradenburg Joy, and to their vision at punctum books. A special thanks must of course be given to all of the contributors in *The Anthology of Babel*, for their hard work and their willingness to commit to an unconventional project (and to everyone's family and friends, who so often constitute an invisible aspect of academic labor). Finally, a special acknowledgement to those past masters of the form, the immaculate Thomas Browne and the divine Jorge Luis Borges, who supplied the inspiration for this volume.

INTRODUCTION

Labyrinths of Imagined Literature

Ed Simon

Sir Thomas Browne possessed veritable shelves of non-existent books.[1] The sadly under-read seventeenth-century prose master oft sat in his Norwich garden and contemplated that infinitely long syllabus which does not exist in our universe. That list includes the epic that Ovid, exiled to the Black Sea's shores by Caesar Augustus, wrote in the indigenous "Getick Language," which is as lost to history as the Roman's poem. Or the letter written to Cicero by his brother, in which the latter described the "State and Manners of the Britains of that Age." Of course there is the ancient Persian king Mithridates' treatise on dream interpretation, and even more stunningly the Stoic philosopher Seneca's lost epistles to Saint Paul.

Not only were these books unavailable to Browne, but the "Antiquities, Pictures and Rarities of several kinds, scarce or never seen by any man now living" were similarly inaccessible, for the simple fact that all of them were the products of the physician's mind. Browne's conceptual Renaissance *Wunderkammer*, his "Wonder cabinet," included paintings of an ancient

---

1 An excellent contemporary treatment of the author is Hugh Aldersey-Williams's *In Search of Sir Thomas Browne: The Life and Afterlife of the Seventeenth Century's Most Inquiring Mind* (New York: W.W. Norton Company, 2015).

submarine, a battle scene of Tamerlane fighting in the moonlight, and artifacts like a "neat Crucifix made out of the cross Bone of a Frogs Head."[2] Such fantastic wonders are recorded in his remarkable 1684 pamphlet *Musaeum Clausum, or Bibliotheca Abscondita* (that is roughly the *Closed Museum,* or the *Hidden Library*), which scholar Claire Preston has admiringly described as being both "playful and melancholy," a testament to Browne's "feelings about the unavailability of precious intellectual treasure."[3]

An admiring Herman Melville once accurately described Browne as a "crack'd archangel," and it's easy to see why that old sailor, with his love of ephemera and scholarly debris, had an affection for the Restoration author, whose interests ranged through literature, religion, and nascent anthropology.[4] In his 1643 *Religio Medici,* Browne explicated his humane, tolerant, and most of all curious worldview, writing that "We carry with us the wonders, we seek without us: There is all *Africa,* and her prodigies in us."[5] Not just Africa, but the entire world as well, the enormity of those catalogues and compendiums collected in his era of wonder where cracked Anglo-Saxon pots and bits of shells shared space with incunabula and parrot feathers to attest to the sheer glowing, transcendent enchantment of everything.

And as *Musaeum Clausum* demonstrates, not just the entire world, but all of the imagined universes as well. For ours is a creation so over-stuffed with wonder, where "every man is a *Microcosm,* and carries the whole world about him" that we also hold

---

[2] Thomas Browne, *Musaeum Clausum, or Bibliotheca Abscondita* (London, 1684).

[3] Claire Preston, "Lost Libraries," *The Public Domain Review,* February 20, 2012, https://publicdomainreview.org/2012/02/20/lost-libraries/.

[4] Ed Simon, "*Religio Medici and Urne-Buriall,* by Sir Thomas Browne. Edited by Stephen Greenblatt and Ramie Targoff," *This Rough Magic: A Peer-Reviewed, Academic, Online Journal Dedicated to the Teaching of Medieval & Renaissance Literature,* December 2013, http://www.thisroughmagic.org/simon%20review.html.

[5] Thomas Browne, *The Major Works: Religio Medici, Hydrotophia, The Garden of Cyprus, A Letter to a Friend, and Christian Morals,* ed. C.A. Patrides (New York: Penguin Classics, 1977), 78.

within our souls not just that which is, but that which could ever be. Which is why despite the sheer exuberance of his prose in works like *Religio Medici* or in *Hydriotaphia,* or *Urne Burial,* his melancholic masterpiece concerning the consideration of death, it is rather that strange little pamphlet *Bibliotheca Abscondita* which most fully holds my heart, for it's there that his mind joyfully enumerates epics unwritten and tomes unpenned, having journeyed to that undiscovered library and returned with intimations of possibility. Browne was a cosmonaut in what I call "imagined literature," that is fiction which produces fictions that are in turn fictions, or less tautologically, the practice and method of interpreting books which never were.

There aren't as many modern Browne's as there should be; those who gather a bouquet of non-existent verse, a bushel of imagined novels. I've tried to correct that with this compendium that I have named *The Anthology of Babel.* Having first planned this project during the final days of my PhD program, it is perhaps congruent with the disciplinary uncertainties which seem to plague my profession, for *The Anthology of Babel* is the first edited collection of academic articles which provide literary analysis of completely fictitious primary texts,[6] its title evoking Browne's dutiful student the Argentine master of the imaginary book review, Jorge Luis Borges. A master of brevity and parsimony, with an preternaturally wide-ranging intellect that encompassed everything from kabbalah and Anglo-Saxon alliterative verse to the gaucho stories of his youth, he was perhaps too energetic to commit to ever penning a door stopper like so many of his magical realist colleagues, and so rather he wrote in his seminal 1963 collection *Labyrinths* that "To write vast books is a laborious nonsense, much better is to offer a summary as if those books actually existed."[7]

---

6 In 1971, Stanislaw Lem published a volume of literary criticism of fictitious primary texts, which was translated under the title *A Perfect Vacuum,* trans. Michael Kandel (San Diego: Harcourt Brace Jovanovich, 1983).

7 Jorge Luis Borges, "Forword" to *The Garden of Forking Paths* (1941), in *Collected Fictions,* trans. Andrew Hurley (New York: Viking, 1988), 67.

Borges's idea is attractive, a means of exploring ideas in a free-wheeling, playful manner that's not indebted to anything as dreary as reality. True to that ethos, during the course of his career Borges penned book reviews of completely invented texts, such as of the Indian detective story "The Approach to Al-Mu'tasim" or exegesis of the nihilistic treatises of the Danish theologian Nils Runeberg.[8] Authors had drafted fictional books to quote, review, and analyze before Borges, but the Argentinian provided a gloss of footnotes, paratext, and connections between imagined books which gave his stories an unsurpassed scholarly verisimilitude.

Long before I conceived of *The Anthology of Babel* I became obsessed with Borges's strange concept, as if I were a fevered character out of one of his *Ficciones*. Easy to assume that the project was incubated out of resentments surrounding the sometimes mind-numbing scholarly monotony that is graduate school, with its oral comprehensives, proposals, grants, and innumerable revisions, the project simply being a joke about journal articles and conference presentations. Such an assumption is easy to make, but wrong. I've been drawn to *The Anthology of Babel* ever since reading Borges in high school, feeling like the narrator in his story "The Aleph" who longs to see that singularity where "all space was [...] actual and undiminished," understanding the infinite and eternal potential of imagined literature as an Aleph of sorts.[9]

So then, if there is any guiding spirit, any muse or daemon to serve as both inspiration and mascot to *The Anthology of Babel*, it is both Browne and Borges. With *The Anthology of Babel* both my contributors and I hopefully try to honor our anomalous innovators, the whimsical Englishman Browne, and his attentive reader Borges. Having fallen in love with literary theory, it is easy to grow tired of some of the strictures surrounding the form. Rather, I choose a different direction in that garden of

---

8   Both available in Jorge Luis Borges, *Collected Fictions*, trans. Andrew Hurley (New York: Viking, 1988).

9   Ibid., 284.

forking paths, turning down the less explored corridors of our literary labyrinth, hoping to create a new type of scholarly writing which holds to the abiding belief that criticism and theory are their own branch of creative writing, and never is this more clear, pure, or true than when the texts under consideration are themselves completely invented.

Listings of fictitious books go back much farther than Browne. More than a century before *Bibliotheca Abscondita*, and the French novelist François Rabelais provided long lists of invented volumes in his *Gargantua and Pantagruel,* with titles like *Bishops' Antidotes for Aphrodisiacs, The Clownishness of Little Priests,* and my favorite, *Folk Dances for Heretics.*[10] But if Rabelais's playful example has echoed in his Latinate ancestors like Umberto Eco with his fictitious Aristotelian treatise on comedy in *The Name of the Rose* or Italo Calvino's visceral descriptions in *Invisible Cities,* than a certain latent Puritanism among Anglophone readers has pushed similar games to the literary periphery.[11]

In Britain and America, such "imagined literature" is associated more with genre fiction; for readers of a certain disposition, such as myself, the horror writer H.P. Lovecraft's mysterious grimoire *The Necronomicon* provides a gateway to considering language's particular power, where a book can be so influential that it doesn't actual have to even be real to have an effect on our world.[12] But while English speakers are seemingly fine with such encyclopedic listings and quoting of imagined literature in weird fiction authors like Lovecraft, or in the science fiction of an Isaac Asimov or a Frank Herbert, Borges's contention about the pragmatism of reviewing books that you wished were real

---

10 François Rabelais, *Gargantua and Pantagruel,* trans. M.A. Screech (New York: Penguin, 2006).

11 Umberto Eco, *The Name of the Rose,* trans. William Waver (New York: Harcourt, 1980); Italo Calvino, *Invisible Cities,* trans. William Weaver (Turin: Einaudi, 1972).

12 H.P. Lovecraft, *The New Annotated H.P. Lovecraft,* ed. Leslie S. Klinger (New York: Annotated Books, 2014), 11.

seems to violate some Anglo-American sense of decorum, of seriousness.

Thus those who risked playfulness, who dreamt of books unavailable in any archive, provided the inspiration for *The Anthology of Babel,* and there are other forerunners from Rohan Kriwaczek's ingenious *An Incomplete History of the Art of Funerary Violin* to the lush Darwinian Victorianisms of Dougal Dixon's post-Anthropocene zoological bestiary *After Man,* but ours is the first gathering of scholarly articles by actual academics reading texts of imaginary books, published by a peer-reviewed scholarly press, providing biographical criticism of unreal authors while charting the course of literary movements which never happened.[13]

Again, none of this was done in cheeky bad faith, as a David Lodge-style parody of academic language's worst excesses thrown as a volley by a grad student grown tired of a scholarly culture emphasizing specialization in inverse relationship to the dwindling number of actual professorial jobs. Nor is *The Anthology of Babel* some kind of trenchant satire of "fake news," of an era where expertise can be subverted with a meme and rigor with a tweet. However my intentions for this project have been read, there must have been a spirit of benevolent anarchism which moved the organizers of the Northeastern Modern Language Association to accept a call-for-papers submission for panels at their annual convention which requested "academic-style works of literary theory and criticism which take as their primary texts completely fictional novels, stories, movements, authors, and films [...] [including] the lost Arthurian play of Shakespeare... the epic American poetry of Enoch Campion, and the 1975 Afro-futurist Blaxploitation biblical film *Akhenaton*," none of which are real of course.

In a seminar room at the Baltimore Marriot overlooking the tired Inner Harbor waterfront on a spring morning in 2017,

---

13 Rohan Kriwaczek, *An Incomplete History of the Art of Funerary Violin* (New York: Harry N. Abrams, 2006); Douglas Dixon, *After Man: A Zoology of the Future* (New York: St. Martin's Press, 1981).

three colleagues and myself presented what was to the best of my knowledge a first in the annals of these sorts of conferences — a panel devoted entirely to the close reading and deep analysis of authors unborn and books unwritten. One colleague remarked to me that a panel titled "The Fine Art of Commenting on Books That Don't Exist" was the sort of thing that would further embolden those "committed to cutting funding for the humanities." Certainly the response from some in the audience indicated that the panel seemed to them like arcane, weird, metaphysical naval-gazing, while others saw the baroque sentences and invented references in our papers as a parodic attack on an ever-beleaguered academy, a Sokalesque satire of Judith Butler language and all of the affectations associated with "post-modern theory."[14]

That's not how I read the project, at least not entirely, nor do I imagine that is how my publishers at punctum books read the nature of what is an admittedly unusual project. *The Anthology of Babel* is not meant to be satirical, yet we often confuse the playful for its more acerbic cousin. And as concerns that which is playful, I'm very serious. As Preston writes of *Bibliotheca Abscondita*, Browne's pamphlet isn't just a spoof of "learned curiosity," where he revels in the "absurdity of some of his own items and is obviously trying for comic effect with certain ones," but where such play was also "reparation and restoration of truth […] a wistful evocation of what might have existed" in collections like those at ancient Alexandria. "Imagined literature" is a way of probing the metaphysics of this strange thing that we call fiction, this use of invented language which is comprehensible and yet where reality does not literally support the representation. Fiction is a lie which reveals the truth, to paraphrase Pablo Picasso. A form that already deals in illusion, artifice, and trickery, how much more true to fiction if the very author herself is imagined, the very book, or poem, or play a similar wisp of the fleeting imagination?

---

14 Consult *The Sokal Hoax: The Sham That Shook the Academy* (Lincoln: Bison Books, 2000) by the editors of *Lingua Franca*.

We've always had a strained relationship to the scandal of fictionality anyhow, our earliest novelists like Daniel Defoe pretended that stories like *Robinson Crusoe* were actually factual accounts, lest readers be overly shocked by ingesting invented narratives.[15] How much more scandalous would a brazenly, unabashed, and open celebration of completely imagined libraries be? What we present is such a brazen, unabashed, open celebration of that quantum field which is literature, containing intimations of all that has ever been written and the infinitely larger category of all that ever could be written. In *The Anthology of Babel* there are the inky fingerprints from those authors living in parallel universes perpendicular to ours, such as Reed Johnson's brilliant essay which explores the anonymous dissidents in Soviet gulags who composed *The Rainberg Variations* not by applying pen to paper but by cutting letters out of the bureaucratic paper work which condemned them; imagined literature as erasure, existing in the very spaces between words. Or Kathleen McLoone's erudite readings of Middle English meter in the medieval *Romance of the Minotaur* which places songs of Crete's beast in the mouths of British bards. And Ryan Marnane's consideration of the archive of author Heidi B. Morton, a massive, digressive, rhizomatic collection of the ephemera of her life from bills to library records.

Across twenty scholarly articles *The Anthology of Babel* spans the sensual Milipian "body-loving philosophers" of ancient Greece as explored by Stephen David Engel to the post-human, Martian future of Elon Musk's colonial descendants in Bruce Krajewski's concluding paper. Real figures from Ernest Hemingway to Jane Austin flit throughout the narrative of the anthology, but the focus of every essay is not the real, but the fake. It is written for those who see more wonder in dreaming than utility in wakefulness, understanding that fiction is always a parallel universe of sorts, and it is in imagining these counter-histories,

---

15 Consult Michael McKeon's *The Origins of the English Novel, 1600–1740* (Baltimore: Johns Hopkins University Press, 1987) for more on early modern fictionality.

these alternative narratives of literature that we can fully plumb the depths of this weird thing called language. As scholar Eamonn Peters told me in an interview for *Berfrois* conducted in 2017, "Imagined literature exists in the infinite space between the letters of recorded literature, between its very words. Imagined literature fills the gaps between these letters, waiting to be birthed in our world." Dr. Peters, of course, is completely an invention of my own mind. His being not real doesn't make his contention any less true — which is precisely the point.

Bibliography

Aldersey-Williams, Hugh. *In Search of Sir Thomas Browne: The Life and Afterlife of the Seventeenth Century's Most Inquiring Mind.* New York: W.W. Norton Company, 2015.

Borges, Jorge Luis. *Collected Fictions.* Translated by Andrew Hurley. New York: Viking, 1988.

Browne, Thomas. *Musaeum Clausum, or Bibliotheca Abscondita.* London, 1684.

———. *The Major Works: Religio Medici, Hydrotophia, The Garden of Cyprus, A Letter to a Friend, and Christian Moral*s. Edited by C.A. Patrides. New York: Penguin Classics, 1977.

Calvino, Italo. *Invisible Cities.* Translated by William Weaver. Turin: Einaudi, 1972.

Dixon, Douglas. *After Man: A Zoology of the Future.* New York: St. Martin's Press, 1981.

Eco, Umberto. *The Name of the Rose.* Translated by William Waver. New York: Harcourt, 1980.

Editors of *Lingua Franca*. *The Sokal Hoax: The Sham That Shook the Academy.* Lincoln: Bison Books, 2000.

Kriwaczek, Rohan. *An Incomplete History of the Art of Funerary Violin.* New York: Harry N. Abrams, 2006.

Lem, Stanislaw. *A Perfect Vacuum.* Translated by Michael Kandel. San Diego: Harcourt Brace Jovanovich, 1983.

Lovecraft, H.P. *The New Annotated H.P. Lovecraft.* Edited by Leslie S. Klinger. New York: Annotated Books, 2014.

McKeon, Michael. *The Origins of the English Novel, 1600–1740.* Baltimore: Johns Hopkins University Press, 1987.

Preston, Claire. "Lost Libraries," *The Public Domain Review,* February 20, 2012. https://publicdomainreview.org/2012/02/20/lost-libraries/.

Rabelais, François. *Gargantua and Pantagruel.* Translated by M.A. Screech. New York: Penguin, 2006.

Simon, Ed. "*Religio Medici and Urne-Buriall,* by Sir Thomas Browne. Edited by Stephen Greenblatt and Ramie Targoff." *This Rough Magic: A Peer-Reviewed, Academic, Online*

Journal Dedicated to the Teaching of Medieval & Renaissance Literature, December 2013. http://www.thisroughmagic.org/simon%20review.html.

1

The Body-Loving Philosophers

Stephen David Engel

The Milipians — often referred to as the Milipian School, and pejoratively referred to as "the body-loving philosophers" — were a collection of thinkers active in the Greek city-state of Milipos from the 6th to 4th centuries BCE. Of all Greek philosophers and movements of that period, from Heraclitus and Empedocles to the Atomists and Eleatics, the Milipians were the only ones to take up the human body as focal point of their theories. For them, the body in its perceptual and kinetic capacities was the instrument and ground of inquiry, its sine qua non. They rejected, vehemently, all doctrines of the soul, making the body and its actions synonymous with the who that someone is, and uprooting along with the soul ideas of the human as immortal, fit for reincarnation, or destined to an underworld for an afterlife as a shade. Philosophizing in their community involved an array of rituals. These rituals aimed at full embodiment; subtle attunement of the senses; mastery of craft, labor, sport, song, conversation, dance, and sex; detailed knowledge of the motions and behaviors of elements; and intimate comprehension of death.

The Milipians provoked intense reactions among the ancients, ranging from admiration to hatred, but usually hatred. Their enduring nickname, "the body-loving philosophers," first appears in Plato's *Symposium* when Socrates, discussing the

"Milipian obsession with the body," says, "Do you think, then, that these body-loving philosophers practice love of wisdom, or is it merely love of body?"[1] Plato himself is said to have wanted to wrestle each and every one of the Milipians to death, on the accusation that they were not philosophers at all and had no business claiming to be.[2] Pythagoras, who championed the immortality of the soul, remarked that they were born as Milipians as punishment for crimes they had committed in previous lives, while Ion of Chios called them "enslaved to their stupidity."[3] Aristotle, their sometimes admirer and most rigorous critic, counted the Milipians among the *phusikoi,* or natural philosophers, though later interpreters resist this categorization, on the basis that Milipians tended to avoid the term phusis, or nature.[4] Zenodoros, Stobaeus, and Polydamma, meanwhile, all told of a feud between the Milipians and the Pythagoreans that culminated in a series of massacres, but they disagreed about where this happened, why it started, and how many philosophers were killed.[5]

Stories like this added to the mystique and controversy surrounding the Milipians in ancient commentaries—a mystique and controversy no doubt related to their city-state and to the inclusion of women, non-Greeks, and former slaves in their school. The furor surrounding them, likewise, had to do with their fierce reverence for the body, their suspicion of abstraction

---

[1] Plato, *Symposium* (Olympia: Ergon Press, 2003), 506b.
[2] Hermann Diels and Walther Kranz, *Die Fragmente der Vorsokratiker* (Zurich: Weidmann, 1985), DK68a10. I rely on the Diels-Kranz collection (DK) throughout this article. From here on, I include only Diels-Kranz numbers in the notes, as opposed to full citations. For more on Plato and his rivalries, see Ava Chitwood, *Death by Philosophy* (Ann Arbor: University of Michigan Press, 2004), 199.
[3] DK68a62 and DK68a65.
[4] Aristotle, *Metaphysics* (Olympia: Ergon Press, 2002), 975b21; Jay Bird, *The Milipians and Their Interpreters* (Cambridge: Harvard University Press, 1996); Benjamina Gass, "Are the Milipians *Phusikoi* after All?" *Studies in Ancient Philosophy* 58, no. 4 (2007): 619–52.
[5] Liz Blettner, *Polemics of the Soul: The Pythagoreans and the Milipians* (Madison: University of Wisconsin Press, 2015), 5–11.

and speculation, their thesis that philosophical contemplation could be pursued through non-verbal and non-written forms of sensual, physical, and craft-based activity, and their biting gnomic criticisms of socioeconomic structures wherein the leisure of some depended on the labor of others. Their enemies were many and their ideas traveled widely, which recommends them, time and again, to our attention.

In this article, I introduce the Milipians for non-specialists within and outside of classics and philosophy. First, I provide historical background on Milipos and the Milipians. This helps contextualize the emergence of their philosophical school, and provides some insight into who they were. Second, I focus on three key areas of the Milipian philosophy: how they thought of the human body and bodies in general, how their idea of knowledge was connected to the body, and how they repurposed the political idea of *ho koinos* (the shared, the common) to establish perceptual and epistemic limits. My hope is that this article will serve as an invitation to future study, as well as a correction to some caricatures of the Milipians that circulate to this day.

Milipos and the Milipians

Milipos was a city-state on the island of Patanos. It was close to the ocean, on the western side of the island, and from the western wall, one could look out on the Aegean. Date of settlement is unclear, but most archaeologists place it sometime in the late 8th or early 7th century BCE.[6] Herodotus supplied just a little information about the founding of Milipos, saying that the city-state was established by former slaves. "Where the Milipians came from," he wrote, "no one knows."[7] According to Alcippe, the city's founders were exceedingly gifted at a variety of crafts, and they had great esteem for the legendary

---

6 Nancy Taylor, *Archaeologies of the Aegean* (Cambridge: MIT Press, 2003), 182; Ezra Alhadeff, "Re-Digging Milipos," *Cambria Archaeological Quarterly* 80 (2014): 76–102.
7 Herodotus, *The History,* trans. David Grene (Chicago: University of Chicago Press, 1987), 7.121.

craftsman Daedalus, who, like them, had escaped from captivity by means of technical wit.[8] Not much more is known about the city's founding. More is known about what it came to be — a city that flourished without slave labor, and a center for innovation in craft.

By the middle of the 5th century, when Milipian philosophy was thriving, Milipos had achieved widespread fame for its technics, including metalworking, carpentry, pottery, and clepsydras. The polis was particularly renowned for its motion machines, which were sometimes, in the fashion of the *agalmata* attributed to Daedalus, statues of gods with moveable eyes and limbs, while at others they were unrelated to gods and not at all anthropomorphic, more like experiments in machinery and in what motions it could be made to perform. Craft was so central to Milipos's culture that it played a role in determining political position. All archons, which in Milipos could include women and hermaphrodites, were selected according to their skill in a chosen craft, the idea being that wisdom, know-how, and attention to detail in technical and artistic spheres would inform, profoundly, one's abilities in statecraft.[9]

Craft was central to citizenship as well. Slavery was outlawed in Milipos, and though there were divisions of labor, all citizens were expected to participate in the production of food and goods. Codes of hospitality, Zeus-given, were taken seriously: Milipos opened its gates to outsiders, including exiles and former slaves from other city-states. However, in order to become a citizen, one had to demonstrate mastery, competence, or promise (which depended on age) at a craft as well as a form of labor. If someone could not demonstrate the requisite skill in two areas, one of two things might happen: after a fixed duration of guest-friendship, the person would be asked to leave; or,

---

8   Alcippe, *Chronicles* (Olympia: Ergon Press, 2001), 62; Ovid, *Metamorphoses*, trans. Charles Martin (New York: W.W. Norton, 2010), VIII.183–235.

9   A.J. Cole, "Technics and Politics in the Milipian City-State," *Urban Taxonomies* 10, no. 1 (2010): 1–27; Nigel Spivey, *Greek Sculpture* (Cambridge: Cambridge University Press, 2013), 59; Cornelius Shih, *Ancient Greek Technics* (New York: Columbia University Press, 2010), 75–100.

alternatively, citizens would volunteer to sponsor the person's citizenship and contribute what was necessary, by way of craft or labor or both, on behalf of that person and to meet that person's needs.[10]

All of this was framed in terms of *ho koinos*, the chief principle of the city, meaning the shared, the common. *Ho koinos* was, in its political meaning, both a principle of conduct and a spatial designation. As a principle of conduct, it governed how citizens interacted, how jobs were assigned, and how goods were shared. As a spatial designation, the term referred to different things at different times. Sometimes it designated the entire city, wall to wall, or both the city within the wall as well as the territory beyond the wall. More often, as Andre Reese argues, it designated certain areas of the city known to everyone as shared and, because shared, sacred.[11] This included the mess hall, the gymnasium, the granary, the streets between houses, and the gathering place of elders. The mess and the gymnasium were at the center of the city, and Reese thinks the mess was established ahead of most everything else, family houses included. Aristotle, in his treatment of public messes in *Politics*, said that all Milipian citizens, including women and children, participated in these meals, and that all meals were provided for collectively.[12] Women and children were also allowed in the gymnasium, for training in the same sports as men, including *pankration*, the Greek martial art. According to Diogenes Laërtius, it was at the gymnasium, at the heart of what was designated *ho koinos*, that the Milipian School first formed.[13]

But who were the Milipian philosophers? Theophrastus inventoried them as "Greek men, women, hermaphrodites, bar-

---

10 Stephen David Engel, *Of Sweat and Shape: Labor and Craft in Ancient Milipos* (Brooklyn: punctum books, 2015), 61–90; Nancy Kay, *To Each According to Their Needs: Labor Organization from the Ancient to the Present* (New York: Verso, 1999), 1–15.
11 Andre Reese, *Spatiality of the Sacred: Temples and Commons in the Mediterranean* (Berkeley: University of California Press, 2006), 153–201.
12 Aristotle, *Politics* (Olympia: Ergon Press, 1999), 1329b25.
13 DK68a4.

barians, slaves, exiles, and children."[14] Such diversity is likely, given what we know about the culture in Milipos. However, the identities of these individuals — when they were born and died, who was part of the early conversations that gave rise to the views of the school, etc. — remain obscure. One reason for this is that Milipian texts were usually attributed to the group as opposed to individuals. Lila Duran notes that there are some exceptions to this pattern, most notably the *Verses* and *Sayings* of Diotima, a 5th-century Milipian who described herself as

> a worshipper among worshippers of the body
> whose piety is expressed in dance, in the trance
> of the craftsman hovering piously over wood,
> in the shaping of all metals, in the fever of
> exacting all motions.[15]

But exceptions like this are rare. Far more often, Milipian custom dictated that the text as a whole be attributed to the group, while attributions to individuals would be made *within* the text to mark specific contributions. This was done by name. The personal name alone was used, or in some cases a nickname. Patronymics, as well as names of neighborhoods, tribes, former owners, and cities of origin, were categorically discarded. "Most Milipian texts," writes C. Donna Commé, "were polyphonic constructions and weavings, the outcomes of collaborative investigations, but with some care taken to preserve distinctness of perspective and the dawning of that perspective in a particular body as it existed in, and responded to, the common."[16] Most ancient commentators, however, did not distinguish between individual contributors, and did not carry their names forward in commentaries. For this and other reasons, not much is known about the Milipians as individuals. What we know more

---

14 DK68a20.
15 DK69b12; Lila Duran, "Milipian Compositions," *Antinominal* 17, no. 1 (2010): 233–87.
16 C. Donna Commé, *Rhetorics of Togetherness* (New York: Columbia University Press, 2008), 43.

about is what they thought of bodies, and of the human body in particular.

Body

The core of the Milipian system was *sōma,* body. The Milipians used the word *sōma* in two ways. First, they meant it in a general sense, applying to any "this" (*tode ti*) that could be individuated, any entity that could stand out, manifestly singular and whole, in the perceptual field. A bear was a body. A cypress was a body. A hunk of iron was a body. A piece of dust was a body. A spear was a body. The moon was a body. A gust of wind was a body. These things were bodies because they could be sensed, and they could be sensed because they were bodies.[17] A human for the Milipians was also a body, which brings us to the second, more refined meaning of *sōma* as a specifically "human body." Sometimes this was marked adjectivally; at others, *sōma*'s meaning as human body was inferable through context or implicit in usage, much as how in English people sometimes use the phrase "the body" to mean "the human body." When Socrates, in *Symposium,* refers to the Milipians as "the body-loving philosophers," he seems to have this second, human meaning in mind. But the Milipians used the word generally as well. I will begin with this general meaning.

A counter-example will start us off. Democritus, a contemporary of the Milipians, advocated the existence of indestructible, uncuttable simples as the basis of everything. Atoms, as he and others called them, are so small that they "escape our senses."[18] They only contribute to the sensible when they glom together and make masses of a certain size. Whereas atoms lie below the threshold of the senses, bodies, in the Milipian sense, lie above it. They are and must by definition be manifest. Some bodies come into being, certainly, but from whence below the sensible

---

17 DK68b4.
18 Jonathan Barnes, *Early Greek Philosophy* (New York: Penguin Books, 2001), 206.

they appear, or what below the sensible gives rise to them, no Milipian would hazard to guess, as it would be too speculative, too conjectural a position to maintain. And this characterizes their philosophy overall. Whereas certain of their contemporaries tended to take detours away from bodies in their manifest appearances, seeking principles beneath or beyond bodies, the Milipians sped toward bodies, in hopes of knowing them well.

The Milipians likewise appear to have been utterly indifferent — or scrupulously resistant — to monisms, arguments that one substance, like fire or water or air, made up all things. This pitted them against thinkers like Thales, Anaximenes, and Heraclitus. If monisms did not tempt the Milipians, cosmogenesis (often associated with monisms) tempted them less. They thought it neither possible nor desirable to tell a story about the origin of bodies, satisfied that bodies existed in the present and were available to the senses, to making and doing, to learning and knowing in their specific details and natures.[19] The origin account given by Anaxagoras, that "All things were together, then thought (*nous*) arrived and ordered them,"[20] would have seemed to the Milipians as both an aggrandizement of *nous* and a groundless abstraction of *nous* away from *sōma*. Human bodies thought, and certain other bodies thought, but to posit thought on its own — as bodiless, as separate from things and as having power to organize those things — would be a category mistake. If what Anaxagoras meant was that it is human understanding — hitched to and confronted by a disorganized manifold — that orders a soupy disorder in the antechamber of experience, this would still be too anthropocentric for the Milipians, who thought of nonhuman bodies as autonomous and self-styled in their behaviors, qualities, and relationships.

To an important extent, the Milipians took appearances at face value, as robust enough to stand on their own. This came part and parcel with a view of perception as reliable, of bodies as "there," so much as to be invulnerable to doubt. As Charles

---

19 DK68b11 and DK68a201.
20 Barnes, *Early Greek Philosophy*, 185.

Pailthorp has put it, bodies were "solidly available to an ecstatic curiosity that soared above and spat upon doubt."[21] Gabriela Eepasou has called this "a methodological credulity grounded in the senses, hostile to all epistemologies that would denigrate them."[22] Bodies, always already tethered to the sensible, *were* everything and *did* everything.[23] More than telling stories about origins, more than positing a unified substance running beneath what appears to us, the Milipians were interested in examining bodies as they appear to us in their variety. They were interested in observing and punctuating the differences between bodies, how they behaved and persisted, emerged and perished in the realm of the perceptible, *not* a realm of the intelligible where the form of the thing could be encountered cleansed of matter. Even the distinctions between four elements or six elements, respectively, were too general. Bodies were more numerous, and less reducible, than that, even if they were groupable according to kind.

The chief proposition of the Milipians, which appears across a number of sources with only occasional variation, is the statement, "Being is bodying; bodying is being."[24] This is, on one reading, an ontological statement, in keeping with the position outlined above, that bodies, for the Milipians, are everything and do everything. Bodies were bound up with motion and activity. They were never fully still, never completely at rest. They were always "humming," always "vibrating," or in less poetic terms, "persisting."[25] The Milipians allowed for a relative stillness, and they also believed in a threshold between the persisting of a body in a certain set of activities, on the one hand, and change and destruction, on the other. They distinguished be-

---

21 Charles Pailthorp, *The Bodies That Motions Make: Milipians, Atomists, and Kinesis* (New Haven: Yale University Press, 2002), 185.
22 Gabriela Eepasou, *Skepticism and Realism in the History of Philosophy: Seven Conjectural Anthropologies* (Palo Alto: Stanford University Press, 2012), 112.
23 DK59b1.
24 DK68b1.
25 DK68b7.

tween water and ice, knowing well that water could change to ice then back again to water. They saw that some bodies could convert back and forth in this manner, and that others, like wood when burned, could not. Transitions, wrote Kleonike, "concerned them to no end."[26] But bodies, so long as they existed, were always in motion. Some of this motion might come from other bodies, through interaction, while some of it would be produced by the body itself.[27] Degree of motion differed from body to body and time to time, with some bodies more active than others. Each body was capable of producing a range of motions, and incapable of others. No body could produce all motions, though some degree of imitation, through dance and other arts, was available to human bodies.[28]

"Being is bodying; bodying is being" was also, specifically, a claim about humans. This brings us back to the second, refined meaning of *sōma* as *human* body, sometimes designated adjectivally and sometimes inferable through context. For the Milipians, humans were bodies, and nothing more than, other than, or separate from bodies. There was no being apart from bodying, and in this way the argument entailed in the statement "Being is bodying; bodying is being" is not only an ontological statement, and not only a statement about motion, but also an argument against the idea of any essence of the human person or source of vitality that could leave the body and exist, or continue to exist, without that body.

In short, the Milipian theory of the body opposed the *psukhē*, or soul, in all its forms.[29] The soul was neither a shade to be led to Hades after being separated from the body upon death, nor was it something that could swim bodiless among eternal and immutable ideas, nor was it something that could be incorporated in a new body, human or otherwise, post mortem. The Milipians rejected, therefore, the Homeric, Platonic, and Pythagorean ver-

---

26 DK68a39.
27 DK68b17.
28 Bradford Willoughby, "Mimesis and the Milipians," *Mimesis Studies* 37, no. 4 (2015): 1104–57.
29 DK68b52–63, DK68b28, DK68b47, and DK68b92.

sions of the soul, all of which had corresponding imaginaries in religious practice, both in Greece and elsewhere.[30]

But there were non-religious, stripped-down views of the soul as well. Aristotle, in *On the Soul,* wrote that Thales "assumed the soul to be something that causes motion." He continued, "The Milipians denounce this view, saying that bodies themselves produce motion, and that the soul is superfluous."[31] It made no sense to the Milipians to look beyond bodies for an explanation of their motions, and they attributed such looking beyond, perhaps unfairly, to a shuddering at death that made the idea of a soul desirable in the first place. When Aristotle said that they thought of the soul as "superfluous," he meant superfluous as an idea in its explanatory function. But the Milipians were harsher than this. They wrote, "Of all the things humans give themselves, the soul is the most cowardly."[32] To the accounts of the soul in the works of Hippo, who claimed the soul was water, and the works of Critias, who said the soul was blood, the Milipians would have responded that there is no one source of motion in the body, but that all parts of the body contribute to its motions, albeit unevenly, and depending on what those motions are.[33]

Finally, the proposition "Being is bodying; bodying is being" was prescriptive. If one wanted to *be* as fully as possible, one would need to *body* in the most alert, observant, disciplined, and energized ways that their body, with its particular characteristics and capacities, afforded. The human body was, so long as it was alive, always existing, because it was always bodying. But the Milipians also devised a range of practices to bring about what they called "full bodily flowering," a state in which sense receptivity and philosophical focus are simultaneously

---

30 M.C.M. Drumm, "Volatility and the Soul," *Liquidity and Theology* 9, no. 2 (2016): 99–114.
31 Aristotle, *On the Soul,* trans. Joe Sachs (Santa Fe: Green Lion Press, 2004), 405a19–21.
32 DK68b49.
33 Aristotle, *On the Soul,* 405b1–11.

and indistinguishably raised to a fever pitch.[34] These practices, as described by commentators, took a number of forms. They could take place in the course of seemingly everyday labor and work, in the preparing of a meal in the mess or in the firing of a bowl, or in any other moment when the body was engaged, concentrated, absorbed in a task. It could happen during a wrestling match, or in the hurling of a discus. But there were also more specialized activities in which it could happen, activities that had no other end but the switching on of the body as receptive philosophical instrument. According to Enyo, the Milipians could be found "at any hour of the day touching things and sniffing things and looking closely at things, on all fours or upright, gazing at the stars."[35] For some of these activities, there were detailed instructions. A practice for rainstorms was to be carried out as follows:

> For the feeling and hearing of rain, only at night. Leave eastern gate, naked, with blindfold. Enter the grove of cypress, or go farther to the forest of oak. Cover eyes with blindfold, loosely, with eyes closed gently. Turn palms upward. Feel all drops land on and roll across skin. Hear drops on every leaf, on every stone, every blade of grass and clump of soil. Measure size of drops with skin. Fathom size of forest by means of rain-sound. Listen deep, trying to find end of rain. If moving calls you, dance in imitation of rain, thunder, lighting, wind. If not, stand or sit — humming, absorbing. If lightning strikes, feel it on skin. If thunder booms, locate its source. Track each boom in relation to you — the body that you are — as center. When rain ceases, remain. If day comes, remain until you feel all drops on skin dry up. Track them as they return to air, as the skin drinks them.[36]

---

34 DK68b2 and DK68b77.
35 DK68a13.
36 DK68b71.

This was a practice in which one sense was shut out for the sake of refining others. In this case it was sight. But there were other rituals that depended heavily on sight, like the tracking of wind as it moved over fields of wheat or disturbed the surface of water. Motions like this were often imitated on the spot in dance, and "brought back" to the community via a dance performance. Dance was seen as a sort of recording device, a way of capturing shapes and motions particular to certain bodies and sharing them with other people who had not seen them. Those other people would then imitate the dancer.[37]

The community abounded with rituals like this. There were poetic contests for singing the shapes and behaviors of bodies, from elements and animals to plants and humans, and detail of description was prized.[38] But the most famous Milipian ritual focused on skin. Philosophers would prepare a special mud, which was applied in thick but even amounts all over the body, face and head included.[39] The mud was slathered in the morning, as the sun was coming up. When the heat of the day increased, the mud would harden then crack. Sitting perfectly still, the person covered in mud would attend to the different sensations, with the goal of becoming aware, all at once, of every inch of skin of their body. At an appointed time, usually at sundown, the person would dance, and the mud casing would break and come off in chunks. This ritual in particular was derided by contemporaries. But the Milipians insisted on it, and others like it, as a way of knowing. What they meant by knowing, however, should be further explained.

---

[37] DK68a79; Laya Datsun, *Corybants and Philosophers* (Bloomington: Indiana University Press, 2010), 72–90; Lorán Carboneto, "Milipians and Performance," *Critical Inquiries* 14, no. 2 (2017): 182–207.

[38] A.J. Wiscobb, "Voices of Elements: Milipian Singing Rituals in the 5th Century BCE," *Orality Quarterly* 36, no. 1 (2015): 21–39.

[39] DK68a96.

Knowing

Most objections to the Milipian dismissal of the soul, in both ancient commentaries as well as more recent debates in philosophy, are made on the grounds that eliminating the soul eliminates all possible locations for the faculties, including and especially knowing.[40] The Milipians, however, did not even posit faculties, so the terms of the argument immediately diverge. Knowing and imagining, remembering and desiring were for the Milipians all activities of the body. There were parts of the body most enlivened during any one of these activities, while other parts were not, but none of these parts were thought of as existing on an immaterial or internal plane, or housed in one part of the body exclusively, with the rest of the body subordinate or irrelevant. The doctrine of full bodily flowering had it that, when the body was doing one of these things, such as remembering, the whole body would be "given over to it," participating in that motion.[41] There did not need to be a specific site for thinking, knowing, imagining, and so on, because all of these activities could be associated by various routes with the sensorium or the body as a whole, a whole that was interconnected, where any one activity was best undertaken by the body in its entirety, instead of with divided attention.

"All knowing," wrote the Milipians, "is knowing by the body."[42] This view, though evidently held with conviction, was at the same time polemical, a rebuke to philosophers of the day who dismissed perception as faulty and unreliable and who worked up concepts of knowledge that divorced it from flesh, the senses, and the ephemeral. The body was the only point of access to nonhuman bodies, and bodies were the only thing one could know anything whatsoever about. At the same time, the Milipian designation of the body as the perceptual and epis-

---

[40] Markus Wheelmann, "Milipian Physicalism," *Cognitive Review* 23 (2014): 10–48.
[41] DK68b6.
[42] DK68b12.

temic point of access to other bodies did not place the human body on the outside of philosophic inquiry. It did not place it on the outside of an observable world. The human body, like any other body, was ripe for accounting, especially so because of the intimate relationship the philosopher, as that body, could have with themselves. For the Milipians, the Delphic imperative to know yourself (*gnōthi seauton*) could apply to nothing other than the body. The Milipians wrote,

> Knowing this body here, the body that I am, can only be achieved in knowing other bodies. I cannot know other bodies without, at the same time, coming to know about this body, the body that I am, in its many-sided potency. Bodying, which is being, is in this way always knowing. But there are better and there are worse ways of knowing.[43]

For the Milipians, nonhuman bodies were teeming with potencies, and the human body was likewise teeming with potencies. When a human body, such as the philosopher-body, went searching — whether by means of metalworking, carpentry, or sensory attunement — for the potencies of a given body — be it hunk of iron or prolonged flute note — potencies of the philosopher-body were made manifest along with those potencies that practice brought out of the nonhuman body. For instance: if with my tongue I find a cup of water to be salty, this triggers a simultaneous revelation that the body that I am can detect that this water here contains salt. When learning about another body, I learn about the body that I am.[44]

This did not mean that the body carried around, or possessed, "knowledge." Nor did it entitle someone, even a philosopher, to say that they knew things that they were not presently doing, sensing, or making. The Milipian view of knowing was not

---

[43] Attributed to Tryphosa. DK68b37. Following Joe Sachs, the Greek I translate as "potency" is *dunamis*.

[44] Constanzia Bresson, *Ways of Knowing in Ancient Greece* (New York: W.W. Norton: 2001), 189–92.

only layered, but also present-focused. "Remembering is not the same as knowing," wrote the Milipians.[45] A famous illustration, given by Diotima, is the forging of a spearhead. A person could remember how to forge a spearhead, but they could be said to know how to forge a spearhead only when forging it. Once the spearhead was forged, the metal cooled and deadly, the period of knowing ceased. To know again, one would have to make another. If one could no longer make a spearhead, then one no longer knew.[46] This made saying that one knew something a rarity for the Milipians. The Milipians wrote, "Nobody should attest to knowing without demonstration, without showing."[47] This was, on the one hand, an antidote to arrogant speech. On the other, it was one of many boundary markers for *ho koinos*, for the common in its epistemological sense.

The Common

As mentioned above, the Milipian idea of *ho koinos* arose through the culture and customs of their city. But whereas in their city it had particular political and physical meaning, associated with the distribution of goods and key gathering places for citizens, the Milipian philosophers adapted the term for ontological and epistemological use. All of the positions sketched above — that bodies are everything and do everything, that being is bodying and bodying being, that knowing and remembering are not the same and that all knowing is knowing by the body — are grounded in, defined by, and bound to the common. "The common," wrote the Milipians, "is where the perceptions of more than one body swarm together in a circle of light." They continued:

> The common is the smell we can all smell, the sound we can all hear, the bread we can all taste, the body we can all touch, the wind on the wheat we can all see. It is where we sense one

---

45 DK68b13.
46 DK69b44.
47 DK68b13.

another. It is where we sense the "here" together. If a body cannot see the common, then they can smell it. If a body cannot smell the common, then they can hear it. If a body cannot hear the common, then they can taste it. If a body cannot taste the common, then they can touch it.[48]

The common, in other words, named a shared perceptual field, where the same bodies could appear to the same perceivers. It was necessarily local, a mutually inhabited frame of reference, a place-based orientation from which the community could — collectively and collaboratively, through ritual, process, and dialogue — experience and describe the universe as given them by the senses, even if not all senses were available to all human bodies. There could be no *ho koinos* without plurality. Proximity of perceiving, communicating bodies was its precondition. Otherwise perception would mean nothing more than solipsism. *Ho koinos* was, in short, the near at hand, and the near at hand was, in addition to being sensed by an individual body, also negotiated by a community of bodies.

The edges of *ho koinos* were always shifting, based on the movements and whereabouts of those members of the Milipian philosophical community. The circle of light was therefore fluid, its horizons migratory. According to Kleonike, the nature and scope of *ho koinos* was a frequent topic of debate.[49] In addition to the question "What is *ho koinos*?" Milipians also asked after the "lower" and "upper" limits of it. Some argued that the lower limit should be set by tiny particles, like dust floating in the sunlight. Others said faint, subtle smells that were neither pleasant nor offensive. Yet others said sounds as they faded away. Some proposed dreamless sleep. The upper limit was likewise debated, but there seems to have been greater consensus about it. The mostly accepted upper limit was the boundary of the visual field at night, "the point where the faintest star gives

---

48 DK68b16.
49 DK68a101.

way to darkness."[50] Despite this interest in limits, the Milipians believed that, by and large, the nearer one was to a body, the more one could come to observe about that body. Someone, for instance, could learn much about iron by firing it, molding it, and hammering it, but they could not do that with the sun, even if they could observe the sun daily, keep track of its movements, and so on. There were more potencies to uncover in a river — swimming in it, drinking from it, tossing rocks so that they splash in it — than a star. The common held within it gradations of the perceivable. There were things one could engage with some senses, and things one could engage with all senses, as well as with techniques of craft.[51]

In committing to *ho koinos*, the Milipians avoided the terms *phusis* (nature) and *kosmos* (order, arrangement, universe), key terms in the works of other early Greek philosophers.[52] The reason the Milipians avoided them was simple: they were too totalizing. Restricting themselves to claims about *ho koinos* was a method for refraining from claims about all things. One could talk about the natures of specific bodies, but not the nature of all things, or nature as all things. The Milipians did not know what existed beyond the common, and claiming to know would have spelled epistemological disaster, not to mention hubris. They did not deny the existence of *phusis*; they did not hold in doubt a *kosmos* as the organized sum of all bodies. But *kosmos* on the whole and *phusis* in general were, as Diotima put it, "smoke so distant we cannot see."[53] Whether Aristotle was right to group the Milipians with the other *phusikoi* can accordingly be argued both ways, but their embrace of *ho koinos* should be understood as a principled check on how far from perception others had gone, or were going, in speculation about the world. This was no

---

50 DK68a102.

51 Howard Nedry, "What Are the Limits of the Common? Milipian Perception at the Extremes," *Space and Sense* 19 (2006): 87–101.

52 Mara D. Higuera and Charlotte A. Beavers, *The Being of Phusis: Number, Notion, Nature* (Annapolis: St. John's College Press, 2015), 3.

53 DK69b39.

faultfinder critique. It grew from an esteem of the body rarely matched in the pantheon of thought.

Bibliography

Alcippe. *Chronicles*. Edited by Alexandra Ullman. Olympia: Ergon Press, 2001.

Alhadeff, Ezra. "Re-Digging Milipos." *Cambria Archaeological Quarterly* 80 (2014): 76–102.

Aristotle. *Metaphysics*. Edited by Manuel Martenyi. Olympia: Ergon Press, 2002.

———. *On the Soul*. Translated by Joe Sachs. Santa Fe: Green Lion Press, 2004.

———. *Politics*. Edited by Thad Curtz. Olympia: Ergon Press, 1999.

Barnes, Jonathan. *Early Greek Philosophy*. New York: Penguin Books, 2001.

Bird, Jay. "The Milipians and Death." *Critical Death Studies* 6, no. 4 (2011): 229–50.

Blettner, Liz. *Polemics of the Soul: The Pythagoreans and the Milipians*. Madison: University of Wisconsin Press, 2015.

Bresson, Constanzia. *Ways of Knowing in Ancient Greece*. New York: W.W. Norton: 2001.

Carboneto, Lorán. "Milipians and Performance." *Critical Inquiries* 14, no. 2 (2017): 182–207.

Chitwood, Ava. *Death by Philosophy*. Ann Arbor: University of Michigan Press, 2004.

Cole, A.J. "Technics and Politics in the Milipian City-State." *Urban Taxonomies* 10, no. 1 (2010): 1–27.

Commé, C. Donna. *Rhetorics of Togetherness*. New York: Columbia University Press, 2008.

Datsun, Laya. *Corybants and Philosophers*. Bloomington: Indiana University Press, 2010.

Diels, Hermann Alexander, and Walther Kranz. *Die Fragmente der Vorsokratiker*. Berlin: Weidmannsche Verlagsbuchhandlung, 1951.

Drumm, M.C.M. "Volatility and the Soul." *Liquidity and Theology* 9, no. 2 (2016): 99–114.

Duran, Lila. "Milipian Compositions." *Antinominal* 17, no. 1 (2010): 233–87.

Eepasou, Gabriela. *Skepticism and Realism in the History of Philosophy: Seven Conjectural Anthropologies.* Palo Alto: Stanford University Press, 2012.

Engel, Stephen David. *Of Sweat and Shape: Labor and Craft in Ancient Milipos.* Brooklyn: punctum books, 2015.

Gass, Benjamina. "Are the Milipians *Phusikoi* after All?" *Studies in Ancient Philosophy* 58, no. 4 (2007): 619–52.

Herodotus. *The History.* Translated by David Grene. Chicago: University of Chicago Press, 1987.

Higuera, Mara D., and Charlotte A. Beavers. *The Being of Phusis: Number, Notion, Nature.* Annapolis: St. John's College Press, 2015.

Kay, Nancy. *To Each According to Their Needs: Labor Organization from the Ancient to the Present.* New York: Verso, 1999.

Nedry, Howard. "What Are the Limits of the Common? Milipian Perception at the Extremes." *Space and Sense* 19 (2006): 87–101.

Ovid. *Metamorphoses.* Translated by Charles Martin. New York: W.W. Norton, 2010.

Pailthorp, Charles. *The Bodies That Motions Make: Milipians, Atomists, and Kinesis.* New Haven: Yale University Press, 2002.

Plato. *Symposium.* Edited by Lester Perseus. Olympia: Ergon Press, 2003.

Reese, Andre. *Spatiality of the Sacred: Temples and Commons in the Mediterranean.* Berkeley: University of California Press, 2006.

Shih, Cornelius. *Ancient Greek Technics.* New York: Columbia University Press, 2010.

Spivey, Nigel. *Greek Sculpture.* Cambridge: Cambridge University Press, 2013.

Taylor, Nancy. *Archaeologies of the Aegean.* Cambridge: MIT Press, 2003.

Wheelmann, Markus. "Milipian Physicalism." *Cognitive Review* 23 (2014): 10–48.

Willoughby, Bradford. "Mimesis and the Milipians." *Mimesis Studies* 37, no. 4 (2015): 1104–57.

Wiscobb, A.J. "Voices of Elements: Milipian Singing Rituals in the 5th Century BCE." *Orality Quarterly* 36, no. 1 (2015): 21–39.

2

Encounters with the Unknown and Manifestations of Fear: Discerning the Purpose of the *Great Darkness Text*

Seth Ligo

In the spring of 2013, the sixth of eight treasure rooms beneath Padmanabhaswamy Temple, Thiruvananthapuram, India was opened. Overshadowed by the discovery of further gold reserves — bringing the value of the temple's holdings to some 22 bn. USD — was the presence of a library including superb editions of familiar texts, themselves priceless masterworks. One volume in particular was evidently unusual: it was penned on silk, a textual substrate known in East Asia but unheard of in the palmleaf-preferential South. Written in Siddhaṃ script, the c. 9th century text is primarily in Sanskrit, with extensive passages in what was initially thought to be phonetically transcribed glossolalia. The idiosyncrasies of the text caused it to be shelved until early 2016, when a team of European Research Council and University of Chicago scholars noticed interlinear notations in Chinese, early (Japanese) Katakana, and Tibetan, leading to the realization that these passages were in fact transliterations of sources written in different Asian languages. The collection and collation of these sources appears to be focused on deities associated with the obscure and the unknown, represented metaphorically as forms of darkness. Taking a cue from this metaphor, and nodding to the application of the epithet "Darkness" or "Dark One" to deities described in the book, scholars have begun to refer to it as In Praise of Darkness, or the Great Darkness Text. (Project Announcement Part 1/2 Purāṇa Pāṇsura Pustakāni, Nov. 2016)

In the year that has passed since the publication of this announcement additional manuscripts discovered at Padmanabhaswamy Temple have been identified as tributary sources coalescing in the *Great Darkness Text* (GDT). Ongoing efforts by the European Research Council and the University of Chicago have been expanded to include specialists at the École Française d'Extrême Orient and the Institut Français de Pondichéry, with teams of specialists working simultaneously on different portions of the manuscript in an attempt to accelerate a complete survey of its contents. Though extensive swaths of the text remain unaddressed, sufficient details have been gleaned throughout the volume to allow for an informed material analysis of the manuscript, and for a cursory analysis of its central theme and purpose. The result of these analyses follow.[1]

The *Great Darkness Text*: A Material Analysis

Material idiosyncrasy first drew attention to the Great Darkness Text, and a careful consideration of its form and attributes reveals much about its composition, context, and purpose. The

---

[1] I am indebted to the dedicated efforts of this diverse and talented multinational team of editors for the glimpse into this text that they make possible. In particular, I'd like to thank Dr. Lucille Womack for allowing me to access this work in progress. As I do not read many of the languages in which the GDT is recorded, I must acknowledge the relevant specialists, whose names are available on the project website. I have made an effort to work closely with these specialists to ensure the accuracy of my analysis. That said, any errors in transcription, translation, or interpretation are wholly my own.

text, which weighs 4.27 kg., comprises some 1,200 distinct writing areas.[2] The silk substrate would have been extremely expensive, and technology for its production had to be imported and adapted, but the resulting volume was lighter and longer-lasting than palm leaf alternatives. The current binding is heavily damaged. Silk sheafs rest between two wooden covers: the obverse with remnants of an hexagonal geometric design, the reverse plain. Impressions spaced around the perimeter of the silk suggest that the volume was once much more substantially bound: on all sides, with closely spaced lashings. Wear on the vertices of the pages suggests an inner cover of leather or heavier cloth, meaning the volume was not only securely bound but sealed on all sides from dust and perhaps moisture. Durable and relatively lightweight, the GDT was designed to be portable.

Though the cover binding does not appear to be original, there are decorated sheafs of heavier-weave silk constituting front and end matter, or inner covers. The obverse includes a benediction addressed to Bhairava, the archetypical subject of the text.[3] The preface includes a list of regions and rulers in *pañcamī,* or the ablative case, suggesting they are sources of the compiled material. Areas beyond South Asia are mentioned, which is highly unusual for Indian religious texts. Just inside the back cover appear archaic forms of the characters 接触未知 — Encounter with the Unknown (Chn. *jiēchù wèizhī,* Jpn. *sesshoku michi*), followed by a small note at the bottom of the inner cover in both characters and katakana to indicate this is the end of the volume, presumably for readers of these East Asian languages who were accustomed to texts flowing from right

---

2 At times there are small frames of text on a single stretch of silk; at other times a block of text will extend beyond the dimensions of the covers, and be folded back on itself. This appears to reproduce South Asian and East Asian norms of textual reproduction on a uniform, cloth substrate.

3 Though there are many names and metaphorical allusions to darkness and the unknown scattered through tributary sources and reproduced in the text itself, chief among these in prominence and prevalence in the compiled GDT is the Sanskrit derived भैरव (Bhairava), meaning "Cry of Fear." More about Bhairava and his relationship with the volume and its project below.

to left. Between this title page and the body of text is a purple swath of silk, the only dyed fabric in the volume.

Tributary Sources

The GDT was a grand collaborative exercise, bringing material from dozens of sources together in a definitive volume rendered in a single script. The original sources from which the GDT pulled were originally written in several languages, most prominently Tibetan, Chinese, and Japanese. They are themselves compendia of other sources, as evinced by shifts in writing substrate, calligraphic style, and regional designation. All told, there are twenty-six distinct textual streams feeding into the GDT. The oldest of the contributing sources appears to be a 7th-century Chinese text, though a Sanskrit source references epigraphy and the existence of a tradition of practitioners linked to this manuscript dating to the 5th or 6th century.[4] The latest source appears in a North Indian pre-Hindi Prakrit, and is coeval with the GDT, putting its composition at the middle of the 9th century.

The range and diversity of sources reproduced in the GDT reflect a network of specialists in different regions investigating disparate aspects of a close-knit nexus of topics. The compilation of this research into the GDT was never completed, a fact made clear by the discovery of source materials in the Padmanabhaswamy archive which both include and extend beyond what appears in the GDT. For example, the 17th section ends abruptly mid-description. A Chinese source for this material appears in the archive, and the point at which the GDT transposition ends is located roughly two-thirds of the way through that source.[5] Compilation of the GDT was itself a sub-divided collaborative

---

[4] E.g., Pāśupatas, Kālāmukhas, and Kāpālikas. See Alexis Sanderson, "Śaivism and the Tantric Traditions," in *The World's Religions*, eds. S. Sutherland et al. (London: Routledge, 1988), 660–704; and David N. Lorenzen, *The Kāpālikas and Kālāmukhas: Two Lost Śaivite Sects* (Berkeley: University of California Press, 1972).

[5] GDT sec. 17; Chn. source 14.2.B.

effort, with sections transposed and rendered by more than one scholar, evinced by variations in writing size and style, and repeated error distribution.

That each of these twenty-six sections was worked on by teams of scholars and scribes parallels the composition of the sections themselves. Each section is not the reproduction of a single work, but several works related by region and original language. Sections 21 and 22 are both in Chinese, with the former covering materials from what is now Bhutan, Sikkim, and other Himalayan regions, while the latter addresses Mongolia and North-Western China. There is occasional cross-commentary, such as Japanese material on China (sec. 24) and Chinese material on India (sec. 19), most likely collected by expatriates. More frequent, however, are stories recorded from incoming visitors. Tibetan accounts include many such stories from India and Nepal.

The early medieval teams of Keralan scholars editing the GDT encountered references to large-scale compilation projects similar to their own. Sections 3 and 5 describe efforts in Kathmandu to collect data from visiting scholars, ascetics, and storytellers. Focused on the Himalayan region, compilers drew from what we now distinguish as Vajrayāna, Śaiva, Śakta, (including Kaula variations on the two preceding), and Bön traditions.[6] Material details indicated a remarkably variegated range of sources represented in the GDT, and subsequent investigation has provided an initial view of the text's complex topography. It is, in essence, a series of nested but repeating structures: a fractal of sorts. Individual voices collected material, mostly from direct observation. Over time and across Asia, various regional authorities collected, and teams of scholars organized, these individual accounts. They collated related stories from other compiled sources or collected directly from outsiders. Eventually these initial compilers became aware of other, similar, regionally collabora-

---

6 The earliest entries in these sources coincide with the spread of written culture in Tibet (7th cent.), though the relation between that diffusion and these efforts remains obscure.

tive efforts. Some regional projects intersected, taking on transregional scope. These transregional projects themselves grew, and they were primarily those sources collected in the pan-regional project that was the GDT. Material evidence lets us know mostly about those who gathered and compiled these sources: language, script, organization, and substrate all show us these were geographically diverse textual scholars with extensive support of regional rulers. What we know about the voices who originally gathered and shared these data we can only gather obliquely though analysis of the GDT's representational mode.

Though the authors of the GDT were educated, travelled, aligned with regional influence, and therefore elite, many of the voices they record are not. There are references to wandering monks and ascetics, and other various groups of people whose identities are caught up in the recognition, veneration, and even emulation of deities described in this text. There are references to local leaders, healers, and shamans, non-elite persons who had direct relationships with such deities. The presence of feminine personal pronouns and adjectives demonstrate the inclusion of female informants. Descriptions of the project teams reveal that, at least in China, there were some female specialists gathering and collating these data.[7] This is further supported by the presence of hiragana, an alternate Japanese syllabary that was used almost exclusively by women. Such details led to the reconsideration of the presence of Prakrit and dialogues written with voices both in Prakrit and Sanskrit: originally presumed to be shuffled sources, they may instead be traditional representations of simultaneous male and female voices recorded in different vernacular registers.[8] This project was considered important by many people, from many backgrounds, making the

---

7 Sections 17; 21.
8 Cf. Wendy Doniger, *The Hindus: An Alternative History* (Oxford: Oxford University Press, 2010) 36–37; *The Implied Spider: Politics & Theology in Myth* (New York: Columbia University Press, 1998), chap. 5; and Sheldon Pollock, *The Language of the Gods in the World of Men: Sanskrit, Culture, and Power in Premodern India* (Berkeley: University of California Press, 2006).

participation of the Other multidimensional: regional, social, gendered, and religious.

The GDT and its tributaries present a staggering amount of material and textual information. It's likely the project was commissioned somewhere in Kerala, where it was eventually found. The *how* of the compilation of this text is evident, if unprecedented: Kerala had both the wealth and interconnectivity to conceive of and accomplish such a task. Ideas and information had long moved through this region from all over Asia and the Mediterranean, along with the spices that made the region wealthy and the silk that served as the foundation for the text. That the text, rich in what we would now call Śaiva material, was found in a temple patronized by Vaiṣṇava rulers indicates effort wasn't merely sectarian.[9] The *why* of this project and its importance to its patrons is less clear. The balance of this essay is an attempt to shed light on this question through an analysis of the text's central topic: a class of wrathful deities encountered across Asia, and the selected prime example who is, in Sanskrit, called Bhairava.

Wrathful Deities, Bhairava, Essence, and Effect

The text deals with a class of deities, ferocious in appearance and wild in behavior, who appear at thresholds between the familiar and the unknown: the margins of wilderness, doorways into sacred spaces, and cemeteries or creation grounds. Though a family resemblance in depictions of liminal creatures across South and East Asia has long been noted, this text is the first evidence that there was ongoing transcultural communication regarding encounters with such beings. The Great Darkness Text — the applied name paralleling recently noted internal self-reference as the Treatise on That Which

---

9   Over the past three millennia Buddhists, Jains, Śaivas, Vaiṣṇavas, Śaktas, and others have vied for philosophical and political influence in South Asia. The tension was, and continues to be, particularly pointed between Vaiṣṇava and Śaiva traditions.

Was Previously Obscure — appears to be a collaborative attempt to classify these creatures, determine their origins, and discern their purpose. Initial analysis seems to allude to a pan-Asian community of specialists who travelled these marginal spaces between cultures and used this text to encounter and engage such deities. (Project Announcement Part 2/2 Purāṇa Pāṇsura Pustakāni, Dec. 2016)

> The following are a few of the names used for a pan-Asian class of deity recorded in the Great Darkness Text:
> — Wisdom King (明王 — Chn. *Míngwáng*, Jpn. *Myōō*; विद्याराज — Skt. *Vidyārāja*);
> — Blood Drinker (胜乐金刚 — Chn. *Shèng lè jīngāng*; ཁྲག་འཐུང་ — Tib. *Khrag'thung*);
> — Great Darkness (大黑天 — Chn. *Dàhēitiān*, Jpn. *Daikokuten*; ནག་པོ་ཆེན་པོ་ — Tib. *Nagpo Chenpo*);
> — Cry of Fear (भैरव — Skt. *Bhairava*).
> (Project Announcement Addendum Purāṇa Pāṇsura Pustakāni, Dec. 2016)

The research team working on the GDT has concluded that wrathful deities are the organizing theme for the corpus.[10] Focusing on Bhairava — who while not an absolute archetype is certainly a privileged ectype in the text — illuminates the purpose of the GDT project. Reading Bhairava through the lens of 9th-century Kaśmīri Śaiva theology paired with theory from Ernst Cassirer and Michel Foucault makes sense of otherwise inconclusive material and textual analyses. It becomes clear that the compilers of the GDT were not supernatural big game hunt-

---

10 Robert Linrothe, in his *Ruthless Compassion,* sketches out the difference between Wrathful Deities and Wrathful Protectors. Though protection falls within the purview of many of these deities, they are not merely protectors, or repurposed demons, domesticated and chained for public benefit. Instead, they are fully developed deities in their own rite, with roles and identities far surpassing that of doorman. See Robert N. Linrothe, *Ruthless Compassion: Wrathful Deities in Early Indo-Tibetan Esoteric Buddhist Art* (Boston: Shambhala, 1999).

ers nor collectors of tales of the macabre and gruesome. Rather, they were explorers: intrepid pursuers of fringe experiences and the physical impressions of encounter with the unknown. It is these encounters they collected and organized in order to map the edges of knowledge, experience, an all encompassing inside, and the beginning of the Other.

There is a tendency, especially in the ex-Manichean Abrahamic-influenced Euro-American arena, to organize with binary classification: good/bad; safe/dangerous; insider/outsider; civilized/crude; sacred/profane. To a mind primed for such binary designations, the deities addressed in the GDT would lie with the latter member of these sets. They have fangs and wild eyes; their hair is unkempt and they are often naked; their jewelry is made of snakes and scorpions; they are known to relish impure substances and death; they are associated with dogs and the border beyond which lies wilderness. Though the phenomena reported in the GDT come with different labels, Bhairava is the most frequently used and overtly preferred name. His example most closely aligns with these creatures' common core.

Asian narrative and artistic territory is populated by myriad supernatural creatures, some similar to those familiar to Euro-American traditions, some less so. A *vetāla,* to take an example from the South Asian context that produced the GDT, is a reanimated corpse (like a zombie) who can feed on a person's life force (like a vampire) and can be controlled by a master (like a golem). *Yakṣas* are localized supernatural characters, often associated with the forces of nature in both their positive and negative aspects; *rakṣasas* are demons that trouble or plague people; *bhūtas* are ghosts or unclassified entities; *pretas* are creatures of disquiet, twisted by desire and dissatisfaction. This range and diversity of seemingly sinister characters appear all over Asia, often in overlapping categories, and often with a degree of internal diversity: not all members of a certain population are good, nor all bad.

Bhairava, the primary ectype of the deities addressed in the GDT, bears traces of this ambivalence. Though his behavior is at times transgressive, and he and his related ritual and devotional corpus warrant fear and caution, he is not perceived as an outstanding threat, nor in opposition to mainstream or orthodox religious practice and its maintenance. Indeed, along with being the chief of the *yakṣas, bhuts, pretas, vetālas*, and other assorted troublesome or terrifying creatures, he is associated with *Bīr Bābās* or local heroes.[11] They, like Bhairava, protect territory and, while unpredictable, are benevolent if remembered and attended.

In particular, Bhairava is famous for defending the sacred Hindu city of Vārāṇasī, or Kāśī, in northern India. There, he protects the city so effectively that even Yama, god of death, cannot enter, and anyone who sets foot within its boundary has all faults expunged, no matter who they are or what they have done. Despite this extremely purificatory effect, Bhairava remains associated with darkness, anger, death, and esoteric religious practice. This apparent ambivalence, his association with the protection and maintenance of borders, his association with death and transgressive ritual action, his wrathful appearance, and his staunch emplacement within Hindu sacred geography are useful points to keep in mind when considering the following summaries of regional accounts found in the GDT.

In GDT accounts drawn from East, Central, and South Asia, a wide range of wrathful deities are described, compared to other known types and instances of supernatural being, and organized accordingly. Throughout, there are a few common features — including fangs, bristling hair, tridents, and a third eye, to name a few — which appear to be of the greatest interest to the compilers. As will become increasingly evident in the following summary excerpts, these features support the theory that the GDT is in essence an effort to catalog and map creatures who appear at the peripheries: points between the known and the unknown. Japanese, Chinese, Tibetan, and Sanskrit are the four primary source languages in the compilation. Not all of

---

11 See Diane Coccari, "The Bīr Bābās of Banāras: An Analysis of a Folk Deity in North Indian Hinduism," PhD Thesis, University of Wisconsin-Madison, 1986.

these Sanskrit sources originated in India. Some clearly refer to Nepal, while other segments appear to be from South-East Asia, Afghanistan, or Pakistan. Though distinct in their vernacular cultures, these regions were all within the region that historically treated Sanskrit as lingua franca, and their scholarly, export-quality work would have been recorded in this transferrable language. Material from what is now Korea and parts of the Tibetan plateau were recorded in Chinese. Japanese material was first noticed due to the use of hiragana script, and some of the presumed Chinese materials have proven to be classical Japanese. The following region-specific summaries are drawn from the as-yet-incomplete findings of the research teams cataloging and translating the GDT and tributary sources.

In Japanese contributions, the greatest attention is given to the Myōō (明王), literally Wisdom Kings, who are ferocious in appearance and protective in nature. They have wild hair and fangs, and they trample demons. Later iconography includes tridents and bulls. These associations might have come from Śaiva influence via Vajrayāna Buddhism, which is generally held to have entered Japan in the 9th century. It is interesting to note that the stories of what come to be labeled Myōō predate this introduction, suggesting, as is true in many cases, longer histories of communication and exposure than we can easily account for, as well as the presence of similar characters or categories in Japan that allowed for the ingress and syncretic reconception of Buddhist Bhairava-type characters.

The sections in Japanese also address a precursor to Bishamonten (毘沙門天), a guardian deity associated with tridents and vanquishing demons. He lives on the northern side of a northern mountain, at the edge of known and accessible Japanese topography. He dwells not at the periphery of a community but at the periphery of a naturally formed territory. There, he is the king of creatures analogous to the *yakṣas* that Bhairava rules in India. It is interesting to note that Śiva, of whom Bhairava is believed to be a form, resides on Mount Meru, high in the

Himalayas, at the northernmost geographical limit of South Asian awareness.

None of the characters in the Japanese contributions to the GDT is otherwise unknown. In fact, many of them appear in Heian Period folktales. What is interesting is the fact that these contributors were not interested in stories of other sorts of phantoms or demonic looking characters, such as Tengu or even predecessors of Yamabushi. Instead, they looked for these strange and frightening creatures, who were associated with protection, and who lived at the farthest fringes of the known world.

The Chinese sources cover similar data: fanged creatures with three eyes and wild hair, often writhing and roiling, crushing or otherwise dominating demons. In these portions, there seems to be greater attention paid to arranging these creatures and instances of their encounter into networks. This directly reflects visualization practices common to Buddhist lineages found in Tibet, China, and Japan. As the Myōō protect the cardinal directions in temples and on maps, Bhairava-type deities protect the margins of imagined territories entered by the meditator in order to organize and better engage myriad personified phenomena. In the case of Chinese sources, *maṇḍalas* are mapped onto physical territory. Concentric circles mark degrees of unfamiliarity, with the known in the center. This fits nicely with the theory of meditative *maṇḍala* visualization practice presented by David Gordon White in "At the Maṇḍala's Dark Fringe: Possession and Protection in Tantric Bhairava Cults." There, he argues that the initial models for these visualized cognitive landscapes were kingdoms: seats of power with concentric regions of diminishing influence, security, and awareness.[12]

Chinese sources also traced the appearance of a slightly different creature: tomb guardians (鎮墓獸 — Chn. *zhènmùshòu*),

---

12 David Gordon White, "At the Maṇḍala's Dark Fringe: Possession and Protection in Tantric Bhairava Cults," in *Notes from a Maṇḍala: Essays in the History of Indian Religions in Honor of Wendy Doniger,* eds. Laurie L. Patton and David L. Haberman (Newark: University of Delaware Press, 2010), 200–215.

tiple disparate encounters with such creatures were organized in relation to the pan-Asian concept of Bhairava-type deities.

It is clear from these summaries that the deities addressed in the GDT share a range of attributes: they are ferocious or terrifying in appearance; they are associated with death and dogs; they appear at thresholds and boundaries, be they cosmological, metaphysical, social, or geographical. The compilers of the GDT were evidently interested in developing a detailed taxonomy of this sort of being. Associated with the unknown, it is not difficult to cultivate a sense that they all reflect the ineffable gestalt experience of encountering the unknown. Just how this might work, and how we can discuss such phenomena and experiences of encounter in developed and precise ways, are made possible through a consideration of the nature of Bhairava in conjunction with some 20th-century theory of myth and knowledge.

The Keystone Case of Bhairava

Though there are many etymologies — of varying provenance and plausibility — presented for the name Bhairava, it is difficult to divorce the meaning entirely from the components भी *bhī* and रव *rava* meaning, respectively, "fear" and "to cry out." In his commentary on the ninth century *Svacchandatantra*, Kṣemarāja's first exposition is of Bhairava's name. Two of Kṣemarāja's four glosses of Bhairava's name get to the core of his identity, and more specifically to the identity so laboriously pursued in the GDT. The first reads:

भयं भीः संसारत्रासः तया जनितो रवः आक्रन्दः भीरवः ततो जातः तदाक्रन्दवतां म्फुरतिः

Bhayam bhīḥ saṃsāratrāsaḥ tayā janito ravaḥ ākrandaḥ bhīravaḥ tato jātaḥ tadākrandatāṃ sphuritaḥ

Fear, that is to say terror, specifically the terror of transmigratory existence, engenders a scream; a wailing is thus born; therefore a cry is manifest.[17]

This explanation, written in the cascading multiple-gloss style that prevents any ambiguity, explains Bhairava to be composed of fear (*bhaya*) and cry (*rava*). Kṣemarāja further designates that it's a wailing cry, one that is issued when terror is experienced. That terror is the fear that arises when one encounters entropic, transmigratory existence. It is true that in the Svacchandatantra Bhairava can be understood to be the supporter of all things, and knowing and understanding him can indeed generate courage. To say this is in any way evident in the name itself is a stretch, at best.

After saying that Bhairava means the cry due to the fear of experiencing transmigratory existence, Kṣemarāja explains that this experience is not necessarily negative. He writes:

अस्यैव भीरवस्य संसारभयविमर्शनस्यायं शक्तिपातवशेनोत्थापकः
asyaiva bhīravasya saṃsārabhayavimarśanasyāyaṃ śaktipātavaśenotthāpakaḥ

Of this indeed, of the cry of fear, of awareness of fear in the world, is this: the awakening that is due to the instillation of power (śaktipāta).[18]

Generally speaking, *śaktipāta* is an initiatory empowerment in which spiritual energy is transmitted from the *guru* to a disciple. Kṣemarāja here identifies the inherently terrifying experience of encountering and considering transmigratory existence as a moment of natural initiatory empowerment: one is awakened due to a *śaktipāta* that occurs as one becomes aware of and

---

17 Paṇḍit Madhusudan Kaul Shāstrī, ed., *The Svacchanda-Tantra with commentary by Kshemarāja* (Bombay: Nirnaya-Sagar Press, 1921). Translations are mine unless otherwise noted.
18 Ibid.

considers the terror inherent in overwhelming, impermanent, illusory transmigration. Experiencing this awareness, fear, and empowerment, a cry naturally erupts. Though the exact order is debatable, the association is unmistakable. This is the essence of Bhairava: he is directly linked to encounters with the unknown, resulting fear, ensuing empowerment, and ultimate expression. As such, he is most representative of the core identities of the characters presented and organized in the GDT. Though varying in style and representation defined by cultural context, all of these wrathful deities share this same relationship with the unknown, fear, and its resolution. Kṣemarāja recognizes this in his philosophical commentary for a medieval tantric text. Though the name isn't necessarily essential, here the essence has a name, and it is Bhairava.

Analysis and Beyond

The *Svacchandatantra* describes Bhairava as the cry of fear that arises due to the awareness of transmigratory existence, a great, overwhelming unknown. The Bhairava-type deities catalogued in the GDT instead appear in a somewhat lesser moment of encounter with the unknown. Resulting not in a shriek of terror but rather a sensory experience, an encounter with the unknown is experienced as a palpable encounter with a creature. Though there is regional and even individual diversity amongst these creatures, they are nevertheless clearly of a type in terms of both appearance and function. The compilers of the GDT were directly aware of such phenomena, but similar experiences are postulated by Ernst Cassirer in his 1925 *Language and Myth*. Cassirer builds upon Usener's theory of momentary deities to offer his own theory of the interconnected origins of religion and language. These beings, as Cassirer summarizes,

> do not personify any force of nature, nor do they represent some special aspect of human life; no recurrent trait or value is retired in them and transformed into a mythico-religious image; it is something purely instantaneous, a fleeting,

emerging and vanishing mental content, whose objectification and outward discharge produces the image of the "momentary deity."[19]

Bhairava doesn't fit this description at only one point: mythic-religious images were and are made of him. The difference is that the momentary deities theorized by Usener and developed by Cassirer were unique not only to a certain place, but a single time. They were one-off experiences. Contrastingly, the basis for the eventual compilation of the GDT lies in a recognition of the fact that these encounters demonstrated great similarity across time and space. People were seeing culturally specific versions of the same sort of creature. The cosmology of the *Svacchandatantra* suggests that we can read these as miniature versions of the initial experience with existence: instead of a fear of everything, humans encountered the unknown, and were afraid. Instead of instantaneous *śaktipāt*, they saw a creature: a form of Bhairava who both marks and helps reconcile this encounter with the unknown.

Michel Foucault's notion of irruption facilitates thinking beyond individual arisings to widespread presence. In *Archaeology of Knowledge,* Foucault calls for discourse to be ever ready for irruption: that point when a shift in circumstance makes something formerly so minor as to be practically invisible into something so pervasive and referenced its ubiquity seems eternal and natural.[20] Bhairava's presence across Asia is such an irruption: a demonic looking deity who marks and protects boundaries, his examples tease the categories of the known and the unfathomed. Now widely recognized and accepted, even normalized, it could be said that his grand conceptual irruption is the coalescence of many minor irruptions, when some hitherto unknown or unexperienced or unexpressed thing was met in a moment

---

19 Ernst Cassirer, *Language and Myth,* trans. Susanne Langer (New York: Dover Publications, 1953), 18.

20 Michel Foucault, *Archaeology of Knowledge,* trans. A.M. Sheridan Smith (New York: Routledge, 2002) 25.

of overwhelming bewilderment, which gave rise to the presence and perception of Bhairava.

Foucault says that "to disconnect the unquestioned continuities by which we organize, in advance, the discourse that we are to analyze," we must embrace the practicality of irruption, the point before which any influence or origin is obscure, making this arrival as though *ex nihilo*.[21] Foucault refers to this irruption in chronological terms. We can always look for, and find, precedent for any major phenomenon we wish. We do not know where Bhairava first appeared, when he was first represented, whether he moved into or out of containing traditions. We do, however, have a metaphysical model for the irruption of individual Bhairavas or Bhairava-type deities. Though perhaps they lay dormant or imperceivable in the fabric of existence, their perception irrupts into the consciousness of the person encountering the unknown. It is possible that the initial moment of fear and its processing modeled in the *Svacchandatantra* is ahistorical and therefore fits well with Foucault's idea that there is apparent chronological irruption. Nevertheless, it is the individual instances of metaphysical irruption of Bhairava that the GDT was attempting to document and analyze.

The GDT's sponsors, compilers, and contributors were mapping points at which there had been overwhelming experiences of unknowing at and the appearance of Bhairava or a Bhairava-type deity. There are several possible reasons for this: they could be interested in knowing where their boundaries lay; why such experiences led to such encounters; or the nature of the relationship between, say, Gundari Myōō (軍荼利明王) in Japan and Ananda Bhairava (आनन्दभैरव) in India. They could even have been interested in cultivating nuanced appreciation for such deities. After all, it is said in the Tibetan Buddhist *Bardo Thodol* that if one reacts to a wrathful deity with disgust or fear, it does not end well.[22] While it is likely that the identification and analy-

---

21 Ibid.
22 Robert N. Linrothe and Jeff Watt, *Demonic Divine: Himalayan Art and Beyond* (New York: Rubin Museum of Art; Chicago: Serindia Publications,

sis of the personification of the frontier experience — the sense of exploration and discovery — could well have driven most of these efforts, there is another possible impetus: the benefits of knowing and understanding Bhairava. Certainly, it would behoove a population to know who dwelt at and protected its peripheries, and to know that these creatures are at once ferocious and not predatory. It would also behoove a people to find a way to engage the Other, and the unknown, and to reconcile this rupture of experience and understanding that gave rise to the perception of Bhairava in the first place. In both India and Japan, we have examples of Bhairava-type deities becoming mainstream and finding place within society. At first, they are recognized and marked at the doorways to sacred spaces: temples, and in some cases tombs. Then, we have instances of Bhairavas who have become mainstream deities themselves, even surrounded by other Bhairavas filling the type of role they once filled. In Vārāṇasī, Kāl Bhairava is central to the city, while its periphery is guarded by eight other Bhairavas. Kāl Bhairava, though he rules over death, is not ferocious, but he is not to be trifled with. He remains calm, but his power can expedite untold cycles of rebirth. Among the Myōō, Fudō (不動) sits calm, with smaller and fewer fangs, unmoving and contemplative. He is surrounded by four other Myōō, who still guard the periphery. In this way, the unknown is incrementally incorporated into the familiar and the mainstream while at the same time a connection providing access to the unknown is made regular and reliable.

The GDT doesn't just map similar cases across space, but also a range of cases within particular spaces. In these models, such as the cases of Kāl Bhairava and Fudō Myōō, terrifying creatures are incrementally integrated into society. Their role and appearance become more familiar. This pattern seems to be reflected in some of the source material. As one Tibetan portion (sec. 9) recounts, a traveler entered a dark, narrow mountain pass, and heard a strange sound. As he tried to gain his bearings and identify the sound, he saw a creature with wild eyes, and flam-

---

2004), 6.

ing flowing hair, bared fangs and lolling tongue, holding out a skull in the traveler's direction. Initially frozen with dread, the traveler was able to continue to observe this Bhairava, noticing that the terrifying figure was also holding flowers, and though hideous made no move to attack. The skull was in fact a begging bowl, which he held out for alms. Placing some dried meat in the bowl, the traveler went on his way. His fear resolved, the mark of that point of transition imprinted emotionally and cognitively in his mind, he entered new and unknown territory.

It is evident that Bhairava-type deities can both mark and resolve encounters with the unknown, or Other, on both communal (i.e., Kāl Bhairava and Fudō Myōō) and personal (the account of the traveler) levels. It follows that explorers, alchemists, and ritual experts would be interested in further investigating these phenomena and newly exposed frontiers. Expanding this understanding, it becomes clear why the GDT wanted to pull material from so many diverse sources, regulate it, and re-present it; why it is written phonetically, and made to be portable. Often, phonetic transcription was based in a theory of the power of speech: Sanskrit mantras had power when recited by Chinese Buddhists not because of their meaning, but because of their sound, making phonetic reproduction paramount. In this case, phonetic transcription wasn't to aid ritual accuracy, but to facilitate conversation. By being able to express to others the findings and further goals of such a project, specialists versed in Sanskrit could travel across Asia, expanding both the spread of information and the project itself. As is evident in the repeated focus on outside territory, participants in these projects knew that whatever the benefit of studying Bhairava-type deities in their own context could provide would be exponentially increased by the inclusion of material from other regions and contexts. Beyond increasing understanding of the process of expanding knowledge by analyzing points of intersection with the unknown, collecting these materials provided connections between networks of periphery: mutual recognition of Bhairava was a way to bridge otherwise restrictive chasms between cultures and peoples across Asia. This could facilitate trade, dialogue, and even physical movement among and across disparate cultural contexts.

While the potential of the GDT was never fully realized, these efforts were not made in vain. Beyond linking contributors through a hub in Kerala, the text cemented a scholarly awareness of the experience of Otherness. The GDT remains relevant to this day. It provides a window back in time to a different cartography of wilderness and civilization, of insider and outsider. Bhairavas, many in place since the time of the GDT, become markers for encounters with the unknown, and as such can guide contemporary religious and social research. Bhairavas helped mediate fear and expand understanding. Is it so ridiculous to suggest that better understanding their nuanced forms and roles might help Euro-American minds reconcile the overwhelming, initially uncomfortable encounter with the diversity and dynamism of Asian religious contexts?

Bibliography

Cassirer, Ernst. *Language and Myth*. Translated by Susanne Langer. New York: Dover Publications, 1953.
Coccari, Diane. "The Bīr Bābās of Banāras: An Analysis of a Folk Deity in North Indian Hinduism." PhD Thesis, University of Wisconsin-Madison, 1986.
Doniger, Wendy. *The Hindus: An Alternative History*. Oxford: Oxford University Press, 2010.
———. *The Implied Spider: Politics & Theology in Myth*. New York: Columbia University Press, 1998.
Foucault, Michel. *Archaeology of Knowledge*. Translated by A.M. Sheridan Smith. New York: Routledge, 2002.
Linrothe, Robert N., and Jeff Watt. *Demonic Divine: Himalayan Art and Beyond*. New York: Rubin Museum of Art; Chicago: Serindia Publications, 2004.
Linrothe, Robert N. *Ruthless Compassion: Wrathful Deities in Early Indo-Tibetan Esoteric Buddhist Art*. Boston: Shambhala, 1999.
Lorenzen, David N. *The Kāpālikas and Kālāmukhas: Two Lost Śaivite Sects*. Berkeley: University of California Press, 1972.
Pollock, Sheldon. *The Language of the Gods in the World of Men: Sanskrit, Culture, and Power in Premodern India*. Berkeley: University of California Press, 2006.
Sanderson, Alexis. "Śaivism and the Tantric Traditions." In *The World's Religions,* edited by S. Sutherland et al., 660–704. London: Routledge, 1988.
Madhusudan Kaul Shāstrī, Paṇḍit, ed. *The Svacchanda-Tantra with commentary by Kshemarāja*. Bombay: Nirnaya-Sagar Press, 1921.
White, David Gordon. *Myths of the Dog Man*. Chicago: University of Chicago Press, 1991.
———. "At the Maṇḍala's Dark Fringe: Possession and Protection in Tantric Bhairava Cults." In *Notes from a Maṇḍala: Essays in the History of Indian Religions in Honor of Wendy*

Doniger, edited by Laurie L. Patton and David L. Haberman, 200–215. Newark: University of Delaware Press, 2010.

3

The *Romance of the Minotaur* Reconsidered

Katherine McLoone

Rarely read and frequently forgotten, the *Romance of the Minotaur* is one of the true orphan romances of medieval British literature. Neither the Broadview nor the Norton anthologies see fit to include it. The TEAMS Middle English Texts series omitted it from *The Middle English Breton Lays*[1] and chose not to make it the fifth entry in the popular *Four Middle English Romances*.[2] Unless one wins a travel grant to Scotland, where the Auchinleck manuscript is held, one must acquire a musty library copy of A.J. Bliss's 1961 edition of *Sir Orfeo* that still includes the rare post-publication corrected insert. Bliss apparently meant to edit the *Romance of the Minotaur* as an appendix to Sir Orfeo, but provides only brief comments on its verb forms and likely end-

---

1 Anne Laskaya and Eve Salisbury, eds., *The Middle English Breton Lays* (Rochester: TEAMS Middle English Text Series, 1995).
2 Harriet Hudson, ed., *Four Middle English Romances: Sir Isumbras, Octavian, Sir Eglamour of Artois, Sir Tryamour,* 2nd edn. (Rochester: TEAMS Middle English Text Series, 2006).

ing.³ Even Derek Pearsall omits it from his exhaustive landmark article on "The Development of Middle English Romance."⁴

The text's unpopularity is odd, given its thrilling plot and unique spin on the Theseus legend. Like many medieval romances that draw on classical sources (Ovid's *Metamorphoses* is the likeliest here), the *Romance of the Minotaur* adapts and amends the original, perhaps under the influence of a now-lost Breton lay. In the romance, Theseus is a king who journeys to Canterbury⁵ in search of a wife: "To Canterbury the king must go / In search of a wife to cure his woe" (ll. 9–10).⁶ He there encounters King Minos, who offers him the hand of Ariadne in exchange for Theseus slaying the Minotaur. Theseus agrees, Ariadne weaves him a girdle, and he enters an ornate labyrinth. As he wanders, he unravels the girdle, so that he might find his way back by following its threads. In scenes nearly as graphic as those in the later *Sir Gowther*, Theseus slays the Minotaur. When he brings the head to Minos, he retraces his steps with the aid of the now-destroyed girdle: "The head he bore with carriage proud / Not knowing the peril of what he'd vowed" (ll. 1027–28). When Minos sees the head of the Minotaur, he recognizes it as the head of his long-lost (and heretofore-unmentioned) son, who had been stolen by an evil steward years before.⁷ Minos demands Theseus marry Ariadne so that he might ascend the throne upon Minos's death in place of the now-dead son. Theseus agrees to do so, and — just as Ariadne is poised to speak, perhaps in agreement or perhaps in rejection — the text cuts off.

---

3   A.J. Bliss, ed. *Sir Orfeo* (Oxford: Oxford University Press, 1961).
4   Derek Pearsall, "The Development of Middle English Romance," *Mediaeval Studies* 27 (1965): 91–116.
5   There is a glancing mention of the significance of Canterbury (rather than Crete, as in Ovid's version of the Minotaur story) in Andrea Wearall, "Place Names, The Place," *Medieval Minutiae: Notes on the Fourteenth Century* 101, no. 17 (Autumn 2007): 19–29.
6   All translations from Middle English are my own, and all citations, unless otherwise noted, are to the Bliss corrected edition.
7   For more on the evil steward trope, see "Sir Orfeo: Introduction" in *The Middle English Breton Lays*.

The little that has been written on the *Romance of the Minotaur* focuses, unsurprisingly, on the character of Theseus and his status as a chivalric hero who negotiates the challenges of courtly love while enacting decidedly exhaustive violence. In "James Bond and Dr. Minos: Gawain and Theseus in the Bedroom," John Shaddeus draws on Cory James Rushton's formulation of Gawain as the "medieval James Bond" to argue that the now-lost ending to the *Romance of the Minotaur* would include Theseus, like his Ovidian counterpart, leaving Ariadne behind.[8] Although the comparison with Gawain is fruitful — I will address it in more detail later — the article deflects notions of loyalty to valorize a "love 'em or leave 'em" ethos that is inimical to medieval concepts of both courtly love and chivalry.

In "Road Rage in the Labyrinth: Theseus' Exhausted Violence," Ilan Mitchell-Smith argues that the extraordinary violence Theseus enacts on the Minotaur is linked to the Middle English concept of *wode,* or unbalanced insanity, created by the exhausting journey through the labyrinth. Mitchell-Smith argues that, since the text itself is nearly inexhaustible at that point — some 50 lines are devoted to descriptions of the labyrinth, another 72 to the killing of the Minotaur — the anonymous author linked the reader's exhaustion to Theseus's, and therefore problematized the violence of medieval heroism.[9]

That Theseus's heroism is problematic is undeniable. But that it is — or ought to be — the focus of scholarship represents a masculinist blind spot in the existing criticism. For that reason, I reconsider the *Romance of the Minotaur* in order to explore not only its hero but also its heroine: the silent Ariadne, sister to a monster and bargaining chip to her father; and her brother, the

---

[8] John Shaddeus, "James Bond and Dr. Minos: Gawain and Theseus in the Bedroom," *Exemplaria* 39, no. 2 (Fall 2012): 25–37. See also Cory James Rushton, "The Lady's Man: Gawain as Lover in Middle English Literature," in *The Erotic in the Literature of Medieval Britain,* eds. Amanda Hopkins and Cory James Rushton. (Cambridge: D.S. Brewer, 2007).

[9] Ilan Mitchell-Smith, "Road Rage in the Labyrinth: Theseus' Exhausted Violence," *Speculum* 291, no. 4 (June 2015): 117–40.

monster who represents a "category crisis."[10] I will argue that by examining the portrayals of Ariadne and her brother the Minotaur, as well as her girdle and the labyrinth, we can see the text's nuanced articulation of the connection between trauma and memory.

To do so, we must begin with the context: the Auchinleck manuscript (NLS Adv MS 19.2.1). Produced in 1330s London, named after an eighteenth-century collector, and now held in the National Library of Scotland, the Auchinleck is an iconic medieval miscellany. Five scribes contributed to the Middle English manuscript, which contains works as dull as *The Battle Abbey Rolls* (as the title implies, it is a list of names) and as delightful as *Sir Orfeo, Le Freine,* and *King of Tars*. Laura Hibbard Loomis argues that Chaucer likely read it, and although that idea has a greater percentage of conjecture than confirmation, the connection with Canterbury (which supplants Crete in the *Romance of the Minotaur*) is tantalizing.[11]

Scribe I (or α) transcribed, among other texts, the anonymously authored *Romance of the Minotaur, Sir Orfeo,* and *Lay Le Freine*. In the Auchinleck, which contains the only extant copy, the *Romance of the Minotaur* is missing its opening lines and its conclusion (assumed to be approximately 50 lines); *Sir Orfeo* is missing the first 38 lines; and *Le Freine* is missing lines 121–33 and 341–408, which are commonly supplied in modern editions by Henry William Weber's 1810 recreation[12], based on Marie de France's twelfth-century "Le Fresne." The *Le Freine* prologue ap-

---

10 Jeffrey Jerome Cohen, "Monster Culture (Seven Theses)," in *Monster Theory: Reading Culture* (Minneapolis: University of Minnesota Press, 1996): 3–25, at 6.

11 Laura Hibbard Loomis, "Chaucer and the Breton Lays of the Auchinleck Manuscript," *Studies in Philology* 38 (1941): 14–33, rpt. *Adventures in the Middle Ages* (New York: Burt Franklin, 1962): 131–49. See also Allison Wiggins, "The Auchinleck Manuscript: Importance," *National Library of Scotland,* https://auchinleck.nls.uk/editorial/importance.html

12 Henry W. Weber, *Metrical Romances of the Thirteenth, Fourteenth and Fifteenth Centuries,* vol. I (Edinburgh: Archibald Constance, 1810), 357–71. Both Margaret Wattie ("The Middle English Lai le Freine," *Smith College Studies in Modern Languages* 10, no. 3 [April 1929]: i-xiii and 1–27) and

pears, with emendations and elisions, in two fifteenth-century versions of *Sir Orfeo*: Harley 3810 and Ashmole 61. For that reason, Bliss argues that the Le Freine prologue ought to function as the prologue to both *Sir Orfeo* and the *Romance of the Minotaur*:

> It may be argued that where the original text is lost, any genuine medieval version is better than a hypothetical reconstruction by a modern scholar; this may be a valid argument, but it is only partially relevant here, for the "prologue section" at least occurs on folio 261a of MS. Auchinleck as an introduction to *Lay Le Freine,* and it is written by the same scribe who wrote *Sir Orfeo,* in the same dialect and orthography [...]. It is sufficient to point out that it is more satisfactory for many reasons to supply the missing lines in a contemporary version which shows the same dialect and the same orthography as the rest of the text of *Sir Orfeo*.[13]

The three texts do have some similarities. *Sir Orfeo* is loosely based on the classical myth of Orpheus as told in Ovid's *Metamorphoses,* Virgil's *Georgics,* and Boethius's *Consolation of Philosophy,* and likely translated from the lost Old French *Lai d'Orphay.* At first blush, *Sir Orfeo* is a straightforward example of *translatio studii et imperii*: the medieval theory of the transmission or movement of knowledge and power from ancient Greece to ancient Rome, and thence to France and England. In that movement, Orpheus the bard becomes Orfeo the poet-king; Thrace becomes Winchester; and Hades becomes a fairy land from which Orfeo successful rescues his wife Heurodis, after which he returns to rule his kingdom. When he and Heurodis die without heirs, the steward takes over the kingdom.

Unlike the inventive *Sir Orfeo, Lay Le Freine* is a faithful adaptation of Marie de France's "Le Fresne" that tells of two women,

---

Anne Laskaya and Eve Salisbury ("Lay Le Freine," in *The Middle English Breton Lays,* 61–87) depend on Weber's recreation for their critical editions.
13 Bliss, *Sir Orfeo,* 10–11. See also A.J. Bliss, "Notes on the Auchinleck Manuscript," *Speculum* 26, no. 4 (Oct. 1951): 652–58.

their knightly husbands, and the tragic consequences of sacrificing family to reputation.[14] One woman gives birth to twin boys, prompting the other to declare her an adulteress. When that woman gives birth to twin girls, she faces the consequences of her rumor-mongering and sends one of the girls away to be left at a convent. After numerous reversals, the woman recognizes her abandoned (adult) daughter, and the twin women marry the twin men. A more personal tale than *Sir Orfeo*, *Le Freine* nonetheless places equal emphasis on parent–child relationships, the significance of recognition scenes, and the importance of continuing the family (or in the case of *Sir Orfeo*, dynastic) line.

As those descriptions indicate, all three texts — *Sir Orfeo, Le Freine,* and the *Romance of the Minotaur* — circle around the same themes, with each romance providing a unique perspective. There is a varying attention to the women: in *Sir Orfeo*, Heurodis, like her classical counterpart Eurydice, is more of a quest-object than a character; her most notable quality is being kidnapped by a fairy-king. But *Le Freine*, like its twelfth-century source text, explores the consequences of its titular character, a young girl abandoned at the doorsteps of a nunnery.

In the *Romance of the Minotaur*, Ariadne is both a quest-object (Theseus slays the Minotaur to gain her hand in marriage) and an active participant in the heroic actions. Although she does not speak, Ariadne is present in every scene that takes place outside the labyrinth. "Minos and his daughter" or "Father and daughter" recur 19 times in the romance, as in the first scene after the putative prologue:

> King Minos and his daughter sat in the hall,
> Theseus bade them greetings and homage.
> "Welcome, traveler," King Minos said,
> And his daughter nodded, graceful and staid (57–61).

---

14 See Howard Bloch, "If Words Could Kill: The Lais and Fatal Speech," *The Anonymous Marie de France* (Chicago: University of Chicago Press, 2006), 51–82, esp. 74–79.

In these lines, we see the repetition of "King Minos...and his daughter" twice within four lines, creating the effect of two interlocked beings: throughout the poem, Minos is never without Ariadne. We might read Ariadne's nod as nothing more than a polite gesture, but we can also consider it a form of speech. Silent, yet communicative, Ariadne does not just acknowledge Theseus but also approves of her father's greeting.

Ariadne's silent communication continues throughout the poem, especially in the girdle she sews for Theseus. The passages that describe her needlecraft rival some of the older French *chansons de toile* ("sewing songs" or "sewing poems") for the description of both craft and result:[15]

> Ariadne Theseus's girdle wrought,
> And as she worked, of her mother she thought.
> Green for luck, and the white turned red,
> For Ariande worked until her fingers bled.
> ...
> Ariadne wove the girdle into a round,
> Around Theseus it circled and wound.
> Ariadne wove memory within,
> Protection that she wove therein (303–307; 321–325).

The poet here interlaces Ariadne's sewing with a memory of her mother, which reflects the reality of a young woman's upbringing (mothers taught daughters to sew), but may also foreshadow some of the work's later developments. In the *Romance of the Minotaur*, unlike the classical versions, Minos's unnamed wife is never described as unfaithful, and therefore the Minotaur's parentage is never explicitly stated to be illegitimate. For Ariadne to think of her mother, in other words, might mean she is also thinking of her missing brother.

---

15 For more on portrayals of sewing and clothes — which less common in the British tradition — see E. Jane Burns, *Courtly Love Undressed: Reading Through Clothes in Medieval French Culture* (Philadelphia: University of Pennsylvania Press, 2005).

The theme of the loss of the mother links the text to both Orfeo's quest to find his missing wife and *Le Freine*'s ultimate reunion with her own mother; read together, the three poems speak *around,* but rarely *of,* the trauma of loss. In the incomplete ending of the *Romance of the Minotaur*, Ariadne does not reunite with her mother, whom we might presume to be dead since she is unmentioned. But the poem does link physical trauma (she "worked until her fingers bled") to the emotional trauma of coming of age without a mother-figure. In the first scene in Ariadne appears without her father, she bleeds while doing the work of a mature woman for the purpose of protecting her potential husband's safety.

Although the poem lacks an accurate vocabulary for needlework, the thirty lines that describe Ariadne's sewing constitute *ekphrasis*: the description of art in narrative. Typically, ekphrasis is an opportunity for the author to demonstrate poetic complexity. From Homer's lines about Achilles's shield to Virgil's description of the frieze that depicts the fall of Troy, ekphrasis in the classical tradition serves the same function as a guitar solo: unnecessary for the melody, yet vital for the song's emotive and artistic power. In *Romance of the Minotaur*, the colors (green, red, gold, and white) and materials (silk, soft wool, and even — improbably — lapis lazuli) are meaningful. Green, as we saw above, is for luck ("fortune"), red is Ariadne's blood, white represents purity, and gold signifies success, which the poem distinguishes from fortune, a term that could mean either good or bad outcomes. The lapis lazuli represents wealth, the silk power, and the wool "a memento of the journey home" (312). The cumulative effect of the ekphrasis is to allow Ariadne the opportunity to communicate.

But with whom? Does Ariadne hope to communicate with Theseus? To craft a protective garment that no one but her would understand? Or to provide a memento, a memory token, to the Minotaur? Following Bliss's editorial suggestions and implications, we might compare the girdle in the Romance the Minotaur to the objects of recognition in its two manuscript analogues. In *Sir Orfeo,* the poet-king repeatedly misinterprets what he sees, or has to see it twice to understand it. When he finally finds Heurodis, it is only "by her attire he knew 'twas she" (408).[16] In *Le Freine*, the mother only recognizes her long-lost daughter by the objects she'd left with the abandoned baby, a mantle and a ring (375–85).[17] There is precedent for objects to signify identity.

In more ways than one. In "Feminine Knots and the Other *Sir Gawain and the Green Knight*," Geraldine Heng posits a contrast between the Gawain's pentangle (a masculine knot) and Lady Bertilak's love-lace (the feminine girdle), which encircles — and ultimately shames — Gawain: "Never requiring to be tied, untied, or retied, the pentangle is the ultimate guarantee […] for the existence of fixed and stable identity […] the pentangle as personal emblem for Gawain is subsequently overtaken by an 'imperfect' knot," the girdle.[18]

In the lines quoted above, we saw how "Ariadne wove the girdle into a round / Around Theseus it circled and wound" (321–22). The rhymes and cognates *round, around, circled, wound* enclose Theseus as much as the girdle itself does. Ariadne effectively wraps Theseus in her language, not for the purpose of communicating with him, but to make him, perhaps, a vehicle for communication. Read in light of Heng's model — in which a girdle represents womanhood itself, an inherent threat to masculine stability — we might consider Ariadne's silent communication as a feminine response to his proposed actions: she weaves as he wanders and slaughters.

The woven girdle ("Ariadne wove memory within / Protection that she wove therein") that encircles Theseus also parallels the labyrinth into which he ventures. In "The Poet as Master Builder: Composition and Locational Memory in the Middle Ages," Mary Carruthers argues that descriptions of architecture, such as the "amphitheater" of Dante's Hell, correspond to the

---

16 "Sir Orfeo," trans. J.R.R. Tolkien, in *Sir Gawain and the Green Knight, Pearl, and Sir Orfeo* (New York: Ballantine Books, 1975).
17 "Lay Le Freine" in *The Middle English Breton Lays*.
18 Geraldine Heng, "Feminine Knots and the Other Sir Gawain and the Green Knight," *PMLA* 106, no. 3 (May 1991): 500–514, at 504.

medieval mnemonic technique of a memory palace, in which a student or reader organized information — and, more importantly, connections between bits of information — in a mental architectural structure.[19] The connection with ekphrasis speaks for itself: a description of art or architecture becomes a glimpse into both the memory structures the author may have drawn on and the mnemonic tools he provides the reader.

The fifty lines devoted to describing the labyrinth that contains the Minotaur emphasize both its architectural structure and its artifice. As Seth Lerer said of the fairyland of *Sir Orfeo*: "A close look at the Auchinleck text reveals a description of fairyland indebted to the technical terms of painting in thirteenth- and fourteenth-century England […] a display of human craft which manipulates surfaces for the awe or delectation of the beholder."[20] The same could be said of the labyrinth of the *Romance of the Minotaur*:

> A hundred towers were raised about
> With cunning wrought, embattled stout;
> With buttress of glass and bronzed gold,
> The walls encircled stones of old.
> By Daedalus these walls were wrought,
> To contain that which might be sought (471–77).[21]

Where the poet lacked the vocabulary of needlecraft, he excelled in the vocabulary of architecture. But the near-parity of the two ekphrases — the thirty lines that describe the girdle, the fifty lines that describe the labyrinth — as well as the focus, in each,

---

[19] Mary Carruthers, "The Poet as Master Builder: Composition and Locational Memory in the Middle Ages," *New Literary History* 24, no. 4, Papers from the Commonwealth Center for Literary and Cultural Change (Autumn 1993): 881–904. See also Frances Yates, *The Art of Memory* (Chicago: University of Chicago Press, 2001) and Mary Carruthers, *The Book of Memory* (Cambridge: Cambridge University Press, 2008).

[20] Seth Lerer, "Artifice and Artistry in Sir Orfeo," *Speculum* 60, no. 1 (Jan 1985): 92–109, at 93.

[21] The first two lines of this excerpt are repeated in "Sir Orfeo" (359–60). I have followed Tolkien's translation.

on colors, crafts, and general bedazzlement links the two artificial, constructed objects with medieval mnemonic techniques.

The girdle and the labyrinth evoke both the concept of memory itself, and the personal memories of what has been lost (Ariadne's mother, the Minotaur's loss of his family through his own exile to the labyrinth). Similarly, the girdle and the labyrinth are described as "encircling": the girdle that wraps around Theseus is like the labyrinth that does the same. Or, to extend the parallel, we might argue that the girdle that encircles Theseus is like the labyrinth that encircles the Minotaur.

In most versions of the story, including Ovid's, the Minotaur lives up to his name: half man, half bull, the illegitimate son of King Minos's wife. Yet, while he is named as the Minotaur throughout the romance, his physical features are never described. He is "fearsome," "rough," and "loath to look upon," but the poet never delineates the specifics of his hybridity (515, 521, 526). In "Monster Culture (Seven Theses)," Jeffrey Jerome Cohen argues that "the monster notoriously appears at times of crisis as a kind of third term that problematizes the clash of extremes — as 'that which questions binary thinking and introduces a crisis.'"[22] The Minotaur, in other words, exists as a wrench in the works: girdle/labyrinth, Theseus/Minotaur, even Ariadne/Theseus — these binary terms are complicated both by the Minotaur's existence and by his fate.Because the Minotaur does introduce a "crisis": the revelation of familial trauma. Just before the poem cuts off, Theseus drags the "heavy head" of the Minotaur out of the labyrinth: "The head he carried, full of woe / Red with blood and fraught with dole" (543). The Middle English here is ambiguous: does "full of woe" modify Theseus or the Minotaur's head? Both, we might presume, are covered with blood, but Theseus, who is victorious should not feel "dole" or pain — he has accomplished his mission.

The mention of blood here also evokes the girdle into which Ariadne wove her blood: "Theseus unwound what Ariadne

---

[22] Cohen, "Monster Culture," 6, quoting Marjorie Garber, *Vested Interests: Cross-Dressing and Cultural Anxiety* (New York: Routledge, 1992), 11.

wrought / In his quest to find what was sought" (492–94). Following Cohen's thesis, the Minotaur — like the labyrinth that contains him — creates a "category crisis" in which objects seems to echo and affect each other. Girdle and labyrinth, hero and monster, Ariadne's communicative needlework and the poem's own language: all unravel upon Theseus's exit from the labyrinth.

This returns us to the question of recognition. In *Le Freine*, the ring and the mantle allow the mother to recognize her long-lost daughter. In *Sir Orfeo*, his wife's clothes allow him to realize identity of the woman before him. These objects are mementos that spur the recollection of memory. But in the *Romance of the Minotaur*, recognition and remembrance become monstrous. Minos does not see the unknown monster that has lived in the labyrinth, but instead recognizes the head of his dead son: "Woe to him, for weal was none / Once he realized what Theseus had done" (557–58). Minos's convenient forgetting of his son, who is unmentioned until Theseus emerges from the labyrinth, signifies a failure of theory of mind: the awareness that another person exists when they are not in front of us. Minos lost his son to an evil steward, and forgot to remember his existence after that. Like many premodern characters, Minos realizes, recognizes, and remembers only when the plot demands it.[23]

---

23 It is worth considering this medieval trope of convenient forgetting in light of Erich Auerbach's distinction between texts that are "fraught with background" (such as the Old Testament) and those that allow recognition objects to emerge only when convenient (such as Homer's *Odyssey*): "Odysseus's Scar," in *Mimesis: The Representation of Reality in Western Literature*, trans. William Trask, new and exp. edn. (Princeton: Princeton University Press, 2013), 1–23. We might contrast that forgetfulness, of course, with a hypothesis about the Minotaur's own state of mind before his death: did the Minotaur remember Minos as much as Minos forgot him? Borges hints at an answer in his own story of the labyrinth from the Minotaur's perspective (See Jorge Luis Borges, "The House of Asterion," in *Labyrinths: Selected Stories and Other Writings*, eds. Donald A. Yates and James E. Irby [London: Penguin, 1964], 170–72). In his retelling, Julio Cortázar emphasizes the Minotaur's own ability to reflect on how others view him, as in his words to Theseus: "It's as if you look straight through me. Yet, you don't see me with your eyes; it's not with one's eyes that one faces a myth. Not even your sword is aimed properly. You should strike with a proven method, a spell: with

But Minos's belated recognition also indicates the deeply pessimistic quality to the romance, especially in light of *Le Freine* and *Sir Orfeo*. In those romances, recognition solves the core problem of each: *Le Freine* reunites with her family and marries, Orfeo reunites with his wife and resumes his throne. Yet both contain trauma: *Le Freine* was the unwed lover of the man who later married her, and Heurodis was kidnapped and possibly raped by Hades, the king of fairyland. Those texts overwrite, even ignore, the terror of what comes before the trauma. The *Romance of the Minotaur*, I would argue, does no such thing. Recognition and remembering are realizations but not solutions.

Especially for Ariadne. If Minos is the forgetful king, Theseus the violent but thoughtless hero, and the Minotaur little more than a "rough" monstrous body to slaughter, Ariadne is the keeper of memory. Her girdle, like the labyrinth, contains the past. But unlike the labyrinth, the girdle does not occlude or erase what came before. Ariadne weaves "memory" into the girdle, as visible as the symbolic colorways and prestige textiles. In doing so, she does the work of the "poet as builder" that Carruthers identifies in medieval mnemonic literature. Ariadne builds, or weaves, to remember and to evoke remembrance.

But, like the women in *Sir Gawain and the Green Knight,* Ariadne also weaves to disrupt. In *Sir Gawain,* the girdle is Gawain's temptation, since it provides protection from the Green Knight's threat to behead the hero, and his shame, since he takes the girdle but does not fulfill his promise to be open and honest with the Green Knight. The girdle in *Sir Gawain* is a chance for Morgan le Fay (and Lady Bertilak, her proxy) to take their revenge on the Arthurian court. In the *Romance of the Minotaur*, the girdle is a chance for Ariadne to provoke category crisis, to instigate a new tragedy, and to thus recollect — to herself, to her father — the memory of what has been lost.

The focus on the missing, the forgotten, and the hidden is all the more bittersweet given the state of the only extant copy.

---

another legend": "Los Reyes," trans. Caridad Svich, *The Brooklyn Rail,* 2008, http://intranslation.brooklynrail.org/spanish/the-kings-los-reyes.

As noted above, the opening lines and the final page of the *Romance of the Minotaur* are lost. Bliss argues that the prologue to *Le Freine* (which he also uses as the prologue to *Sir Orfeo*) ought to introduce the tale. But, perhaps because of his own incomplete edition of the romance, Bliss never states precisely how the *Romance of the Minotaur* ends. Shaddeus and Mitchell-Smith, like Wearall, take this tacit omission as evidence that the story would likely end with Ariadne giving verbal assent to Theseus's marriage proposal. The *Romance of the Minotaur* would end happily. Most medieval romances do, after all.

But, as I said above, all three texts — *Sir Orfeo, Le Freine,* and the *Romance of the Minotaur* — circle around the same themes, with each romance providing a unique perspective. In *Sir Orfeo*, the hero regains his wife but they die without issue. In *Le Freine*, the trauma of abandonment is occluded by the joy of marriage. We are meant to forget these trauma in favor of the normative stylistics of medieval romance, which are, like the pentangle, an "ultimate guarantee" of "stability" (recalling Heng). But Ariadne's girdle, like the girdle in *Sir Gawain*, weaves to disrupt, weaves to recall, and provokes an unraveling category crisis through trauma and recollected memory. Bearing that in mind, we might wonder if Ariadne's now-lost speech would be as surprising as the identity of the now-dead Minotaur: not an assent to marriage, but a mournful acknowledgement of what has been lost and what has been forgotten.

Bibliography

Auerbach, Erich. "Odysseus's Scar." In *Mimesis: The Representation of Reality in Western Literature,* translated by William Trask, New and Expanded Edition, 1–23. Princeton: Princeton University Press, 2013.

Bliss, A.J. "Notes on the Auchinleck Manuscript" *Speculum* 26, no. 4 (Oct. 1951): 652–58. DOI: 10.2307/2851220.

———, ed. *Sir Orfeo.* Oxford: Oxford University Press, 1961.

Bloch, Howard. "If Words Could Kill: The Lais and Fatal Speech." In *The Anonymous Marie de France,* 51–82. Chicago: University of Chicago Press, 2006.

Borges, Jorge Luis. "The House of Asterion." In *Labyrinths: Selected Stories and Other Writings,* edited by Donald A. Yates and James E. Irby, 170–72. London: Penguin, 1964.

Burns, E. Jane. *Courtly Love Undressed: Reading Through Clothes in Medieval French Culture.* Philadelphia: University of Pennsylvania Press, 2005.

Carruthers, Mary. *The Book of Memory.* Cambridge: Cambridge University Press, 2008.

———. "The Poet as Master Builder: Composition and Locational Memory in the Middle Ages." *New Literary History* 24, no. 4, Papers from the Commonwealth Center for Literary and Cultural Change (Autumn 1993): 881–904. DOI: 10.2307/469399.

Cohen, Jeffrey Jerome. "Monster Culture (Seven Theses)." In *Monster Theory: Reading Culture,* 3–25. Minneapolis: University of Minnesota Press, 1996.

Cortázar, Julio. "Los Reyes." Translated by Caridad Svich. *The Brooklyn Rail,* 2008. http://intranslation.brooklynrail.org/spanish/the-kings-los-reyes.

Garber, Marjorie. *Vested Interests: Cross-Dressing and Cultural Anxiety.* New York: Routledge, 1992.

Heng, Geraldine. "Feminine Knots and the Other Sir Gawain and the Green Knight." *PMLA* 106, no. 3 (May 1991): 500–514. DOI:10.2307/462782.

Hudson, Harriet, ed. *Four Middle English Romances: Sir Isumbras, Octavian, Sir Eglamour of Artois, Sir Tryamour.* Second Edition. Rochester: TEAMS Middle English Text Series, 2006.

Laskaya, Anne, and Eve Salisbury, eds. *The Middle English Breton Lays.* Rochester: TEAMS Middle English Text Series, 1995.

Lerer, Seth. "Artifice and Artistry in *Sir Orfeo.*" *Speculum* 60, no. 1 (Jan. 1985): 92–109. DOI: 10.2307/2852135.

Loomis, Laura Hibbard. "Chaucer and the Breton Lays of the Auchinleck Manuscript." *Studies in Philology* 38 (1941): 14–33. rpt. in *Adventures in the Middle Ages,* 131–49. New York: Burt Franklin, 1962.

Mitchell-Smith, Ilan. "Road Rage in the Labyrinth: Theseus' Exhausted Violence." *Speculum* 291, no. 4 (June 2015): 117–40.

Pearsall, Derek. "The Development of Middle English Romance." *Mediaeval Studies* 27 (1965): 91–116.

Rushton, Cory James. "The Lady's Man: Gawain as Lover in Middle English Literature." In *The Erotic in the Literature of Medieval Britain,* edited by Amanda Hopkins and Cory James Rushton. Cambridge: D.S. Brewer, 2007.

Shaddeus, John. "James Bond and Dr. Minos: Gawain and Theseus in the Bedroom." *Exemplaria* 39, no. 2 (Fall 2012): 25–37.

"Sir Orfeo." Translated by J.R.R. Tolkien. In *Sir Gawain and the Green Knight, Pearl, and Sir Orfeo.* New York: Ballantine Books, 1975.

Wattie, Margaret. "The Middle English Lai le Freine." *Smith College Studies in Modern Languages* 10, no. 3 (April 1929): i–xiii and 1–27.

Wearall, Andrea. "Place Names, The Place." *Medieval Minutiae: Notes on the Fourteenth Century* 101, no. 17 (Autumn 2007): 19–29.

Weber, Henry W. *Metrical Romances of the Thirteenth, Fourteenth and Fifteenth Centuries,* Vol. I. Edinburgh: Archibald Constance, 1810.

Wiggins, Allison. "The Auchinleck Manuscript: Importance," *National Library of Scotland.* https://auchinleck.nls.uk/editorial/importance.html.

Yates, Frances. *The Art of Memory.* Chicago: University of Chicago Press, 2001.

4

"The Very Globe Came Undone": Ontological Negation in Enoch Campion's *The Tragedy of Dracule*

Ed Simon

"I thrice shall nail the papal crown to his head/ as nail'd I the Saracens' turbans theirs."[1] In act 4 scene 4 of Enoch Campion's 1592 play *The Tragedy of Dracule*, the titular antagonist confronts with reptilian efficacy three Ottoman envoys sent by Sultan Mehmed II. The Wallachian prince, described as having serpent eye and tongue, hisses to his prisoners, saying "Your charge Constantinople's scourge may be/but now a high'r god your souls sent to be/not to the sheep Nazarene false as yours / nor to the stiff-neck'd Jews' God of Mos'ic law / for three in one, and one in three, all these / gods strut, lie, and die, three imposters all."[2] The dramatic action is placed in a Hungarian monastery, where the plays massive central personality, Vlad Tepes, son of Vlad Dracule of the House of Dragon has spent the entire scene torturing the unfortunate diplomats. The scene isn't out of character for Vlad, as the scholarly and apocryphal tradition which has accumulated around the fragmentary text has it that the character

---

1 Franklin Mercer, *Source Materials for Campion's Dracule* (New York: Hudson University Press, 1987), 7.
2 Ibid. 12.

has spent four acts murdering his way across Hungary, Romania, Saxony, the Balkans, and the Ottoman Empire.[3] Now, after scenes which apparently included implement, dismemberment, rape, infanticide, and cannibalism, we reach the narrative denouement in which the arch-heretic sinner explicates his nihilistic non-theology, his "ontological negation" as philosopher Adolph Trachtenberg describes it.[4]

Mathias Blum writes in *Akiva's Garden* that "No play in the Renaissance canon, no play in the English canon, no play in literature is as terrifying as *The Tragedy of Dracula,* not because of what it says, but because of what it doesn't say."[5] This play will examine these themes of negation which surround the rich folkloric extra textual tradition associated with a play none of us have ever been able to see performed in its entirety, fusing both the archival scholarship of Eamonn Peters with the hermeneutic interpretations of Trachtenberg.

In the only surviving monologue from the mythic play which exists more as lacunae than as reality, Vlad continues his speech, saying "Nor to Asmo'dus, Belial, or Moloch / shall a scorch'd sacrifice of you be made / for as true as their persons shall be / truer still is King Nothing, the only / God beyond me."[6] Campion's unwieldy stage directions which follow read "Vlad does nail the Saracen's turbans to their pate, using the real actors as real sacrifice, collects real blood to make Cornish pasty for later."[7] Say what you will about Shakespeare's "Exeunt, pursued by a bear," what Campion lacks in pithiness he makes up for in sheer horrifying shock value. Plays are rarely notable for their stage directions; amazingly the previously quoted section isn't even the most infamous one in *The Tragedy of Dracula,* that distinc-

---

3 Mercer remains the best resource for narrative description of Campion's play, albeit his is a study that is light on theoretical interpretation.
4 Adolph Trachtenberg, *The Peterson Aphorisms* (New York: Vilna Press, 1984), 342.
5 Mathias Blum, *Akiva's Garden: A Metaphysical Explication of Unknown Literatures* (Arkham: Miskatonic University Press, 1979), 66.
6 Mercer, *Source Materials for Campion's Dracula,* 38.
7 Ibid.

tion being reserved for the paradoxical and counterintuitive one which ends the play in act 5 scene 5 which reads with an intense apophatic minimalism "Thus God dies."[8]

A fitting ending to an unsettling play, or at least an unsettling play insomuch as we're able to piece together any details about it, the entirety of that which remains from the cursed text fitting on less than five pages. *The Tragedy of Dracula,* as it survives in quotation, fragment, conjecture, description, innuendo, rumor, curse, and incantation is almost less a work of literature than it is a type of spell, a lost grimoire unraveling the fabric of reality itself. Nothingness is at the core of this play, which itself has become a nothing. But where other scholars have gone through the painstaking work of compiling secondary quote and praying for some archival magic where a complete manuscript exists, hoping that some palimpsest in some dingy English library contains all of Campion's eponymous work, I argue that the play itself never actually existed, and that as a type of potential non-existent literature its most potent aesthetic and philosophical contribution is in its very Nothingness. Note that I am not claiming that the play's existence is a hoax per se, but rather that *The Tragedy of Dracula* is itself its own type of textual object which could be viewed as an ontological negation.

Despite the non-existence of either foul or fair papers, much less a complete printed version, *The Tragedy of Dracula* has haunted the periphery of textual scholarship. For those familiar with the critical murmurings about the text, no play in the Jacobeathan repertoire has had the reputation for pure unmitigated violence, horror, or perversion as Campion's gothic stage nightmare. According to secondary contemporary sources, in his highly fictionalized retelling of the rule of the sixteenth-century Wallachian prince Vlad Tepes, the shadowy Campion presented a blood-soaked drama which was not to be matched by *Titus*

---

8   Ibid. 66.

Andronicus, 'Tis a Pity She's a Whore, The Duchess of Malfi, or *Tamburlaine.*[9]

Departing from the already nebulous moral world of Senecan revenge tragedy, Campion's only written text gained a reputation not just for licentiousness and barbarism, but indeed occult powers as well. William Prynne in his 1640 *Diabolicon* wrote,

> Of the whoremongers and blasphemers who plyed their infernal trades amongst the dens and brothels and bear-pits of Southwark, not even Marlowe matched the demonic Campion, the strange wizard and reviled master of necromantic arts, whose hateful Dracule charged a power that made the threads unravel, the knots come loosed, and the very Globe came undone, so that being itself should be strangled.[10]

Indeed while *The Tragedy of Dracule* was performed supposedly only three times, it was that final performance which would draw Prynne's horrified reaction.

First staged in the attic of The Bishop's Miter in 1592, before its author had yet disappeared, scholar Eamonn Peters has made a convincing case that the work was performed as a sort of ritualistic closet drama, with its various roles read by members of the infamous School of Night, possibly including Marlow, Walter Raleigh, Thomas Harriot, John Dee, and Campion itself, though as Peters reports the actors only got to the fourth act, as a fire below had broken out and interrupted their performance.[11] The wider London public would not be presented with the play until 1620 at the Blackfriars, when halfway through the second act a representative of the Privy Council arrived and stopped the production. The players, as well as Cuthbert Burbage, one of the theater's shareholders, were all sent immediately to New-

---

9 A decent overview of the play's textual history can be found in Tucker Ayeslboro's "A Play that You'll Never See," *The Pittsburgh Review of Books* 38, no. 2 (1997): 24.

10 William Prynne, *Diabolicon* (London, 1640), 4,367.

11 Eamon Peters, "The School of Night's Infernal Play," *Journal of Seventeenth Century Literature* 48, no. 2 (1967): 182.

gate.¹² Ostensibly the production was interrupted because James I feared that the anti-Catholicism of *The Tragedy of Dracule* would offend representatives of the Hapsburg Crown, as Prince Charles was involved in negations to marry the Spanish infanta, but even Prynne for whom nothing could be too anti-Catholic didn't believe that this was the actual reason for the play's closing.¹³ *The Tragedy of Dracule*'s final and only complete performance supposedly occurred at midnight on Walpurgis Night at Tyburn Field in 1640, on the eve of civil war.¹⁴ According to Prynne, several observers, and general legend surrounding that event, the words of the occult play itself were so powerful that "meaning was if as no meaning," the very substance of reality becoming terrifyingly nullified.¹⁵

The play itself supposedly saw only one printing, though only some paratextual remnants of dubious legitimacy remain, and the only portions of the play's dialogue that survive are in quotation from Campion's critics. Needless to say the play was never listed in the Stationer's Register. While I concur with Peters's contention that the play should be read as occult closet drama — more ritual than play — I further his argument concerning the deficit of actual archival material. The small community of scholars familiar with *The Tragedy of Dracule* hold out hope that a printing or even a manuscript might exist in its entirety; Peters, on the other hand claims that the play was an unusual instance of oral, performed literature where participants were formally forbidden from recording the play in its entirety, rather agreeing to commit the ritual to memory.

Though Campion's biography is slightly more transparent than that of his infamous play, the details of his life are still difficult to fully verify. Prynne claims that he was "raised in the old abominable faith of popery," though whether he has any familial connection to rescuency is impossible to ascertain.¹⁶ Other

---

12 Ibid. 185.
13 Ibid. 186.
14 Ibid. 187.
15 William Prynne, *Diabolicon* (London, 1640), 4,368.
16 Ibid., 4,366.

sources claim that Campion was born in Devonshire in the mid-sixteenth century amongst a community where a still surviving Celtic paganism endured. In the realm of the more verifiable, there are in the records of the parish of Torbay, baptismal records indicating that an "Enoch Campion" was welcomed into the Church of England in 1562 at the Church of St. Barlaam and Josaphat, and most scholars have agreed that this record refers to the author of *The Tragedy of Dracule*.[17] In his only extant, verified book entitled *Of the Seventh Generation,* Campion gives little biographical information himself, other than to write "I come from that West Country where the sun dies at night and the pitter-patter of the old gods' feet still beat out their demon rhythm at midnight," which would seem to verify his Devonshire origin.[18]

Campion's presence in the necromantic circles of Elizabethan London is well established, though his origins were shadowy to his compatriots, men like Dee and Simon Forman. Both knew Campion, though neither could speak with any authority about the man's circumstances, with Dee writing in 1601, "Some have seen the Cornishman in the scrying mirrors, some call for his Enochian magic, though none know his true name."[19] The occultist William Lilly, who did not know Campion personally but who had some associates in common wrote in 1658 that "In the years before war many have spoken of the Druid Campion whose words could undo words."[20] Indeed one of the most provocative aspects of the Campion mythos is that for as shadowy as the circumstances of his birth may be, there is simply no record of his death. Similar to the legends of immortality which surround figures like the Count St. Germaine, a tradition grew which claimed Campion never died, with anecdotal stories of his presence as a member of Sir Francis Dashwood's Hell-Fire Club of rakes in the eighteenth century, his presence in French

---

17 Mercer, *Source Materials for Campion's Dracule,* ix.
18 Enoch Campion, *Of the Seventh Generation* (London, 1590), 52.
19 John Dee, *Ecstasticks I Hath Known* (London, 1601), 17.
20 William Lilly, The *Theocosmologiometaphysinopticon* (London, 1658), 139.

Symbolist poetics circles in the nineteenth, and even a reported sighting of Campion in Manhattan by noted occultist Crowley Jean Bucknell at a diner at 1st Ave. and 62nd in 1957.[21] Lilly claimed that Campion's colleagues hewed to a more Faustian understanding of the master's demise, writing that Campion "walked with Satan: and he was no more; for Satan took him."[22]

For all of the richness of Campion apocrypha, I argue that a close examination of the available references to where and when the play was performed, as well as the contents of the play, should avail us of the belief that the play ever really existed at all, whether as material object or as performed piece. Indeed the non-existence of *The Tragedy of Dracula* is its chief aesthetic and metaphysical accomplishment, for the spoken play is not the real play, and whereof we cannot perform we must remain silent. I base this interpretation on a single cryptic line from the only extant text by Campion, an unusual commonplace book that doubles as a type of grimoire entitled *Of the Seventh Generation*. This heterodox compendium of folklore, heretical theology, theurgy, metaphysical speculation, and memoir is the only verified writing of the shadowy Campion. Recalling both the prose style and the varied interests of writers a century later, like Thomas Browne and Robert Burton, Campion provides an engaging and full portrait of a human mind — unfortunately that human mind was one that was undeniably twisted. The lurid content of the text has helped it to develop a reputation of being a sort of sadist's Voynich Manuscript, which may speak to the fact that the trustees of Wordsworth & Southey College whose special collections department owns the only copy *Of the Seventh Generation* set a strict quota of the number of scholars allowed to consult the work and placed a time limit of one hour per decade for all approved researchers. Scholars sign a waiver promising to quote no more than 1% of the book in any of their publications. As such, few have read the book, even less in its entirety, and no one should expect a comprehensive edi-

---
21 Ayeslboro, "A Play that You'll Never See," 27.
22 Lilly, *The Theocosmologiometaphysinopticon*, 142.

tion available to the wider public anytime soon, as the gift of the book to Wordsworth & Southey College by trustee Andrew Carnegie in 1898 stipulated that "This is a wicked book for wicked men, and none but the prepared shall read it."[23]

It was during my reading *Of the Seventh Generation* that I came across an unpublished line, where Campion writes, "The Romists worship a cracked statue after the schismatics smash idols and rood screens, but the Puritans make a Pope of paper; rather in the ending there will be the word and the word will not be with us for the word will unravel, and the chief word shall be that which was never uttered but shall still have been heard."[24] Though my hypothesis remains tentative, I conjecture not that Campion did not write *The Tragedy of Dracule,* rather that he did in another dimension, and that the incantatory power of the play was such that it did just what it promised to do — literally erase itself from the very fabric of reality. The play did once exist, but like a god who commits suicide, it achieves the new status of never having existed even though it once did, in a past that no longer is, in a universe just next door that we can never go to.

Trachtenberg writes in his classic *The Patterson Aphorisms* that

> [t]he English play of the Dracule is not just an atheistic nihilism, but a nihilism beyond mere nihilism, that negates negations themselves, a negative assertion beyond both paradox and tautology so as to be a type of hyper-paradox, a negation of a negation that is neither Hegelian dialectic generating a new positive, nor simply negation, but an apophatic nothingness that gestures to an emptiness which undoes existence.[25]

---

23 Andrew Carnegie, letter to trustees of Wordsworth & Southey College, June 9, 1898.
24 Campion, *Of the Seventh Generation,* 66.
25 Adolph Trachtenberg, *The Peterson Aphorisms* (New York: Vilna Press, 1984), 355.

What could be more vexing than a text for which there is no text, where we have nothing we are able to interpret, but that we fear still has the power to interpret us?

Bibliography

Ayeslboro, Tucker. "A Play that You'll Never See." *The Pittsburgh Review of Books* 38, no. 2 (1997): 20–38.

Blum, Mathias. *Akiva's Garden: A Metaphysical Explication of Unknown Literatures.* Arkham: Miskatonic University Press, 1979.

Campion, Enoch. *Of the Seventh Generation.* London, 1590.

Dee, John. *Ecstasticks I Hath Known.* London, 1601.

Lilly, William. *The Theocosmologiometaphysinopticon.* London, 1658.

Mercer, Franklin. *Source Materials for Campion's Dracule.* New York: Hudson University Press, 1987.

Peters, Eamon. "Argument about an Image of Enoch Campion." *Journal of Seventeenth Century Literature* 47, no. 4 (1966): 270–86.

———. "The School of Night's Infernal Play." *Journal of Seventeenth Century Literature* 48, no. 2 (1967): 165–90.

Prynne, William. *Diabolicon.* London, 1640.

Trachtenberg, Adolph. *The Peterson Aphorisms.* New York: Vilna Press, 1984.

5

"All My Heroines Must Like Him": Circumscribing the Spouse in Jane Austen's *Plan of a Husband*

Tom Zille

Ever since the publication of J.E. Austen-Leigh's *Memoir of Jane Austen* in 1869, literary critics have been intrigued by the fact that the inventor of so many a subversive marriage plot herself remained unmarried throughout her life. The recent rediscovery of Austen's lost *Plan of a Husband* has further stimulated this interest. Written in December 1815, around the time of her fortieth birthday, the text in many ways anticipates its natural counterpart, *Plan of a Novel* (1816).[1]

In the *Plan of a Husband,* Austen develops a vision of the perfect spouse, "a man so abominably excellent that I must be determined to marry him," as the letter to her niece Fanny Knight

---

1 For a detailed account of the text's rediscovery in 2016, see Djane Dott, "Jane Austen's Lost Text on the Perfect Husband Rediscovered," *Oxford Review,* Dec. 15, 2016. All quotations in this essay will cite the first fully-edited publication of the *Plan,* in Laylac Messler, ed., "A Rediscovered Letter to Fanny Knight, Containing a 'Plan of a Husband,'" *Canon Revision* 15, no. 3 (Autumn 2016): 334–65, hereafter referred to as *Plan.*

in which the *Plan* is embedded explains.[2] The main intention of the text seems to have been to amuse Fanny, to whom it is also dedicated. As the description of this "abominably excellent" man unfolds, however, it quickly starts to contradict the jocular rhetoric of its paratext. The first part of the *Plan* is headed by a list of physical and character traits, outlining the fictional husband's features and qualities in such an extremely specific way as to appear positively obsessive.[3] The same holds true for the second half of the *Plan*, in which the narrative of an imagined visit to London is used to present an absurdly detailed account of the husband's habits and actions, and the effect he has on each and every person the couple encounter on their way through streets and shops.

Following the rediscovery of the *Plan*, most critics have engaged with the text on the basis of biographical readings. The present essay, by contrast, will trace the obsessive undertones that are present throughout the whole of the *Plan of a Husband* in order to argue that it is best understood as a mock-autobiographical experiment turned literary project. An examination of passages from both parts of the *Plan* as well as the letter that frames it will show that the way in which Austen conceives of her ideal husband resembles the construction of a literary character more than anything else. Freed from the necessity of embedding this character in a continuous narrative, the writer embarks on a literary experiment that is strongly reminiscent of her juvenilia. The essay will also look at some of the connections and influences between the *Plan* and Austen's novels, *Persuasion* in particular. Finally, it will consider the exaggeratedly prescriptive tone of the *Plan of a Husband* in relation to Austen's characteristic use of irony. In doing all this, it hopes to make a contribution

---

2 *Plan*, 342.

3 Sid Omen tells me that his upcoming paper, "Spenser–Sidney–Austen: The Petrarchan Tradition in *Plan of a Husband*" will examine hitherto unknown traces of the Petrarchan blazon in Austen's text; while the present essay proposes an altogether different interpretation, the interested reader would do well to attend Sid's presentation at the *Fourteenth International Colloquium on Literary Influence*, to be held in Boston, MA, in October of 2019.

not only to a better understanding, but to the canonization of this undeservedly forgotten literary masterpiece as well.

The Paratext

The *Plan of a Husband* is contained in a long letter Austen wrote to her niece Fanny in December 1815, shortly before Christmas. Unlike their usual correspondence, the letter starts not with an acknowledgement of recent correspondence or an account of family events, but directly introduces the *Plan*:

> [...] — I have the shameless pleasure of also sending you a perfectly new peice [sic] of Perfection. Recovering from my little cold, I amused myself by composing these very serious lines, my *Plan of a Husband*; I think it is very clever, & you must think it very amusing at least.[4]

Much of this introduction is devoted to a prefatory apology of the project. Austen cautiously hopes that her niece "will not think me too presumptuous in venturing upon such an enterprise — yet I beleive [sic] you will agree that ladies are always the best judges of men."[5] Judgment is indeed a recurring motif of the *Plan*, and it is invariably the author-narrator herself who fills this role.[6] The introductory paragraphs closes with the proclamation: "All my Heroines must like him."[7] Pointing to the fictional nature of the husband in a way that would already seem to strongly discourage biographical readings, this is only the first

---

4 *Plan*, 342.
5 This sentiment is echoed in an almost verbatim fashion by Admiral Croft in *Persuasion* (Jane Austen, *Northanger Abbey and Persuasion,* ed. R.W. Chapman, 3rd edn. [Oxford: Oxford University Press, 1988], 172).
6 While some critics (esp. Dott, "Jane Austen's Lost Text") have argued that since the *Plan* is embedded in regular correspondence, its speaker must be Austen herself, it seems more adequate — especially if we regard the text as literary to at least some extent — to conceive of the speaker as a blend of author and conventional narrator. Hence, in this essay, the voice of the *Plan* will consistently be referred to as the "author-narrator."
7 *Plan*, 342.

of many instances in the text in which the subject of the *Plan* is clearly conceived of as a literary character.

The layout of the manuscript letter as a whole provides some evidence of how highly Austen rated this product of her imagination. The *Plan* itself starts on a fresh page, which leaves the second half of the letter's first page blank, an almost singular instance of deliberate wastefulness on Austen's part. In fact, the *Plan* can in many regards be treated as an entirely separate text, even though the occasional "you" in the text is usually interpreted as directly addressing the intended reader, Fanny Knight.[8] While the paratext covers only the first half manuscript page of the letter, the *Plan* is a full three and a half pages long.

Biographical Readings

A complete absence of reliable evidence notwithstanding, a number of critics have entertained speculations about the *Plan*'s supposed background in Austen's biography. The leading theory interprets the text as a "history" of Austen's relationship with Tom Lefroy — no less than the long-lost key to her adolescent love life, or at least a "literary rendering" of the same.[9] The majority of these studies rely on what meagre information about these relationships J.E. Austen Leigh's *Memoir* yields: "In her youth, she had declined the addresses of a gentleman who had the recommendations of good character, and connections, and position in life, of everything, in fact, except the subtle power of touching her heart." Austen Leigh also relates the even vaguer story of an acquaintance between the Austen sisters and "a gentleman, whose charm of person, mind, and manners was such that Cassandra thought him worthy to possess and likely to win

---

8 Dott, "Jane Austen's Lost Text."
9 For a representative account, see Djane Dott, "Boyish Love: Tom Lefroy and Jane Austen's 'Plan of a Husband,'" *Studies in Regency Literature* 65, no. 2 (July 2017): 168–84.

her sister's love," an acquaintance of which, however, nothing ever became.[10]

Djane Dott has pointed out that Austen conceived of the *Plan* on a momentous date: It was written almost exactly twenty years after her youthful infatuation with Tom Lefroy. In 1795, he and Austen had flirted with each other at Ashe Rectory — in a letter dated January 9, 1796, she described him as "a very gentleman-like, good-looking, pleasant young man" –;[11] in 1815, Austen put pen to paper to compose her outline of a perfect husband.[12] One might add that this was also shortly after she had begun work on *Persuasion* — a novel, among other things, about the regret over an unfulfilled relationship.

All this notwithstanding, there are numerous arguments that refute this logic, only one of which shall be discussed in greater detail here. Evidence may be gleaned from the very letter in which Austen praises Lefroy: "[W]e received a visit from Mr. Tom Lefroy and his cousin George. The latter is really very well-behaved now; and as for the other, he has but one fault, which time will, I trust, entirely remove — it is that his morning coat is a great deal too light."[13]

It seems surprising that critics should fail to recognize the significance of this passage. The "one fault" mentioned here is a grave one indeed — at least in Austen's eyes, whose fondness of heavy coats cannot possibly be overestimated. Eileen Kalvini has noted that Austen's heroines all prefer men in heavy coats; she even goes so far as to say that in the realm of male attire, heavy coats in these novels "certainly rank as the garments with the greatest pulling power."[14] Prime examples can be found in

---

10 J.E. Austen Leigh, *A Memoir of Jane Austen* (London: Bentley & Son, 1882), 27.
11 Deirdre Le Faye, ed., *Jane Austen's Letters*, 4th edn. (Oxford: Oxford University Press, 2011), 1, hereafter referred to as *Letters*.
12 Dott, "Boyish Love," 178.
13 *Letters*, 2 (original emphasis).
14 Eileen Kalvini, "Formen von Männlichkeit in Austen," in *Große Schriftstellerinnen und ihre Männer*, eds. Annie E. Verslob and Eileen Kalvini (Grimma: Mitteldeutscher Philologinnenverband, 1996), 118.

Northanger Abbey, the heroine of which loves a man who on occasion makes an entrance by coming "booted and great coated into the room" where she sits,[15] while Catherine Morland herself admiringly thinks that "the innumerable capes of his great coat looked so becomingly important!"[16] To Austen, the fact that Tom Lefroy's coat was "too light" would indubitably have marked him as too light a suitor himself. As we shall see, moreover, the husband of the *Plan* is anything but a light-coated man.

Last but not least, readings which interpret the *Plan* as a melancholy attempt at recapturing the experience of a past love will be unable to account for its comic elements. As a recent critic put it, "the tone of the *Plan of a Husband* is not primarily wistful, but playful."[17] This text does not look back at any of Austen's early suitors, but painstakingly constructs a new, better one.

The Outline of a Character

In her seminal study, *The Construction of Literary Characters,* Firey Lee Dread develops the concept of "obsessive characterization." Her theory assumes that "[g]enerally speaking, the care which a novelist lavishes on a particular character is directly proportional to their sense of attachment to, sometimes identification with, that same character."[18] According to Dread, "obsessive characterization" often relies on long, overly specific lists of attributes and qualities associated with a particular character and tends to be "repetitive in its attention to minute details."[19] Dread also links this to the issue of an author's control over their characters: "When developing their fictional personnel, obses-

---

15 Austen, *Northanger Abbey and Persuasion,* 210.
16 Ibid., 157.
17 Lorene Hech, "'Happiness in marriage is entirely a matter of chance:' Matrimony, Masochism, and Masculinity in Jane Austen's novels,' in *Jane and Gender: Feminist Perspectives on Austen's Life and Work,* ed. Djane Dott (London: Litter Demon Press, 2017), 182.
18 Firey Lee Dread, *The Construction of Literary Characters* (Cambridge: Richardson & Smith, 2004).
19 Ibid., 45.

sive writers usually rely on reported speech rather than dialogue to rule out any chance of their characters' turning out to be unruly."[20] While Dread's concept is quite — not to put too fine a point on it — obsessive itself, several of its key components can certainly be detected in the *Plan of a Husband*.

In Austen's novels, characterization usually takes place through dialogue and direct action — "when it comes to showing versus telling, Austen is heavily in favour of the former."[21] The letters, on the other hand, more commonly rely on reports and succinct descriptions of the writer's friends and acquaintances. Stylistically, the *Plan* occupies a middle ground between the two; at the same time, its two parts lean towards different ends of the spectrum.

The first part of the *Plan* consists mainly of a list of required physical and character traits that covers almost two manuscript pages. The standards are not only exceedingly high, but extremely specific as well. Most of Austen's heroines have either a rather simple or a rather vague idea of what they are looking for in a potential spouse. For instance, we learn of Catherine Morland that "her general notions of what men ought to be" are "unfixed."[22] By stark contrast, the author-narrator of the *Plan* knows exactly what her husband, the "handsomest man of my acquaintance," must look like.[23]

The imaginary gentleman's face has "not too red, nor too pale a look, but with just the right degree of colour in his complexion [...] and a forehead two inches high." He possesses "a most intelligent and animated eye" as well as, unsurprisingly, "the most becoming great coat you could imagine."[24] While many of the qualities contained in the list belong to the standard equipment

---

20 Ibid., 47–48.
21 Sootheana Randgras, "'Men have had every advantage of us in telling their own story. [...] I will not allow books to prove any thing': The Metafictional Gender Discourse in Jane Austen's *Persuasion*," in *Discourse into Literature*, ed. Col. Horatio Springfield (New Orleans: Mosaic, 2002), 38.
22 Austen, *Northanger Abbey and Persuasion,* 66.
23 *Plan,* 343.
24 *Plan,* 344.

of the desirable male in early nineteenth-century literature, the artful blend of physical and mental capacities is characteristic of Austen's style in particular.[25]

As for the husband's other qualities: "His manners are affectionate, and thereby engage the affection of others." His conduct "can only excite the greatest admiration."[26] This idea of reciprocity will become more important in the second part of the *Plan*. Furthermore, his is "a sanguine temper joined with an earnest concern for worldly propriety." He is "a most gallant man who moves with a natural grace."[27] Unusually, the description of the ideal husband makes no mention of his being a good, or even an adequate dancer — which, given the relevance attached to balls and dancing in Austen's novels, might seem surprising; yet at the time of the *Plan*'s composition, the dinner party had already begun to slowly usurp the social role of eighteenth-century entertainments such as the ball.[28]

The list continues describing the husband as, among other things, "liberal but prudent," "naturally fond of […] company," and possessing a "decided, steady manner."[29] It does by no means limit itself to qualities of character and manner; as a matter of course, the man described here "is of consequence wherever he dwells," and by his social status "commands the respect of everybody in the world." There appears to be only one (perhaps unavoidable) limitation to his greatness: the husband of the *Plan* only has "a Mind <u>almost</u> as strong as my own."[30] This playful qualification marks the first instance in which the author-narrator explicitly refers to herself. While the format of the exercise naturally invites an almost exclusive focus on the husband, es-

---

25 See R. Merta Chaplawn, "Jane Austen's Ideal of Beauty," *Proceedings of the Hampshire Philological Society* 34 (1921): 468–77, at 469, who takes the metaleptic "intelligent eye" as the starting point of her investigation.
26 *Plan*, 344.
27 *Plan*, 345.
28 Cf. Kalvini, "Formen von Männlichkeit," 121.
29 *Plan*, 346.
30 *Plan*, 348 (original emphasis).

pecially later parts of the text tend to increasingly emphasize the relation between the two spouses.

A further, decidedly unusual quality of Austen's would-be husband is that he plays the pianoforte "as well as, nay, better than any accomplished young lady." In addition to this, he has "the pleasantest singing voice imaginable."[31] While this combination is by no means unique among literary descriptions of gentlemen in this period, in the context of Austen's novels it is a thoroughly eccentric characteristic.[32] Leaving aside the issue of biographical readings, this is one of numerous elements of the description that also suggest the husband of the *Plan* was not inspired by, or derived from, any of the heroes of her novels. In fact, there is quite a strong discrepancy between the kind of man with whom Austen's heroines are supposed to experience marital bliss and the spouse she envisages for herself. As Snatij Tirić-Anker puts it in her recent monograph:

> The "perfect husband" in the *Plan* is [...] unlike Austen's heroines' choices, constructed with a care that goes beyond anything we find in her novels. Whereas each of the young men in her published works has a series of obvious character flaws that both make them human and underline the compromising nature of marriage, the husband she "imagines" for herself is both physically and character-wise infallible, at least according to Austen's standards.[33]

This becomes most evident towards the end of her rundown of the husband's qualities. It concludes with the observation that he is, "in short, all that a man <u>should</u> be."[34] If further proof of this

---

[31] *Plan*, 348.
[32] For a broader survey, consult Vertika Leerump, *Men and Music in the Regency Period* (Bath: Pump Room Press, 2012), 81–134 in particular.
[33] Snatij Tirić-Anker, *Reclaiming Spinsterhood and Lesbianism: (Auto)biographical Backgrounds of Nonconventional Gender Dynamics in Women's Fiction in Britain, from Jane Austen to Jeanette Winterson* (Manchester: Glass & Co., 2017), 203–4.
[34] *Plan*, 350.

figure's fictional nature were needed, this would be it. Moreover, we can detect a note of mock-exasperation attached to the modal verb here, a reminder that the text has a familial addressee at a marriageable age, the author's niece.

As mentioned before, the complete list (less of a quarter of which has been quoted here) makes up almost half of the whole text. Despite the great lexical variety and stylistic accomplishment Austen displays, the physical characterization seems obsessively detailed to the point of absurdity, especially in contrast to the comparatively succinct descriptions of gentlemen's qualities and features in the novels.[35] At the same time, we encounter a narrator no longer bound by the limits a conventional narrative would impose on characterization, and Austen exploits that freedom to its fullest extent. While the second part of the *Plan* exhibits a completely different structure and style than the first, it is nevertheless characterized by this same tension.

The Narrative Turn

To some extent, the very title, *Plan of a Husband* suggests a text of a somewhat facetious nature, similar to Austen's subsequent project, the *Plan of a Novel*. The title definitely points to the artificial construction of the husband, which from the outset puts him in a kind of ontological proximity to the fictional characters in Austen's novels.

The second part of the *Plan* is characterized by a change of tense, and is framed in a different manner than the first. It comes under the subheading, "A Visit to London / an interesting history, written by Jane Austen for the amusement of Miss Knight." While at many points, this section of the text is again suggestive of Dread's concept of "obsessive characterization," its most noticeable feature is the increasingly narrative character of the text. Instead of listing attributes of her spouse, the author-narrator now lets his actions speak, in a sequence of scenes that

---

35 See Firey Lee Dread, *The Romantic Hero, 1750–1850* (Nashville: Blockhouse, 1999), 129–31.

revolve around the couple's activities during a visit to the city. The issue of control becomes even more dominant now, with the detailed accounts of the verbal contributions made by the husband, and the overly precise depiction of the effect he has on each and every single person he and his wife encounter in the streets, shops, and theater they visit. Due perhaps to the use of the past tense, this part of the text in particular has attracted biographical readings, all of which, however, have remained unsatisfactory.[36] The stylistic discrepancy between the way Austen reports on her activities and encounters in the extant letters and the idiosyncratic style of the *Plan* once more suggests that the latter is best understood as a literary experiment.

Virtually every person the couple encounter on their way through the streets "expressed their admiration of his figure" and "witnessed his general benevolence," while on every occasion, the husband "spoke and acted exactly as he ought to," in other words, without showing the slightest vanity with regard to his appearance. To the narrator, walking at his side provides "the most exquisite felicity."[37] While this introductory account is still quite vague, the "narrative" part of the *Plan* is characterized by a steady move from the general towards the specific. One of the first scenes in which this becomes noticeable involves an extremely detailed description of a visit to a shop where the author-narrator purchases a new bonnet, accompanied by a long conversation (in reported speech) between her and the adoring husband.[38] Among other experiences, the author-narrator also describes a visit to a London theater, a scene that would be very difficult indeed to relate to a concrete biographical background:

> We had a private box at the theatre, where we talked of his recent promotion to Captain, and he amused me with stories of his adventures at sea, while we paid scarcely any attention to the amusing scenes acted out in front of us. He would

---

36 See esp. Dott, "Boyish Love," 177–79.
37 *Plan*, 352.
38 *Plan*, 353.

> not cease giving me new proofs of love at every occasion, by laughing heartily at every witty comment I made, professing his due admiration of my cap, and generally being attentive and entertaining. — He talked wit all night.[39]

The reference to the husband's "adventures at sea" also exemplifies the way Austen's preoccupation with naval matters bled into her texts around the time she was working on *Persuasion*. The theater scene moreover contains what Messler in her comment has called "the single most remarkable sentence in the whole of the *Plan of a Husband*."[40] Speaking of the way fellow audience members watch the couple's behaviour in their private box, the author-narrator vouches "for their beleiving [sic] we were flirting shamelessly; and why indeed should matrimony be allowed to put an end to flirting?"[41] In the context of Fanny Knight's recurrent plans to marry, which Austen's letters regularly comment upon, this provocatively unconventional statement can also be read as a kind of tongue-in-cheek advice to the much younger woman.

The "Visit to London" turns fully narrative in its last paragraphs. The husband is now almost exclusively characterized by his words and actions, in scenes that continue the trend towards greater specificity in all descriptions. One of the most remarkable of these passages is the one in which, after the couple have left the theater, husband and wife board the carriage that will drive them back home:

> He handed me into the carriage with his usual grace, and glancing — as is his wont — towards my foot as to be perfectly sure I should not stumble and fall; — all in the <u>most</u> decorous manner you can imagine. Once we had taken our seats, he beg'd that I should read to him after dinner, the Lady of the Lake we both find very agreeable. The beauty of my

---

39 *Plan*, 354–55.
40 *Plan*, 363.
41 *Plan*, 355.

reading is so gratifying to him, etc. I should mention that my husband addresses <u>me</u> always by my name, and indeed I would never suffer a My Dear or some similarly unfeeling denomination.[42]

The overall prescriptive tone and uncharacteristic verbosity of the final passages — all of which read like the above — mark them out as perfect instances of "obsessive characterization." While at its outset, the "Visit to London" relies on somewhat general notions of perfect male behavior, a trend towards the more specific and anecdotal continues until at its end, the *Plan of a Husband* comes full circle, in narrative passages that recall the obsessively detailed lists of character traits at the text's beginning.

The Question of Irony

Given Austen's reputation as a great ironist, it should come as no surprise that ever since the *Plan*'s rediscovery, critics have debated whether its intention was serious or ironic, with the majority favoring the latter interpretation.[43] As we have seen, the author-narrator of the text obsessively paints a picture of perfection — yet to Austen herself, the concept of personal perfection was always a highly dubious one.

In *Sense and Sensibility*, Marianne Dashwood complains that "the more I know of the world, the more I am convinced that I shall never see a man whom I can really love. I require so much!"[44] The *Plan*, of course, requires infinitely more of its husband than Marianne would ever dare to ask. The "peice of Perfection" which Austen's prefatory announcement in the let-

---

42 *Plan*, 356–57. *The Lady of the Lake* is also mentioned in *Persuasion*, 100.
43 Cf. e.g. Tirić-Anker, who believes that the text's "irony and cynical undertone [...] make it obvious that Austen imagines a [...] creature [...] that, even if brought to life from the pages of her manuscript, would remain an empty cadaver controlled by her" (*Reclaiming Spinsterhood and Lesbianism*, 204).
44 Jane Austen, *Sense and Sensibility*, ed. R.W. Chapman, 3rd edn. (Oxford: Oxford University Press, 1987), 18.

ter promises is exactly what the text sets out to create.⁴⁵ Yet this very formula recalls statements of the writer's that bespeak little attachment to that very concept. In a letter to Fanny dated November 18–20, 1814, Austen had mockingly promised that

> [t]here are such beings in the World perhaps, one in a Thousand, as the Creature You & I should think perfection, where Grace & Spirit are united to Worth, where the Manners are equal to the Heart & Understanding, but such a person may not come in your way, or if he does, he may not be the eldest son of a Man of Fortune, the Brother of your particular friend, & belonging to your own County.⁴⁶

Gary Hillinspur has proposed passages like this one "are tinged with regret over the perfect husband Austen herself never had."⁴⁷ Yet firstly, the deliberately overblown rhetoric clearly marks this as a facetious remark, and secondly, only two and a half years later, a letter to the same addressee would include the passing remark, "pictures of perfection as you know make me sick and wicked."⁴⁸ The "Plan of a Novel," Austen's other return to the style of her juvenilia written in 1816, as ironically as desultorily would introduce its hero as "all perfection of course."⁴⁹

All this strongly suggests that the *Plan* was at least partly ironic in its intent. And even if we look beyond the broad issue of "perfection," there are a few obviously ironic passages in the text. Its first part, for instance, among other things describes the husband as "an officer of the navy [...] with ten or twenty thousand pounds a year; and the son of a priest, like the great

---

45 *Plan*, 342.
46 *Letters*, 292.
47 Gary Hillinspur, *Austen When Old: The Novelist's Later Life* (London: Holloway & Penn, 1996), 469.
48 Letter to Fanny Knight, March 23–25, 1817 (*Letters*, 350).
49 Jane Austen, "Plan of a Novel, According to Hints from Various Quarters," in *Minor Works*, ed. R.W. Chapman (London: Oxford University Press, 1975), 430.

Nelson."[50] The fact that Austen was far from sharing in her ages' adoration of Nelson can be gathered from a letter to her sister Cassandra, in which she complains that she is "tired of Lives of Nelson, being that I never read any."[51]

Not infrequently, however, the irony of passages like this one are in clash with the overall serious tone of the text. It seems most adequate, therefore, to regard the *Plan of a Husband* as a serious literary experiment infused with, but not solely determined by, Austen's characteristic use of irony. The "obsessive characterization" that runs through the text certainly relies on an overblown rhetoric, sometimes to comic effect. At the same time, it betrays the author's deep attachment to the issue discussed. There is no evidence to suggest that Austen was tackling sorrow over a past or unfulfilled relationship, but the *Plan* is nevertheless a genuine attempt at fashioning an ideal husband at least in theory. Features such as the two-page long list of character traits and personal features demonstrate that at points, this attempt developed a dynamic of its own.

Conclusion

As this brief study of Austen's *Plan of a Husband* has demonstrated, the widespread biographical readings of this text can once and for all be dismissed. In her letter to Fanny Knight, Austen does not look back wistfully on any of the light-coated men of her past. When the author asserts that "all [her] heroines must like him," she likens the husband more to his equally fictional counterparts in the novels.[52] Yet the man introduced here is more impressive than Mr. Darcy and Captain Frederick Wentworth combined (and, one might add, he wears a heavier coat than either of them). What might indeed have once been intended to become a mock-autobiographical project quickly

---

50 *Plan*, 347.
51 October 11–12, 1813 (*Letters*, 245).
52 *Plan*, 342.

turns into an exercise in rigidly controlled fiction that goes beyond anything we encounter in the novels.

Using Dread's concept of "obsessive characterization," it has been shown that the process in which the author-narrator of the *Plan* describes the husband in both parts of the text is characterized by an extreme attention to minute details, a propensity for drawing the character's outlines a little too sharp, and an overall prescriptive tone. The husband's many minor and major perfections notwithstanding, the reader is never meant to forget who is in control of this experiment; the man described will only ever have "a Mind <u>almost</u> as strong as my own."[53] When read in conjunction with its paratext, the *Plan* appears as a remarkably self-aware text. If Marianne Dashwood says, "I require so much!"[54] the author of the *Plan of a Husband* has discovered that the only way to be sure a husband meets all the necessary requirements is to leave nothing to chance — no detail of his person and character, nor even the way he will behave in any given situation. The fact that this literary self-indulgence turns out everything but trivial is due to the literary genius of its creator. It is high time that this text take its rightful place among the oeuvre of Jane Austen.

---

53 *Plan*, 348.
54 Austen, *Sense and Sensibility*, 18.

Bibliography

Primary Literature

Austen, Jane. *Northanger Abbey and Persuasion.* Edited by R.W. Chapman. 3rd edition. Oxford: Oxford University Press, 1988.

———. "Plan of a Novel, According to Hints from Various Quarters." In *Minor Works,* edited by R.W. Chapman, 428–30. London: Oxford University Press, 1975.

———. *Sense and Sensibility.* Edited by R.W. Chapman. 3rd edition. Oxford: Oxford University Press, 1987.

Le Faye, Deirdre, ed. *Jane Austen's Letters.* 4th Edition. Oxford: Oxford University Press, 2011.

Messler, Laylac, ed. "A Rediscovered letter to Fanny Knight, Containing a 'Plan of a Husband.'" *Canon Revision* 15, no. 3 (Autumn 2016): 334–65.

Secondary Literature

Austen Leigh, J.E. *A Memoir of Jane Austen.* London: Bentley & Son, 1882.

Chaplawn, R. Merta. "Jane Austen's Ideal of Beauty." *Proceedings of the Hampshire Philological Society* 34 (1921): 468–77.

Dott, Djane. "Jane Austen's Lost Text on the Perfect Husband Rediscovered." *Oxford Review,* Dec. 15, 2016.

———. "Boyish Love: Tom Lefroy and Jane Austen's 'Plan of a Husband.'" *Studies in Regency Literature* 65, no. 2 (July 2017): 168–84.

Dread, Firey Lee. *The Romantic Hero, 1750–1850.* Nashville: Blockhouse, 1999.

———. *The Construction of Literary Characters.* Cambridge: Richardson & Smith, 2004.

Hech, Lorene. "'Happiness in marriage is entirely a matter of chance:' Matrimony, Masochism, and Masculinity in Jane Austen's Novels.' In *Jane and Gender: Feminist Perspectives on Austen's Life and Work,* edited by Djane Dott, 174–86. London: Litter Demon Press, 2017.

Hillinspur, Gary. *Austen When Old: The Novelist's Later Life.* London: Holloway & Penn, 1996.

Kalvini, Eileen. "Formen von Männlichkeit in Austen." In *Große Schriftstellerinnen und ihre Männer,* edited by Annie E. Verslob and Eileen Kalvini, 112–26. Grimma: Mitteldeutscher Philologinnenverband, 1996.

Leerump, Vertika. *Men and Music in the Regency Period.* Bath: Pump Room Press, 2012.

Randgras, Sootheana. "'Men have had every advantage of us in telling their own story. ... I will not allow books to prove any thing': The Metafictional Gender Discourse in Jane Austen's Persuasion." In *Discourse into Literature,* edited by Col. Horatio Springfield, 34–49. New Orleans: Mosaic, 2002.

Tirić-Anker, Snatij. *Reclaiming Spinsterhood and Lesbianism: (Auto)biographical Backgrounds of Nonconventional Gender Dynamics in Women's Fiction in Britain, from Jane Austen to Jeanette Winterson.* Manchester: Glass & Co., 2017.

6

Linus Withold and the Birth of the Rhizomatic Text

Eric D. Lehman

"Novels should not grow in straight lines, like trees, but in all directions, like fungi," wrote Linus Withold in the *Hartford Courant* in 1811. This was no idle theory, but rather what this intrepid Yankee scribbler considered the founding metaphor of his own work. A few years earlier he had begun a three-decade attempt to write a book that could be read not only chronologically, but also by character, thematically, and dozens of other ways. Through a remarkable indexing system, he attempted to change the way books were written and consumed, creating an "ideal text" and putting the reader in charge of the story.

A recent revival of regional interest in Withold has been occasioned by a local bookseller's recovery and collection of more pieces of his *Root-Book*.[1] This novel, if we can actually call an ever-growing text a novel, was by all standards a failure due to a variety of problems, some material, some stylistic, some legal. A century after the author's death and Withold was unfamiliar

---

[1] "Linus Withold's Strange Book," *Hamden Historical Society Newsletter*, Winter 2016. And David K. Leff, "Who Is Linus Withold and Why Don't We Remember Him?" July 1, 2016, http://davidkleff.typepad.com. The local bookseller in question is the famed Whitlock's Book Barn in Bethany, CT.

to all but a few literary historians. This should be no surprise. After all, he never finished his book; it *could* never be finished. Nevertheless, his ambitious attempt to write the world's first non-hierarchic, rhizomatic story was a seminal moment in the history of the American novel, one that only now in the age of the Internet, hyperlinking, and digital technology can we truly appreciate.

∞

When Linus Withold was born in 1771, his parish of Mount Carmel was still considered part of New Haven, and he remembered enough of the 1779 British attack to write a version of it in his novel.[2] His family had been one of the first to settle the Colony in the 1600s, and its scions could be found in nearly every village. They had never prospered, refusing (or being rejected from) community leadership, failing in mercantile ventures to the Caribbean, and leaving only headstones scattered amidst Connecticut's rocky hills. We find their names on both Loyalist and Continental Army registers, but none distinguished themselves as officers. An Archibald Withold (1707–1765) apparently fought with some distinction in King George's War, helping to capture the fortress of Louisbourg on Cape Breton Island. However, his letters comprise the only evidence, and his name appears on none of the Connecticut rolls.[3]

It seems scarcely worth mentioning, since it was so common in those times, but Linus was the last surviving child of eight brothers and sisters, all of whom died when he was a boy.[4] Like many too young to fight in the Revolution, he became an overachiever, trying to measure up to the uniformed titans just a few years older than he. Entering Yale College at age 15, he recalled

---

[2] In Withold's version, Mount Carmel, also known as the Sleeping Giant, wakes up and smashes the British fleet with its stony arms.

[3] Archibald Withold to Emiline Withold, May 10, 1744, Derby Historical Society. Historian Marian O'Keefe posits that the man was really disguising a clandestine "business" (smuggling) trip to Montreal.

[4] We find their names repeated as characters in the *Root-Book*.

engaging in debates about the Constitution, drinking coffee in the public houses, and bowling on the New Haven green.[5] During his last year he tutored Eli Whitney, who was just entering school, even though Linus was actually significantly younger.

Upon graduation, he took a job with a printer of religious tracts, walking to and from his parents' house in Mount Carmel, a significant commute of several hours a day. He certainly could not afford a horse. Throughout the 1790s we find his writing in the *New Haven Torrent,* though articles also appear in the *Courant* and various "literary journals" like Timothy Dwight's *Sermonalia*.[6] Some of these are opinions on political or social topics of the day, but some are fantastic stories that can only be called fiction. Here is one example from 1798, at the dawn of the Quasi-War with France.[7]

> The real danger, fellow Connectors, is *not* from the French, our allies of old. Nay, tis as our forebears knew, from savages of the Long-Island, whose whale-boat raids harassed our shores during the splendid *Revolution,* and now threaten to carry off both *maids* and *midwives*. These sand-loving devils from across the Devil's Belt are not *content* with our corn and carrots, but *covet* our very skins.

This is no doubt a sort of satire, though we cannot discount it as an actual concern of the conspiracy-loving public, which was as likely to believe such tales in those times as in ours.[8]

---

[5] Linus Withold to unknown, October 27, 1813, MS399, New Haven Historical Society.

[6] These are barely recognizable to us today as "literary journals," but rather as bound anthologies of disparate material, from sermons to poems to treatises on onion-farming.

[7] "The Real Threat," *New Haven Torrent,* July 14, 1798. Withold's politics generally seem to be Federalist, while his social ideas are generally those of a reformer. However, they are eclectic, and usually diverge wildly from any ideology or platform.

[8] See Joseph E. Uchinski and Joseph Parent, *American Conspiracy Theories* (New York: Oxford University Press, 2014), and Peter Knight, ed., *Conspir-*

During the 1790s there are hints of a love affair, possibly with the wife of Noah Webster, Rebecca Greenleaf. By the time he arrived in New Haven, Webster was already famous for his blue-backed speller, and the two men did not become friends, though they traveled in some of the same circles. The hint comes from the *Root-Book* itself, in which a Becky Redleaf is pursued and won by the narrator of one of the volumes. It is probable that he simply loved her from afar, though Webster himself was notoriously hard to live with; one could hardly blame Greenleaf for a dalliance or two. Other than that, we have no indication that Withold ever wooed a lady, and he never married. Any speculation on his bachelorhood can be left to more dexterous interpreters of his fictions like Prof. Caleb Three (see below), because no evidence exists in the historical documentation.

For a few years, in addition to writing for the newspapers, he reunited with another classmate, Eli Whitney, tramping down the dusty high road to the new, bustling factory on the edge of town, keeping records, drawing diagrams, answering letters. It could even be that Whitney's use of transposable parts gave him the idea to apply this concept to literature. To be fair, interchangeability is only one aspect of Withold's project, but it is a startling concurrence. They had a falling out sometime in 1806–1807. Neither left a record of the cause, but there is evidence it may have been an argument over Whitney's cotton gin lawsuits.[9] We know Withold had a loose regard for literary "property," and so perhaps he had a similar point of view about Whitney's invention, stolen by plantation owners in the 1790s.

No paintings exist of Withold, but we do have a description by Timothy Dwight, poet, minister, and president of Yale.[10]

---

acy Theories in American History: An Encyclopedia (Santa Barbara: ABC-CLIO, 2003).

9 Eli Whitney Blake to Linus Withold, March 15, 1826, MS399, New Haven Historical Society. "My uncle and yourself disagreed on the gin, but he had high regard for your opinion."

10 Timothy Dwight, *Diary for 1809,* Dwight Family Papers 1713–1937, MS187, Series 1, Manuscripts and Archives, Yale University Library.

July 4. Spoke with one Linus Withold today at the fireworks, a tall, gangly fellow with a nest of brown hair. Strange fellow with Stranger ideas. Have read one or two things of his in the *Torrent* — amusing and light. The man himself though is Deadly Serious. Would be a bore in company.

His parents both died in 1810, leaving their only son the house and small farm. He seems to have rented out his fields, and the income from that kept him afloat through many years of literary work. The house, a blue saltbox with a handsome central chimney, stood for over two centuries in Mount Carmel. It is scheduled for demolition by the local university.

∞

For the rest of Linus Withold's life, his primary concern was the *Root-Book*. All of his publications in newspapers 1805–1836 are pieces from this growing novel. But he was not satisfied with newspaper publication, and in 1811 began to assemble the manuscripts, some of which end up at the printer, and some that do not. Only a few were published as individual books or "chapters of the novel" as he called them. We thus call the *Root-Book* a novel because Withold did, but it could as easily be called novels, plural. After all, the manuscripts contain at least 8,499,000 words, not counting the various books they "connect" to, or devour, depending on our perspective.

The problem with novels, he often complained, was that they were forced into an orderly linear narrative, despite any "time-hopping" within that narrative. Sequels proceeded linearly, as well. Worse, the specificity of setting and character limited rather than expanded the possibilities of story for both writer and reader. "Most authors are like land surveyors," he grouched. "They only think in straight lines."[11] And so, his underpinning idea was to write a novel that grew in all directions, like a "fun-

---

11 Linus Withold to Mrs. Brimfield. June 15, 1814. MS399, New Haven Historical Society.

gus" as he said. It would have an incredible freedom in this way, and at the same time increase the possibility of connection by subject, theme, setting, character, etc.

He began by collecting his published pieces and finding ways and places to connect them through an elaborate index. He then wrote the first new "sectals" (his word for chapters, since he used "chapters" for what we would call short or long "novels"), which at first must have provided a center for this growing manuscript. However, any center was quickly lost, which seems to have been his intention.[12] Connections were provided with an elaborate system that allowed readers to choose their own paths. A reader could jump from Sectal 5A in one novel to G16 in another, then TH40 in another, then back to Sectal 6A. But Sectal G16 could lead to 47Z in another, and connections could also be designated by footnotes in the middle of chapters, or even paragraphs, allowing the reader to spend weeks just reading one sectal, by jumping out at various footnotes to a place where the subject or character is explored more thoroughly, and then jumping back.[13]

As one might guess from these unusual designations, the sectal system takes an advanced degree in mathematics to decipher, with combinations of letters and numbers, along with various codes for readers to use to navigate, each one of which could create a new "plot." These were supplemented by an increasing number of indexes, each of which presented thematic and linguistic "guides" that could also be used by a reader to build a different story.[14] However, as the novel grew, the codes changed, and it seems that Withold lost track of his own system. Or it could just be that a cypher to decrypt the old and new codes

---

12 We might note a similarity to a novel like Laurence Sterne's *Tristram Shandy* in this lack of center. However, Withold's idea was much more ambitious, and as mentioned above, put the onus on the reader to create the story.

13 The obvious problem with this method is that a reader needs to own all the chapters. However, this could possibly have been an incentive to purchase.

14 Some unattributable footnotes and indexes must refer either to lost pieces of the *Root-Book* or to sectals and chapters that Withold planned to write but never got around to (before ending his life in Hartford's Retreat for the Insane).

has been lost. Whatever the case, we cannot speak of plot in the *Root-Book,* because each plot is new, created by the choices of the reader.[15] We can approach the plots of some (but not all) the individual sectals.

Because of the strange way that the books and individual plots interlocked, an even stranger thing happened with *time* in the *Root-Book.* The wars and development of early America was certainly one of his favorite subjects, and about half the material involves the years 1600 to 1787. However, this was not historical novel per se, and lacks many of the hallmarks of the genre. Furthermore, many parts leap into possible futures, include supernatural events, and delve back into the times of the Roman Empire, which in some variations of the *Root-Book*'s puzzling timeline seems to happen contemporaneously with the founding of the United States. Characters sometimes seem to grow older the further back in time the stories go, or die and then appear again without comment.

But more interesting than the compressions or extensions of time that happen on different readings (and often within the text itself), are the circular and spiral forms that time seems to move through. Imagine if *Huckleberry Finn* ended with the opening scene of its own prequel *Tom Sawyer,* or if the final scene of *Hamlet* is continually approached in time, getting closer and closer to it each time but never reaching the prince's death. Those examples give a small idea but do not begin to approach the temporal complexity of the *Root-Book.* It is not clear whether this was intentional or simply an after-effect of Withold's obsession with connection.

The hundreds of characters include figures from all over the globe, but since at least a quarter of the extant manuscripts take place in the colonial and post-colonial United States, we certainly have a wide range of American types. One archetypal Yankee wit seems to be based on Phineas Barnum, grandfather

---

15 We might add to Roland Barthes's various "pleasures of the text" this additional pleasure. Roland Barthes, *The Pleasure of the Text,* trans. Richard Miller (New York: The Noonday Press, 1975).

and namesake of the more famous showman. In the early 1800s Barnum was noted throughout western Connecticut for his practical jokes, and the character of Porphyry Custom takes on many of the attributes noted later by the grandson in his autobiography.[16]

Looking at just one of his original characters is instructive as to difficulties of development, timeline continuity, and plot. For example, Ricard Merton appears in twelve different chapters and sectals. He fights in the Revolution, spies on King Louis XIV in France, and invents a steam-powered fire hose. He speaks in an antiquated fashion, more appropriate to his apparent birthplace and time of England in 1554: "Who hath filled the lands of Columbia with the hands of sloth? A special clause of the will is pure enough to finde a noble cause?"[17] He falls in love with Becky Redleaf (who should not yet be born according to some timelines) but she is promised to another. One connection has him discoursing on the nature of love for fifty pages in a book in which he otherwise does not appear. He marries the daughter of George Washington and in one variation their child seems to become his grandmother. Along with these original creations, the Root-Book contains characters from *Robinson Crusoe, Paradise Lost,* and dozens of other popular works of literature. He then used footnotes and indexing to connect his sectals and chapters with these other works. This made perfect sense, because his goal was an interrelated, unending, and ever-expanding fungus of fiction. He used cathedrals as an example of collaborative art to defend this practice, which eventually got him into trouble, as we will see below.

Another problem that Withold never solved, or perhaps was not even aware of, was created by changing narrators. In long, time-hopping texts such as Marcel Proust's *Remembrance of*

---

16 Phineas Taylor Barnum, *Life of P.T. Barnum* (New York: Redfield, 1855). Similarity noted by Malcolm Cowley in his unpublished notes on Withold held in the Archives of American Art.

17 Quote only from Linus Withold, *The Ball of Middle Years* (Hartford: River Press, 1818).

Things Past or Karl Ove Knausgaard's *My Struggle*, we have one narrative voice to bind together such unwieldy "novels." However, Withold may have lacked either the desire or the skill to unite the texts with one voice. Regardless of his intention, the narrative voice changes throughout the text(s), jumping from omniscient to limited, from first to third person, and so on. This often has the effect of disconnecting the various pieces into separate stories, separate worlds. We might see this as a failure on his part, creating a contrary effect to the main scheme of the *Root-Book*.[18]

In his 50s, he began to try to physically connect the various documents and texts. He had already dabbled with a three-dimensional index, but that had simply led to a pile of wooden blocks in his living room. Frustrated with the linear nature of a bookshelf, he built in his barn a spherical one, in fact a series of spheres inside each other.[19] At one point he tried to attach the books at various pages with strings and ropes, but this quickly created a tangle of incredible proportions. With a heavy heart, he resorted to a scissors. However, he soon commissioned a local blacksmith to forge small interlocking pieces, which he could then attach to metal rods, chains, and other books with similar pieces.[20]

Unfortunately, perhaps, this focus on physical connection distracted him from his original plan, which was to interweave the texts of different books, poems and essays, by a process of plot, character, word, phrase, and index connection. However, the retreat is more understandable when we look at the legal trouble he was facing at the time.

∞

---

18 On the other hand, see the discussion of Mikhail Bakhtin below.
19 It is unfortunate that this astounding piece of furniture was not preserved, as he intended. However, it was difficult to move and store, and the bewildered trustees at Yale finally gave up, leaving a brief note on its design and their struggle in the archives of the Trumbull Gallery.
20 A few of these strange pieces remain on display at the Hamden Historical Society's Jonathan Dickerman House.

One reason Withold's *Root-Book* (or rather its various separate "chapter" novels) disappeared from public view, is the series of lawsuits attached to it, beginning in the 1820s and continuing through the 1830s. As one might have already guessed, his use of the characters from the works of other authors is where he finally got himself into trouble. Beginning with "foreign" writers including Goethe and Plato, he began using fictional characters and events freely as early as 1808. Sir Walter Scott's *Waverley* was the first contemporary novel to be devoured, a year after its publication in 1814. In Withold's "Sectal FD5: Plum Sauce for the Captain," Edward Waverley comes to America and enlists in the fight for American independence, joining the Sons of Liberty and convincing an equivocal George Washington that England was not to be trusted. Reader feedback was immediate and ecstatic; sales jumped from a few hundred to a few thousand. One particular reader noted the move in her journal. "Finished Withold's latest triumph after bean pot last night. Waverley and Washington evermore!"[21] However, sales plummeted after the spring, perhaps caused by the so-called "Year Without a Summer" and the subsequent migration from New England. Few had time to read novels.[22]

Nevertheless, he tried again in 1822, and this time chose an American author, James Fenimore Cooper. *The Spy* had just been released in 1821, and Withold immediately used the lonely character of Harvey Birch in several published pieces that hover around the American Revolution.[23] The response was again favorable from readers, but not from the author, who called Withold a "honey-fuggler."[24] Cooper and Withold may have met

---

21 Margaret Crane Fuller, *Diary,* MS Am 1086, Margaret Fuller Family Papers, Houghton Library, Harvard Library, Harvard University.

22 Although this dark, cold summer was a productive time to create literature. See the origin of Mary Shelley's *Frankenstein,* among others.

23 Published in the *New Haven Torrent,* and reprinted in various papers throughout the region.

24 I.e., "thief." James Fenimore Cooper to Linus Withold, December 16, 1822, MS399, New Haven Historical Society. Withold often assumed that other authors would be excited about his project, and was just as often misled in his assumptions.

when the former was at Yale (before being expelled for misbehavior), because they both spoke with a familiarity born of former close contact. However, no records exist of this relationship.

Characters in imaginary works were not covered by any sort of law at the time. Today, based on the ruling of Judge Learned Hand of the U.S. Court of Appeals of the Second Circuit in *Nichols v. Universal Pictures Corp.* (1930), a character that is "sufficiently unique and distinctive" can be protected, though often this muddy area can still be circumvented by clever authors, or more permissive judges. So Withold could comfortably or at least legally ignore the threatening letters sent by Cooper's lawyers. Where Withold got into trouble, though, was using other authors' actual writing, something he had done before but not with living writers.[25] And so, in 1827, with his publication of Chapter XG456, "Hawk-eye Flies Away," he made a fatal error.

The chapter, a novel-length paper booklet of 80,000 words published by Crown and Sons of Hartford, Connecticut, not only uses the character of Natty Bumpo, also known as Hawk-eye, but plagiarizes several large sections of *The Last of the Mohicans,* particularly those surrounding the attack on Fort William Henry. Cooper's lawyers found here a true point of attack, and their lawsuit intended not only to take Withold's meager royalties, but asked for damages from the publisher and the author amounting to $10,000, a staggering sum that neither could hope to pay.

The lawsuit dragged on for years, slowed by primitive legal systems, differences in state laws, and lack of precedent that generally hampered civil courts in the early Republic. "This nutmeg thief continues to plague me," Cooper told a friend in 1831, though it was something he rarely commented on.[26] It's possible he didn't want to publicize the ongoing case, and so kept quiet

---

25 One of his favorite games was to put the speeches of Shakespeare into the mouths of other characters. Marquis de Lafayette using language from *Julius Caesar,* etc.

26 James Fenimore Cooper to Mr. River, July 20, 1831, "I Remain: A Digital Archive of Letters, Manuscripts and Ephemera," Lehigh University Digital Library.

for the most part, letting his lawyers do the work. However, several other authors were alerted, and after a quick read found that their own works had also been cannibalized, though to a lesser extent.[27] Their lawsuits joined Cooper's.

For his own part, Withold remained defiant, and we see here his philosophy of fiction bleeding into his philosophy of life.[28]

> No self-respecting author would assault another for what surely must be the highest compliment, which is to take his words as your own. All stories are connected, all stories are one. That Huron dog [Cooper] is free to use mine own, as I am his.

Publishers had always been wary of the ever-expanding and foggy nature of the *Root-Book,* and by the 1830s no one wanted to touch his material, afraid that they would lose money in court. By the time of the author's death a few years later, his works were all out of print.

∞

Despite its scarcity, Withold's work did inspire a few other 19th-century writers like Walt Whitman, who tried to build a poetic version in *Leaves of Grass*.[29] Even Whitman's title may allude to Withold's project, with the "leaves" standing up like individuals, but connecting underneath the ground, their roots intertwined. Whitman's attempt fell victim to his constant revisions, though, and his need to control and limit the material ruined what could have been a successfully interconnected "Root-Poem."

---

27 These lawsuits name Washington Irving, William Cullen Bryant, Fitz-Greene Halleck, and other members of Cooper's Bread and Cheese Lunch.
28 Linus Withold to Eli Whitney Blake, January 15, 1832, MS399, New Haven Historical Society.
29 Whitman's line in *Song of Myself,* "Root of wash'd sweet-flag! timorous pond-snipe! nest of guarded duplicate eggs! it shall be you!" is a direct reference to Withold's book, which features sectals called, "Sweet Flag," "Pond Snipe," and "Duplicate Eggs."

A few modernist critics, including Connecticut's Malcolm Cowley, rediscovered the manuscript, and attempted to explain or even catalog the multiplicity of connections and variations, including Withold's indexed editions and further potential versions. However, Cowley and the others admitted defeat, leaving incomplete their own critiques of an incomplete text. It may be that Cowley found what first appeared a "modernist" project, with the reader as detective of a complex *Ulysses*-like text, turned out to be nothing of the sort. The meaning, if there was any, seemed to lie in the connections themselves, not the words or ideas Withold connected.

In the late 20th century, only University of San Diego professor Caleb Three attempted criticism of the *Root-Book,* restricting himself to a psychological interpretation of the genesis of and subsequent expansion of the project. "Withold's lack of a strong father figure is an important consideration," Three writes. "When speaking of his writing, in particular the lack of centrality and free-form connection, we can see a reaction to the absence of authority and also an attempt to create the emotional connections he lacked as a child."[30] The value of this article is questionable to say the least. Armchair analysis of a long-dead author through a few fragments of historical documentation is usually a fool's errand. Doing the same by examining his fiction is an even less productive exercise. Dr. Three would have been better served to spend his own obsessive energies elsewhere.

In recent decades, we have witnessed authors unconsciously repeat elements of Withold's experiment, from the casual assemblage of characters by Bret Easton Ellis to the physical thread "hyperlinks" of German artist Maria Fisher. However, in the age of the internet, hypertexts, and wikis, it seems surprising that none have attempted such a far-reaching and ambitious novel. Now that a larger portion of this work has been recov-

---

30 Caleb Three, "The Freudian Interplay of the Hierarchy in Linus Withold's *Root-Book,*" FAKE *Life: A Journal of Thoughtculture* 1, no. 3 (Spring 1999): 25–38.

ered, we should examine it more closely through the jeweler's lens of modern literary theory.

Approaching the "sectals" of the *Root-Book* seems to call for a re-examination of Roland Barthes's idea of "brief, contiguous fragments" or "lexias." These "units of reading" that Barthes cuts up texts with are in Withold's case already present through his strange "hypertext" method.[31] Can we take agency as readers if the author has already given it to us? Likewise, the multiple voices within the text(s) point to a consideration of Mikhail Bakhtin's "heteroglossia" or "heteroglot multiplicity," which is certainly present, if not in the way Bakhtin imagined. The Russian theoretician is more interested in "meaning" and diversity of language, and while his "system of intersecting planes" sounds like Withold's structural ideas, it is not quite the same thing. However, this theory might be interesting when applied to such a vast work, since the sectals are ostensibly all "one novel." Withold also unintentionally creates many "hybrid utterances" and multiple discourses, and his apparent failure in creating and controlling literary voice might through Bakhtin's eyes be a positive result.[32]

The digression and reference inherent to postmodernist maximalism seem to fit the *Root-Book* very nicely. He revels in quantity and accumulation to excess. However, the elaboration of minute detail that characterizes David Foster Wallace or Samuel Beckett does not fit Withold's style, and in fact his lack of descriptive or emotional detail is often his Achilles heel. Witness this passage from "The French Hen" (Sectal GY894).[33]

> Lafayette turned to go, hastening upon his errand. The last of the kings was dead, and the oaths all kept. Once he would have wept, but his eyes were dry. Then the soldiers walked to the river, where the stags had supped, and began to berate

---

31 Roland Barthes, *S/Z*, trans. Richard Miller (New York: Hill and Wang, 1975).

32 Mikhail Bakhtin, *Dialogic Imagination: Four Essays,* ed. Michael Holquist (Austin: University of Texas Press, 1982).

33 *New Haven Torrent,* August 30, 1824.

the crowds who walked along it. There was much to do in the republic of the just. God knew the answer. Profligacy would be the next virtue. Soon God turned to the door and walked up to Jacob Huntsman. "I forgive you," he said. Huntsman left on his own errand, to fight the next war.

A lack of rhythmic or syntactic flow leads to a flat passage that moves through multiple ideas and even entire scenes without linguistic punch or the opportunity for reflection. Furthermore, the baffling aspects of this piece are never answered, the confusing ideas never advanced. He may indeed be writing the "literature of exhaustion," as John Barth once called it,[34] but he is doing it by spreading out, not digging in.

Alan Kirby's reaction against postmodernism—digimodernism—provides another methodology. "The digimodernist text in its pure form is made up to a varying degree by the reader or viewer or textual consumer," he writes. "This figure becomes authorial in this sense: s/he makes text where none existed before."[35] Kirby's ideas about social and anonymous authorship would also have found a home in Withold's mind, and no doubt the latter would have embraced "digital technology" as a method for building stories. However, Kirby is more interested in the ways technologies have demolished "cultural postmodernism" and operate to create a new intellectual moment, while Withold's concerns were with the principles of fiction itself. Still, this is a fruitful area for critics to explore.

Though they remained unaware of Withold's attempt, Gilles Deleuze and Félix Guattari's post-structuralist idea of a "rhizome book" in *A Thousand Plateaus* allows for what might be the most interesting interpretation. They begin talking of the "root-book" as the taproot of a tree, and then move toward something that

---

34 John Barth, "The Literature of Exhaustion," *The Atlantic* (1967): 29–34. See also John Barth, "A Few Words about Minimalism," *New York Times Book Review,* Dec. 28, 1986, 1.

35 Alan Kirby, *Digimodernism: How New Technologies Dismantle the Postmodern and Reconfigure Our Culture* (London: Bloomsbury Academic, 2009), 51.

more closely resembles his *Root-Book,* a rhizomatic structure, "a map and not a tracing," with "linear multiplicities," which is "in the middle, between things, interbeing, *intermezzo*." Using their theory, each sectal or chapter of Withold's book would be an assemblage, a neuron in a system of dendrites, which operates "by variation, expansion, conquest, capture, offshoots." The meaning, as they put it, is in the connections themselves. They command us: "Make rhizomes, not roots, never plant! Don't sow, grow offshoots! Don't be one or multiple, be multiplicities!"[36] It seems as if Linus Withold heard this command, almost two hundred years earlier.

∞

Whatever approach we take to understanding Linus Withold's iconoclastic work, it gives modern scholars and authors a new way of thinking about the novel and its future. After all, why *not* write books this way? Most novels do not follow a traditional A → B → C narrative, shifting perspective, leaping around in time. In our digital age, we have a method for exploring and demonstrating this in more detail. The first step is to attempt to digitize Withold's entire *oeuvre,* at least what remains to us. There seem to be two options for rhizomatic "publication" — putting his construct on a single, expanding website or wiki, or using the Internet itself as the connective tissue of story. Problems of methodology, design, and control will arise with each. But with willing support and a publisher with a visionary outlook, these challenges could be solved. Perhaps later hardbound editions could be offered and even sold in "puzzle" format, with chapters that can be rearranged according to the reader.

Let me propose two more radical steps to accompany this digitization, which with a dedicated team will take at least a decade. Novelists of our own age could steal a page from Withold,

---

36 Gilles Deleuze and Félix Guattari, *A Thousand Plateaus: Capitalism and Schizophrenia,* trans. Brian Massumi (Minneapolis: University of Minnesota Press, 1987), 3–25.

and begin rhizomatic books of their own. These could find ample opportunity to connect with the original *Root-Book,* and taking this idea farther, with each other. Indeed, this forgotten Connecticut author's ambitious idea calls for such a step, calls for the radical (could we say *fungal*?) transformation of literature.

I close with an anecdote that may well be apocryphal, but any assessment of Withold's work seems incomplete without it. In January 1836, just before his death, he shared dinner in New Haven with his old rival Noah Webster. Apparently, they had not spoken since the 1790s, because Webster seems unaware of the *Root-Book* even at this late date. For decades, he had been assembling his own vast project, the *American Dictionary,* and had recently sold the final copy of the first edition. A mutual friend, Edvard LeRoche, recorded the following in a letter.[37]

> Webster listened to Withold describe his scheme for over an hour, while picking at his election cake. Finally, his temper—which has been the bane of his life—came forth against the man. "But what's the *story*?" he asked. "Ah, that's too intricate to describe," Withold replied. "There are many possible plots, many beginnings, many endings." Webster would not be put off. "No one will read a novel without a story." "We'll see about that," Withold said.

---

[37] Edvard Leroche to Ryan Parker, May 15, 1836, MS399, New Haven Historical Society.

Bibliography

Bakhtin, Mikhail. *Dialogic Imagination: Four Essays*. Edited by Michael Holquist. Austin: University of Texas Press, 1982.

Barnum, Phineas Taylor. *Life of P.T. Barnum*. New York: Redfield, 1855.

Barth, John. "The Literature of Exhaustion." *The Atlantic* (1967): 29–34.

———. "A Few Words about Minimalism." *New York Times Book Review,* Dec. 28, 1986.

Barthes, Roland. *The Pleasure of the Text*. Translated by Richard Miller. New York: The Noonday Press, 1975.

———. *S/Z*. Translated by Richard Miller. New York: Hill and Wang, 1975.

Blake, Eli Whitney. Letter to Linus Withold, March 15, 1826, MS399, New Haven Historical Society.

Cooper, James Fenimore. Letter to Mr. River, July 20, 1831, "I Remain: A Digital Archive of Letters, Manuscripts and Ephemera," Lehigh University Digital Library.

Deleuze, Gilles, and Félix Guattari. *A Thousand Plateaus: Capitalism and Schizophrenia*. Translated by Brian Massumi. Minneapolis: University of Minnesota Press, 1987.

Dwight, Timothy. *Diary for 1809*. Dwight Family Papers 1713–1937, MS187, Series 1, Manuscripts and Archives, Yale University Library.

Fuller, Margaret Crane. *Diary*. MS Am 1086, Margaret Fuller Family Papers, Houghton Library, Harvard Library, Harvard University.

Kirby, Alan. *Digimodernism: How New Technologies Dismantle the Postmodern and Reconfigure Our Culture*. London: Bloomsbury Academic, 2009.

Leff, David K. "Who Is Linus Withold and Why Don't We Remember him?" July 1, 2016. http://davidkleff.typepad.com.

Leroche, Edvard. Letter to Ryan Parker, May 15, 1836, MS399, New Haven Historical Society.

"Linus Withold's Strange Book." *Hamden Historical Society Newsletter* (Winter 2016).

Three, Caleb. "The Freudian Interplay of the Hierarchy in Linus Withold's *Root-Book*." fake *Life: A Journal of Thought-culture* 1, no. 3 (Spring 1999): 25–28.

Withold, Archibald. Letter to Emiline Withold, May 10, 1744, Derby Historical Society.

Withold, Linus. *Root-Book*. Various publishers, 1805–1836.

———. *The Ball of Middle Years*. Hartford: River Press, 1818.

———. To Eli Whitney Blake, January 15, 1832, MS399, New Haven Historical Society.

———. To Mrs. Brimfield. June 15, 1814. MS399, New Haven Historical Society.

———. To unknown, October 27, 1813, MS399, New Haven Historical Society.

———. Untitled article. *New Haven Torrent*. August 30, 1824.

Whitman, Walt. *Leaves of Grass: Comprehensive Reader's Edition*. Edited by Harold W. Blodgett and Sculley Bradley. New York: New York University Press, 1965.

7

Eighth Draft of "First-Order Variables & Repression: Oedipal Relations in 'The Sandwich' by Rubiard Whimp" by James Lichtenstein

Austin Sarfan

Though not recognized by scholars of intellectual history, Rubiard Whimp played an important role in the American New Critics' reception of psychoanalytic theory. I want to provide a reading of Rubiard Whimp's short story, "The Sandwich,"[1] which links it to William Wimsatt, a foundational figure of New Criticism. In interpreting the ways that Whimp's writing influenced Wimsatt, I believe that we can detect, at the roots of New Criticism's formalist conception of poetry, an unappreciated model of repression that challenges a strictly Oedipal model of relative difference and instead situates difference within the context of the numinous or infinite.

"The Sandwich" by Rubiard Whimp was published as a short story, spanning about seven pages, in 1947. Originally planned as an eight-chapter novel, the short story has been described

---

1 Rubiard Whimp, "The Sandwich," in *Collected Writings and Other Writings*, ed. Marie Still (New York: Hackett Publishing Company, 1978).

by one critic recently as "a phrase by Proust repeated so many times that a genetic mutation occurs somewhere along the way"[2] — apparently a compliment. Accordingly, the story consists of vague and wandering recollections of the unnamed protagonist's childhood, through a sensorium of domestic scenes, with a climax in which the protagonist meets the child of another family after eating Thanksgiving dinner at this other family's house. Because the child whom the protagonist meets in the story shares the name "Rubiard" with the author of the story, I will call the child character Rubiard and the author Whimp, in order to avoid confusion.

At the latest, Whimp began working on drafts of "The Sandwich" in Fall 1940, when he was in his second year as an undergraduate at Yale. As we know from his autobiography and letters, in his first years at Yale, he was in close communication with his professor of English, Wimsatt, a foundational figure of New Criticism. Wimsatt was particularly regarded for his arguments against the "Intentional Fallacy"[3] and the "Affective Fallacy"[4] which he developed with M.C. Beardsley, a philosopher of art, in the latter half of the 1940s. It is to Wimsatt's elaboration of the "Intentional Fallacy" essay that I eventually want to relate "The Sandwich."

Family relations between the mother, the father, and their child are at the center of "The Sandwich." In his paper "Effects of Prosocial Behavior in the Psychoanalytic Tradition,"[5] Benjamin Trey uses "The Sandwich" to argue that the Oedipal structure functions as a "first-order variable," that is, as an immutable factor whose actualization informs subsequent second-order vari-

---

2   Elaine Prav, "Rubiard and Proust?," in *Reading Whimp from the Start: The Sources of a Style,* ed. Jim L. Kairy (London: Bloomscurrant, 1999), 32.
3   W.K. Wimsatt and M.C. Beardsley, "The Intentional Fallacy," *The Sewanee Review* 54, no. 3 (1946): 468–88.
4   W.K. Wimsatt and M.C. Beardsley, "The Affective Fallacy," *The Sewanee Review* 57, no. 1 (1949): 31–55.
5   Benjamin Trey, "Effects Of Prosocial Behavior in the Psychoanalytic Tradition: What, How, and Why?" *The American Journal of Psychoanalysis* 38, no. 6 (1984): 781–91.

ables of consciousness, like personality. However, I would argue that what we might call the biographical context surrounding "The Sandwich," particularly Whimp's interactions with Whimsatt, challenges Trey's reading. "The Sandwich" demonstrates that, though we may be different from others, this difference is not explained adequately through the closed-model of psychoanalytic relativism which posits the Oedipal structure as a first-order variable. I think that Whimp's story, while clearly engaging in questions surrounding psychoanalytic relativism, actually rethinks difference and opens up a new way to think about psychoanalytic relativism. Following Whimp's claim in a later interview that the "The Sandwich" intends to think difference beyond relativism, we should ask how in fact the Oedipal relations of the story reveal a mode of difference that does not simply confine difference to the first-order triangle constituted by the parents and child. Whimp says in this interview: "At the time [of writing "The Sandwich"] I was thinking a lot about an alternate view of the developmental process, not discrediting consciousness as a product of the family, but at least reframing the family as an aesthetic or literary element."[6] In my opinion, we can best begin to answer the question of how "The Sandwich" rethinks psychoanalytic relativism by examining the relation between Whimp's story and its effect on Wimsatt, particularly in the latter's "The Intentional Fallacy" essay.

The psychoanalytic triangle of Oedipal relations comes to the fore most prominently in the story's Thanksgiving scene. In an attempt to emulate American society, Rubiard's family, recently immigrated from France, decides to invite the protagonist's family over for a Thanksgiving dinner whose rituals are largely lost in translation; Rubiard's mother, taking English lessons from the protagonist's mother at church, hosts the holiday with excitement, but does not realize, to Rubiard's father's dismay, that a "turkey" is a specific kind of bird. In the scene of the dinner,

---

6 Rubiard Whimp, "Two Scenes of Consciousness in Fiction," in *Interviews: On Time and Process*, ed. Jim L. Kairy (Philadelphia: University of Philadelphia, 1994), 76.

the triangular relations between the unnamed protagonist, his mother, and his father, converge with this other set of triangular relations: those of Rubiard, his mother, and his father. In a sense, the two sets of Oedipal triangles actually converge in an exponential fashion. As the protagonist narrates the Thanksgiving scene, after meeting the parents of Rubiard, he notes that, "The clock on the wall read 6, but all I could think was that I wanted it to be 9, since the dinner must then soon be over. 27 times I must have thought this, 27 times." This exponential series begins the various fantasies which constantly interrupt the protagonist's attention during of the dinner scene and condense in images of flight, transcendence, and diminution of scale. In relation to these fantasies which yearn for the infinite during dinner, and which only end when the protagonist properly meets Rubiard, it seems that the singular event of convergence represented by Thanksgiving is helpless to preserve its actual position against every and any larger quantity, real or imagined. The familial relations converging in the Thanksgiving scene are already outstripped by a numinous ideal incapable of being incorporated sufficiently into any vision.

What interests me here is the precise role of the Oedipal complex in the Thanksgiving meeting, and why the encounter between two Oedipal triangles provides occasion for this fantastic and infinite transcendence. The numinous ideal towers over the Oedipal triangle of relations, providing energy for a differentiation far beyond its relative limits. I believe that the fantastic nature of this familial convergence is designed to rupture the actuality of family relativism in a radical way. Freud's theory of psychic structure and libido inspired some of the most influential accounts of revolutionary praxis in the 20th century, for example in the work of Wilhelm Reich and Herbert Marcuse. Specifically, in Reich's work, frequently championed by proponents of radical sexual politics, the Oedipal family is thought to be an after-effect of repression, which inhibits sexual revolution. It is regarding this revolutionary potential of Freud's work that the author exerts a simultaneously profound but muted influence on Wimsatt, who came into contact with Reich's brand of psychoanalysis while it still made pretensions to clinical validity, even if it was only just then being tentatively greeted by academic circles decades prior to its weaponization in the countercultural politics of the later decades.

As I previously mentioned, Wimsatt and Whimp had been in close communication during the academic year 1939. In numerous letters to Wimsatt, Whimp had given voice to the problems facing him in writing "The Sandwich." Whimp speaks of the journals he filled by transcribing passages from the literature he admired — an activity which Whimp hoped would teach him how to write. Four of the eight chapters originally planned for the novel version of "The Sandwich" are entirely comprised of reorganized passages from existing literature, such as from novels of Ernest Hemingway, chivalric romance, and Homeric poetry. Seemingly rejecting Whimp's method of transcription, Wimsatt replied in one teacherly letter to Whimp: "Your paper on aesthetics last term was splendid — I do not think there is a need to immerse yourself further in the actual material of literature. Choose one or two authors. Their context is not important." Whimp, however, did not take this advice. Yale's collections still hold a number of Whimp's early writings, most impressively fourteen folio volumes dated between 1939 and December 1940 filled with his transcriptions of literary sources ranging from ancient Greek to American modernism, as well as copious notes taken by Whimp on the biographical, social, and political circumstances surrounding many of the works cited.

In late December of 1940, Reich gave a lecture at Yale, which Wimsatt attended. From the existing evidence, we can conclude that Reich, during the lecture, spoke of the revolutionary power of sexual libido and of his plans to build a therapeutic machine which he called the "Orgone Energy Accumulator." In the "Glossary" of Reich's *The Structure of Mass Psychology*, orgone energy is defined as: "Primordial Cosmic Energy; universally present and demonstrable visually, thermically, electroscopically, and by means of Geiger-Mueller counters. In the living organism: Bioenergy, Life Energy. Discovered [...] between 1936 and 1940."[7] The Orgone Energy Accumulator was designed by Reich in order to collect the primordial cosmic energy of the orgone, to a therapeutic effect. As one historian writes, the Orgone Energy Accumulator was "an almost magical device that could improve its users' 'orgastic potency' and, by extension, their general, and above all mental, health."[8] The machine liberates the individual's relation to orgone energy otherwise repressed. Throughout the 20th century, the Orgone Energy Accumulator that Reich designed gained significant popularity and was used by prominent figures such as JD Salinger, Saul Bellow, Allen Ginsberg, Jack Kerouac, William Burroughs, and Sean Connery.[9] In addition to them, we have also to add the New Criticism's Wimsatt.

Though Reich's lecture on sexual libido and the Orgone Energy Accumulator was generally not well-received at Yale, it exerted a profound effect on Wimsatt and his understanding of literature. In fact, Wimsatt was so moved by Reich's lecture that a few months after, he visited Reich's workshop to undergo therapy in the Orgone Energy Accumulator. There is little evidence testifying to the exact nature of Wimsatt's experience of the Energy Accumulator, aside from a single letter which he sends to Whimp briefly after his therapy. As Reich intended, the Energy Accumulator seems to have liberated Wimsatt's repressed energy. In the letter which Wimsatt writes to Whimp after his therapy, Wimsatt describes his disillusionment with the very idea of a literary object, and apparently agrees that Whimp's practice of transcription may be the only means to access literature. Whimp writes that there is no discrete literary object but only a "series [...] [which is] an enormous undifferentiated object,"[10] at

---

[7] Wilhelm Reich, *The Structure of Mass Psychology,* trans. Mary Higgins, ed. Michael Terry (New York: Farrar, Straus, and Giroux: 1980).

[8] Christopher Turner, "Wilhelm Reich: The Man Who Invented Free Love," *The Guardian,* July 8, 2011, https://www.theguardian.com/books/2011/jul/08/wilhelm-reich-free-love-orgasmatron.

[9] Ibid.

[10] Rubiard Whimp, "Letter dated 2 March 1942." Personal letter. Unpublished.

its limit, infinitely extended, and which encompasses all literature as a cosmic totality.

The tone of the letter is bizarre, simultaneously desperate and ecstatic. At one point, comparing Whimp to Heraclitus, Wimsatt writes, "My only solace is that you have shown me how to step into this river with you." Concluding the letter, Wimsatt equates his therapeutic realization with a divine or spiritual experience of revelation. He says:

> I cannot of course count upon being fully understood because things are dealt with which cannot be expressed in human language; they exceed human understanding. […] After all, I too am only a human being and therefore limited by the confines of human understanding; but one thing I am certain of, namely that I have come infinitely closer to the truth than human beings who have not received divine revelation.[11]

As we see, Wimsatt's revelation regarding the infinity of literature which outstrips the understanding has a specifically noumenal quality — and this is envisioned only through Reich's therapy of repressive forces. Three days after receiving this letter by Wimsatt, Whimp sent, without any explanation, the first draft of the short story of "The Sandwich," which was the last written exchange the two ever had with each other.

In the years which followed his therapy, Wimsatt published nothing, and was reportedly in deep despair over his capacity to write, until beginning to work on what would become the famous 1946 essay "The Intentional Fallacy," co-authored with M.C. Beardsley. While the essay's analytic style hardly betrays the sense of Wimsatt's struggling with the numinous during these years, doubtlessly nonetheless one can detect that Beardsley's philosophical positions influenced Wimsatt's understanding of his revelation in the Orgone Energy Accumulator. Beginning in 1941, Beardsley constantly recommended William James to Wimsatt, which may have had something to do with the liter-

---

11 Ibid.

ary scholar's ultimate recovery. Regardless, I argue that it is only on the basis of Wimsatt's revelation regarding the infinity of literature that the formalism of "The Intentional Fallacy" essay can be properly understood. The essay charts a difference between a "psychology of composition" and a "public science of evaluating poems."[12] To put it simply, the thesis of the essay is that the psychology of composition has to do with the author's private life, and hence is biographical; whereas on the other hand, the science of judging poems has only to do with the internal dynamics and coherence of the poem as object, only accidentally related to the biographical. As such, Wimsatt and Beardsley's definition of the poetic object definitely contradicts Wimsatt's own prior experience of orgone energy which he expressed to Whimp in their discussions of transcription and literature. One may speculate that this apparent reversal in Wimsatt's position regarding literature is a symptom of a sincere recovery, given that, following the evidence of psychoanalysis, resolving the anxieties provoked by traumatic experience necessitates disavowing its relevance. In this case, the trauma of Wimsatt's shock both attracts and finally repels his understanding of a cosmic aesthetics.

What I want to stress, in any case, is that in order to make this distinction between the biographical and the poem in science, Wimsatt and Beardsley have no choice but to repress the infinitely undifferentiated elements of lived experience. We see here an aversion to, and suppression of, the literary infinite, which, biographically speaking, Wimsatt had privately glimpsed when liberated from repression in Reich's Orgone Energy Accumulator. The ambiguously undifferentiated series of the biographical is excluded in order to isolate the singular content of the poem — both by Wimsatt's disavowal of biographical evidence in relation to poetry and in the formalism of his conception of a science of poetics. In their essay, Wimsatt and Beardsley write, "There is a gross body of life, of sensory and mental experience, which lies behind and in some sense causes every poem, but can never be and need not be known in [...] the poem." While this

---

12 Wimsatt and Beardsley, "The Intentional Fallacy," 476.

undifferentiated mass of experience intersects with and causally determines every poem, Wimsatt and Beardsley nonetheless choose to characterize it as a superfluous *externality* that is irrelevant from the perspective of the internally consistent poem, which alone is the singular, proper object of any science of evaluating poems. Life as an undifferentiated series necessarily must be disregarded or, we might say, repressed, in order to isolate the poem as a singular object for science. As Wimsatt and Beardsley write, "For all the objects of our manifold experience, [...] for every unity, there is an action of the mind which cuts off roots, melts away context — or indeed we should never have objects or ideas or anything to talk about."[13] The production of discourse requires a forceful action mitigating the prevalence of biographical context. Following this idea, the science of poetic analysis operates according to already constituted syntheses, that is, already accomplished and fictitious divisions from life, only valid in its pretensions to separate writing from life — just, as Wimsatt and Beardsley write, so that we should have something to talk about. A science of poetry, if we want to talk about that, requires the repression of biography, which, taken literally, would mean that a science of poetry requires the repression of any actual correspondence between *writing* and *life*.

If Reich derives economic property from sexual repression, ultimately a repression of orgone energy, does Wimsatt derive literary property, or the formalist self-sufficiency of the literary object, from a similar bio-repression? If so, there would be a more fundamental and un-differentiated outside of the literary object, which nonetheless provides the conditions for its genesis. Acknowledging this outside of the literary object, or the infinite, would require recognizing the dissolution of any boundaries between work and ownership, or work and originality, in order to gain an intuition of literature's involvement rather than separation from life. Otherwise speaking, liberation from bio-repression would require embracing the method of work practiced by Whimp and revealed to Wimsatt in order to learn what

---

13 Ibid., 480.

writing is, properly in relation to the cosmic — ideally, the practice of transcription expanding through the cosmic, a relativism that is an infinite repetition.

This definition of writing disrupts the supposed unity of the literary object postulated by Wimsatt and Beardsley convergent on an unconscious cosmos. To what extent can we see this definition already operative in the conversation between the protective mother and the guilty father in Whimp's "The Sandwich?" How does Whimp's story dissolve the form of the Oedipal matrix as first-order variable? We know, in fact, from the extant outlines, notes, and drafts that were involved in the final construction of the short story, which again was originally planned as a novel, that some sort of repression of content seems to have played an essential role in the story's creation. From seven meticulously outlined and prepared chapters, spanning hundreds of pages of notes, only a short story composed of a handful of pages finally emerges. How is such a quantity of content condensed into the final work?

So long as we speak of the relationship between preparatory notes and the final work, everything seems fine. However, the notes themselves read largely as a series of transcriptions; transcriptions of conversations with friends and family members, various news sources and works of fiction, and thoughts which have occurred to Whimp throughout the day. In a sense, from the perspective of the preparatory notes, it is clear that life is always impinging on the work's construction, if we understand by that work a definite, closed entity. It forces the documents to be incomplete, always open to further contributions, always sensitive to the living development of the work as an exercise in responsibility to life. The biographical material that may appear in the notes and drafts of the text is in fact already removed from life, but one gets the sense that Whimp's most artful abilities are revealed in the construction of the biographical legibility that exists between the extant drafts and an invisible, undisclosed, at least unwritten, life. In other words, Whimp's genius consists not so much in the finely sculpted literary production, as in his commitment to a life that, when compared with its textual recording, reflects a dramatic conflict between the process of living and its representation in discourse. The supreme aesthetic value of Whimp's literary production consists in his deliberate formation of a relationship between his life and his texts which collapses the formalist self-sufficiency of a literary object.

The space between life and discourse haunts Rubiard's notes for "The Sandwich," where one has the sense that within the finally published short story there are nearly endless potentialities of symbolic content waiting to be revealed through biographical research. How many elements of life have been displaced and condensed into the text? Ultimately, what appears to be the work as a self-sufficient object is the final short story, but nonetheless the real work concerns the indifferent and undifferentiated relationship between life and the notes. As in Sigmund Freud's *Interpretation of Dreams,* where apparent significance is merely one product, and merely the terminal point, of mental labor,[14] so too Whimp's texts seem to be produced only as terminal points of a more extensive life. The dream or the text is the visible form, the trace, of a mental work which remains invisible, primarily unconscious. This insight regarding the invisibility of a production whose effort disappears insofar as it is terminally condensed into a significant object, in fact, clarifies Whimp's otherwise obscure notebook entry, written the day after his completion of the final draft of the short story: "The final draft is certainly done, but it is the least of the work which has concerned me."[15]

With this in mind, recall that the dream sequence in the drafts of the work is supposed to be the initial action of "The Sandwich" — although in the final version it is nowhere to be found. As Whimp states in an early outline of the chapters, the book's second chapter is supposed to demonstrate how "Rubiard's parents meet in a dream in the United States of America,

---

14 Sigmund Freud, "Interpretation of Dreams," in *The Basic Writings of Sigmund Freud,* trans. and ed. Dr. A.A. Brill (New York: Random House, 1995).
15 Ibid., 232.

spitefully."[16] Regarding the extant drafts for the chapters (up to chapter five, out of seven), the second chapter, outlined by Whimp beginning with this parental dream-sequence, is by far the most elaborate. However, the dream itself remains invisible. Following the outline of the chapter, we would expect to find a dream sequence in the written drafts which develop its structure. But we do not. Is the stated description of the chapter its true intention? Is there a dream event proper? I would say that the impossibility of an answer to these questions constitutes the genius of the transition from the novel envisioned by Whimp — divided according to discrete chapters — to the short story, a construction of pure *durée,* written by Whimp, it seems, swiftly over one single night. Altogether, in Whimp's case, the mental effort of not writing or at least preparing for writing far exceeds the amount of work involved in the story's final and most concentrated expression. The work of not writing both achieves access to an unconscious language logically supporting the narrative and retains an organic purity of expression that can never be located in the representation of the finished work.

This is precisely how psychoanalytic relativism must frame the process of mental development: as one which continuously finds its claims to discovering significance already undone by the secret labor of the unconscious. It must be said that, following the most recent theory, Oedipus is always folded into a series of mediated applications that continuously transcribe the real while delegating to an agent the responsibility of a finite application of the terms of the real: at once the site, the convergence, but also the "de-vergence" of the familial as real.[17] In this sense, de-vergence describes how relations of power and control appear entangled in their own unconscious self-reciprocity, as the "auto-mechanical" underbrush of directives which can do noth-

---

16 Rubiard Whimp, *Outlines for a Novel and Other Drafts,* ed. Bill Janey (New York: Schocken, 1981), 5.

17 Heimlich Nowte. "Family and Population: An Outline of a Theory of Practice," in *On the Use and Abuse of Oedipus: Contemporary Thought on The Triad* (Chicago: University of Chicago Press, 1980), 58–93.

ing but posit their own "unshakeable" ground in retrospect.[18] I see de-vergence precisely in Whimp's "The Sandwich" where the community, formed by Rubiard, his mother, and the trace of the father (whose intoxication over the course of the dinner risks ultimate unconsciousness), resolves itself in a specific stage of the development of the productive forces of Oedipal relations, namely that of "a psychosis against the fake standard" of the insoluble question of relativism: "Why do we get so much pleasure out of being so different not only from others but from our own past?" the story ultimately seems to ask.[19] It is because the fake standard, or the first-order variable, claims a past that only appears in the present, already constituted without the subject's consent. Yet, even if a sham, the fake standards that claim significance are the only kind of significance consciously available to the subject. Apparent significance is but the most superficial layer of a denser symbolic environment. However, transcription is a production of difference since what consciousness attends to is always a process of mediation actively being discovered. This is why, according to the relativist position, mediation and immediacy are never separate. It is through mediation that the immediate is always promised, if only after a certain activity in relation to the given material, both presently awaiting transcription and organizing consciousness toward its presence in the future.

So long as the history of desire serves as an organon for planetary negotiations over the relative universals that we are groping to construct in the future, Oedipus haunts all societies, indeed even this microcosm of the society that presides over the Thanksgiving table in Whimp's story, but which is really just the nightmare of something which has still not happened. Does the promise of relativism require anxiety over the revelation of unconscious, cosmic investments? The transcription and revelation of the Oedipal triangle during the Thanksgiving scene of Whimp's story responds to this question clearly enough. The dishes are passed around, and everyone eats, but in preparation

---

18 Ibid., 165.
19 Trey, "Effects Of Prosocial Behavior in the Psychoanalytic Tradition," 784.

for another kind of composition or decomposition of the subject involving more than simply nutrition. Here, the family dinner becomes the transcribed sign of a communion that Whimp formulates in terms of the reception of a promise, attributed to an absent Word. After the dinner begins with a toast by Rubiard's mother, it is the phrase "without a word from us" that Whimp keeps repeating, again and again, throughout the narrator's account of the dinner scene. The food is passed, the wine is consumed, and even the conversation is made, all somehow "without a word from us."[20] There is, then, a passivity of transcription which seems to nullify the being of the subject in the event that is supposed to have transpired. Ultimately, the Word that would provide its logic is never spoken, but is still remembered and heard in this very absence.

It is here that we see the appearance of Venus constituting the essential turn in the narrative, demonstrating the "gravitational" reduction that clearly necessitates at least a revision of the relativist position. If logic is absent, at least large objects attract us. While the relativist position does assume the mutual involvement of mediation and immediacy, the gravitational attraction of the future promise — the immediacy that is known to be concealed by the mediator — decomposes even the pretensions of the subject to be responsible for the comprehension of the future state that the subject intends to transcribe. Therefore, the Oedipal triangle is not a first-order variable, since it is in its own way disrupted by something outside of it, a more primary source that is the cosmic. This is what continues to go unrecognized so long as the relativist position ignores the mortal weight of life which far outweighs the superficial significance of narration. Though Rubiard is missing from the dinner scene, after the meal which transpires "without a word from us," the first meeting of the narrator and Rubiard indeed involves the cessation rather than the inspiration of the Word. As Rubiard is studying his astronomical texts in order to observe the appearance of Venus that night, Whimp writes:

---

20 Whimp, "The Sandwich," 26–28.

> We entered the study quietly so as to not disturb him [Rubiard]. At the desk, he sat hunched over, furiously scribbling amongst open books. Their colorful illustrations, battered spines and exhausted pages were bathed by the warm, yellow light of a candle which delicately flickered in the corner of the room. An old globe sat next to it, shimmering against its flame. Then, without a word from us, he ceased writing, and pushed his chair from the desk.[21]

As the narrator continues, however, it is clear also that this cessation of writing and the introduction of Rubiard who has been preparing for the cosmological event produces a fractured rather than simply enduring memory. It is in fact Rubiard's mother who must provide the logic for Rubiard's intentions in this scene. After an unclear question by Rubiard regarding whether the narrator is "ready," the mother intervenes: "He [Rubiard] means for Venus — tonight, it will be visible. Rubiard is so excited! Would you like to stay and watch?" Moreover, there are constantly retentions in memory that are not forgotten (the stench on Rubiard's jacket), even very remote ones (the cockroach scurrying across the floor).[22] The enduring memory of the subject (here the narrator's) is a collection of these disparate fragments, which overwhelm the mind tasked with simply transcribing them (when could one note the first smell, the first sight? Their significance depends on their attraction). There are fragments "perceived" just now that disappear, but only to reappear again as phenomena formally indicating their own horizons, which displace and disrupt the subject since they always trail off into corners that cannot be contained by the narrator's priorities and perceptions. The fragments of memory obtain a gravitational force.

Yet, we have to ask, is there ever, in fact, an original and singular transcription that would be outside a gravitational system, like that of memory? At least, each subject at the Thanksgiving

---

21 Ibid., 29.
22 Ibid.

table would seem to *intensively* recreate entire genealogies of the event for his- or herself, thereby producing *real* effects that we must indeed respect. Clearly, then, as Trey himself even implies at certain moments of his essay with which I began, we must revise the current theory of relativism only insofar as it determines the common rejection of transcription by the first-order model. To reject transcription too hastily would be to side with the supposedly first-order variable of Oedipus — the sham image that produces productivity only by mutually (clandestinely) exchanging immediate realities with the mediating symbols and phenomena of social relations. Oedipus cannot be a first-order variable since not everything is pulled in. We then return to the old problem of "de-vergence" — how are new relations formed between variables? Perhaps the anthropological matrix, inarguably immanent within the formation of the subject itself, first gains its own transcendental ground from a self-referential entanglement. But then, is there anything that could be considered a variable? It is worth noting, incidentally, that the fundamental ambiguity between transcription and creation is a fact recognized by embryologists, by the term *foetalization,* which determines the prevalence of the so-called superior apparatus of the neurax, and especially of the cortex, the use of which is more so a symptom of originality as a problem, less so than its solution.

Bibliography

Freud, Sigmund. "Interpretation of Dreams." In *The Basic Writings of Sigmund Freud,* edited and translated by Dr. A.A. Brill. New York: Random House, 1995.

Nowte, Heimlich. "Family and Population: An Outline of a Theory of Practice." In *On the Use and Abuse of Oedipus: Contemporary Thought on The Triad,* 58–93. Chicago: University of Chicago Press, 1980.

Prav, Elaine . "Rubiard and Proust?" In *Reading Whimp from the Start: The Sources of a Style,* edited by Jim L. Kairy, 23–47. London: Bloomscurrant, 1999.

Reich, Wilhelm. *The Structure of Mass Psychology.* Edited by Michael Terry and translated by Mary Higgins. New York: Farrar, Straus, and Giroux: 1980.

Trey, Benjamin. "Effects Of Prosocial Behavior in the Psychoanalytic Tradition: What, How, and Why?" *The American Journal of Psychoanalysis* 38, no. 6 (1984): 781–91. https://www.jstor.org/stable/11117883.

Turner, Christopher. "Wilhelm Reich: The Man Who Invented Free Love." *The Guardian.* July 8, 2011. https://www.theguardian.com/books/2011/jul/08/wilhelm-reich-free-love-orgasmatron.

Whimp, Rubiard. "The Sandwich." In *Collected Writings and Other Writings,* edited by Marie Still, 20–33. New York: Hackett Publishing Company, 1978.

———. "Two Scenes of Consciousness in Fiction." In *Interviews: On Time and Process,* edited by Jim L. Kairy, 73–77. Philadelphia: University of Philadelphia, 1994.

———. "Letter dated 2 March 1942." Personal letter. Unpublished.

———. *Outlines for a Novel and Other Drafts.* Edited by Bill Janey. New York: Schocken, 1981.

Wimsatt, W.K., and M.C. Beardsley. "The Intentional Fallacy." *The Sewanee Review* 54, no. 3 (1946): 468–88. http://www.jstor.org/stable/27537676.

———. "The Affective Fallacy." *The Sewanee Review* 57, no. 1 (1949): 31–55. https://www.jstor.org/stable/27537883.

8

Under Imaginary Skies: Scholarly Variations on *The Rainberg Variations*

Reed Johnson

"Telling stories about stories — this is our role as critics," the Hungarian scholar László Karol-Wald writes in his essay collection *These Strange Days*. "The storytelling task is liberating, but not one of complete liberty: if we are to write critical fictions, they must be *worthy* fictions."[1] Karol-Wald does not provide an exact definition of "worthy fictions," though his own four decades of criticism provide their own sort of primer for the concept. "Worthiness," in his view, is not an objective quality that inheres within the work, but is instead a relational measure. A work of criticism must, first and foremost, be worthy of that which it claims to study. It must answer complexity with complexity, playfulness with playfulness. Instead of attempting to occlude the original literary work with its own vision or version, the critical essay should instead seek to stand beside it. The critic's job is not to render meaning, but instead to multiply,

---

1 László Karol-Wald, *These Strange Days* (Budapest: Lorem Press, 1998), 47. Emphasis in the original.

deepen, complicate the potentials of the original.[2] In short, the writer and critic are not antagonists, but partners in the very same project.

It is in the spirit of the late Karol-Wald that the present essay explores the potentials of *The Rainberg Variations* — that is, not in order to fix its meanings, but to unfix them wherever possible.[3] The immediate focus will not be so much on the *Variations* themselves, however, as the scholarly variations on the *Variations* — that is, what types of meaning different critics and interpretive communities have discerned in this literary work. Such a metacritical approach is thrice-removed from the *Variations* — that is, it tells stories about stories about stories — but will nonetheless strive to remain worthy, in the Karol-Waldian sense, to the original work. Before exploring the critical responses to the *Variations,* however, a few words should be said about the manuscript, particularly in light of its relative obscurity in the West and the unconventional circumstances surrounding its creation and discovery.

Unlike painting, where an artwork's medium — oil on canvas, say — takes pride of place beside its title, the material aspects of literature are generally viewed as immaterial, perhaps because the raw materials of literature in some deeper sense come from the intangible play of language and culture. In the case of the literary texts known collectively as *The Rainberg Variations,* however, discussion of the physical process of creation is unavoidable. While almost everything about the work has been contested in the three decades since its discovery, the material facts of the manuscript are not in question. *The Rainberg Variations* were "written" with a #3-9 N-301 standard sewing needle of Soviet manufacture, an object that might have easily passed

---

2 Ibid., 49. Karol-Wald was not a postmodern thinker and wouldn't have approved of anything smacking of relativism in criticism. Rather, he thinks we should apply the same quest for truth to criticism as to literature: Does it speak some deeper truth, reveal something new about ourselves?

3 The word "fix" of course, also carries two meanings: to pin down, and to repair something that is defective. Often these meanings prevail in equal measure in literary criticism.

into NKVD archives hidden in a hem or hat brim of one of its workers.[4] For its "pages," the *Variations* made use of over sixteen thousand official documents — interrogation transcripts, forced confessions, denunciations from informants, etc. — found in the case files of convicted (and, in most cases, executed) political prisoners during the years of 1937–38. Thus the *Variations* were quite literally inscribed across the vast bureaucratic corpus of Stalin's Great Terror. Over the intervening years, many of these case files were moved, others destroyed when a radiator in the archives burst in the mid-1970s, still more records were interpolated into the dossiers of convicts, often transferred along with the convicts themselves as they were scattered across the vast prison colonies of the Soviet Empire, making the *Variations* fragmentary and incomplete, so that even the size of these lacunae may only be guessed at.

Similarly, the identity of the *Rainberg Variations*'s author is shrouded in uncertainty. The manuscript takes its name not from the author, but from Viktor Rainberg (1924–1997), who found the work hidden in the secret police archives of a provincial capital in the Soviet Union just weeks after the fall of the Berlin Wall. Rainberg writes about the discovery in his self-published autobiography, *Written for the Drawer,* shortly before his death in 1997. A historian who was, by all accounts of his contemporaries, painfully shy in real life, he makes only the briefest of mentions about his own personal life, but writes lovingly of *The Rainberg Variations,* which became his project for the last decade of his life.

Of this momentous discovery, the provincial historian writes that he was allowed into the KGB archives that summer on the strength of a letter of recommendation from a high-school classmate who'd climbed the ranks of the civil service. He spent much of the summer under the gaze of the senior archivist in

---

4 For a fascinating discussion of the actual forensic analysis done on the archival materials, including a comparison of needle gauges and the holes they produce in typing paper, see James Arnold, "Finding a Needle in the Stacks: Analysis of Perforations in the *Rainberg Variations,*" *Paratexts* 12, no. 3 (April 2013): 81–98, at 87.

the closed section of the record-keeping area, a woman whom he describes as having "a great hooked nose, like Baba Yaga, but with an essentially kind and forgiving soul, someone who'd been cursed with an appearance that manifestly did not fit her inner qualities."[5] Interestingly, Rainberg provided conflicting accounts of the day of his discovery — to the critic Mark Rudensky, he said that he'd first come across part of what would be later known as *The Rainberg Variations* on an April morning in 1989, while in his own autobiography he gave the day as a "rainy and windy August afternoon" of the same year.[6] In one story, he was alone; in another, the head archivist was sitting in her usual spot. In both cases, however, the essential mode of discovery is the same. While paging through the file of a "repressed person," he felt a strange stipple on the pages, "as if it were written in a sort of sparse braille."[7] To get a better look, he held the page up to the dim bare bulb of the archives, and saw that the paper had been pierced in several places with a sharp object, presumably a pin or needle, and these tiny holes glowed brightly ("a constellation of tiny stars", as he describes them[8]) when held up to the light. Baffled, he scanned more pages of the case file, and found all the pages were marked invisibly in the same manner. But it wasn't until he noticed that the holes all neatly fell in the center of individual letters in the typescript that he understood: the markings were not random, but instead indicated letters. These transpierced letters spelled words, the words made sentences, the sentences could be strung together to form narrative threads of stories that leapfrogged across archival documents and case

---

5   Viktor Rainberg, *Written for the Drawer,* trans. Catherine Humboldt (Geneva: Ad Infinitum, 1999), 47.
6   The discrepancy has led to various claims over the years that Rainberg fabricated the entire document himself. In her discussion of the "hoax hypothesis," the critic P. Bortnikova asks whether it even matters if it were fabricated by Rainberg or created by an unknown author. But surely it does matter, because we must then read an entirely different intent into the document. (P. Bortnikova, "On Rainberg's Missing Author," *Vologda Philological Bulletin* 56, no. 2 [June 2014]: 456–76, at 457.)
7   Rainberg, *Written for the Drawer,* 67.
8   Ibid., 54.

files. Assembling these stories was a monumental task, one that Rainberg was unable to complete before his own death ten years later, and which he likened to a "vast puzzle in which most pieces have been lost and the only colors are grays."[9]

One way to view this puzzle is as a cipher text — specifically, the type created in the encoding process known as steganography. Steganographic cipher texts are concealed inside other, innocuous, texts, so that, unlike other coded messages, whose content but not existence is hidden, they may escape detection altogether. In this sense, the *Variations* are concealed within the larger archival corpus in such a way to escape any casual detection from the authorities.[10] This may have protected the author, but by creating his work on papers that would remain in a closed secret-police archive, they were essentially guaranteed never to find an audience.

Enzo Brigande, the essayist and scholar who wrote about the *Variations* in his posthumously published volume *Avant La Lettre,* speculates that this was precisely the author's aim. In other words, this work posits no actual reader besides the author himself, for whom the work represented, in Brigande's view, "an act of literary penance, resolutely performed in private."[11]

---

9 Ibid., 78.
10 Some scholars have used the theoretical model of steganography, and coded forms of communication more generally, to explain how dissident literature can reach its audience in totalitarian societies. Most everyday speech acts follow the Jakobsonian model, with a speaker and a receiver using a shared language to communicate in some medium. But for writers in a totalitarian environment, there are, in fact, two receivers, two entirely separate audiences — one is the intended reader, the other is the censor, the secret police. So how does a person communicate his true intent to his intended audience without revealing it to the secret police? Soviet literature was well-known for its Aesopian language, that is, elaborate disguises for satires of the authorities, and this can be viewed through the lens of cryptographic theory, since the problem is the same: how to communicate with your intended audience without alerting the "enemy" — in this case, the censor who can close your channel of communication. Thus, cryptographic theory is better suited to the task here than Jakobsonian models of communication.
11 Enzo Brigande, *Avant La Lettre,* trans. Simone Verdure (Somerton-Upon-Swindale: Terra Incognita Publishing, 2015), 17.

In this way, Brigande presupposes that, because the author had privileged access to these secret police files — this is, in fact, the *only* fact we know about him (or, indeed, her) — it follows that the author was almost certainly complicit in the Stalinist purges, and his awareness of this complicity was what drove the author to compose the *Variations*. In his discussion of the work, Brigande employs a psychoanalytic framework in his reading of the various narratives, which, in his analysis, center on a series of "micronarratives" of guilt and repression that represent the author's own struggle with his role inside the regime's murderous machine.[12]

Other scholars, chief among them A.M. Grudnitsky, dispute that the *Variations* might have been written (as Grudnitsky acidly remarks) for "therapeutic reasons, a soothing balm for the troubled secret-police soul,"[13] and instead ascribe the encoded format of the work to the need to keep the work hidden until a more propitious time for its release. In this reading, the code is a sort of "time-release" mechanism, a bomb with a fuse of several decades — or, to use the baroque metaphors that Grudnitsky favors, "a missive corked into empty wine bottle and tossed into the high seas, so as to wash up on the shores of the future."[14] This argument depends on the supposition that the author expected future generations — of scholars, if not the general public — would be granted access to the archives, and that this opening up of the archives would thus indicate that society would at last be ready for the *Variations*'s release.[15]

Belarussian critic and translator Lyudmila Shvarts has argued that undue attention has been paid to situating the work in a

---

12 That the language of political persecution and Freudian psychoanalysis both use the same word, "repression," is a fact that Brigande's analysis relies heavily upon.

13 A.M. Grudnitsky, "The Case of the *Rainberg Variations*: Suppositions and Conjectures," in *Festschrift for Petr Romanovich Volynsky*, ed. R.A. Laurita (Frankfurt: Postscriptum, 2009), 89.

14 Ibid., 92.

15 This is in fact precisely what happened, historically speaking, with the discovery and release of the *Variations*.

political/historical context while ignoring its literary lineage.[16] The *Variations*, in her view, fits neatly in the tradition of early-twentieth century textual experiments, in particular the "cut-up poems" of the Dadaists and others. As Shvarts points out, the *Variations* is a derivative work formed from an underlying non-literary text in much the same way that the French surrealists drew from newspaper articles, advertisements, and other ephemera to create new literary works. One might consider more recent examples, such as the Bosniak installation artist Miroslava Begić, who used a six-hundred-page volume of the United Nations publication *On the Prevention and Mitigation of Territorial Conflict Arising from Ethnic Strife in Central Europe, 1991–1999*, to detonate an anti-personnel landmine left behind in a beet field in south-central Tuzla after the Balkan Wars, after which she collected the resultant scraps of paper from the destroyed volume, rearranged them, and affixed them with transparent resin to a concrete floor in Sarajevo's War Childhood museum.[17]

Despite a few superficial similarities, however, the *Variations* differs from these literary and artistic experiments in its use of raw material. For the Dadaists, the underlying source of the words was largely unimportant; presumably the more mundane or commonplace their origin, the better. In this type of textual play, which continues today in erasure poems and the Internet-derived verse of so-called "flarf poetry," composition is often driven by chance or probability-based procedures, unlike the meticulous drafting of the *Variations*. Many of these avant-garde literary works are composed by destroying their raw material, either through cutting, erasure, or more extreme acts of violence, such as Begić's exploding landmine. In such works, the literary work supersedes and displaces its source material. This is not the case, however, with the *Variations*, which exists

---

16 Lyudmila Shvarts, "Literary Influences in the Rainberg Variations," *Journal of Synesthetic Investigations* 34, no. 2 (May 2013): 374–86, at 376.
17 For a detailed discussion of Begić's installation, see Martin Speers, "Miroslava Begić's New Installation Creates Shock Waves in the Art World," *Balkan Arts Quarterly* (May/June 2008): 23.

in a strange sort of superposition alongside the documents from which it was derived.

The complex interrelations between the source material — in Genettian terms, the work's *hypotext* — and the *Variations* has been the subject of much scholarly debate. P. Bortnikova characterizes the relationship as a symbiotic one, contrasting her approach with earlier scholars (viz. Nikolenko) — who, in her terminology, saw it as a "parasitic" work, at least in the sense that it could not exist without the underlying case files,[18] although her negative characterization of Nikolenko's work has been recently challenged.[19] Daniel Alcoser, the Spanish translator of the *Variations*, likens the work instead to a palimpsest, stating that "there is no reading the *Variations* without reading the case files; one must read them both, ideally at the same time, reconstructing the embedded narrative one letter at a time from the files just as they were originally created."[20]

Whether through symbiosis or palimpsest, the *Variations* draws on the case files in deeper ways than traditional steganography. In many instances, the stories of the *Variations* are, in fact, fictional variations on the lives of the accused, using their real names, their professions, their families and friends. In this sense, one might see the work as the imaginings of an archivist who wishes to tell himself stories about the people he encounters in the files. These lapidary vignettes speculate on the loves of the prisoners, their inner lives, their moments of joy and sadness. Crucially, the stories that make up the *Variations*

---

18 Bortnikova, "On Rainberg's Missing Author," 59.
19 See Stephen Newcomb, "Revisiting a Lost World: Reflections on Rainberg's Found Manuscript," *Proceedings of the Hermeneutic Circle* 2 (August 2017): 84–99, at 89.
20 Daniel Alcoser, "Simultaneous Translation: (Re)reading the Rainberg Variations," *The Albuquerque Review* 5, no. 4 (July 2018): 30–43, at 38. Until recently, all published versions of the *Variations* are the text itself, without the underlying case files, which are too voluminous to include in a single volume. In the last decade, however, the graduate student and digital humanist Jacob Vilensky has created a computerized version of the *Variations* that allows the reader to see both the text of the case files alongside the fictional variations.

are devoted almost entirely to imagining quotidian moments and simple pleasures, in stark contrast to the often-lurid descriptions of the case files themselves. In these fictional speculations, no one is ever arrested, interrogated, executed for spying or industrial sabotage. Four single-spaced pages of typescript that describe — in harrowing and almost certainly invented detail — a plot by a certain Comrade Yermolayev to assassinate Regional Committee Secretary Usmanov with an injection of carbolic acid becomes, when transformed in the *Variations,* a single sentence:

> Yermolaev bit into a strawberry, squinting into the sunlight while he watched the barges float down the river, thinking of nothing more than shoes, a good sturdy pair of shoes, how satisfying it would be to polish this pair of shoes to a lustrous gleam.

Reading this passage, one finds not the slightest whiff of the subversive. Indeed, the sentence might have been taken from a story written by Chekhov written in the fading light of the nineteenth century, decades before the revolution. There is no ideology in the *Variations,* no class struggle or so-called enemies of the people. There is little drama, and almost no plot.[21] The lives of these characters (who, it must be recalled, bear the names of real-life political prisoners), are not without event, but they are free of politics, of grand historical forces and cataclysms. They dwell in a world where no one is ever awakened by the sound of a Black Maria idling curbside. As Gerhard Blumfeld notes, "the silences of the *Variations* speak louder than its words."[22] And the work's most deafening silences are reserved for the revolution and for Lenin and Stalin, who merit not a single mention

---

[21] "Plot," of course, can mean both the sequence of causal events of a narrative as well as the sorts of conspiracies that NKVD sought to uncover — or to fabricate, using the devices of narrative plots.
[22] Gerhard Blumfeld, "Facing the Void: Emptiness in the *Rainberg Variations,*" *Pareidolia* 14, no. 1 (January 2017): 96–111, at 98.

among the *Variations*'s eighty-three thousand two hundred and fifty-two known words.

Blumfeld again:

> The conclusion that one must draw is that the *Variations* represent an attempt to build an entirely imaginary world — a world in which the Bolshevik revolution never took place, where Stalin never rose to power, a make-believe realm in which each of these convicted prisoners could be allowed to live out his or her life uninterrupted by the midnight knock at the door.[23]

In this light, we might classify the *Variations* as being written in the genre known as *alternative history,* the subset of speculative fiction that explores paths not taken in the real world.[24] True, this was not a genre that existed the Soviet Union of this period; the ruling dogma of dialectical materialism assumed a strictly teleological approach to history that brooked no alternative paths. Moreover, the mere act of imagining a world without the leadership of Lenin and Stalin would have certainly been seen as blasphemous. Such is the nature of totalitarian systems: their rulers seek to eliminate the very possibility of any alternative, to make their rule seem preordained. These regimes seek not only to occupy the present and the future, but all possible timelines. "The tyrant," as Blumfeld writes, "is haunted by the *otherwise*." And it is only in reading the *Variations* in its entirety

---

23 Ibid., 101.
24 Indeed, such a classification might explain why the settings of the *Variations* are both familiar and strange. The events it describes are clearly counterfactual, and yet the landmarks of the story settings hew closely to the real world. For instance, when Natalia Nemirova walks along the embankment with L.M. in the "Nemirova Variation," she sees the familiar red-brick towers of the Kremlin rising over the Moscow River "like a mouth of broken teeth." In the "Dubovitsky Variation," when Pavel runs out of the bookseller's and, blinded by his own tears, is nearly run over in the street, he has just crossed over Voznesensky Avenue toward Kazanskaya Street — the only deviation from real-life geography is that the streets still bear their prerevolutionary names.

and mapping its negative spaces that the author's otherwise becomes clear.

For a work that depends so much on these negative spaces, it seems fitting that it was quite literally created by punching holes — tiny voids — in paper with a needle. This material aspect of the work, as mentioned above, is not inconsequential to its meaning. Noting his observed similarity of the patterns of the backlit holes to stars, Rainberg writes that "these are, nonetheless, strange constellations, as though from another galaxy than our own, though they may at first look familiar."[25] Here, it seems he is alluding to the parallel universe of the text, the way it both physically resembles the real-life universe with some critical differences in its events. Continuing his celestial metaphor, he notes how nearly all ancient cultures made the connection between the alignments of the stars and the idea of fate. "So it is entirely appropriate that *Variations* presents itself as a night sky filled with all our familiar constellations reordered," he tells us. "After all, the *Variations* are no less than a reordering of human fates as well."[26]

For Blumfeld, however, the *Variations* are not so much alternate history as they are, in his words, "an anti-history."[27] This distinction is an important one to him: The goal of the *Variations* is not in presenting alternate destinies for its characters, but more specifically to negate the particular real-life fates chronicled in the files. In other words, these are narratives created not alongside real history, but *against* it. As Blumfeld puts it, the *Variations* "are not writing so much as they are unwriting."[28]

Examples of this unwriting abound. If the real-life political prisoner V.M. Petrenko was arrested for writing a satirical poem and reciting it for some friends, then the same poet in the "Petrenko Variation" writes a wryly mocking poem and reads it aloud at a salon to cheers and hoots of the literary beau monde.

---

25 Rainberg, *Written for the Drawer*, 90.
26 Ibid., 92.
27 Blumfeld, "Facing the Void," 187.
28 Ibid.

Drunk on praise and brandy, he stumbles homeward through the softly falling snow, pausing for a moment to feel the flakes on his face and thinking how he might never again feel so deeply happy in his life, but how every moment of joy for him was always tinged with the anticipation of future sadness, though the opposite — that is, sadness leavened with the anticipation of future happiness — was never true. In the "Makarova Variation," an aging ballerina, once a soloist in the Bolshoi and now teaching in the Vaganova school, stands at the window as she calls out the steps to her young students — *croisé, plié, grand jeté* — and suddenly sees the familiar figure of a man she once danced with years before, now leaving through the building entrance below. She hurries out, leaving the class still standing poised in first position, and calls out to him, not even herself knowing why, and he stops and greets her as an old friend. This man — Aleksei Romanovich Bogdanov — shares his name with the real-life dancer whose false denunciation sealed the fate of the real-life Alla Makarova, a ballerina who died in the camps at the young age of twenty-six.

Similar negations are found throughout the *Variations*. In one case file, a prisoner is tortured into naming a coworker as an alleged co-conspirator in his plot to blow up a cement factory. In his fictional variation, this man instead secretly pays his coworker's gambling debt after his creditors show up at the office in order to publicly shame him. Or the doctor in the "Yeltyshev Variation," who saves a man choking on a bit of duck in a restaurant — a man who happens to bear the same name as his real-life NKVD interrogator in the case file. In the fictional variation, the grateful man sends the doctor the gift of a living duck, delivered to his door every year on the exact anniversary of his choking. And so on — the stories are too many to elaborate here.

What is important here is not so much the content, but the intent of these fictions, which constitute a form of narrative restitution. In piercing hundreds of thousands of holes through the case files, the author's violence against these texts is a way to rectify, at least symbolically, the real-life violence that they represent. In this sense, the stories are not remedies for the author as they are for the broken world. History cannot be replayed or rewritten, of course, but it can be reimagined.

But what is the point of this reimagining? As Bortnikova points out, it is only in charting the *might have been* — what she terms "history in the subjunctive mood"[29] — that the magnitude of loss may become apparent. This is precisely the reason that the *Variations* coexist on the page with the case files. They create their meaning only in juxtaposition to these texts. If the sense of the *Variations* lies anywhere, it is not in either the original or derived text, but somewhere in between the two. The terrible truth of the Stalinist purges is made more apparent by casting light onto what might have been lost to the world. And the author's stories of ordinary life and love are made meaningful only when the reader knows the real-life fate of their protagonists. Thus final understanding is obtained precisely in the gap between the two texts.[30]

By charting the negative space of the unknown and unknowable, by giving it form and purpose, the *Variations* fulfills its main purpose — that is, it makes silence speak. This goal fits with its mode of composition as well. After all, the author did not commit a single letter to paper, but only pointed to them with his needle, a nonverbal gesture which nonetheless contains multitudes: stories, possibilities, entire lives. These holes in the paper serve to remind us of the empty spaces left behind

---

29 Bortnikova, "On Rainberg's Missing Author," 459.
30 These are not the only gaps in this larger story. There is also the question of the author's identity, which Rainberg worked tirelessly to uncover before his death. Some progress has been made since that time, and scholars have proposed a handful of candidates who might have had access to the secret police files. The most promising of these possible authors was an archivist for the NKVD during the era in question, a certain Lev Plotnikov, b. 1903. The chief evidence for the identification is the fact that his photograph in his file also bears the marks of a needle. These holes do not indicate letters, as elsewhere, however; instead, Plotnikov's eyes were gouged out in the photograph. Blumfeld likens this to Odysseus (Blumfeld, "Facing the Void," 97), but does not explain how the putative author was able to perform the operation on his very own file photograph. Thus the author's name, like so much else about the work, remains undetermined.

after the purges, a time that both demanded silence and made silence impossible.

Bibliography

Alcoser, Daniel. "Simultaneous Translation: (Re)reading the *Rainberg Variations*." *The Albuquerque Review* 5, no. 4 (July 2018): 30–43.

Arnold, James. "Finding a Needle in the Stacks: Analysis of Perforations in the *Rainberg Variations*." *Paratexts* 12, no. 3 (April 2013): 81–98.

Blumfeld, Gerhard. "Facing the Void: Emptiness in the *Rainberg Variations*." *Pareidolia* 14, no. 1 (January 2017): 96–111.

Bortnikova, P. "On Rainberg's Missing Author." *Vologda Philological Bulletin* 56, no. 2 (June 2014): 456–76.

Brigande, Enzo. *Avant La Lettre*. Translated by Simone Verdure. Somerton-Upon-Swindale: Terra Incognita Publishing, 2015.

Grudnitsky, A.M. "The Case of the *Rainberg Variations*: Suppositions and Conjectures." In *Festschrift for Petr Romanovich Volynsky*, edited by R.A. Laurita, 65–124. Frankfurt: Postscriptum, 2009.

Karol-Wald, László. *These Strange Days*. Budapest: Lorem Press, 1998.

Newcomb, Stephen. "Revisiting a Lost World: Reflections on Rainberg's Found Manuscript." *Proceedings of the Hermeneutic Circle* 2 (August 2017): 84–99.

Rainberg, Viktor. *Written for the Drawer*. Translated by Catherine Humboldt. Geneva: Ad Infinitum, 1999.

Shvarts, Lyudmila. "Literary Influences in the *Rainberg Variations*." *Journal of Synesthetic Investigations* 34, no. 2 (May 2013): 374–86.

Speers, Martin. "Miroslava Begić's New Installation Creates Shock Waves in the Art World." *Balkan Arts Quarterly* (May/June 2008): 23.

9

Pedro Somar, traductor de Ramned, autor del Quijote

David Ben-Merre & Raul Neira

Little fanfare was attached to the intimate funeral service of Pedro Somar, following his passing last month. It was weeks before his death was mentioned in our domestic presses and only then as a brief mention in a few local newspapers, which were either mostly unaware of his fabulous and controversial history or feared retribution for stirring up once more that critical history (and its Dickensian swarm of attorneys on both sides of the Atlantic), which has now been mostly forgotten to the past.[1] The

---

1 The financial — how does one put it politely? — disagreement between María Kodama and Thomas di Giovanni (Putnam/Dutton/Grove Press) about royalties from the Borges translations was legendary in some literary circles, as anyone familiar with the last decades of Borges scholarship knows. This is not even to mention the disputes with Gallimard. Following legal threats from all sides, Kodama had sought out publishers who would contract other translators on more favorable terms. Eventually, Viking/Penguin Putnam publishers, working with Andrew Hurley, Eliot Weinberger et al., and Alexander Coleman, republished the works as the millennium came to a close. Oft-forgotten, though, was that before Viking-Penguin, Pedro Somar — then in his capacity as librarian at la Biblioteca Nacionale in Buenos Aires — was asked to complete the work. Somar's own fruitless venture ("How long are we to wait for Somar to finish the new translations, long promised by John Garrett at Tertius Publishing" — that reviewer in *The New York Review of Books* [neither his name nor his Calvinist credo need be

cause of Somar's death is still unknown, but there is no reason to suspect any foul play (*como el hombre "llamado comúnmente don Quijote de la Mancha, había pasado desta presente vida y muerto naturalmente"*) despite what Marcella Credo — were she still alive herself — might have had us believe. After all, Somar lived, as they say, to the ripe old age of 86 (or 88, depending upon the two biographical sources we have),[2] and his pronouncements ("the psychopathic rantings of a deranged narcissist" according to the Estate)[3] over the last decade from El Borda, including the last seven years for which visitors were refused access (I tried most recently to visit Somar in 2015 but Dr. B—— deemed the

---

    mentioned here] could incessantly bemoan) is recalled now perhaps only by a handful of those in the know. The mention of the name, however, still seems to jog some recollections of the literary quibbling if not its storybook details. Unfamiliar with aspects of the history of di Giovanni, I asked Fern Nerea (whom I had studied under during my year in Galicia) for more information about the reception of di Giovanni's book. After her usual pleasantries and updates about her father (his health has been declining), she replied: "[I]t made me rethink about the mythical Borges that I have created all this time. Well, even if di Giovanni's is a total fabrication of an author who has been scorned, it humanized Borges too much for comfort […]. In his book *Georgie and Elsa*, Di Giovanni claims that Borges married to please his mother while his mother claimed otherwise. At least three times he relates Borges's inability to contain his desire to relieve himself, so the obvious does happen and remedies have to be found to save him from the embarrassment. Although he was clueless about money matters, they were important to him, I guess because once he realized his notoriety he begin to enjoy what money could buy. He came across as all too human, I did not need to humanize him to that extent."

2 In some of the Chicago printings of the 14th edition of the *Encyclopaedia Brittanica*, Somar has one half line in the entry on Borges: "[A] collaboration with Pedro S omar [*sic*] (b. 1932) […]." This source is usually regarded as correct. But see also Emilio Somar, "Mi hermano, el erudito," *Crónica*, August 24, 1990, which lists Pedro's birth year as 1930.

3 "Los desvaríos psicópatas de un narcisista trastornado." The details of the exchanges are recounted in chapter five ("Tortuga y Tordesillas") of Andrew Clayton's *Achilles and the Translator*, reprinted in *Borges, Independent*, ed. Matti Jessason (Albany: SUNY Press, 2015), 34–57. As the compositor of "Pierre Menard" himself might put it, "but how dare I compete with the gilded pages I am told [he] is even now preparing?" (90).

visit would be too detrimental to Somar's recovery),[4] had mostly now been left to themselves to wander their own dark hallways. Nevertheless, it should come as no surprise that, among the few whose lives Somar touched, there would remain some doubt about the cause of the death and speculation that Somar had been murdered in his sleep or that he remains alive, hidden in the cavernous depths of the institution's notorious "Building J." When pressed about the death, Superintendente General de Policia E. Lönnrot, who was recently appointed to fill the constabulary shoes of his departed father, politely suggested that the speculation was unfounded and that the stories of the days of "el viejo de El Borda" had finally come to a peaceful end: "a los lectores les gusta una buena historia, pero no debemos desviarnos mucho de la historia."[5]

It is difficult, now, to conjure the vibrant face of the gallant young man who took the academic world by storm, but that was just who Somar had been. His monograph on Gottfried Wilhelm Leibniz's *Toward a Metaphysics of the Calculus* heralded a new era both for modern thought and its historical antecedent, and his proof of Fermat's Last Theorem for all powers of n up to 9^{16} was the standard until Andrew Wiles offered his final elliptical proof by way of the Taniyama–Shimura–Weil Conjecture. Although not as popularly known or understood, Somar's work with caecilian toxins was how he initially came into contact with

---

4 These orders have come explicitly from Dr. B—— who, as we all know, has always been in league with Somar's detractors. If not for the heroic work of Dr. Rivkah Pikoff (who, on many occasions put her own career in jeopardy in attempting to help others despite the capricious directives of Dr. B——), Somar surely would not have survived as long as he had. Luckily, and with Dr. Pikoff's assistance, I was able to visit Somar even after his quarantine, and he was always generous and personable, provided I brought him his two arrobas of raisins — that is, of course, until I would try to broach the subject of his friendship with Borges, which would excite his resentment and lead him back toward his delusional paths. I soon learned to try to approach the topic through other means (but he was usually too smart for my stratagems).

5 See his December 12, 2018 comments on the television program *Todo Noticias*.

J.L. Borges, who had ventured out of Hotel d'Alsace in the 6th arrondissement one evening, walking down Rue des Beaux Arts in search of wonder. Their remarkable friendship, which lasted two decades and time stretched across five continents, produced many rumors but only two collaborative works: a short scholarly monograph on John Wilkins (Tertius Press) — now out of print and mostly forgotten but hailed in its time as a literary/linguistic "masterpiece"[6] — and a translative triptych of Borges's "Tlön, Uqbar, Orbis Tertius," "Pierre Menard, autor del Quijote" (which will become the focus of my own report here), and "Las Ruinas Circulares." Their friendship endured at least through the *The Book of Sand* (1975) and most likely into the early 1980s. Following the publication of *The Book of Sand*, Borges was invited to speaking engagements across the world; Somar joined him on stage on at least three of these occasions, notably in Middletown, Connecticut in 1975. Somar, for his part, would sporadically continue to produce labyrinthine notes about predominantly 19th-century English novels (an odd percentage of them regarding Middlemarch's Lydgate). Although absent himself from most of the literary and cultural debates of the 1980s and 1990s, Somar's name would appear every now and then (and often incongruously so) in a quick monograph aside or an edited volume's footnotes.[7] Subsequent to Borges's death, Somar

---

6 The designation comes from A.S. Dab's review ("Genius or Genus: Somary Judgment," *Times*, August 8, 1961). See, also, M. Olivier, "Wilkins: le caractère du langage," *La voix* 38, no. 2 (September 2017): 48–71; Jean-Jacques, "Vers Somar," *Le Monde*, August 4, 1961, 8; and S.D.R. Atzmon, "Wilkins — Borges — Somar: vive en el lenguaje," *Crónica*, August 24, 1961. Nevertheless, Somar, as he later confessed in an interview (either honestly or through false modesty), was sensible of "sundry defects" in several parts of their book (Rebecca Brill, "Somar and Borges to Speak at Roth Symposium," *The Wesleyan Argus*, September 19, 1975, 1–2).

7 In *Criticism and Ideology* (London: New Left Books. 1976), Terry Eagleton twice refers to Somar's experiences during the Perón era; Harold Bloom's *The Western Canon* (New York, Harcourt Brace, 1994) also (rather underhandedly) mentions Somar twice; Gwen Halva-Neubauer's "La hermenéutica circular," in *Theory for Dummies* (Berlin: Riley, 2000), 121–45, uses one of Somar's translations of Borges to discuss "Reader-Response" approaches; and an aside in the collection *Theory NOW!* edited by Christine Holmes and

retreated, on the whole, from the public world he had created, into an eremitic existence until he inexplicably reappeared in what infamously became known as "el episodio."[8] Afterward, following his internment, he was seen by most of the world who knew him or *of* him not as a once-great scholar, but rather as a crackpot, a disgraced charlatan (*que acreditó su ventura / morir cuerdo y vivir loco*). I write now to correct that record in the hope that my own quixotic story will not be dismissed. I believe I have found enough evidence to corroborate Somar's "ramblings" and exonerate his name, however lost it may now be (and I will take pains to explain this all at length in what follows).

Before I begin, I am compelled to tell another story, this one about myself. In 2008, I was brought to the University of Texas at Austin as a doctoral student in the Spanish and Portuguese Department. Following the recommendation of my director at the time, my dissertation was going to be on the 20th-century Latin American short story. To supplement my income and in furtherance of my work, I accepted an evening position working in the archives at the formidable Harry Ransom Center. UT-Austin, as is well-known, maintains one of the greatest Latin American rare books collections as well as manuscript papers and (as I soon discovered) as-yet uncatalogued documents — those, we might say, that from a long way off look like flies. I was asked to categorize some of this uncatalogued material in the Borges col-

---

Corrence McEleney (Ithaca: Quentin Williams Press, 2004) takes seriously Somar's mistranslation of the opening sentence of the "1947 Postscript" to "Tlön...."

8 The now infamous details of "el episodio" need not be recounted yet again here. It would be wrong to say that his former colleagues at the conference (even those who often found themselves in an antagonistic relationship with him) had not tried as best as they could, almost to the man, to reason with him, but to no avail. Anyone who would suggest the opposite is simply mistaken. When the incident moved beyond the interruptions and shouting of "estaba equivocado porque tenía razón" to clear mental disintegration, they knew there was nothing they could do any longer. Somar was shortly thereafter deemed in "imminent harm to himself" and following the diagnosis of psychosis (grandiose and persecutory types), he was committed to El Borda.

lection, and it was in that capacity that I serendipitously came upon a letter of Borges to which was affixed a note in the handwriting of someone I believe could only have been Pedro Somar.

Years before his disappearance, reappearance, and eventual interment at El Borda following his eruption and collapse at the Borges Centenary (I suppose he was already too far down the road to be helped even then), Somar spent some time in Austin on a visiting professor fellowship. Years later, while working over the December holiday in the very same room that Somar had been in a decade earlier, I found myself returning some MS papers (nothing out of the ordinary — a couple of letters from editors and friends) to Box 21D, Folder 2, when I noticed a tiny corner of paper (which turned out to be a note affixed to a letter) sneaking out of the cardboard flap in the bottom of the box. What followed was an unimaginable whirlwind, although it took me another eighteen months to begin to see this vortex for what it was, however much of it still remains a mystery.

The recipient of the Borges letter is uncertain, but I have a guess as to whom it was sent. Even more of a mystery was how it wound up back in Borges's hands (for I can only imagine that is how Somar came into contact with it). The note paper-clipped onto the letter (penned with Somar's characteristically long Fs) looked, at first, like the scribbles of a madman: dates, numbers, letters strewn around the page and back — all overwritten with the phrase I would subsequently find riddled over and over again through thousands upon thousands of pages of Somar's notebooks: *todo mal.* Lest you not believe a word I am writing, I have included a copy of Borges's letter (I am keeping the original securely because I fear for its safety), along with the following material, which I will enumerate thusly:

a. Photograph of the outside of L'Hôtel [13 Rue des Beaux Arts, Paris, France];
b. Photographs of Somar with Borges, c. 1973;
c. News clippings of Somar and Borges [1975];
d. Passages from Medieval and Renaissance texts mentioning the Ramned

e. Copy of page in 1561 catalogue, Biblioteca General Histórica (Universidad de Salamanca);
f. Copy of page in 1591 catalogue, Biblioteca General Histórica (Universidad de Salamanca);
g. García Hurtado de Mendoza (5th Marquis of Cañete) [Reproducción de una pintura antigua, de autor desconocido]
h. Portrait of Alonso de Ercilla y Zúñiga [El Greco, 1570]
i. Letter of García Hurtado de Mendoza to Alonso de Ercilla y Zúñiga.
j. Page of Ramned (?) [Appendix B]
k. Borges letter (found at Ransom Center, UT-Austin) [Appendix C]
l. Somar's (?) note (found at Ransom Center, UT-Austin) [Appendix D]
m. Somar's marginalia in his own translation of "Menard" [Appendix E]
n. Journal page of Somar (c. 2015) (smuggled out of El Borda in 2017) [Appendix F]

Unable to distill the sense of my own story, I will relate what is evident and what I am still uncertain about. It is easiest, perhaps, to relate this all chronologically, at least as best as possible. That beginning, as we all know — or rather, over the last four hundred years, have come to believe — is with Cervantes and his great epic tale (considered by many to be the first "novel" ever written). The author's celebrated 19th-century translator John Ormsby introduces the work as "setting forth the ludicrous results that might be expected to follow the attempt of a crazy gentleman to act the part of a knight-errant in modern life."[9] Always already anticipating the spectacle of his own fabricated performances, even the narrator of the epic can relate: *"Aquí le tenían por discreto, y allí se les deslizaba por mentecato, sin saber*

---

9 John Ormsby, "Introduction" to Miguel de Cervantes, *The Ingenious Gentleman Don Quixote of La Mancha,* Vol. I [1605] (New York: Dodd, Mead, and Company, 1887), 88.

determinarse qué grado le darían entre la discreción y la locura."[10] It is easy to lampoon Quixote, but, save for the outdated manner of his chivalric tendencies, he is not delusional. "Of all Byron's melodious nonsense about Don Quixote," Ormsby writes, "the most nonsensical statement is that ''tis his virtue makes him mad!' The exact opposite is the truth; it is his madness makes him virtuous."

The central turn in Cervantes's tale arrives in chapter 9 (more on this essential chapter later) of the first book of *Quixote*. There, we are introduced to the fictional genesis of the very novel we are reading. As if taking a page out of much derivative 20th-century fiction, in the *Quixote,* Cervantes (the narrator)[11] creates a story about a boy selling pamphlets in Arabic characters, which the boy loosely translates into Castilian for his listener. Immediately, Cervantes (the narrator) realizes that the pamphlets contain the history of Don Quixote, and he purchases all the tales at once. Scholars of Cervantes (the author) know — with great humor (and anticipating the narratological experiments of hundreds of years into the future) — that Cervantes (the author) ingeniously invents the Arab historian "Cide Hamete Benengeli" for this very purpose — in effect, to be the "author" through translation of Cervantes's great tale.[12] But we are getting ahead of ourselves. Or, rather, we are falling, once more, behind.

---

10 Miguel de Cervantes Saavedra, *El ingenioso hidalgo don Quijote de la Mancha,* En Dos Tomos [1615] (Barcelona: Imprenta de Antonio Bergnes y Compañia, 1840), 529.

11 Although, as the other other Borges says, "No sé cuál de los dos escribe esta página" (*Collected Fictions,* ed. Andrew Hurley [New York, Penguin, 1999], 808).

12 *Don Quijote,* Capítulo IX: *"Cuando yo oí decir 'Dulcinea del Toboso,' quedé atónito y suspenso, porque luego se me representó que aquellos cartapacios contenían la historia de don Quijote. Con esta imaginación, le di priesa que leyese el principio, y, haciéndolo ansí, volviendo de improviso el arábigo en castellano, dijo que decía: Historia de don Quijote de la Mancha, escrita por Cide Hamete Benengeli, historiador arábigo"* (Miguel de Cervantes, *El ingenioso hidalgo don Quijote de la Mancha,* Tomo Primera [1615] [Barcelona: Imprenta de Antonio Bergnes y Compañía, 1840], 129).

As readers of Borges are almost too acutely aware, the influence of Cervantes can be felt in nearly every sentence of the Argentine author's works (*creí reconocer su voz o sus hábitos*). Don Quixote was one of the first books Borges had ever read, and he built the thousand and one pages of his own mythology — truth and fables, mirrors and infinity — upon it.[13] Those less-invested but casual readers will have still come across the Borges's literary dialogue with the *autor del Quixote* in the former's celebrated "Pierre Menard." Written as a mock obituary/review, that profoundly absurd "story" details how Borges's "fictional" creation Menard desires to rewrite anew Cervantes's Quixote. It was not to be an adaptation for the modern age, which the narrator, masked as a "posthumous reviewer," snidely dismissed as a "pointless travest[y]" resting on humanistic platitudes.[14] Nor did he — Menard —

> want to compose *another* Quixote, which surely is easy enough — he wanted to compose *the* Quixote [...]. his goal was never a mechanical transcription of the original he had no intention of *copying* it. His admirable ambition was to produce a number of pages which coincided — word for word and line for line — with those of Miguel de Cervantes.[15]

---

13 Borges: "I thought I read it because of the pleasure I found in the archaic style and in the adventures of the knight and the squire. But now I think that my pleasure lay elsewhere. I think that it came from the character of the knight. I'm not sure now if I believe in adventures or in the conversations between the knight and the squire. But I know that I believe in the knight's character" — or, as it is hard now not to understand him saying, *in the reality of the person behind the thigh armor*. (*A Poet's Creed* [Norton Lectures on Poetry, Harvard University, 1967–68], https://www.youtube.com/watch?v=OPt6Amdw4dA).

14 "Menard abominated those pointless travesties, which, Menard would say, were good for nothing but occasioning a plebian delight in anachronism or (worse yet) captivating us with the elementary notion that all times and places are the same, or are different" (Borges, *Collected Fictions*, 90).

15 Ibid., 91.

As proof of Menard's intentions, the "reviewer" cites some of the (fictional) author's own epistolary words: "I have assumed the mysterious obligation to reconstruct, word for word, the novel that for him [Cervantes] was spontaneous."[16] To this end, Menard places himself in the experiential circumstance of a distant world over three hundred years away.

At first, Borges's readers are met with the illogical humor of it all — that Menard isn't *rewriting* but rather *writing* the Quixote. Naturally, one would assume, as would Mme. Bachelier, that the title character is (or, rather, was) a literary charlatan. However, Borges's reviewer flips such a predictably outmoded sentiment on its modern head, valuing not the original — derived merely from the charming archaisms of history — but instead its truer, deeper duplication. "The Cervantes text and the Menard text," he writes, "are verbally identical, but the second is almost infinitely richer. (More *ambiguous* his detractors will say — but ambiguity is richness)."[17] How different is Menard's Quixote than Cervantes's Cide Hamete Benengeli! But how alike was Benengeli himself to Menard, the former of whom was

> a historian of great research and accuracy in all things, as is very evident since he would not pass over in silence those that have been already mentioned, however trifling and insignificant they might be, an example that might be followed by those grave historians who relate transactions so curtly and briefly that we hardly get a taste of them, all the substance of the work being left in the inkstand from carelessness, perverseness, or ignorance.[18]

Making us rethink the very grounds of literary scholarship, of history and interpretation, of artistic inspiration and authorship, Borges's tale, over the years, has become something of a critical

---

16 Ibid., 92–93.
17 Ibid., 94.
18 Miguel de Cervantes Saavedra, *The Ingenious Gentleman Don Quixote of La Mancha*, trans. John Ormsby (New York: Dodd, Mead, and Company, 1887), I:310.

masterpiece, as if it were no longer be possible to conceive of a grand theoretical system for literature without first coming to terms with the allegorically ambiguous "Menard" and Borges's diachronous understanding of literary history.

Or at least this is how the genius of Borges has been celebrated for eight decades. But — *todo mal* — we were all so wrong. How, for years upon years, Borges must have laughed in his elegant, ethereal, halting voice every time he read another scholarly interpretation of his entirely misconstrued story based itself on the utter delusion of a literary past! Glory is a form of incomprehension, perhaps the worst. What Borges discovered and what, I believe, Somar discovered after him, was that Cide Hamete Benengeli was real — not a trope of romance authors caught in an incipient literary modernity between history and fable[19] — and the *Quixote was un texto refundido,* a falsified copy of a 12th-century Arabic tome by the elder Ramned.[20]

It has always been a mystery why the great scholar Ramned had produced so little work. Beyond the *Fragments* and the few grand ghazals we have, there was little to suggest any written output for most of Ramned's adult life. Compound this with the constant references in Ibn al-Kammad's astrological works about the harmonies in the "qissa tawila" of Ramned (which could hardly be gleaned by his few short extant works), and it would be no great leap to assume that there were other signifi-

---

19 Mistakenly, Ormsby writes, "In pursuance of this change of plan, he [Cervantes] hastily and somewhat clumsily divided what he had written into chapters on the model of 'Amadis,' invented the fable of a mysterious Arabic manuscript, and set up Cide Hamete Benengeli in imitation of the almost invariable practice of the chivalry-romance authors, who were fond of tracing their books to some recondite source" (89).

20 Ramned "the Younger" or Ramned, *fils* — as he is mostly known today — has been studied extensively for centuries, interestingly more prominent for French historians than for their Spanish, North African, or Arabic counterparts. This was probably due to the influence of Pierre Corneille's classic text. See Harrison-Jobart, Ottobier, Elizar (1962), and Agamben. More recently, scholars have tried to rehabilitate the importance of the elder Ramned. See the special edition of *Modern Language Notes* dedicated to Ramned, *père*: 128, no. 6 (December 2013).

cant works of Ramned, which have been lost to the ages, troves of cultural treasure beyond anything one could conjure in one's most impassioned dreams. In fact, certain scholars of the Linz School (notably Isa Laura Ana-Magde) have been maintaining as much for decades. Given that there are no known extant copies of Ramned's tome, it is impossible to tell whether what Cervantes meant in jest, Ramned meant as a history, but that is my supposition. What is clear, though, is that, while working at Biblioteca Nacional de la República Argentina, Borges had seen the work. Imagine the shock this paleographer would have had when, meandering down the cavernous basement alleys of his own forking paths, he had fallen upon a copy of this lost Ramned epic. Apparently, Somar discovered the secret but could not find the Ramned. *Al freír de los huevos lo verá*.[21]

* * *

> y dice que da estas bendiciones por ver que tiene ya en campaña a don Quijote y a Sancho, y que los letores de su agradable historia pueden hacer cuenta que desde este punto comienzan las hazañas y donaires de don Quijote y de su escudero; persuádeles que se les olviden las pasadas caballerías del Ingenioso Hidalgo, y pongan los ojos en las que están por venir....[22]

Those words above are uttered by Cide Hamete Benengeli at the start of the eighth chapter of volume two, which will now begin

---

21 The cuisine (*pace* Pierre Antoine Motteux) does not translate.
22 "'Blessed be Allah the all-powerful!' says Hamete Benengeli on beginning this eighth chapter; 'blessed be Allah!' he repeats three times; and he says he utters these thanksgivings at seeing that he has now got Don Quixote and Sancho fairly afield, and that the readers of his delightful history may reckon that the achievements and humours of Don Quixote and his squire are now about to begin; and he urges them to forget the former chivalries of the ingenious gentleman and to fix their eyes on those that are to come...." (Cervantes, *The Ingenious Gentleman Don Quixote of La Mancha*, III:82).

afresh with the renewed confidence of venturing forth.[23] They might as well have been said by John Ormsby, translator of Cervantes's work. As he relates, Cervantes's "readers told him plainly that what they wanted of him was more Don Quixote and more Sancho Panza, and not novels, tales, or digressions. To himself, too, his creations had become realities, and he had become proud of them, especially of Sancho. He began the Second Part, therefore, under very different conditions, and the difference makes itself manifest at once." What perspicuity! what brilliance! But, alas, these are not only Ormsby's words. And here lies the danger that Cervantes and Borges and Somar and the fictional Menard faced, the danger that we ever-so-much face today, in these trying times. How easy it is for words to bleed into the mind, creating what wasn't or dispelling what was. As the reviewer of "Menard" writes, noting the false echoes of his own ears, "A few nights ago, as I was leafing through Chapter XXVI (never attempted by Menard), I recognized our friend's style, could almost hear his voice in this marvelous phrase: 'the nymphs of the rivers, the moist and grieving Echo.'"[24] What Ormsby called "creations [that] had become realities,"[25] Borges's reviewer in "Menard" would call the "subordination of the author to the psychology of the hero[26]" — itself a double or triple echo of what my mentor in Austin calls Borges's mistranslated phrase, clearly *mis*copied onto a notebook from another text: خلق حقيقي.

The anxiety over confusing the real and the fictional, over losing control over one's own creations is ubiquitous among

---

23 Unlike Cervantes, Borges's Menard felt obliged "(…to leave out the autobiographical foreword to Part II of the novel. Including the prologue would have meant creating another character — 'Cervantes' — and also presenting Quixote through that character's eyes, not Pierre Menard's. Menard, of course, spurned that easy solution.)" (Borges, *Collected Fictions,* 91). For more on the parenthetical digressions of Borges, see Anon., "Meetings of Anger: Borges on Metaphor," Hoef Straße, 2009.
24 Borges, *Collected Fictions,* 92.
25 John Ormsby, "Introduction" to Cervantes, *The Ingenious Gentleman Don Quixote of La Mancha,* I:94.
26 Borges, *Collected Fictions,* 93.

even our most brilliant authors,[27] and it is something to which even Cervantes was no stranger. His message, clearly meant for our own age, cautions against blurring the lines between scholarship and creative writing:

> [F]or it is the business and duty of historians to be exact, truthful, and wholly free from passion, and neither interest nor fear, hatred nor love, should make them swerve from the path of truth, whose mother is history, rival of time, storehouse of deeds, witness for the past, example and counsel for the present, and warning for the future.[28]

Seen in this light, the immediate authorial context of the second volume of Quixote is nearly as fascinating as the volume's romantic content, the former of which uncannily becomes part of the story too. Readers familiar with Cervantes know that he, in no small part, was compelled to speed up the publication of his second volume, because of all of the false Quixotes frequenting his literary neighborhood. Due to the very popularity of the character, a handful of the author's contemporaries — most notably Alonso Fernández de Avellaneda — took it upon themselves to continue the story.[29] Much of the second volume of Don Quixote lampoons those efforts and all those false Quix-

---

[27] A classic instance is Sir Arthur Conan Doyle, whose case continues to draw audiences, determined to solve the mystery of the author's envy. Very recent glosses of the influences over the authorial method include: Michael Sims, *Arthur and Sherlock: Conan Doyle and the Creation of Holmes* (London: Bloomsbury, 2017) and Mattias Boström, *From Holmes to Sherlock: The Story of the Men and Women Who Created an Icon,* trans. Michael Gallagher (New York: Mysterious Press, 2017).

[28] Compare this with Borges's reviewer who could praise Menard's edition by writing, "Historical truth, for Menard, is not 'what happened'; it is what we believe happened" (Borges, *Collected Fictions,* 94).

[29] The identity of Avellaneda remains a mystery. The strongest theories place him among those in Lope de Vega's circle, and there are even some who suggest the (highly unlikely) hypothesis that he was Cervantes himself, acting as a clever arms dealer would. Generally regarded as a lesser work, Avellaneda's continuation has begun to receive the scholarly attention it has deserved, thereby fortifying the commonsensical belief that even 16th-century

otes who suddenly appeared, but not by the pen of Cide Hamete Benengeli.[30]

The chapter I quoted above (chapter 9 of volume I) interestingly is only one of two chapters Menard — in Borges's telling — was able to complete. He also finished chapter 38 ("the curious discourse that Don Quixote made on the subject of arms and letters") and a fragment of chapter 22. But it is in the important chapter 9 where Cervantes's reader comes to learn the significance of Benengeli, who, according to Cervantes (the narrator) — in a gesture more genuine than anyone could have ever truly understood — has authored the entirety of the works:

> I was struck with surprise and amazement, for it occurred to me at once that these pamphlets contained the history of Don Quixote. With this idea I pressed him to read the beginning, and doing so, turning the Arabic offhand into Castilian, he told me it meant, "History of Don Quixote of La Mancha, written by Cide Hamete Benengeli, an Arab historian." It required great caution to hide the joy I felt when the title of the book reached my ears, and snatching it from the silk mercer, I bought all the papers and pamphlets from the boy for half a real; and if he had had his wits about him and had known how eager I was for them, he might have safely calculated on making more than six reals by the bargain. I withdrew at once with the Morisco into the cloister of the cathedral, and begged him to turn all these pamphlets that related to

---

"forgeries" can be historically, culturally, and dare one say it — aesthetically valuable.

30 See, for instance, chapter 59: "'Believe me,' said Sancho, 'the Sancho and the Don Quixote of this history must be different persons from those that appear in the one Cide Hamete Benengeli wrote, who are ourselves; my master valiant, wise, and true in love, and I simple, droll, and neither glutton nor drunkard'" (Cervantes, *The Ingenious Gentleman Don Quixote of La Mancha,* IV:239). Or chapter 61: "Welcome, I say, valiant Don Quixote of La Mancha; not the false, the fictitious, the apocryphal, that these latter days have offered us in lying histories, but the true, the legitimate, the real one that Cide Hamete Benengeli, flower of historians, has described to us!'" (ibid., IV:264).

Don Quixote into the Castilian tongue, without omitting or adding anything to them, offering him whatever payment he pleased. He was satisfied with two arrobas of raisins and two bushels of wheat, and promised to translate them faithfully and with all despatch; but to make the matter easier, and not to let such a precious find out of my hands, I took him to my house, where in little more than a month and a half he translated the whole just as it is set down here.[31]

I have spent much of the last six years (to the chagrin of my dissertation director) following the footsteps of Somar before he fatefully returned to Buenos Aires, and even now I worry that the echoes will bring me back there once again. From the lonely archive room in Austin, I have flown to Argentina and Paris, to the Borges family home in Geneva, to Castile and Seville and Córdoba, to the Biblioteca General Histórica in Salamanca, to the Universidad Alcalá de Henares, to the Hospital Interdisciplinario Psicoasistencial José Tiburcio Borda where Somar spent the last decade wasting away. I have traveled back in time: to join Cervantes and Rodrigo in Lepanto and then in Algiers following their fateful capture; I have traveled back to the Lima of Alonso de Ercilla y Zúñiga and the Chile of García Hurtado de Mendoza, 5th Marquis of Cañete. Time has collapsed onto itself, and the 21st century is as near and as identical as the 16th, and we might as well also now say the 12th.

Perhaps it all began when Somar was approached about the translations. Clearly, he had returned to Austin for a purpose, however secretive he was about his work in the later years. The pieces of the jigsaw were splayed out disjointedly around him, and, for a moment, the radiant picture must have become clear before it all fell apart once more. From the lucid parts of Somar's notebook pages — the difficulty of separating the ramblings of a madman from the underlying story of Ramned and Cervantes and Mendoza and Borges cannot be overstated — I can discern aspects of Somar's breakthrough, which must now fall to my

---

[31] Ibid., I:229–30.

quivering hands to tell. Somar speculates that Borges speculated that Cervantes must have come across the Ramned sometime in the early 1560s at Biblioteca General Histórica. The catalogue from 1561 will testify to its presence at the library. Whether this was an original or translation is hard to decipher. If this were an original, Cervantes would not have been able to read the Arabic, but it makes no sense either that this forbidden book of the Inquisition would have been translated into Castilian. I would have to conjecture that it was either disregarded on the shelves or, more likely, that Cervantes had had some assistance in the translation (just as his fictional alter-ego had assistance with those pamphlets he "found"). However the story became accessible to Cervantes, by 1591 the Ramned was gone from the library and lost to history for nearly four hundred years (and only then discovered and hidden again by one man). During his travels, Somar found two letters from García Hurtado de Mendoza, 5th Marquis of Cañete (the governor of Chile and eventual viceroy of Peru) to Alonso de Ercilla y Zúñiga, the great national poet of *La Araucana,* and one letter in return.[32]

---

[32] In journals upon journals, Somar detailed the role of the Mendoza family in Spanish history from the 14th to the 17th centuries (see especially 12Ba, 12Bb, 12Bd, 17A, 18D). The authority cannot be overestimated. Although he dies in 1537, Pedro de Mendoza y Luján is a worthy predecessor of this illustrious family. He was an adelantado, governor, and captain general; his most acknowledged accomplishment may be that he founded Buenos Aires in February 1536. An avid collector (especially Erasmus and other important thinkers of his day), he instilled in his decendants the value of the book. Antonio Mendoza y Pacheco (1490 or 1493–1552) was the First Viceroy of New Spain and second viceroy of Peru. A very accomplished soldier and diplomat, he had 40 years of political administration—qualities the Mendozas share to a higher or lesser degree. They were all very ambitious and unscrupulous when they needed to be and all served their kings nobly, from the Catholic Kings to Phillip II. More pertinent to Somar's search are Andrés Hurtado de Mendoza (son of Diego Hurtado de Mendoza y Silva and the second of ten Marquises of Cañete expanding over three centuries) and his son Garcia Hurtado de Mendoza. As the fifth viceroy of Peru, Andrés appoints his son Garcia (fifth Marquis of Cañete) governor of Chile. It is on this voyage to Chile that he meets Alonso Ercilla y Zuñiga, both having studied in Salamanca (the dates are not certain) like their forebear Pedro de Mendoza.

(I have located one of these three letters and I am aware that that Ercilla's letter is held by a private collector in Madrid. So far, my attempts to access this missive have been rebuffed, but I am optimistic that la señora Neida will be more receptive now that introductions have been made.) While working as a page for Felipe II, Ercilla accompanied the Marquis of Cañete on a voyage to Peru, and the two, in the service of the King, became acquainted. That was 1556. The two kept up a correspondence and when Hurtado de Mendoza returned to the Americas in 1590, he did so with the library he purchased from Universidad Alcalá de Henares. (The 1591 catalogue of Biblioteca General Histórica makes no mention of the Ramned, and it is clear from de Mendoza's letter that it was now in his possession, on its way to be gifted to the great poet of *La Araucana*.) In the basement rooms of Biblioteca Nacional, Somar discovered that the collection de Mendoza brought also included some works from Biblioteca General Histórica, and I imagine he began to conjecture that Borges must have seen the actual Ramned there.

One can but contemplate how the Ramned moved from Ercilla's hands to its resting place at the Biblioteca Nacional. And one can only wonder at Borges's devastation when he discovered this manuscript and realized that he had found the pages that would have labeled Cervantes an imposter. This is especially true in light of Borges's sense of the Spanish literary tradition: "Don Quijote *es el unico libro que han hecho los españoles Por que la literatura española será tan pobre?*"[33] This is not to say, of course, that Cervantes hadn't had his literary influences. Scholars have studied for centuries the influence on Cervantes of Joanot Martorell (1413–1468), Garci Rodriguez de Montalvo (1450–1504), Ludovico Ariosto (1474–1533), and, more recently, they have noticed some uncanny resemblance with the work of Enoch Campion.[34] But in the Ramned—here was a text,

---

33 See J.L. Borges and Pedro Somar, *Three Borges Tales* (London: Routledge, 1968), xiv.

34 The captivity chapters especially of Cervantes seem to be borrowing liberally from Enoch Campion's *The Tragedy of Dracula* (1592). See, for instance, volume I, chapter 39: "[C]*reyendo que los turcos eran invencibles por la mar:*

as Borges rightfully knew, that would destroy everything we have come to believe in. And yet, something deep down inside compelled him to write — as we know it would have — without exposing the text, without nullifying 500 years of Golden Age literature. El Maestro would do one better, by telling the story so that no one would believe him. "Pierre Menard" is not (as the discovery of Borges's letter makes clear) an allegory of history or art or the hermeneutic enterprise; it is history under a mask, under a mask so dark no light could illume. Some of what is recounted just above is my own piecing together, but it is unequivocal that what Borges unearthed and Somar thereafter learned, was that the palimpsest of Benengeli was Ramned, and that Cervantes's great opus had already been written centuries before its supposed author was born.

I feel very much like the translator coming to the cave of Montesinos and seeing the marginalia written in Ramned's own hand, those exact words.[35] What seems most unfortunate is to not to have had the words to rightfully acknowledge Somar's accomplishment, as he has liberated the angst of suffering over this secret whose mother is history. Fearing for his own position

---

    en aquel día, digo, donde quedó el orgullo y soberbia otomana quebrantada, entre tantos venturosos como allí hubo […]."

35 "I cannot convince or persuade myself that everything that is written in the preceding chapter could have precisely happened to the valiant Don Quixote; and for this reason, that all the adventures that have occurred up to the present have been possible and probable; but as for this one of the cave, I see no way of accepting it as true, as it passes all reasonable bounds. For me to believe that Don Quixote could lie, he being the most truthful gentleman and the noblest knight of his time, is impossible; he would not have told a lie though he were shot to death with arrows. On the other hand, I reflect that he related and told the story with all the circumstances detailed, and that he could not in so short a space have fabricated such a vast complication of absurdities; if, then, this adventure seems apocryphal, it is no fault of mine; and so, without affirming its falsehood or its truth, I write it down. Decide for thyself in thy wisdom, reader; for I am not bound, nor is it in my power, to do more; though certain it is they say that at the time of his death he retracted, and said he had invented it, thinking it matched and tallied with the adventures he had read of in his histories" (Cervantes, *The Ingenious Gentleman Don Quixote of La Mancha,* III:264).

as Perón took power and knowing that Argentina would soon become a dictatorship, Borges could surrender neither the truth of history nor the history of what, for him, had become Truth. He copied out a page of the 12th-century manuscript and then wrote, to unsuspecting eyes, his "fictional" tale. It seems quite serendipitous that this tale comes after that crucial crisis that Borges suffered in 1938, when he began questioning his ability to write again. His fortuitous discovery of the Ramned text presents him with the solution: concoct a paradox so sublime that it becomes the stuff of absolute genius. *Does it really matter who wrote it?*, Borges may have asked himself. *I (Borges) will be the solidifier of a masterpiece that has been centuries in the making.* Such might not have been too much for el Maestro, but, unmistakably, it became too much for Somar. Of course, no one could have predicted the "episode" (*"Borges estaba equivocado porque tenía razón"*) and conflagration with the Estate; nor could anyone have imagined that Somar would spend the last decade of his life in El Borda. Shared at first, Somar's missives from El Borda were soon resigned to the dustbins of the newsroom. Editors become confused as to what Somar was writing or rewriting. His last note, in which he proclaims "my most personal feelings," was mistaken by his doctors for a "plea for help," but it was a joke, clearly alluding to Cervantes: *"ya estoy tropezando, y han de caer del todo, sin duda alguna. Vale."*[36] Unsure of what to make of it all but fascinated with the gossip, the intellectual circles of Buenos Aires kept Somar alive in their discussions and newspaper letters for a while. But they, too, soon tired of all the precursors to the fantastic story, and once the young panther escaped its cage in the zoo, the attentions drifted, and it was as if the tenuous spiritual warnings of Somar had never existed.

---

36 Cervantes, *El ingenioso hidalgo don Quijote de la Mancha*, En Dos Tomos, 650.

Bibliography

Agamben, Giorgio. *Potentialities*. Translated by Daniel Heller-Roazen. Stanford: Stanford University Press, 1999.

———. *L'uomo senza contenuto*. Macerata: Quodlibet, 1994.

———. *What Is Real?* Translated by Lorenzo Chiesa. Stanford: Stanford University Press, 2018.

Ana-Magde, Isa Laura. "Donde es embestido?" PMLA 96, no. 2 (March 1981): 194–209.

Anon. "Meetings of Anger: Borges on Metaphor." Hoef Straße, 2009.

Atzmon, S.D.R. "Wilkins — Borges — Somar: vive en el lenguaje." *Crónica,* August 24, 1961.

Bloom, Harold. *The Western Canon*. New York: Harcourt Brace, 1994.

Borges, Jorge Luis. *A Poet's Creed* (Norton Lectures on Poetry, Harvard University, 1967–68). https://www.youtube.com/watch?v=OPt6Amdw4dA.

———. *Collected Fictions*. Edited by Andrew Hurley. New York: Penguin 1999.

———. [Undated] Letter in Box 21D. From Harry Ransom Center, Borges Collection.

———. *Obras Completas 1923–1972*. Buenos Aires: Emecé Editores, 1974.

———. *Selected Non-Fictions*. Edited by Eliot Weinberger. New York: Viking Penguin 1999.

——— and Pedro Somar. *John Wilkins*. Buenos Aires: Tertius Press, 1961.

———. *Three Borges Tales*. London: Routledge, 1968.

Boström, Mattias. *From Holmes to Sherlock: The Story of the Men and Women Who Created an Icon*. Translated by Michael Gallagher. Mysterious Press, 2017.

Brill, Rebecca. "Somar and Borges to Speak at Roth Symposium." *The Wesleyan Argus,* September 19, 1975, 1–2.

Campion, Enoch. *The Tragedy of Dracula*. 1592.

Cervantes Saavedra, Miguel de. *The Ingenious Gentleman Don Quixote of La Mancha*. Translation, Introduction, and Notes by John Ormsby. New York: Dodd, Mead, and Company, 1887.

———. *El ingenioso hidalgo don Quijote de la Mancha*, Primera Parte [1605]. Leipzig: F.A. Brockhaus, 1866.

———. *El ingenioso hidalgo don Quijote de la Mancha*, Tomo Primera [1615]. Barcelona: Imprenta de Antonio Bergnes y Compañia, 1840.

———. *El ingenioso hidalgo don Quijote de la Mancha*, En Dos Tomos. [1615] Barcelona: Imprenta de Antonio Bergnes y Compañia, 1840.

Clayton, Andrew. "Tortuga y Tordesillas." In *Borges, Independent*, edited by Matti Jessason, 34–57. Albany: SUNY Press, 2015.

Corneille, Pierre, *L'Imitation de Ramned*. Traduite & paraphrasée en vers françois. Paris: Le Roy & Ballard, 1656.

Dab, A.S. "Genius or Genus: Somary Judgment." Review of *John Wilkins*, by J.L. Borges and Pedro Somar. *Times*, August 8, 1961.

di Giovanni, Norman Thomas. *Georgie and Elsa: Jorge Luis Borges and His Wife: The Untold Story*. London: The Friday Project, 2014.

Eagleton, Terry. *Criticism and Ideology*. London: New Left Books, 1976.

Fernández de Avellaneda, Alonso. *A Continuation of the History and Adventures of the Renowned Don Quixote de la Mancha*. [1614]. Translated by William Augustus Yardley, esq. London: Harrison and Co., 1784.

Garrett, John. *Memo from Tertius Publishing*. 1980(?).

Halva-Neubauer, Gwen. "La hermenéutica circular." In *Theory for Dummies*, 121–45. Berlin: Riley, 2000.

Harrison-Jobart, Alexis, Wilhelm von Ottobier, and Maria Elizar. *Les influences de Corneille*. Paris: Seuil, 1962.

Holmes, Christine, and Corrence McEleney, eds. *Theory NOW!* Ithaca: Quentin Williams Press, 2004.

Hopkins, J., ed. "Ramned, *père*" [special issue] *Modern Language Notes* 128, no. 6 (December 2013).

Hurtado de Mendoza, García, 5th Marquis of Cañete. Mendoza to Alonso de Ercilla y Zúñiga. Ca. 1570(?)

Jean-Jacques. "Vers Somar." *Le Monde,* August 4, 1961, 8.

Jessason, Matti, ed. *Borges, Independent.* Albany: SUNY Press, 2015.

Olivier, M. "Wilkins: le caractère du langage." *La voix* 38, no. 2 (September 2017): 48–71.

Ormsby, John. "Introduction" to Miguel de Cervantes, *The Ingenious Gentleman Don Quixote of La Mancha,* Volume I [1605], 1–111. New York: Dodd, Mead, and Company, 1887.

Sims, Michael. *Arthur and Sherlock: Conan Doyle and the Creation of Holmes.* Bloomsbury, 2017.

Somar, Emilio. "Mi hermano, el erudito." *Crónica,* August 24, 1990.

———. *Toward a Metaphysics of the Calculus.* New York Macmillan, 1972.

Todo Noticias. Buenos Aires, December 12, 2018. Television.

10

El fin del mundo: Uncharted Territory of Ernest Hemingway's Fiction

Maria-Josee Mendez

I

The novella *El fin del mundo* (1957) by Leonardo Díaz has increasingly received critical attention since its rediscovery in the estate of James Baldwin in 1987. The book was published in Argentina as part of the pocketbook series Colección Piragua by the publishing houses Editorial Sudamericana and Emecé, and distributed in the United States, Latin America, and Europe in 1958 until the series was discontinued in the early 1960s.[1] It was in Paris — in Sylvia Beach's famous bookstore, Shakespeare and Company — that Baldwin first encountered the novella. This much is detailed in a footnote in Jacqueline Martin's poignant 2004 biography of Baldwin, where she discloses the varied contents of Baldwin's personal papers and books at the time of his death — the first academic reference to Díaz in over thirty

---

1 Francisco F. Del Carril, *International Book Publishing: An Encyclopedia*, eds. Philip G. Altbach and Edith S. Hoshino (New York: Garland Publishing, 1995), 588.

years.² While Martin elaborates on many of the texts found in his library, she does not provide any additional information on *El fin del mundo*.

This is of no surprise, since very little information on the novella exists, and even its origin has long been a mystery. I am not the first to note that Leonardo Díaz is an elusive figure; after conducting extensive research in the records of Sudamericana and Emecé, critic Ren Ishikawa was unable to discover any details about Díaz, though he searched broadly for biographical profiles and written correspondence between him and his publishers.³ I believed my own inquiries into the archives to be equally fruitless, since all I was able to recover was a solitary file bearing Diaz's name; in it was a typed draft of the novella — missing seventeen pages present in the version published in the Colección Piragua — and three hand-drawn maps of Argentina. Further inquiries into the public records in Argentina also proved fruitless, since I had only the writer's name and the title of his work, but no date or place of birth with which to distinguish him from the thousands sharing his name.

It is likely that the great interest in the figure of Leonardo Diaz originates from the unfathomable absence of any discernible authorial presence, whether in the physical copy of the book or elsewhere. The edition of *El fin del mundo* published in the Colección Piragua — the *only* edition of the novel ever to have been published — has recorded on its back cover only the title and author of the work, followed by a short review of the novel composed by the pocketbook series's editor-in-chief, Francisco Porrúa:

> Mucho se pudiera decir de esta novela, hasta en más páginas de las que el librito tiene. Basta decir que esta obra habla por si misma. En ella el autor ha dejado una huella muy grande

---

2 Jacqueline Martin, *The Knowledge the Mind and Heart Refuse: On the Life of James Baldwin* (New York: Knopf Doubleday, 2004), 647.
3 Ren Ishikawa, "Into the Archives of Colección Piragua," *Latin American Literary Review* 39, no. 78 (Fall 2011): 80–97, at 89.

en la imaginaria cultural de nuestro país. Es mi gran placer compartir esta obra con nuestros leyentes, ambos aquí y en todo el mundo.

[Much could be said of this novel, perhaps even in more pages than compose the text. It suffices to say that this novel speaks for itself. In it the author has left a deep impression on the cultural imaginary of our country. It is my great pleasure to share this work with our readers, both here and abroad.][4]

In its six years of circulation, *El fin del mundo* was distributed internationally in thirty-two countries, selling especially well in Argentina and Chile and even in non-Spanish speaking nations like Brazil, France, and England — in spite of the fact that the novel has never been officially translated into any other language.[5] Nevertheless, *El fin del mundo* was for the Colección Piragua a successful venture, and might have continued to sell well if the series had not been discontinued. Yet it was by no means considered the most important book of its generation; Feliciano Costa remarks that the "very fact that a novella could have been lost and rediscovered in the span of twenty years reflects well on neither the book nor on the memory of its reader."[6] A fair assessment of the novella's popular reach, perhaps, but an altogether impoverished understanding of its critical reception. Indeed, the novella was not entertained as a text of literary importance until Jacqueline Martin cited it in her biography *The Knowledge the Mind and Heart Refuse: On the Life of James Baldwin* as one of the many books in the author's possession at the time of his death. Scholars invested in unraveling the discrete influences on Baldwin's writing at the time of the biography's publication immediately remarked upon the little cited novella — a particularly

---

4   All translations appearing here have been completed by the author of the article.
5   Elena Gómez, ed. *Global Perspectives on the Latin American Novel* (Chicago: University of Chicago Press, 2008), 201.
6   Feliciano Costa, "The Mysterious Fernando Díaz," *Journal of Latin American Studies* 43, no. 2 (May 2011): 327–49, at 329.

interesting inclusion because it was the only work in Baldwin's personal library written in Spanish, a language Baldwin is not known to have spoken.[7] It was the proximity to this American writer that formally introduced *El fin del mundo* to the academic, for no formal study of the novella had been conducted before 2004. But in the years since much work has been done: Edith Williams's essays on temporality and love in Diaz's text are revelatory and beautiful; and Matthew Duhamel's upcoming book on the geography of the archipelago and the indigenous body in *El fin del mundo* will continue to enrich the body of scholarship on the novella.

I nevertheless remain entranced by the figure of Leonardo Díaz, that elusive author of whom nothing is recorded in the archives of his only publishers. Over the course of several years I attempted to gain access to Baldwin's copy of the novel, hoping to find within it some indication of the author's origin, or at the very least the relationship between Baldwin and this obscure novella marked in the margin of the text. Aware that Baldwin found the novella in Shakespeare & Company, I wondered whether Baldwin's relationship with Sylvia Beach had brought him into proximity with Díaz, as it did Scott Fitzgerald, Pablo Picasso, and James Joyce. But up until this point, I have been denied access to the novel, which remains along with the rest of Baldwin's personal effects restricted by his estate.[8] Ultimately, however, my search for the imponderable Leonardo Díaz took an unanticipated turn when, immersed in a project entirely unrelated to either Baldwin or *El fin del mundo,* I began to entertain the possibility that Leonardo Diaz has not been entirely lost

---

7 Leslie Donaldson, "On James Baldwin," in *The Books That Make Us,* ed. Michael Higgins (Austin: University of Texas Press, 2014), 480.

8 While in the process of writing her biography on Baldwin, Jacqueline Martin was similarly barred from accessing Baldwin's personal library and was only able to reproduce a list of the books contained within it due to the generosity of an employee of the Baldwin estate who recorded the names of the texts and their authors so that they might be included in the biography. See Martin, *The Knowledge the Mind and Heart Refuse,* 506.

to history, but that he is merely remembered under a different name.

II

It is worth noting that in 1956, the year before the novella was published, Ernest Hemingway spent several months in Cabo Blanco, Peru, in order to film part of *The Old Man and the Sea*. Onboard his yacht, the *Miss Texas,* Hemingway and his wife Mary Welsh traveled up and down the Pacific coast, ultimately arriving at Tierra del Fuego in Argentina — the southernmost point of South America and the setting of *El fin del mundo*.[9] I had not initially chosen to focus my project on the Hemingwayan presence in Peru and Argentina but was instead pursuing a broader analysis of Cabo Blanco in the 1950s: a small fishing village that in addition to gaining notoriety for its 1,000-pound black marlin was frequented by the likes of Marilyn Monroe, John Wayne, and Paul Newman but has in the decades since fallen into ruin.[10] The manuscript for this project remains yet unfinished, not merely because of the extensive research required to complete a work so rich with different personalities but due in large part to my own particularized interest in Hemingway's role in Latin America.

Much has been written — both by biographers and Hemingway himself — of the writer's time spent abroad in Europe, Asia, and Africa. *The Sun Also Rises,* which has been called Hemingway's most autobiographical novel, takes as its setting both France and Spain; and *A Farewell to Arms* fictionalizes Hemingway's own experiences serving in the Italian campaigns of the first World War. Furthermore, Hemingway spent time in Hong Kong, China, and Burma when Martha Gellhorn — a gifted war correspondent and the writer's third wife — was sent there on

---

9 Michael Shane Reynolds, *Hemingway: The Final Years* (New York: W.W. Norton, 2000), 295.
10 Andrew Vietze, *The Biggest Fish Ever Caught: A Long String of (Mostly) True Stories* (Guilford: Lyons Press, 2013), 19.

assignment for *Collier's* magazine, and was later accompanied by his fourth wife Mary Welsh on safari through the Belgian Congo, Rwanda, and Kenya. Hemingway's experiences while on safari provided him with the inspiration and material that filled the pages of his novel *Green Hills of Africa* and the short stories *The Snows of Kilimanjaro* and *The Short Happy Life of Francis Macomber*. His works were deeply marked by his own experiences — the running of the bulls in Pamplona, battle in Europe during the Great War, and the hunting of big game in Africa. It appeared more than reasonable to me that a writer who so frequently transcribed his own experiences into fiction should have written something, anything, about his experiences in Peru and Argentina in the 1950s.

It was this hypothesis that drove me to seek out any texts written by Hemingway during the time spent in Peru, in Argentina and beyond, up to the time of his death in 1961. Michael Reynolds recounts in his biography of the writer that from February to June of 1955 — the year preceding his trip to Cabo Blanco — Hemingway was working prolifically on a second African novel that was promptly put on hold at the time his presence was required on the set of *The Old Man and the Sea*. It was not until the next summer that, having returned to Cuba, Hemingway reportedly began to write again, composing six short stories about his experiences in World War II "to resharpen his blunted pen" before continuing work on the African novel.[11] Then in August of the same year, Hemingway took his wife Mary to New York City, where the couple saw nobody and were heard only by phone from Sylvia Beach,[12] who was in town negotiating publishing terms for her memoirs.[13] Nothing points to an additional text written by Hemingway during those months spent

---

11 Reynolds, *Hemingway*, 297.

12 Ibid., 298.

13 This has been reiterated in Mary Welsh Hemingway's memoir *How It Was* (New York: Knopf, 1976), 481, in Florence Wirth's *Beyond Attainment: A Hemingway Biography* (Princeton: Princeton University Press, 1988) and by Sylvia Beach in her correspondence. See *The Letters of Sylvia Beach,* ed. Keri Walsh (New York: Columbia University Press, 2011), 237.

in Cabo Blanco except for one note scribbled by Mary Welsh to Peter Viertel — who adapted the screenplay for *The Old Man and the Sea* — requesting that a Spanish dictionary be brought to their accommodations in Peru, since "Papa[14] [is] writing, can't remember how to spell a word he heard today. Needs Spanish dictionary."[15] No other suggestion appears in either the letters of Mary Welsh, the person most often responsible for typing the novels and short stories handwritten by Hemingway or in Peter Viertel's memoir *Dangerous Friends*.[16] But this short scribbled note does indicate that Hemingway was writing something related to neither his time in Europe during the World Wars nor his time on safari in Africa.

Surely, this is a tenuous detail on which to base a theory that there has been for several decades now a Hemingway novella lost to time and the best scholars of the writer's work. It certainly would not have been enough for me to pursue this project, if it had not been for a reference I then found in the archives of Sudamericana and Emecé to an untitled project by Ernest Hemingway to be published in the Colección Piragua in June of 1957. It would not have been absolutely unthinkable that a novel by a prominent American writer should be published through either of those houses. In 1950, Emecé published a translation of William Faulkner's *Absalom, Absalom* by Beatriz Florencia Nelson and another of his works, *Knight's Gambit,* by Lucrecia Moreno de Sáenz in 1951 as part of the Colección Piragua.[17] And indeed, Editorial Sudamericana would in 1966 and 1967, respectively, publish Julio Cortázar's novel *Rayuela* (*Hopscotch*) and Gabriel García Márquez's *Cien años de soledad* (*One Hundred Years of Solitude*). Normally, exchanges concerning the publication of a novel — particularly one written by an American author who

---

14 "Papa" was the nickname affectionately given to Hemingway by many who knew him, not merely his wives and children.

15 Hemingway, *How It Was,* 619.

16 Peter Viertel, *Dangerous Friends: Hemingway, Huston, and Others* (London: Penguin, 1992).

17 Doreen Fowler and Ann J. Abadie, *Faulkner: International Perspectives* (Jackson: University Press of Mississippi, 1984), 321.

just three years earlier had been awarded the Nobel Prize in Literature — would have been well documented, almost certainly with legal involvement to ensure the protection of the writer and of the publishing houses. But within the archives of both Emecé and Editorial Sudamericana, Hemingway's name appears but once, and only in the letter of a copyeditor named Moises Berrocal to a colleague named Xiomara Perez,[18] which reads thus:

> Mirá, Mara, estoy trabajando en está novela del Americano que no se decide de donde es, si no español entonces africano o talvez [sic] cubano, pero ahora se cree argentino? Necesito el quinto capitulo de la novela porque si no lo termino ahora me cuelga el jefe, asique mandámelo [sic] ahora, eh? Todo hay que hacerlo más rápido para el Hemingway.[19]

> [Look, Mara, I'm working on this novel by the American who can't decide where he's from, if he's not Spanish then he's African or maybe Cuban, but now he thinks himself Peruvian? I need the fifth chapter of the novel because if I don't finish it soon the boss will kill me, so send it to me now, okay? We have to do everything faster for Hemingway.]

None of this evidence could in isolation convince me of the Hemingwayan authorship of *El fin del mundo*; but in considering the details systematically I am led to believe that this could in fact be the last novel written and published by Ernest Hemingway. Working under the assumption that Hemingway is the novella's true author, I suggest that for the recent Nobel laureate, to write and publish under a *nom de plume* and in a language other than his native tongue was no caprice, but rather an attempt towards expression outside of the increasingly unman-

---

18 After cross referencing all the employees at both Emecé and Sudamericana, I was only able to find one person whose name could have reasonably matched with the nickname, Mara, that appears in the text of the letter.

19 From the archives of Sudamericana and Emecé.

ageable demands on one of the American literary masters of the twentieth century.

III

In his Nobel lecture, Ernest Hemingway wrote that

> For a true writer each book should be a new beginning where he tries again for something that is beyond attainment. He should always try for something that has never been done or that others have tried and failed. Then sometimes, with great luck, he will succeed. [...] It is because we have had such great writers in the past that a writer is driven far out past where he can go, out to where no one can help him.[20]

Michael Reynolds suggests that the impetus for this speech was at least in part a response to a complaint made previously by William Faulkner that Hemingway "never took chances by attempting the impossible."[21] Faulkner, Reynolds goes on to say, was not alone in assuming that the simplicity of Hemingway's novels and short stories reflected the effortlessness of their construction or that each text was merely a reiteration of the same themes without any perceivable evolution.[22] This approach to his writing was a constant source of frustration for Hemingway, who continually endeavored to rework the genres within which he produced. The recognition afforded him by the Nobel Prize in Literature, furthermore, was for the writer a double-edged sword. Hans-Peter Rodenberg indicates that Hemingway "felt offended by the justification of the award, which spoke of a triumph of 'a manly love of danger and adventure' over his early 'brutal, cynical and callous period.'" It appeared to him that acceptance of the award was essentially submission to a critical

---
20 Ernest Hemingway, "Banquet Speech," Nobel Banquet, Stockholm, December 10, 1954.
21 Reynolds, *Hemingway*, 283.
22 Ibid., 283–84.

atmosphere that would devour him—one that expected that "each new book by him had to surpass the past ones."[23] Overwhelmed by the prospect of meeting public expectations with his next work, Hemingway began to work a fictitious diary about his second safari to Africa but did not complete it with the intention of immediate publication. Rather, he set the manuscript aside with instructions that it be published in 1998 (in all likelihood, posthumously) to mark his hundredth birthday. The fictional journal, he decided, would be titled *True at First Light: A Fictional Memoir*.[24] This act of deferral, likely chosen for a number of reasons including Hemingway's own anxieties about the diary's reception, has for many of my contemporaries awoken and encouraged optimism in the belief that there is another Hemingway text, "[a]nother manuscript, a trunk, a letter, something [to] be found."[25] I believe that if there is one to be found, it is *El fin del mundo*, written under the name Leonardo Díaz and published clandestinely in South America.

It would not have been impossible for Hemingway to compose an entire novella in Spanish. In a letter to Arthur Mizener composed in June of 1950, Hemingway explained that he can "speak and read French but not write it; nor Italian, nor German. But can write Spanish. English sometimes too, maybe."[26] And in another letter to Adriana Ivancich written in the same month, he explains that

> Here in the house, we talk Spanish always. Mary corrects my grammar altho [*sic*] she had never heard of the language until 1945 and cannot follow it if it gets fast, or rough, or takes her out of her depth. It is the roughest language that there is and we can say anything in front of her because she knows

---

23 Hans-Peter Rodenberg, *The Making of Ernest Hemingway: Celebrity, Photojournalism and the Emergence of the Modern Lifestyle Media* (Berlin: LIT, 2015), 182.

24 Ibid., 182.

25 Dawn Trouard, "The Last Safari," *The Washington Post*, June 27, 1999.

26 Ernest Hemingway, *Ernest Hemingway: Selected Letters 1917–1961*, ed. Carlos Baker (New York: Scribner Classics, 2003), 696.

nothing of the dirty part or old gallows language. But if she does understand she will correct the grammar.[27]

René Villarreal, an employee of Hemingway's for fifteen years at the Finca in Cuba, has confirmed in interviews that "Papa spoke primarily in Spanish to the Finca staff" and had newspapers brought in daily from Havana in both Spanish and English so that he could stay informed via *The New York Times* and the Cuban editorial *El Pais*.[28] But even before moving to Cuba in 1946, Hemingway was already deeply immersed in the language, having visited Spain frequently in the preceding years. Many scholars have noted how the Spanish spoken by Hemingway influenced or even infiltrated his novel *For Whom the Bell Tolls*. Edward Fenimore argues that the although this novel was written in English, there is throughout "the tacit assumption that it is Spanish."[29] Milton Azevedo, furthermore, observes that "Hemingway manipulates English and Spanish syntax and vocabulary to convey the impression that the characters are speaking Spanish"[30] and even includes phrases in the text that continually reemphasize the language in which communication between the characters is occurring: the narrator remarks at one point in the novel that Anselmo "spoke rapidly and furiously in a dialect that Robert Jordan could just follow. It was like reading Quevedo. Anselmo was speaking old Castilian"[31]; and elsewhere in the text, "it sounded wonderful in Spanish."[32] Additionally,

---

27 Ibid., 704.
28 René Villarreal and Raúl Villarreal, *Hemingway's Cuban Son: Reflections on the Writer by His Longtime Majordomo* (Kent: Kent State University Press, 2009), 55.
29 Edward Fenimore, "English and Spanish in For Whom the Bell Tolls," in *Ernest Hemingway: The Man and His Work,* ed. John K.M. McCaffery (Cleveland: World Publishing Company, 1956), 210–11.
30 Milton M. Azevedo "Shadows of a Literary Dialect: For Whom the Bell Tolls in Five Romance Languages," *The Hemingway Review* 20, no. 1 (2000): 30–48, at 30.
31 Ernest Hemingway, *For Whom the Bell Tolls* (London: Arrow Books, 2004), 13.
32 Ibid., 96.

Hemingway incorporated Spanish words and phrases throughout the novel, relying heavily on context to communicate meaning wherever it would otherwise have remained unclear — or even, as is the case with many of the expletives incorporated into the text, neglecting to translate them into English.[33]

But perhaps the greatest argument for the Hemingwayan authorship of *El fin del mundo* proceeds from a reading of the novel, in which one may see the style of the author typified. In *El fin del mundo* one notes comparably simple syntax as well as an "intense awareness of the world of the senses" most frequently explored in the detailed depictions of the body and the physical world it resides in.[34] This is especially important given the specificity of the location where the novel is set in light of Hemingway's own experiences in Peru and Argentina. The title *El fin del mundo*, which might be translated *At World's End* or *The End of the World*, refers to Tierra del Fuego, the Land of Fire — the archipelago at the southernmost extreme of the American continent. Its name originates with the fires built by the indigenous Selk'nam people upon the arrival of the Portuguese explorer Ferdinand Magellan in 1520. But, as journalist Laura Mallonee has explained, it is "better known for spectacular scenery and ceaseless wind" that blows without respite and even changes the shape of growing trees into unusual shapes.[35] Tierra del Fuego is considered one of the best locations in the world for fishing trout and salmon and remains one of the most impressive geographical sites in the world, boasting peat bogs, lenga forests, and snowy mountain ranges. Ultimately, the appellation of this land as "the end of the world" serves as a beautifully posed metaphor for the conflict between Santiago and his wife Felicitas as they find themselves on holiday in the archipelago, attempting to restore the love that has slowly dissolved from their marriage.

---

33 Azevedo, "Shadows of a Literary Dialect," 38.

34 Robert Penn Warren, "Ernest Hemingway," in *Ernest Hemingway*, ed. Harold Bloom (Philadelphia: Chelsea House, 2005), 36.

35 Laura Mallonee, "Journey to Tierra del Fuego, the End of the Modern World," *Wired*, April 12, 2017.

Because Hemingway's habit of working his life into his fiction has been well documented, it is perhaps quite a pedestrian undertaking to attempt to demonstrate the manner in which the relationship between Santiago and Felicitas mirrors that of Hemingway and Mary, particularly during their time at sea in Peru and Argentina. But at that point Hemingway and his wife were in fact very disconnected; in a note to her husband, Mary pleaded with him, asking if it "[h]as ever occurred to you how lonely a woman of yours can get. Wake up alone, breakfast alone, garden alone, swim alone, sup alone… It may be too much to expect that any of this will cause you to change your mind in thinking of you versus The Other," signing the message "M. who feels her life slipping away in a welter of chaos."[36] And indeed, Felicitas does find herself an isolated figure, especially with regards to her marriage; her husband — a successful businessman and entrepreneur — has drifted from Felicitas, frequently engaging in flirtations with younger women and avoiding physical intimacy with his wife. In one particularly moving scene, Felicitas stands alone outside the house in which they are staying as she waits for her husband to return:

> El sol iba bajando, y ya quedaría sola. Tuviera de compañía solamente el viento que soplaba sin parar, y a la distancia la luna solitaria como ella. Las estrellas salían una por una y todavía ella permanecía afuera, esperando. Sentada en la rama de un árbol bifurcado veía el horizonte vacío.[37]

> [The sun was setting, and she would soon remain alone. She would have for company only the wind that blew without ending, and at a distance the moon, lonely like her. The stars came out one by one and still she stayed outside, waiting. Sitting on the branch of a bifurcated tree she watched the empty horizon.]

---
36 Quoted in Reynolds, *Hemingway,* 294.
37 Leonardo Díaz, *El fin del mundo* (Buenos Aires: Editorial Sudamericana y Emecé, 1957), 39.

Speaking about Hemingway's novels, Robert Penn Warren has suggested that the "beauty of the physical world is a background for the human predicament, and the very relishing of the beauty is merely a kind of desperate and momentary compensation possible in the midst of the predicament."[38] This scene in *El fin del mundo* achieves exactly that: Felicitas finds herself alone, the world as she knows it crumbling before her as her husband seeks to ease his own solitude with another woman. It is a painful moment for the reader, who knows what Felicitas does not and must nevertheless wait in vigil with her in the moonlight.

There are many such moments in *El fin del mundo* that, if cited, could testify to the Hemingwayan authorship of the novella. But to conclude it is perhaps more efficacious to consider why Hemingway, a Nobel laureate and celebrity of international renown, would choose to write a work such as this under a different name to be published quietly in South America. I believe that the key is in his Nobel address, in which he emphasizes that each new book should be for its writer a "new beginning where he tries again for something that is beyond attainment." To write a novella in Spanish would certainly have challenged Hemingway's intellectual and creative abilities; that he might have been able to compose a text as beautiful and moving as *El fin del mundo* in a language other than his native tongue would be a testament not only to his genius, but also to his diligence and perseverance. If so, then why publish the novella under a different name as part of a pocketbook series in South America when it could have been published in any major publishing house? By 1957, the year of the novella's publication, Hemingway had long been overwhelmed by the viciousness of fellow writers and literary critics, and yet he did not want to stop writing. Michael Reynolds reports that when he was asked if he would ever run out of ideas for fiction, Hemingway replied, "'I don't see how I can quit.'"[39] It would appear that until the very end of his life, fiction remained essential to his existence, but in order to continue

---

38 Warren, "Ernest Hemingway," 36.
39 Quoted in Reynolds, *Hemingway*, 287.

expanding his artistic boundaries without the weight of critical reception, another means of publication would be necessary. How indeed Hemingway would have arranged the details with Editorial Sudamericana and Emecé — especially with regards to the confidentiality of his identity — I cannot say. But although I will not be able to say this with absolute certainty until I can hold James Baldwin's copy of *El fin del mundo* in my own hands, I suspect that the famous bookstore owner Sylvia Beach might have had a hand in the process, facilitating the publication and even carrying the series at Shakespeare and Company, where a young Baldwin would have picked it up and taken it home.

Bibliography

Azevedo, Milton M. "Shadows of a Literary Dialect: For Whom the Bell Tolls in Five Romance Languages." *The Hemingway Review* 20, no. 1 (2000): 30–48. DOI: 10.1353/hem.2000.0007.

Beach, Sylvia. *The Letters of Sylvia Beach.* Edited by Keri Walsh. New York: Columbia University Press, 2011.

Costa, Feliciano. "The Mysterious Fernando Díaz." *Journal of Latin American Studies* 43, no. 2 (May 2011): 327–49.

Del Carril, Francisco F. *International Book Publishing: An Encyclopedia.* Edited by Philip G. Altbach and Edith S. Hoshino. New York: Garland Publishing, 1995.

Díaz, Leonardo. *El fin del mundo.* Buenos Aires: Editorial Sudamericana y Emecé, 1957.

Donaldson, Leslie. "On James Baldwin." In *The Books That Make Us,* edited by Michael Higgins, 465–90. Austin: University of Texas Press, 2014.

Fenimore, Edward. "English and Spanish in For Whom the Bell Tolls." In *Ernest Hemingway: The Man and His Work,* edited by John K.M. McCaffery, 205–20. Cleveland: World Publishing Company, 1956.

Fowler, Doreen, and Ann J. Abadie. *Faulkner: International Perspectives.* Jackson: University Press of Mississippi, 1984.

Gómez, Elena, ed. Global Perspectives on the Latin American Novel. Chicago: The University of Chicago Press, 2008.

Hemingway, Ernest. "Banquet Speech." Nobel Banquet, Stockholm, December 10, 1954.

———. *Ernest Hemingway: Selected Letters 1917–1961.* Edited by Carlos Baker. New York: Scribner Classics, 2003.

———. *For Whom the Bell Tolls.* London: Arrow Books, 2004.

Hemingway, Mary Welsh. *How It Was.* New York: Knopf, 1976.

Ishikawa, Ren. "Into the Archives of Colección Piragua." *Latin American Literary Review* 39, no. 78 (Fall 2011): 80–97.

Mallonee, Laura. "Journey to Tierra del Fuego, the End of the Modern World." *Wired,* April 12, 2017.

Martin, Jacqueline. *The Knowledge the Mind and Heart Refuse: On the Life of James Baldwin.* New York: Knopf Doubleday, 2004.

Reynolds, Michael Shane. *Hemingway: The Final Years.* New York: W.W. Norton, 2000.

Rodenberg, Hans-Peter. *The Making of Ernest Hemingway: Celebrity, Photojournalism and the Emergence of the Modern Lifestyle Media.* Berlin: LIT, 2015.

Trouard, Dawn. "The Last Safari." *The Washington Post,* June 27, 1999.

Viertel, Peter. *Dangerous Friends: Hemingway, Huston, and Others.* London: Penguin, 1992.

Vietze, Andrew. *The Biggest Fish Ever Caught: A Long String of (Mostly) True Stories.* Guilford: Lyons Press, 2013.

Villarreal, René, and Raúl Villarreal. *Hemingway's Cuban Son: Reflections on the Writer by His Longtime Majordomo.* Kent: Kent State University Press, 2009.

Warren, Robert Penn. "Ernest Hemingway." In *Ernest Hemingway,* edited by Harold Bloom, 25–54. Philadelphia: Chelsea House, 2005.

Wirth, Florence. *Beyond Attainment: A Hemingway Biography.* Princeton: Princeton University Press, 1988.

11

The Unfinished and Lost Texts of Richard A. Conlan: An Examination of an Obsession, by Mark Conlan, Ph.D.

Introduced and Annotated by James Speese, Ph.D.

INTRODUCTION

Editor's note: While I worked on a chapter on bildungsroman novels in my dissertation, I discovered references to a coming-of-age novel entitled *Darkness Rains,* written by Richard A. Conlan and published by Putnam in 1969. The novel was, apparently, fairly popular for a time, and sold well enough for several paperback printings before finally going out of print in the 1980s. Intrigued, I attempted to find the novel; it was not an easy task. Every copy seemed to have been lost. Then, while vacationing in Yellowstone, I came upon a bookstore in Bozeman, MT, called Vargas Books, and in the dark bowels at the rear of the store, I discovered a single, well-worn copy (as well as a complete collection of all the Doonesbury books, for which I was eternally grateful!). I read the book voraciously, despite its having a few missing pages. While there were far better books for the purposes of my dissertation, including obviously J.D. Salinger's *The Catcher in the Rye,* I was transfixed by Conlan's forgotten novel.

Despite the somewhat pedestrian writing, the novel's main character, Nelson Peterson, was fascinating. Hoping to one day be a writer himself, he finds himself incapable of being in any way satisfied with his work, seeing his prose as a "pale imitation, a shadow of a ghost, moments chained to weak words."[1] Indeed, he writes poems and stories throughout the narrative, writing that he almost always immediately destroys. In perhaps a nod to Salinger, Conlan's novel concludes with Nelson being finally committed to a mental ward in a local hospital.

While Conlan's novel ultimately wouldn't feature in my dissertation, I decided that once I received my degree that I would devote time to examine Conlan and his writing more deeply. Unfortunately once I was able to begin a further study of Conlan, the author was already long dead. Conlan died in 1992, killed by perhaps the cruelest of diseases for a writer — Alzheimer's. However, he left his voluminous papers to his son, Mark. Those papers, however, were mostly destroyed when Mark's house burned in a tragic fire in 2006, a fire that killed both him and his family. Mark's estate, executed by his now-deceased sister, had willed Conlan's papers to Bard College, where Mark had taught for years. My interest was piqued, so I approached the estate, now run by a grandson, Charles Johnson, to ask if I might examine the papers. He asked to meet me and I readily agreed. The interview was not as enlightening as I'd hoped, but I did receive permission.[2] There was precious little material left. Indeed, it took quite some time to convince the librarian at Bard that the papers even existed, let alone that they resided in her library.[3]

---

1   Richard A. Conlan, *Darkness Rains* (New York: Putnam, 1969), 71.
2   Charles had little to say about his grandfather or his family, but did grant me exclusive permission to examine the papers at Bard, so long as I agreed to get further permission for any extended quotations, particularly of *Darkness Rains*, as he hopes for future publishing rights for what he believes will be the "rediscovered masterpiece." His hopes are, I suspect, in vain.
3   The librarian in the rare and antiquities section at the Bard Library was Heather Summers. She claimed never to have heard of either Mark (who had, after all, worked at the college for decades) or his father. After some searching, she discovered a small closet which held reams and reams of papers from both men. The pages had never been examined, nor, in fact,

Still, I found Richard's papers strangely fascinating. However, the most interesting piece among the papers in his estate was an essay his son, Mark, wrote shortly after Richard died, incorporating part of Richard's writing journal. This essay is remarkable. Here, then, is Mark's, essay. My annotations reflect my own research into Mark and Richard's writing while attempting to explain both Richard's obsession with prose and Mark's obsession with his father. These obsessions can certainly be examined through a Freudian lens, but I've eschewed incorporating much, if any, critical theory here. I'll let the reader draw their own conclusions and perhaps open the door to others for more in-depth study. The following are Richard's (and Mark Conlan's) words:

The Unfinished and Lost Texts of Richard A Conlan: An Examination of an Obsession, by Mark Conlan, Annotated by James Speese

"All lives, in passing, leave tasks undone and paths untrodden." So spoke the hero, Nelson Peterson, in my father's (Richard A. Conlan's) one published full-length novel, *Darkness Rains*.[4] It's an off-hand line, often overlooked by college and high-school students as they type their term papers, delving into the mind and soul of Nelson, an archetypical adolescent tragic hero. But the line is a subtle indication of an obsession of Nelson's, and, indeed, my father's. The protagonist is obsessed with the efficacy

---

indexed. It was, literally, a pile of papers waiting for some future librarian to organize.

4   Richard A. Conlan's lost American coming of age novel *Darkness Rains* tells the story of a young Nelson Peterson as he faces both madness and adulthood in a time of cultural conformity. The novel garnered at least one evocative review. An *LA Times Book Review* was among Richard's papers and it noted, "This is the sort of book that works like the sense of smell upon the memory, teasing a nostalgia for what was once, we hope, real" (Jonah Harris, "*Darkness* Will Tease Your Dreams," review of *Darkness Rains*, by Richard A. Conlan, *LA Times Book Review*, May 15, 1969, 12) However, *Darkness Rains* has largely faded from our cultural memory.

of moments, with how everything constantly changes, and how no moment is ever complete.[5]

Darkness Rains is of course a fairly popular novel, especially in literary circles where it is both praised and maligned. Every now and then it makes one of those lists of "Great American Novels," though more often even those who admit many aspects of the novel are "brilliant" pass it over.[6] In fact, at the time of its publication, *The Pennsylvania Quarterly Review* summed up the opinion of most, though not all, literary critics and scholars:

---

[5] Quoting from the published version of the novel, page 131, will give the uninitiated reader some view of the prose and Nelson's first person ruminations:

> As I relived all these memories of Jill, [Nelson's ex girlfriend] it occurred to me that it's not *people* we love. It's *moments*. People fill moments and the memories of these moments masquerade as love. Everything we love is a memory, a ghost of something shining bright and gone. Lost.
>
> I didn't love *Jill*. I loved the moments we'd shared.
>
> And I didn't miss her. I missed those *moments*.
>
> I wondered briefly and somewhat heretically (for a lover of Romantic literature such as I) if Keats had, in fact, loved moments and not a woman. If Yeats had. If the love the Brownings had felt for each other was really a love of each other rather than a love of the moments they'd shared. Perhaps all love, even the immortal love of the greatest lovers, is really a selfish desire for meaningful moments. What did such a possibility mean to a Romantic such as I? Or was this simply the basic truth of Romanticism, after all?
>
> Rather than attempt to come to grips with these heresies, and what they meant to me, I again retreated to *another* sort of love, the unconditional and dependable love of alcohol.

[6] "Harold Bloom, for instance, listed as among the 'best books of its time.'" [This is the only footnote by Mark Conlan in this essay. I could find no such quote, though I did discover a quote in one of Bloom's literary anthologies, in which, while not including any works by Conlan, he writes: "Another whose work could potentially be included in this volume is Richard Conlan, though his best work, the novel *Darkness Rains,* is inappropriate." Why the work was "inappropriate" remains unsaid; I assume either Bloom did not receive Conlan's permission (indeed, Conlan, in his papers shows derision for both Bloom and the concept of anthologies completely, referring to them as "editors deboning writers"), or that the piece was too long. The anthology was of coming-of-age novellas after all. See bibliography page for more information. Harold Bloom, ed., *Anthology of 20th Century Coming of Age Novellas* (Norton: London, 1980), 15. — James Speese]

"A fine first effort, with extraordinary promise, but in the final analysis, too incohesive to be dealt with seriously."[7]

My father was aware of such criticism of course. He read everything ever printed about his prose, I think.[8] And it has been well-documented (again, especially in the literary community) that he didn't publish much of anything afterwards, in part because of such criticism, and in part because he felt such criticism might be valid. (And also because of more than a few well-documented disagreements he'd had with every publisher he'd ever submitted to, including the publisher of *Darkness Rains* and several magazine publishers — Kevin Angstadt, once his best friend in the business, among them.)[9] The few pieces my father did publish were short stories that rarely approached the promise of *Darkness*. He, himself, admitted as much in one of his rare letters to me.[10]

Still, despite his self-imposed exile (or maybe because of it), *Darkness* sold steadily over the years. It was published in 1969, when my father was only twenty-five and I was only two. He was a man desperately trying to provide for a new family, and, as it turns out, the novel did just that. It has since provided, almost on its own, a home, a couple of college educations, and a healthy nest egg for the future of us three children. Incidentally,

---

7   Not only have I found no such quote, but no such literary journal seems to exist.
8   The only actual contemporaneous review of the novel that I found is the LA *Times* review by Harris quoted in footnote 4.
9   A Kevin Angstadt did work at Putnam, which published *Darkness Rains,* but evidence suggests he started at Putnam after the publication of the novel.
10 Most of these letters — if they ever did exist — are gone. I did find among the estate several letters that Richard wrote to his son, but, like most letters from family members, these mostly focus on family issues. That noted, one letter, dated December 12, 1990, includes the following quote: "Sometimes I wish I had worked harder to please the critics. But then I remember that writing is for the author and the moment, and not for the critic. Indeed, at my old age, I don't even care about the reader anymore. That, however, does not mean the critics are wrong."

for some reason, after the U.S., the novel has sold the most copies in Argentina, where it was made into a major three-act play.[11]

When my father died this past fall after a long and desperate battle with early on-set Alzheimer's disease, the few literary obituaries were still laced with barely disguised criticism, mostly directed at his meager output, his lack of published material. "Obsessive, talented, but somewhat lazy, a writer who screamed of potential never realized, a man content to rest on the laurels of one major promising but ultimately unsatisfying work," read part of his eulogy in the *New York Times Book Review*.[12] The story was pretty much the same everywhere: That of a unique but quixotic talented loner whose potential was never fulfilled.[13]

These criticisms may be true, except that my father was not lazy. He never did personal appearances and rarely published, but he wrote every day, from six in the morning until five at night. I can attest to this as I witnessed it every day of my upbringing. He had boxes and boxes of manuscripts that he never allowed anyone, including his own family, to read.

His pages survived, and I have spent the months since his death reading and indexing as many of these pages as possible. I did this not with the idea of posthumous publication (I respect

---

11 The play *Here Rains Darkness* must be what Mark is referring to. Copies of the play exist, and reviews of performances can be found in contemporaneous Argentinean journals. The play does follow the story of the novel in vague ways, however, and while the playwright, Julian Diaz, does thank Conlan in the acknowledgements, he never actually refers to the play as an adaptation. The novel, meanwhile, was in print for over a decade and did sell well over that time; it is strange, then, that so few copies remain. I only note this fact because it seems quite true that its sales could have supported a family for quite a while.

12 Phillips Rogers, "The Passing of a Forgotten Author," *New York Times*, August 24, 1993, 43.

13 Indeed, it is Conlan's later works that befuddled both critics and publishers alike. Seemingly obsessed with the idea that all texts are unfinished, Conlan's work became more and more chaotic and thus simultaneously more demanding of the reader. In time, the author quit publishing altogether, and it remains a critical truism that his reclusive nature was due to two factors: Because he felt publishers and editors treated him unfairly and because he now had a family to raise.

my father's obvious, if unspoken, wishes) but rather, to try to come to terms with his obsessions, to try to get to know the man that nobody ever really knew and yet judged nonetheless. This is the right, I believe, of every offspring. And I will attempt here and now, to expose and explain some of my father's obsessions. In short, I will attempt something he would never have considered: I will try, using the remarkable body of work that survives him, to answer his critics.

Which brings me back to the beginning. "All lives, in passing, leave tasks undone, and paths untrodden."[14] To my father, it seems, this was not just an off-hand line spoken by Nelson Peterson. In fact, it seems almost central to the obsession that drove my father to write in the first place. The line first appears in his journal, a disjointed work, entries of which often went undated. The line (and occasional permutations of it) is often repeated here, and eventually finds its way to the protagonist of *Darkness Rains*. And it is this journal, which, obviously, sheds the most light on my father as a writer.

Shortly after the novel was published, the line appears for a final time in this journal, after which my father writes:

> We do not curse mortality because we are afraid of death, but rather because we haven't the time to finish our life's work, whatever it may be. Were I given ten lifetimes, I would never complete all that has been set upon me to accomplish. And I have but one lifetime, and most of it is wasted on the mundane…[15]
>
> Aside from that, despite my continual deluge of words and ideas, I am truly (as many critics have graciously pointed out)

---

14 A discerning reader will note the addition of a comma in this second reference to the quote. In fact, there is no comma in the version of the novel that I have, but Mark did, in both cases, leave out the word "must." "All lives, in passing, must leave tasks undone and paths untrodden," says the character Peterson on page 124 of the novel.

15 Remarkably, or perhaps unsurprisingly, Mark skips over part of this quote, in which his father defines the mundane: "[M]ost of it is wasted in the mundane, dealing with family and home life."

no writer of worth. I cannot compare to Shakespeare or Hugo or Melville. Were I blessed (or cursed) with their ideas in their times, *Hamlet* would remain unfinished. *Moby Dick* would end up as a bare ten-page short story, compromised to fit some tasteless magazine's format. And *Les Miserables* would be nothing more than a passing sentence in another story.

At this point my father began to list some of his ideas that he wanted to complete before he died. I suspect that most of the projects based on these ideas were eventually completed (more or less). All evidence points to this list of ideas being something of an obsession. Each idea is numbered and listed separately, apparently jotted down just as the concept hit him. It was a list he could use for reference later. Each entry seems to have been added much later than the previous one, and some are, in fact, dated.

It would seem that the various ideas he actually bothered to jot down would take up a great portion of his writing time until the next one would occur to him, which he would then write down, and which would then take priority, forcing my father onto a different path. This list was, in many ways, the primary obsession of my father's, and certainly it is what we need to study if we are ever to truly know him. This was the veritable literary garden he would toil in for decades.

Above the list he added these words: "These ideas are for my future self to remember and put into words when (if) I am ever capable. Or, failing that, for someone else, perhaps a writer of worth, to do so."

Then the extraordinary list begins.

1. A tale of someone waking up from a dream in his own house, only to discover that he can't remember where the light switches are! In panic, he ransacks the entire house, fearing demons from his childhood nightmares, in an attempt to simply turn on the lights.

A version of this story, written respectfully in the style of early dime novels and '50s horror magazines, was published by my father in *Weird Tales* magazine. Apparently his distrust of editors and critics had not yet completely overpowered him. However, my father had two versions of this tale in his collection; the published version he obviously considered inferior, a toned down version of the original, a concession to the editors.

In the published version, the man can't find the light switch, and all his childhood fears return and drive him mad. The next day the authorities find him in his home, mad, staring into space, lying in his own urine, his fingers raw and bloody, just beneath a hole that he had scratched in the plaster of the wall in search of the switch. Just above the bloody hole in the wall is the light switch. It's a simple but effective irony (the editors obviously liked it, or perhaps they bought the story simply for my father's name, *Darkness Rains* being a recent release), but my father still preferred the original, which was, I believe, never submitted for publication.[16]

---

16 Mark Conlan describes this story quite well. I am not sure it is an "homage," as it seems to be more or less Conlan's style. While he apparently had grand delusions of literary brilliance, much of his work is pedestrian. This piece, available at weirdtales.com/conlan/darkness holds up as a horror story for children. Some samples of the prose, as the protagonist finally finds a light switch:

> He tried not to think of roaches scurrying away into the cracks as he flipped the switch. And in that same split-second, he remembered horror movies from his youth that had inspired nightmares of tiny demons borne of darkness who snuck out from corners and chimneys and closets at night, hissing, whispering of murder, of stealing souls, of taking people down into the darkness, but scurrying like roaches in retreat from the light, disappearing once again into their crack. Until, of course, the lights went out again. (13)

Of course, the light switch doesn't work. It should also be noted that many of the images evoked in this story do seem reminiscent of some old horror movies. The paragraph quoted above, for instance, bears a striking resemblance to the TV horror movie *Don't Be Afraid of the Dark,* directed by John Newland. The short story predates the TV movie by years (it debuted in 1973) so, if anything, Conlan's story provided the image for the movie and not the other way around, though the story itself seems to suggest the opposite.

In this version, the man finally manages to turn on the lights, only to wake from this nightmare in his dark house. And as he lies in the dark he wonders where his light switches are. Thus the story takes on a cyclical nature and begins again, a dream within a dream. In fact, my father's notes suggest that his original plan was to submit both stories, one after the other, as one tale. This would have assumed some incredible patience on the part of the reader since both stories are essentially the same until the last few paragraphs. The man wakes from the dream, can't find the light switches, finally finds them, only to wake from a dream unable to find the light switches, and finally is driven mad. Had he somehow published this version, he could have expected more critical derision (which is not to suggest the published version was universally acclaimed. It went largely unnoticed), since critics often disapprove of reader manipulation of such magnitude.

It's interesting to note, though, that my father's concept was such that he provided no true ending to the tale. To him, it was unfinished, and it could be argued that including both endings hinted paths to the reader to imagine other endings, other ironies, more than my father could ever conceive.

Now let's return to my father's list.

2. Huckleberry Finn on I95: Rewrite Twain's novel and alter it so that Huck in 1960 could walk down a huge eight lane highway instead of rafting down the Mississippi. The tale should be able to follow the entire novel.

And it does, but tediously. A version of this attempt exists, (unpublished) though a lot is missing. It appears my father was rather unhappy with it (with, I think, good reason) and disposed of most of it. Some of the didactic analogies work—the reaction, for instance, of many of the characters to Jim (the escaped slave in Twain's version, an educated African-American SDS member in my father's) is interesting since, one hundred years after slavery, and despite the difference in circumstance, those character reactions to Jim are virtually the same. This suggests, of course, that for African Americans, little has truly changed in the course of American history. There is even a white supremacist character who suggests that there will soon be a "world racial war," replacing Twain's allusions to the upcoming Civil War. But most of the analogies fall apart rather quickly, and my father obviously abandoned the idea. Still all evidence seems to suggest that this work occupied my father for years.

Indeed, there even exists among his papers pages of a similar rewrite of *Tom Sawyer* as well, and part of an updated *Connecticut Yankee in King Arthur's Court*. Apparently my father had decided that all of Twain's works could be rewritten. I wonder how many rewritten Twain (or other authors') works he considered. Indeed, his last (and I believe most effective piece) was an updated "Letters from Earth." In the margins next to this particular journal entry, my father later wrote: "To attempt such a task is to attempt to live at least two lifetimes in the span of one. Even if I were as prolific as Twain, I would never come to complete any of my own ideas and works. Also, why Twain? Why not Hemingway or Kafka or Fitzgerald? Thus, this idea can only be dropped, somehow forgotten, and passed on to another future writer with more stamina than I."[17] I admit I'd hoped to find more rewritings of different authors, but, in the end, I could only find hundreds of pages of Twain's works rewritten.

Still my father was already "cursing mortality" for his being unable to complete this single concept, while other paths opened ahead of him. Still, he hoped to hint at completion, to pass on the idea for someone else to finish, to talk [sic] that path. His ideas, it seems, were not his personal property.

Back to the journal and the list:

3. An argument between two friends as to the meaning of a particular song (or any artwork). This idea comes from

---

[17] None of these pages still exist. The interesting link to Jamesonian postmodernity here needs to be mentioned. Jameson essentially argued that all literature in the postmodern era subconsciously does what Richard Conlan admits to doing consciously here: rewriting what has been written before, updating it, and quoting it outright (without attribution.) This is pastiche, a parody without a point.

my own experience, listening to a song—"Cat's Cradle" [*sic*] by Harry Chapin[18]—with my friend Kevin (Angstadt). We discussed the song; he believed it was a happy song since it ended with a father's son being "just like me," from the father's perspective. I saw it as a sad song since the father had no time for his son as the boy grew, and in the end, the son had no time for his father — they *were* just like each other, *both* distracted from moments that matter by the mundane, and both ended up missing so much, and saddened by life." (Incidentally, this entry illustrates one of the critics' greatest criticisms of my father — that he underestimated and insulted the reader by *italicizing* (or in this case, printed out, *underlining* too much.)

A version of this story was published in the *New Yorker*, which, more or less, seems to be a direct narrative of my father's discussion with Angstadt. It ends with my father being amazed that two people could view a piece of artwork, whose proper reading would seem to be clear, so differently. This piece was praised by many for its prose, but criticized for its many digressions.[19] It

---

18 This is of course the song "Cats in the Cradle" written by Sandy and Harry Chapin, and performed by Harry, published by Story Songs, Ltd, ASCAP. I wonder what Mark thought about this discussion of lyrics in a song about a lack of a son's connection to his father, something that surely Mark must have considered given his father's obsessions that drove him to write everyday and, presumably, spend time away from his son. Perhaps tellingly, Mark does not comment directly.

19 I could find no critical mention of the story, so I am not sure what Mark is referring to with his comments about praise and criticism. The best I can conjure is that, two weeks after the publishing of the story in the April 1, 1976 issue of *The New Yorker*, a letter to the editor from Donna Miller of Brooklyn, NY, sums up both views: "What a beautiful sentiment in the story. It makes me question how we can ever really understand each other or the artists we love. That said, the author could probably have said as much in half as many words. Harry Chapin could probably do better. You don't need to explain his work, which is exactly what this beautiful story tries to do." I quote Miller without permission since, understandably, I have not been able to contact her. Miller, Donna, "Response to Conlan Story," *The New Yorker*, April 1, 1976, 13.

was the last piece of work my father ever published, just a few years after I was born.

After this piece was published, my father wrote another story about two people reading the former story and discussing it, only to find that they had viewed the story itself completely differently. One thought it sad that one of the characters had misunderstood the author of the story. The other believed it was the author's *intent* to be misunderstood, and in that context, he had been understood. In my father's papers was a rejection slip from the New Yorker for this story. (How could he have expected more?)

Shortly after that story was written, however, my father wrote another story about two people reading the second unpublished story, with predictable results. They, too, disagreed over *its* meaning. As you can see, my father was becoming, more and more, a man obsessed.

Finally he wrote a (never completed) story about an author arguing with himself as to the meanings of his own stories.[20]

Then, my father turned to other concepts. Or so it seemed.

4. I remember well my first year of summer-camp as a Boy Scout and especially the intense ghost story that was told around the campfire. I think I will attempt to write a story of the story being told. It would center on myself hearing the story, and perhaps later as a father telling the same, slightly altered tale, at his son's Boy Scout camp, and maybe someone else one day writing the story, and then someone subsequently reading parts of it around a campfire to a group of Boy Scouts, including a young me.

After this my father adds, in somewhat enlighteningly and somewhat needlessly:

---

[20] Mark Conlan offers no evidence of this story and as far as I could tell, it no longer exists in Richard's papers. Either it burned in the fire or Mark invented the idea out of whole cloth.

I am fond of such contrivances, even if they are manipulative — or perhaps because they are. I enjoy stories within stories, each leading to the cycle once again, a continuous and eternal cycle of tales within tales, none of which are ever completed, but suggest completion, none of which truly belong to the author or the reader. This is another of my literary weaknesses, I suppose.

It may have been a weakness, but it was one my father was by now completely obsessed with. Each story wore the same obsessive themes like a suit, a different mask that hid the same face. At times I believe this obsession led to genius, but apparently not with this particular story idea. I could not find a shred of this story in any of my father's papers. If he ever attempted to write it, he disposed of all evidence.[21]

---

21 In fact, I found a version of this tale, amusingly called "The Story of Gombi," in Conlan's papers. How Mark missed it, I have no idea. The tale starts off with a Ray Bradbury-esque introduction:

I have many memories of many camp-outs with the boy scouts, nights among the crickets, hiding in tents from rain, or sweltering under the summer afternoon sun. But few memories stir my spirit as much as the campfires at night, singing songs, playing games, telling stories, and then, the incredible stillness afterwards, the embers of the fire a reflection of the stars above.

And of all those hundreds of campfire nights, none is as clear in my mind as the third night of my first week of summer camp. As the songs died and the stillness grew, I remember, with intricate detail, that the big moment had come.

From this point on, however, the story is remarkably circuitous, as it jumps around in time and perspective — sometimes we are hearing the eleven year old narrator listening to a "Tom Dempsey" telling the tale, sometimes we are hearing the thoughts of Dempsey as he tells the tale, and sometimes we even get the thoughts of the now adult narrator, named Richard, looking back on the tale as he tells the story to his son, (sometimes named James, sometimes Tom, sometimes Mark) around a campfire. The tale itself, about a young Vietnam vet whose house is accidently burned to the ground by two Boy Scouts, is hard to follow. In revenge for the killing of his family in the fire, "George Gombi, horribly disfigured," takes to stalking and murdering (with an ax) camping Boy Scouts. Still, at almost a hundred pages, the piece, jumping around as it does without explanation or warning, loses any

5. Written as history from the future: The story of how, after the Third Racial War, blacks everywhere commit mass suicide in an attempt to bring peace to the world. It does no good, of course, and hatred continues to exist as people find other excuses to kill each other.

Shortly after he wrote this entry, my father added: "This idea is unworkable. It is just too preposterous, too ponderous. Perhaps it can only be written as a dream."

This idea must've been very daunting for my father, and no complete stories based on it still exist. There are only three pages from any attempt to write this story, and they are the last three. In these pages, a white supremacist wakes from the aforementioned dream to find he can't find his light switches! Now my father's stories and ideas begin to keep folding back on themselves, and my father seemed to believe that here was where true brilliance lay. Nothing was ever complete. Everything simply suggested more paths. To my father, this was almost a metaphor for life in general, and his muse in particular.[22]

His next entry will interest fans of his novel.

6. A new version of *Darkness Rains*. I will, without rereading the first, published version, write it again. The prose will

---

sense of drama. Not only is the writing pedestrian here, but also largely ultimately indecipherable.

22 I found no evidence of these pages, and the handwriting of this entry in Richard's journal is noticeably different from the rest. I should also note that race would seem an important subject for both Richard and Mark — Richard, a WASP from New Jersey, married Toni, an African American woman from New York City, shortly before his writing career began. Indeed, Toni worked as a secretary for a law firm for a year or two while Richard toiled away before being published. Strangely, given the time period, I have found nothing written by Richard that touches on race. Indeed, the character Nelson Peterson is never fully described. He could certainly be African-American or white, but it does seem strange that the question is never raised. Mark, however, focused much of his career on race, teaching African-American history at Bard College, and being twice arrested at civil rights protests. I believe he added this section out of embarrassment for his father's silence on the issue.

> be different, if only because I am different because several years have passed. Different themes will be stressed, not from any definite purpose, but simply because age and experience has changed my perspective.

I never found any new versions of the novel, but evidence suggests (in the form of a letter to Putnam) that he did, in fact, rewrite it. The letter (which may or may not have been sent) asks the publisher to begin to publish the new version, which, he writes, "I have just finished writing," rather than the original. It goes on to suggest that every two years he plans to write and publish a new version. The letter ends by suggesting that, "one day, all novelists will do this."

It's hard to say whether the publisher rejected this idea (though how could they do otherwise?) or my father simply realized the idea was unpublishable before he sent the letter. Regardless, after his journal entry, he adds: "It would be impossible, of course, to ever write anything else in my short lifetime."

As I said, no new versions of my father's novel exist, save for earlier drafts, but there does exist pieces of a short story (or novel) about a novelist, Jonathan Menard, who writes a different version of the same novel every two years. This tale is, appropriately enough, incomplete. My father was growing more obsessed with the paradox of stories within stories, all incomplete. He was also freely realizing the limitations of himself (and any mortal) and his ideas. Rather than follow through on his idea, he decides to write instead about someone else who does, yet he never even finishes the story. This concept is completely valid to him since all of the different possibilities exist — the altered novel, for example — if only in the mind of the reader, all stemming from one simple idea.[23]

---

[23] Here is another point where Mark manages to miss something obvious. He says he finds no evidence of these attempts. But in fact, there are several manuscripts of *Darkness Rains* in the papers I studied at Bard. I can only assume that Mark assumed they were "earlier drafts" of the original novel but evidence — such as the apparent new technology of the manuscripts, suggest they were written after the original. I read through these with care,

7. An argument around a table about the "meaning of life" — the existence or non-existence of God, predestination vs. free will, etc... As each person speaks, it becomes clear to the reader that the speaker is right, and each man in turn alters the make-up and history of the entire universe unknowingly as he argues for his beliefs.

This somewhat muddy concept must've kept my father working for years. Many stories exist, as each person argues and my father would write a virtual philosophic history of the world based on that argument. Each history is a story unto itself, and they are all, admittedly, quite tedious. Included are glossaries of invented religions and histories of art and literature. Even several languages are invented here. My father's obsessions were certainly getting the best of him at this point. Much of time was had also clearly been taken up in research, as he has long tracts of notes of differing philosophies and religious views, complete with citation explanation. If the argument that he wrote was actually taking place in real-time, the characters would've been sitting around that table for months, perhaps years. Finally, after several hundred pages of this (all that remains, apparently, of several thousand), one of the men at the table claims that as they argue, the universe itself changes. At this point another laughs and asks, "What if we are but the dream of a madman, a storyteller who uses our very existence to tell a story?" and then the tale (thankfully) ends.

---

constantly comparing them with the published version. Some are definitely quite different. In one version, Nelson Peterson wakes up an old man remembering the events of the novel as if in a fog of dementia. This "fog" appears from time to time in the prose. Having promised the estate that I would not quote from any different versions of the novel I'd discover, I really cannot say a lot more on this subject. I will add that, remarkably, one manuscript is entirely the same as the published version save for the addition of a comma on page 25 of the published version, and the fact that Nelson leans on an chestnut tree on page 234 of the published version while leaning on an oak tree in the manuscript.

Once again my father obviously enjoys his manipulation of the reader, and once again, he tries to express that no story is ever really complete, that all are part of each other, and that any ideas that exist therein are purely in the mind of the writer or reader, and are only suggested rather than shown.[24]

8. The last tree on Earth, after environmental short-sightedness has destroyed all the others, is illegally climbed by some typical boys seeking adventure.

This is, in fact, the last major piece my father wrote, in his last year. The story is even complete, in several different versions. In one (written in first person), governmental forces capture the boys. In another (written in third person), the boys are killed in a minefield that surrounds the prized tree. In another, they succeed in climbing the tree and manage to escape into the night, bearing acorns, and telling the story to their friends. However, my father, in his obsession, jammed all these and several more versions into one, never explaining, for instance, how the boys, killed earlier, were now in jail, and on the next page, climbing the tree, nor does he explains the changes in point of view.[25]

My father was apparently trying to express the idea of unlimited ideas based on one concept into a single story. It was a

---

24 Again, no pages of this tale exist. While Mark found this work "tedious," I find this to be the most potentially intriguing tale in this list. I wish I had found just one or two of these glossaries or histories. Also this tale represents the concept of post-structuralism (itself, of course, deeply related to postmodernism). Here Richard Conlan seems to be commenting on post-structuralists like Derrida and Foucault. Post-structural linguists argue that, while we assume language describes reality, in fact, language constructs reality for all intents and purposes, by defining and thus limiting it. Conlan's story simply makes this concept more direct and literal—here the discussion literally creates the reality around the speakers, suggesting, I think, something about the importance of language and how we choose to use it. It also has a remarkably postmodern ending, allowing the characters in on the jest, making a space for play for the characters, author(s) and the reader.

25 Unfortunately these pages, too, are lost. One wonders if Richard's advancing illness was, in part, a cause for this disjointed work. Mark never mentions the possibility that Alzheimer's may be affecting Richard's prose.

valiant but vain attempt, since the story (which ends with the words "Or maybe it happened a different way...") is virtually incomprehensible. But with my father's next and final journal entry, he almost succeeded where earlier he had failed.

9. A story about a list of stories by an obsessive writer, perhaps dead, each tale unfinished or simply sketched-out ideas, that leave endless options for other writers, or in the imaginations of the readers. This story could express all of the ideas of a writer's lifetime, all the different versions and permutations of those ideas, since the stories themselves would exist only as ideas, suggestions for infinite possibilities. The list itself would be incomplete, like all important work of a lifetime, but in this way, a lifetime's work could at least suggest completion, could almost leave no tasks undone.

These are the last words my father apparently wrote as he was now facing the specter of Alzheimer's disease. I believe, in a way that his critics and readers never guessed, that he did finally realize his potential as a writer. And I daresay many writers could, and doubtless will, learn something from him, perhaps even attempting to cope, in their own ways, with the theories that drove his obsession, and, as he no doubt guessed and hoped, these theories will spawn many different interpretations.

Including, I fear, his son's.[26]

— Mark Conlan, April 1992

---

26 [And, of course, mine. Richard Conlan's remarkable career has opened up play for characters, readers, writers, and critics. Some more notes to complete this tale of incomplete tales: when authorities examined the house fire that apparently killed Mark Conlan and his family, and which destroyed most of the papers that Richard Conlan had left his son, they discovered two remarkable facts that the reader may already be guessing. The fire was apparently caused by two Boy Scouts who had wandered into Mark's yard, adjacent to woods adjacent to a Boy Scout camp, and Mark Conlan's body was never recovered. — James Speese, Ph.D.]

Bibliography

Bloom, Harold, ed. *Anthology of 20th Century Coming of Age Novellas.* London: Norton, 1980.

Conlan, Richard A. *Darkness Rains.* New York: Putnam, 1969.

Diaz, Julian. *Here Rains Darkness.* Buenos Aires: Arturo Publishing, 1972.

Harris, Jonah. "*Darkness* Will Tease Your Dreams." Review of *Darkness Rains,* by Richard A. Conlan. *LA Times Book Review,* May 15, 1969.

Miller, Donna. "Response to Conlan Story." *The New Yorker,* April 1, 1976.

Rogers, Phillip. "The Passing of a Forgotten Author." *New York Times,* Aug. 24, 1993.

12

Stirring the Sentient Dust: Marie-Rose Souci's *The Grey Moth*

Claire Daigle

"The grey layer of dust covering things has become their best part."
— Walter Benjamin

"Maybe meaning is in gazing till it hurts."
— Santiago Vizcaíno

The Grey Moth (1968) is the only known novel by Marie-Rose Souci.[1] While it is tempting to speculate that "Marie-Rose Souci"

---

1   Marie-Rose Souci, *The Grey Moth* (Paris: Editions Lits et Rature, 1968). Information about the author is scant. It arrives in the novel's short preface, quoted here in full:
    "Insects horrify me, not because of their alien monstrosity, but because I am wracked with guilt.
        At the age of eight, I collected butterflies. Wonder turned to gnawing anxiety as their delicate corpses piled up in airless jars. I became aware of the human capacity for cruelty.
        Years later, on a night in June, a pale green Luna moth landed just below my left collarbone. Its wings spanned the length of a large hand. The beast, quivering with exhaustion, was so fragile that any attempt to brush it away would crush it. The intimacy was excruciating. When it gathered the force to fly off, tears streamed down my face.

is a *nom de plume* — whose, we may never know.[2] Souci's *The Grey Moth* received mean-spirited reviews upon initial publication in France. Pierre Rocher, for example, wrote: "Box the old girl up with naphthalene. The rest of us are writers. Souci just gathers dust."[3] Souci's style was repeatedly denigrated as an es-

---

> I learned that Luna moths do not possess a mechanism for eating. They cannot and do not consume. Their ravishing imago stage lasts for less than a week, time only to astonish with airy luminescence and to produce ravenous grubs that will gorge themselves on the tender leaves of sweet gum, walnut, and birch trees.
>
> I am haunted by that encounter. This book is the result of yearning for that stranger.

Souci takes pains to stress that the artist, the only (human) character in the book, becomes fully sensate by rendering a world that is, in and of itself, sensate. This authorial stance anticipates the realization of the world's imperiled existence in the waning light of the Anthropocene Era.

2   The writer's name echoes "Rrose Sélavy" (itself the homophone of *"Eros, c'est la vie."*). Rrose Sélavy was the female alter ego of artist Marcel Duchamp. He performed Rrose in drag and she often provided the signature for works attributed to him. Might Duchamp, modern art's *éminence grise*, lurk somewhere in Souci's environs? Once one has caught whiff of dada hijinks, associations proliferate. It would do *The Grey Moth* and its author a disservice to suggest overt affiliation with Duchamp, however.

   Nevertheless, with the mere addition of an acute accent over a feminizing second "e", the name Marie becomes *"la mariée"* ("bride"). One work begs noting here: Duchamp's diabolically enigmatic *La mariée mise à nu par ses célibataires, même* (*The Bride Stripped Bare by her Bachelors, Even*) — also known as *The Large Glass*. The work, begun in 1915, was left "definitively unfinished" in 1923. It is accompanied by copious annotations gathered in *The Green Box*. *The Grey Moth* was completed in 1968, the year that Duchamp died. Ultimately, this reader would argue that any Duchampian allusions are illusions, perhaps meant to put the reader off the trail of the Author (or to kill him off altogether). Souci seems to prefer to raise the wraith of Rrose.

3   Pierre Rocher, "La mite poussiéreuse," *La Planète*, January 4, 1969, 27. In what is likely a paraphrase, Rocher misconstrued the closing line of John Cage's verbal composition, "26 Statements Re Duchamp" from 1964: "History / The danger remains that he'll get out of the valise we put him in. So long as he remains locked up — / The rest of them were artists. Duchamp collects dust." Cage knew full well that his conceptual conspirator, Marcel Duchamp, was art's Harry Houdini. (John Cage, "26 Statements Re Duchamp," in *A Year from Monday — New Lectures and Writings* [Middletown: Wesleyan University Press, 1968], 70).

pecially egregious instance of purple prose.⁴ Alain Robbe-Grillet was "bored stiff" by the book. He claimed that its writer failed to obey the rigid strictures of the New French Novel.⁵ When the English translation appeared in the United States in 1973,⁶ Norman Raymond chided Souci for "doing little more than conjuring up the tedious specter of a desiccated spinster."⁷ Raymond,

---

4 This reader would propose an alternative term to counter the disparaging term "purple prose": *l'écriture mauve*. The coinage is meant to call to mind, glancingly, *l'écriture féminine*, associated primarily with the French theorist Hélène Cixous. *L'écriture féminine* is defined, *essentially*, as writing that issues from specifically female bodies. While the "too-much" of Souci's prose style was derided by critics, the term *l'écriture mauve* means to describe writing like hers that issues from eccentric bodies of many proclivities. The chromatic tinge of this term takes on specific and powerful significance in *The Grey Moth*.
   The affective tone struck by Souci's pale purpling of the yellowing page calls to mind director Lars von Trier's poignant palette in the twelve-minute, slow motion prelude to the film *Melancholia* (2011). In both, the eerie hue establishes crepuscular calm tinged with dread and anticipating a cataclysmic end. At the close of von Trier's opening sequence, the planet *Melancholia* collides with Earth, sending up great plumes of dust.
5 Alain Robbe-Grillet, *For a New Novel* [1963], trans. Richard Howard (Evanston: University of Illinois Press, 1989). The writing that Robbe-Grillet called for was to be characterized by multiple visual perspectives, attention to the matter and surface of things, phenomenological orientation, and strict avoidance of expressions of interior states of being. There is no small irony in his critique since one is hard pressed to find a novel more fitting of this definition than *The Grey Moth*.
6 The English translation was published by Nightwood Press, which seems to have only one other title in its catalog: Georgina Peacher's *Mary Stuart's Ravishment Descending Time* (New York: Nightwood Press, 1972). The ear catches something uncannily familiar in Peacher's "mesmeric" prose: "Mary's eyes syncopated spectrums; oranged coppered yellowed pumpkined ambered lava-fountained blued primrosed, rheostated golds in bolder flakes… Irises thinned; gilded eminences embraced night jewels. Onyx breathed. Stars fainted" (5). No translator is credited for *The Grey Moth*. One might make the cautious assumption that Souci translated the book herself.
7 It seems possible that Souci may have been up to another Duchampian trick. The name Man Ray crouches within that of Nor*man Ray*mond. Given that the only mention of Raymond's review occurs in Banes and Barnes (see note 8) without citation, this reader would speculate that Souci penned the review herself (Deirdre Banes and Susan Barnes, "Dust and the Moth's Do-

and the French critics preceding him, were countered with tepid defense of Souci by feminist scholars.[8]

While the assumption that Souci's single character — the moth-artist — is a woman has long held, nothing in the novel overtly supports this. Souci avoids most possessive pronouns and eschews gendered pronouns altogether. Such difficult verbal maneuvering is particularly challenging in the original French. The writer performs a feat as deft as the linguistic acrobatics of the writers involved with Oulipo (*Ouvroir de littérature potentielle*). Rumor has it that Souci was associated with the mysterious *L'hache au cou*, the clandestine group within Oulipo, said to be comprised mainly of its few female participants.[9] But Souci's

---

    mestic Rebellion," *The Mistress of the House* [New York: The Feminist Press, 1974], 178–97, at 182).

    In 1920, Man Ray photographed Duchamp's *The Large Glass* lying prone, after a year's worth of gathering dust. The image, the result of a two-hour exposure, depicts a complex topography of indeterminable scale. When the photograph was published in the journal *Littérature* in 1921, it was accompanied by a caption that read: "Behold the domain of Rrose Sélavy / how arid it is / how fertile it is / how joyous it is / how sad it is!" (David Campany, *A Handful of Dust: from the Cosmic to the Domestic*, exh. cat. [Paris: Le Bal and Mack, 2015], 10).

8 Deirdre Banes and Susan Barnes, "Dust and the Moth's Domestic Rebellion," 178–97. Banes and Barnes describe "the artist's labors as the desperate expression of a housewife suffocated by the confining role assigned to her by patriarchal dominance. Souci's insistence that the only creative path open to the woman artist is her refusal to keep the home 'neat and tidy' is devastating" (194). Another characteristic statement reads: "Refusing the cultural imperative to be a mother, she stubbornly remains a moth" (187). The importance of Banes and Barnes breaking of feminist ground should not be underestimated, yet the particular and peculiar creative labors performed by both Souci and the (indeterminately gendered) moth-artist are pulverized by such a blunt argument. If the reader will excuse a lapse into popular culture: "You can't use a bulldozer to study orchids." (The Magnetic Fields's "The Death of Ferdinand de Saussure," *69 Love Songs*, Merge Records, 1999).

9 The possibly mythic L'hache au cou is said to have been the short-lived "Sister Society" within the Oulipo group, formed by the American writer Alice Bee. L'hache au cou is a homophone for *L.H.O.O.Q.*, Duchamp's salacious send up of the *Mona Lisa*. L'hache au cou translates "Axe to the neck." (For more, see Clementine Finn, *Flamboyant Conceits* [San Francisco: A Press of One's Own], 2006).

wordplay functions not only as a generative conceit, it clears space for other forms of force and agency to emerge. Souci radically challenges the traditional Western subject, queerly dislodging the obstinate gender binary that accompanies it, as well as the presumption of human control — manifested most markedly by the I/eye — over other worldly ways of being and becoming.

Marie-Rose Souci and this astonishing work — like its eponymous, anonymous moth-artist — have almost fallen beneath notice. This essay's primary aims are to acknowledge the writer's extraordinary literary achievement, to draw scholarly attention to the book, and to posit its considerable significance in the present moment. Otherwise, this reader hopes only to extend a retelling of the odd tale of the moth before it vanishes.

The Grey Moth is a thicket of idiosyncrasies that is dense with literary, mythological, and art-historical allusions. Thus far, the knotty strands of its associative web have yet to be disentangled.[10] The novel — now over half a century old — anticipated many contemporary bookish and artistic concerns. The literary genre of the New Weird, for instance, certainly owes much to the writer. Souci's themes, narrative strategies, peculiar style, and dark tone haunt a growing number of artists, filmmakers, and writers, whether they recognize "the Souci effect" at work or not.[11] In time, readers and researchers might catch up with the relentlessly patient Souci.

Deserving of particular consideration is Souci's linguistic virtuosity. Taking on a subject that could not be more parched, her writing is plush with precise description and glimmers with poetic effects. Souci persistently struggles, struggles extravagantly,

---

10 For example, art historians have yet to consider the work of Souci's artist in relation to kin laborers. The moth-artist's work calls immediately to mind Vija Celmins's trompe-l'oeil drawing of a dustscape of in *Irregular Desert* (1972).
11 American novelist Nicholson Baker's sharp powers of observation that carve thin temporal slices of mundane experience might serve as one literary point of comparison. In The Mezzanine, for example, he details a lunch hour escalator ride in one-hundred-and-forty-four pages with copious, digressive footnotes (Nicholson Baker, *The Mezzanine: A Novel* [London: Everyman Paperbacks, 1988]).

to defy the limited capacity of words to register the multifarious substances of life. The challenge to render sheer matter legible is met by the writer's surfeit of prose.

The Grey Moth opens with the figure of an ordinary moth[12] warming itself on a slate windowsill. Camouflaged, it almost fades into stone. A slight twitch catches the eye of an artist on the other side of a dusty glass windowpane:

> The residual markings of "false" eyes looked back. Inconspicuous as they appeared, the displaced eyes had the power to deflect the perilous gaze of a predator. The moth's tiny setae, feathery and finely tuned, quivered and reached, but reached toward what? A kind of knowing of the world in a manner and at a scale that was altogether alien. Its wings tentatively […] incrementally spread open, offering the revelation of pale pigment, a pinkish-purple reveling in the reserved dominion of grey. Harkened, the artist became something other — became determined to seek and to see harder.[13]

---

12 Vera Nadeau (who shares her initials with the avid pursuer of blue butterflies Vladimir Nabokov) is a lepidopterist based in Toulouse, specializing in the genus *Hyles*. She has determined that the moth Souci describes, in nearly forty pages of exhaustive detail (24–63), is of the species *Hyles verspertilio*. "*Vespertilio*" refers to its batlike appearance. Most would not find the creature visually appealing. It measures between two-and-a-half-to-three inches from wingtip to wingtip and has a stout, hairy body. *Hyles vespertilio* is awkwardly proportioned: it wings seem too small to lend flight to such bulk. It is uniformly pigeon-grey when its wings lie flat. However — and of utmost significance to the novel — when its top wings unfold, a startling glimpse of pigmentation appears on the hind wings. The color is an embarrassed blush pink. Important, however, is the fact that Souci describes the shade as *pinkish purple*. This slight color distinction suggests to Nadeau that the author refers to a subspecies of *Hyles vespertilio* that is now extinct.

13 Souci, *The Grey Moth*, 4. Roland Barthes's words on color never seemed more apt than when applied to the swoon caused by the tender gift at the crook of those untucked wings: "But what is color? A kind of bliss […]It suffices that color appear, that it be there, that it be inscribed like a pinprick in the corner of an eye […] it suffices that color lacerate something, that it pass in front of the eye, like an apparition — or a disappearance, for color is like a closing eyelid, a tiny fainting spell." (Roland Barthes, "Cy Twombly: Works

This tiniest of wing tremors is of greatest consequence. The artist senses the sentience of other-than-human existence and is driven to move toward it, closer to the "soft, glimmering grains of pollen that nuance trembling wings [...] [their thinness] as bewilderingly slim as the space between the recto and verso of a leaf of tracing paper."[14] This extraordinary instant of encounter flows in slow motion through the honey-dense span of a life spent searching for significance. Once the artist's eyes shift downward to the walnut tabletop burnished by the pressures of hand heel and pencil on page, the humble specks gathering there upon it fall into focus. From that point on, the artist patiently strives to draw dust — just dust in all its humility — with pencils of sharper and sharper points:

> Friable threads of lead encased in slivers of silvered wood, honed with a glinting razor to superlative fineness. The pencil-pin tips met specifications suited to registering particulate distinctions.[15]

Thus the field of vision narrows as attention intensifies — magnifying, granting magnitude, to that which is infinitesimal and utterly abject.

The moth-artist remains nameless and faceless, back turned to the reader, hunched over the page. What emerges from the

---

on Paper," trans. Richard Howard, in *The Responsibility of Forms* [Berkeley: University of California Press, 1985], 166).

An oblique tangent: the meaning of the name Souci encompasses a small range of emotions: "care," "worry," "anxiety," "trouble" — as well as, quite surprisingly, the burst of orange that is "marigold."

14 This phrase bears close resemblance to Duchamp's "as thin as the space between the front and the back side of a sheet of paper." For such nearly inconceivable intervals, Duchamp used the neologism, "the *inframince*." The term gestures toward liminal passages in which the slightest degrees of material exchange occur: "when the smoke of the tobacco smells also of the mouth from which it comes" or "the warmth of a seat which has just been left." (Marcel Duchamp, *Notes,* arr. and trans. Paul Matisse [Boston: G.K. Hall, 1983]).

15 Souci, *The Grey Moth,* 67.

shade of solitude, from the no-place with dust-felted contours, is a hand. What can barely be beheld is that the hand is never still. Its innumerable gestures are not meant to stave off dust's inevitable encroachment, but only to bear witness to the tiniest degrees of difference, nearly not there, in the stuff of the world.[16] As a scrutinizing, haptic gaze attends to the nubby dustscape, an illegible microscript comes to flannel countless sheets of fine-grained paper.[17] The marks are signs destined, perhaps, for other modes of sensing. Particles of graphite shimmer at the threshold of human perception.[18]

---

[16] Roland Barthes, *The Neutral: Lecture Course at the Collège de France (1977–1978),* trans. Thomas Clerc (New York: Columbia University Press, 2007), 51: "[T]he Neutral is the shimmer: that whose aspect, perhaps whose meaning, is subtly modified according to the angle of the subject's gaze." The seminar Barthes taught on the neuter blossomed from the following incident. Barthes, while purchasing ink, became curious about what color was contained by the bottle labeled "Neutral" might be. So eager to find out, he spilled it all over his desk, and discovered that it was violet-grey.

[17] While vision generally dominates the hierarchical scale of sensory perception, Souci attends on nearly every page to the sense of touch (and as the novel progresses, to smell and sound, as well). While turning the pages of the book, readers come to feel the dust clogging skin pores. Fingertips become tender from fine abrasion.

[18] The book design of *The Grey Moth* is extraordinary in that it redoubles the shimmering effect. Whenever the word "dust" appears, it is printed in dark grey ink, just a degree or two lighter than standard black printer's ink. Typographically, a slim margin of extra space has been left between the word "moth" and the words preceding and following it. In each instance, the page quivers; the gaze trembles. The latter is only one small example, among others, of the care Souci pays not only to words, but also to the meaningful silences between them.

This flickering of altered intervals on the page is nearly as subtle as that of film projected at twenty-four frames per second. The blank spaces between frames are *nearly* perceptible, extending into the realm Walter Benjamin described as "the optical unconscious," the site of images that the brain thinks it does not see (Walter Benjamin, *The Work of Art at the Age of Its Mechanical Reproducibility and Other Writings on Media,* trans. Edmund Jephcott et al. [Cambridge: Harvard University Press, 2008], 37).

Grey-scale gradations range from the most luminous white toward the most devouring black.[19] And yet the grisaille is haunted by prismatic apparitions:

In this situation of drastically reduced sensory stimulation, it seemed to occur to the moth-artist, perhaps erroneously, that the enveloping dust was comprised in large measure of wing-loosed scales. This resulted in scintillating variegations of color. What seemed to a careless eye to be duly and dully grey, appeared to the artist as possessing infinite chromatic modulation, resplendent with fugitive flashes of violet and far rarer mercurial glints."[20]

The narrative action of the novel, of a perversely protracted sort, can be summed up in two words: "becoming dust." The verb here functions transitively and intransitively, doubly meaningful: "the moth-artist becomes dust" and "the dust merely becomes." After the initial encounter with the moth,[21] whatever

---

19 "Whether all grow black, or all grow bright, or all remain grey, it is grey we need, to begin with, because of what it is, and of what it can do, made of bright and black, able to shed the former, or the latter, and be the latter or the former alone" (Samuel Beckett, *The Unnamable* [1953], in *Three Novels: Malone, Malone Dies, The Unnamable* [New York: Grove Press, 2009], 295).

20 Souci, *The Grey Moth*, 94–95. The violet-ing of grey, occurring in the novel's most moving passages, is so effective because the reader has, under Souci's spell, come to inhabit this moth-grey realm. It is perhaps worth mentioning that moth vision greatly extends far beyond human vision into the ultraviolet range.

21 The impact of this encounter, accompanied by heightened sensitivity, might have been influenced by Virginia Woolf's essay "The Death of the Moth." Woolf extends compassion at its smallest scale as she witnesses the death throes of a moth and acknowledges its mortality (and her own). Consider the following passage: "Also, when there was nobody to care or to know, this gigantic effort on the part of an insignificant little moth, against a power of such magnitude, to retain what no one else valued or desired to keep, moved one strangely. Again, somehow, one saw life, a pure bead." (Virginia Woolf, "The Death of the Moth," in *The Death of the Moth and Other Essays* [New York: Harcourt Brace Jovanovich, 1974], 6).

A similar instinct compelled filmmaker Stan Brakhage to make his cameraless, labor intensive three-minute film *Mothlight* (1963): "Over the

narrative action unfolds, unfolds at a table in the confines of a hushed room.[22] At one point the author questions urgently: "What is the thrum of dust? Dry scratching at an itch? The susurrations of belabored breath? Insect wing beats? The seething of mites? Silence."[23] In this realm, the sound-dampening dust is the only marker of time — or rather, it serves not to measure but to thicken time.

Well into the narrative, an unexpected occurrence — quite momentous in this context — indicates that other spaces exist outside the room: "an errant, redolent scent — agitated molecules in porous air — insinuates itself."[24] The odor calls for a differently adapted means of perception. Drawing fails it.

---

lightbulbs there's all these dead moth wings, and I hate that. Such a sadness; there must surely be something to do with that. I tenderly picked them out and start pasting them onto a strip of film, to try to give them life again, to animate them again, to try to put them into some sort of life through the motion picture machine." (Stan Brakhage in a 2002 interview with Bruce Kawin, for By *Brakhage: An Anthology*, Volumes 1 and 2, DVD, Criterion Collection, 2003).

22 The space might be imagined like a paper construction of another great dust dweller, Bruno Schulz: "From the rustle of sheets, from the ceaseless turning over of pages, arose the squared empty existence of that room" (Bruno Schulz, "The Night of the Great Season," in *The Street of Crocodiles and Other Stories*, trans. Celina Wieniewska [London: Penguin Books, 2012], 134).

This reader also imagines, perhaps too romantically, the moth-artist's room as a vision of intensified quietude much like the exquisite, nearly monochromatic painting *Dustmotes Dancing in the Sunbeams* (1900), by the Danish artist Vilhelm Hammershøi. The painter perfected the backscatter effect by which dust particles floating midair become visible and grant substance to light. Note also that the closed door depicted in *Dustmotes Dancing* lacks a knob.

23 Souci, *The Grey Moth*, 246.

24 The aroma Souci might have had in mind could have been that of Un Air Embaumé. The perfume — with a bouquet of ambergris, heliotrope, bergamot, and almond — was produced by Rigaud and sold between 1915 and 1968. It was initially packaged in a coffin-shaped box. A flacon of Un Air Embaumé was used by Duchamp for his *Belle Haleine, Eau de Violette* in 1921. The label featured Rrose Sélavy in a photograph taken by Man Ray. (For more see Bonnie Jean Garner, "Duchamp Bottles Belle Greene: Just Desserts for His Canning," *tout-fait: The Marcel Duchamp Studies Online Journal* 1, no. 2 [May 2000], http://www.toutfait.com/issues/issue_2/News/garner.html.)

The moth-artist, for the first time, turns away from the work on the table. The frame of vision expands dramatically to register that the room has become a grey garden of shambolic grace. Specks have succumbed to electrostatic tugs. Impossibly delicate filaments have formed dust-spun webs, shivering with each faint gust of breath. Another force reveals its slow, incessant labor. Something apart from human endeavor is coming into play.

The lengthy, deceptively predictable denouement of *The Grey Moth* involves the attenuated process by which the artist slowly goes "dustblind," then crumbles like a doddering entomologist's specimen in a reliquary napped with grey velvet.[25] As though in mourning, moths amass.

> Countless ghastly woolen bodies scramble and softly thud their plump bellies against the window, leaving smudged blooms of pollen as offerings. Frenzied wings flutter in wild grief, glinting light and casting off swarms of untamed gazes.[26]

Then, in an instant, the moths disperse. Time becomes inconceivably slow. "The window panes thicken at bottom. In response to gravity's tug, glass reveals its liquid nature. But reveals it to whom?"[27]

Like the moth-artist, Souci cloaks the page with attention. In passages as uncompromisingly perceptive as those drawn on the moth-frayed tatters of paper piled up and abandoned on the

---

25 If one asks the enigmatic David Wilson, Director of the Museum of Jurassic Technology in Los Angeles, about museum conservation, he might recount a favorite incident (that might or might not have occurred). After the San Fernando earthquake in 1971, the museum's display of extinct nineteenth-century French moths remained nearly intact. But one moth was reduced to a little pile of opalescent dust around an obsolete pin, "More beautiful than the others," he might say, fiddling with his accordion. "Beautiful, just beautiful."

26 Souci, *The Grey Moth*, 288.

27 Ibid., 289.

table, Souci feels her way through the dark to the moment when the gaze loosens its grip:

> The artist faithfully recorded, but did not remember, will not be remembered. The moth-artist just barely existed at the pale of perception. It is as though the grey moth might never have alit on the warm sill, or as though the dust might never have settled, might never have been set upon by the most generous gaze. Each fleeting event occurred only as the tiniest particular teeming among countless others.[28]

At this moment, something else takes (its) place — with the turn of what might be described as "particulate gazes," issuing from the entropic stuff of dust.[29]

What begins to stir upon the moth-artist's death is something other than human. The most miniscule forces — of dust, of pollen, of spores, of mites — quicken to stave off the nullity of night. Draft-stirred motes are backlit by "faint vespertine incandescence," gaining in intensity.[30] The dust scatters the silver and violet light[31] as it surges through widening fissures in the brittle

---

28 Ibid., 302.

29 Souci anticipates the power that Reza Negarestani would attribute to dust in his singular *Cyclonopedia*: "Each particle of dust carries with it a unique vision of matter, movement, collectivity, interaction, affect, differentiation, composition and infinite darkness. […] There is no line of narration more concrete than a stream of dust particles" (Reza Negarestani, *Cyclonopedia: Complicity with Anonymous Materials* [Melbourne: re.press, 2008], 43).

30 Souci, *The Grey Moth,* 330. The phrasing, "faint vespertine incandescence," might be a sly reference to the title of Vladimir Nabokov's deliriously annotated novel, *Pale Fire* (New York: G.P. Putnam's Sons, 1962).

31 The long-awaited unbridling of color has an overwhelming effect after the unrelenting immersion in grey. While color has appeared as foreshadowing — in the glimpse at the hind wings of the *Hyles vespertilio,* in the violeting of dust by wing scales — such glimpses have served only to make the reader's yearning for color stronger. When chromo-luminescence breaks through, it is an exquisite gift to the patient reader, offering nothing short of the bliss Barthes describes (see note 13). By no other means than the preposterously thick felting of language could Souci have produced a reader so precisely calibrated to be ravished by color and light. The effect is reminiscent of the scene in director Andrei Tarkovsky's film *Stalker* (1979) when a

panes.³² Ultimately, the gloom of the artist's moth-grey microcosm — at once enchanted and horrific — twins the precarious twilit world outside, as it ceaselessly, splendorously, grinds down. Yet becomes, never still.³³

---

guide and two searchers make slow passage into the realm known as the Zone. As they approach, green seeps up to stain the grey film stock. The coming into being of color indicates the men's arrival in the mysterious realm that has its eyes turned upon the seekers. Geoff Dyer describes the force of Tarkovsky's restrained use of color: "Technically this concentrated sepia was achieved by filming in colour and printing in black-and-white. The result is a kind of sub-monochrome in which the spectrum has been so compressed that it might turn out to be a source of energy" (Geoff Dyer, *Zona: A Book about a Film about a Journey to a Room* [New York: Pantheon Books, 2012], 8).

32 In 1926, Duchamp's *The Large Glass* cracked, too.
33 The novel's ending is neither apocalyptic nor redemptive. Like the moth-artist that Souci conjures, her work hovers wraithlike at a burgeoning threshold.

Bibliography

Baker, Nicholson. *The Mezzanine: A Novel*. London: Everyman Paperbacks, 1988.

Banes, Deirdre, and Susan Barnes. "Dust and the Moth's Domestic Rebellion." In *The Mistress of the House*, 178–97. New York: The Feminist Press, 1974.

Barthes, Roland. "Cy Twombly: Works on Paper." Translated by Richard Howard. In *The Responsibility of Forms*, 157–76. Berkeley: University of California Press, 1985.

———. *The Neutral: Lecture Course at the Collège de France (1977–1978)*. Translated by Thomas Clerc. New York: Columbia University Press, 2007.

Samuel Beckett, *The Unnamable* [1953]. In *Three Novels: Malone, Malone Dies, The Unnamable*, 332–474. New York: Grove Press, 2009.

Benjamin, Walter. *The Work of Art at the Age of Its Mechanical Reproducibility and Other Writings on Media*. Translated by Edmund Jephcott et al. Cambridge: Harvard University Press, 2008.

Brakhage, Stan. *By Brakhage: An Anthology*, Volumes 1 and 2, DVD, Criterion Collection, 2003.

Cage, John. "26 Statements Re Duchamp." In *A Year from Monday — New Lectures and Writings*, 70–72. Middletown: Wesleyan University Press, 1968.

Campany, David. *A Handful of Dust: from the Cosmic to the Domestic*. Exhibition catalog. Paris: Le Bal and Mack, 2015.

Duchamp, Marcel. *Notes*. Arranged and translated by Paul Matisse. Boston: G.K. Hall, 1983.

Dyer, Geoff. *Zona: A Book about a Film about a Journey to a Room*. New York: Pantheon Books, 2012.

Finn, Clementine. *Flamboyant Conceits*. San Francisco: A Press of One's Own, 2006.

Garner, Bonnie Jean. "Duchamp Bottles Belle Greene: Just Desserts for His Canning." *tout-fait: The Marcel Duchamp Studies Online Journal* 1, no. 2 (May 2000). http://www.toutfait.com/issues/issue_2/News/garner.html.

Negarestani, Reza. *Cyclonopedia: Complicity with Anonymous Materials.* Melbourne: re.press, 2008.

Robbe-Grillet, Alain. *For a New Novel.* Translated by Richard Howard. Evanston: University of Illinois Press, 1989.

Rocher, Pierre. "La mite poussiéreuse." *La Planète,* January 4, 1969.

Schulz, Bruno. "The Night of the Great Season." In *The Street of Crocodiles and Other Stories,* translated by Celina Wieniewska, 132–44. London: Penguin Books, 2012.

Souci, Marie-Rose. *The Grey Moth*. Paris: Editions Lits et Rature, 1968.

The Magnetic Fields. "The Death of Ferdinand de Saussure." *69 Love Songs.* Merge Records, 1999.

Virginia Woolf, "The Death of the Moth." In *The Death of the Moth and Other Essays,* 9–12. New York: Harcourt Brace Jovanovich, 1974.

13

Traduttore, Traditore: Authorial Inconsistencies in the Works of Redondo Panza

Julia Coursey
Originally published in the Collagist Issue Ninety-Two

"Todas las familias felices se parecen unas a otras; pero cada familia infeliz tiene un motivo especial para sentirse desgraciada," or, roughly, "All happy families are similar to one another; but every unhappy family has its own special reason to feel itself wretched," is the phrase that begins the now standard Editorial Iberia translation of Tolstoy's *Anna Karenina*.[1] From the very start, then, the reader can see that Panza's *Karenina* would diverge from the Russian—"Todas las familias felices se parecen unas a otras; pero cada familia infeliz tiene un motivo especial para matar," or "All happy families are similar to one another; but every unhappy family has its own motive to kill."[2] Despite his long reign as the preeminent translator of Russian literature into Spanish, Juan Carlos Redondo Panza's later works have long been a subject of some speculation, as they quite clearly diverge

---

1 Liev Nikoláievich Tolstói, *Ana Karenina*, trans. Editorial Iberia (Madrid: Austral, 2010), 1.
2 Liev Nikoláievich Tolstói, *Ana Karenina*, trans. Redondo Panza, Juan Carlos, and Panza Martín (Madrid: Ediciones Halcon, 1939), 1.

from his customary translation style and the original texts. Panza's early work has been seen as influential in the Spanish intelligentsia's resistance to Franco, even more so than his overtly political anti-fascist organizing. *Anna Karenina* is the turning point in his oeuvre, the transition from the political tirades of his earlier works to the almost entirely fabricated later volumes.

For many years, very little was known about the life of Redondo Panza. Thanks to the generosity of the Fulbright Foundation and the Ministry of Sports, Education, and Culture (MEDC), I was able to go to Madrid and consult the small number of drafts that have turned up in various contexts as well as the original manuscripts sent to Panza's publisher. Additionally, I traveled to Cádiz and conducted original research into the life of his stepsister, Panza Martín. In this way, I was able to determine conclusively that not only was Redondo Panza dead by the time *Anna Karenina* was published, his later translations were almost certainly written by his stepsister, Maria de los Angeles Panza Martín. For the purposes of this paper, I have translated her translations into English.

A thorough perusal of the Cádiz archives reveals that Redondo Panza was arrested upon using the informal *tú* with a fascist officer, and, after resisting this arrest, was slated to be killed. His execution was recorded, but three weeks after his presumed death his publisher received a final copy of his translation of *War and Peace* sent by Panza while in hiding. This edition appears to be entirely authored by Redondo Panza, albeit with a looser interpretation of the text than one might anticipate. Tolstoy's theory of history is radically altered, with a new focus on the power of collective action to change the course of history. The unrest among the serfs that brings together Marya and Rostrov in the original book ends with a kind of utopian workers state. Unhindered by the shackles of serfdom, the workers implement various farming improvements and spend their free time educating themselves with the books they find in the estate's library. The movement spreads and Napoleon's soldiers desert en masse, preferring to live out their lives in the Russian countryside.[3]

While this diverges wildly from Tolstoy's plot, much of Panza's translation remains wholly faithful to the original (in particular, Pierre's time as a prisoner of war), requiring the author/translator to have a working knowledge of Russian. It is this text that most fully aligns with the Marxist school of Panza studies, as his earliest translations are more faithful to the original texts and the later translations seem less directly concerned with the plight of the working class. While Simmons and Hammerschmidt have both put forward plausible interpretations of a few of the later translations (most notably in Hammerschmidt's analysis of *Brothers K*[4]), neither has been able to fully integrate *Anna Karenina* into their theories.

It appears that the beginning of Anna Karenina was also translated, though heavily edited. The level of accuracy observed in the first half of the text and the wild disregard for Tolstoy's story in the second half give the work an almost schizophrenic feel—as if it had been authored by more than one person. According to Águila, Redondo Panza was in Cádiz to visit his stepsister at the time it would have been translated, with whom he had always had something of a fraught relationship. The two of them were the same age, the brother always preferred by his mother. Both were ignored by her father, who drank heavily.[5] While Redondo Panza remained in school through his teenage years, Panza Martín was pulled out at age eight to help her stepmother around the house. When she was 14, Maria de los Angeles married Miguel Joaquim Repiso Martín, a greengrocer who often gave her stepmother good deals on produce.[6] Her new husband died in rather mysterious circumstances a month

---

3   Liev Nikoláievich Tolstói, *Guerra y paz,* trans. Redondo Panza (Madrid: Ediciones Halcon, 1938), 759.
4   Hans Hammerschmidt, *Spanish Inquisition: Redondo Panza's Brothers Karamazov* (Chicago: The University of Chicago Press, 2006)
5   Eduardo Rafael Revilla Águila, *Picturing Panza: A Translator's Biography* (Madrid: Grupo SM, 1998), 17.
6   Ibid., 23–45.

or so after the wedding — official cause of death was listed as choking on an orange, but the mortician originally suspected suffocation.[7]

Panza Martín took over the business, which she was very adept at running, though she had little respect for the deals her late husband had worked out with various townspeople.[8] Official reports indicate that she was hiding Redondo Panza in her attic for almost six months before he was discovered, having ventured into the store on the ground level for a snack when one of the nosier members of the community, Marta Gutierrez, was passing by.[9] Gutierrez maintains that she did not intend to inform on him, but told a few people about the apparition, unsure if he was a ghost.[10] The building was soon searched, and Panza Martín was found standing over the corpse of her brother, a revolver in her hand. She told the soldiers that he had been hiding there without her knowledge, that he had been stealing her food. She killed him herself, for that was how committed she was to Franco. She called upon God to "forgive [her], but to damn [her brother] to hell for the way he had betrayed his country."[11] A brief review of her accounts provides evidence that there was an immediate drop off in customers, and one month after the death of her stepbrother the shop was closed.[12] Six months later, Redondo Panza's publisher received a manuscript for *Anna Karenina*. Not knowing that Redondo Panza was actually dead, as opposed to his previous position of pretending to be dead, the publisher reviewed it and printed it without much fuss, opening the door to further pseudotranslations from his stepsister, Panza Martín.

Reading Panza Martín's *Karenina* through the lens of her life provides a new perspective on the translation. The novel first begins to go off the rails when Vronsky and Anna are travel-

---

7 "Chisme y chistes," *Diario de Cádiz*, May 26, 1934, C4.
8 Maria Julia Gutierrez, Personal interview, April 1, 4, 5, 7, 11, 2017.
9 "Ha muerto un traidor," *Diario de Cádiz*, April 4, 1939, D9.
10 Gutierrez, Personal interview.
11 "Ha muerto un traidor," D9.
12 Ibid.

ling through Europe. Anna grows tired of Vronsky's pretensions and finds herself increasingly unable to communicate with him. This comes to a head when the two of them stop at the Atocha Station in Madrid, a historical impossibility as the station was not built until several years after the initial publication of the novel.[13] Anna and Vronsky drink a relaxing cup of cafe con leche and split a plate of churros while they wait for the train to Barcelona. Vronsky spends pages monologuing about his "new theory of art," which he believes will render all previous artistic endeavors useless.[14] Meanwhile, Anna feels the baby kicking and wonders what kind of life her child will have with this man as his father. Anna reaches for the last churro, but Vronsky unthinkingly snaches it from the plate, resulting in an emotional turning point: "Anna felt as though she were a ghost, an invisible presence who could only be seen when she was angry."[15] Anna decides to remain silent, to see how long it will take Vronsky to notice that she has removed herself from the conversation, and he manages to speak to himself for another two hours, only acknowledging her when insisting she hurry up so they would not miss the train. As the engine approaches the platform, Anna bends down to get something from her suitcase, knocking the bag that contains Vronsky's paintings onto the tracks. Panicked, Vronsky jumps in front of the train, willing to die for his art in a scene that mirrors the early death of the railway worker.[16]

Her train delayed and her lover deceased, Anna spends a few hours looking at the paintings in the Prado, noting "the sad eyes of the women, forever trapped in their poses."[17] Still pregnant, Anna feels compelled to return to Moscow and throw herself on the mercy of her husband. But a miscarriage while the train is stopped in Paris causes her to reconsider. She checks into a hotel near the Louvre to recover, and spends some time exploring

---

13 "Estación de Madrid Atocha," *Ferropedia,* May 24, 2015, http://www.ferropedia.es/wiki/Estaci%C3%B3n_de_Madrid_Atocha.
14 Tolstói, *Ana Karenina* [1939], 566.
15 Ibid., 568
16 Ibid., 570–78.
17 Ibid., 578.

the collections, fascinated by the Japanese scrolls painted with scenes from *The Tale of Genji*. In the mornings she rests in bed and reads until she feels strong enough to eat something. When she finishes *Madame Bovary*, she weeps for an entire day.[18]

Both the general plot and the pages of impressionistic narration — descriptions of the city, of paintings, of the steam of the trains — seem to have their counterparts in Panza Martín's life. After losing her livelihood, Panza Martín sold everything she owned and set out across the border to France. She lived for a time in the town of Aix-en-Provence, and may have been Cezanne's mistress for a brief but tumultuous period. Picasso, too, was in exile from Spain in this region during the time, and she may have had lunch with him one sunny afternoon, on the patio of the large house he lived in there, and perhaps watched a single white horse canter up and down the field in front of it.[19] When she grew tired of Provence, she moved to Paris, where she worked as a shop girl, having taught herself French when she first crossed the border and being more than qualified to run the store. The scenes from Anna's time in Paris seem to come from this experience, allowing Panza Martín to have an outlet for the flâneuse she had become.

The segments in Japan, however, appear largely produced from thin air. After her adventures on the Trans-Siberian Railway, Anna comes to a country made of tiny islands, each one only big enough for a single house. The people that live in the houses are all young, always smiling. They take her in, and feed her a variety of soups throughout the day. That night, a tremendous wailing wakes Anna, who rushes from the house toward the source of the sound. The sea is roiling, the young women throwing baskets of flowers and herbs into an ever-growing whirlpool. By the light of the moon, Anna is able to make out shifting shapes under the water, a sinister mass making the ocean move angrily. The young women motion her back to her

---

18 Ibid., 580–96.
19 Pablo Picasso, Letter to Gertrude Stein, May 18, 1947. MS.

room, where she lays awake for hours listening to the screams that come from the sea.

The next morning the women explain to her that there is nothing to fear. This is how the sea is made, they tell her, "without their tears we would have no water.[20]The breakfast soup is particularly salty that morning. That night, Anna sneaks out of her bedroom and dives into the ocean. It is full of all the old women that did not live on the islands, and they are not happy. The old women dance and scream, each twirl causing the water to eddy, each scream accompanied by a sob. The onlookers weep until they too are compelled to dance, full of *duende,* showing every crushed desire, every small betrayal. The book concludes with Anna's death song, for as she sings and screams and wails the water fills her lungs; she ages, and perhaps she is drowned, perhaps she lives forever in the sea.

While the physical descriptions of the locale are disconnected from Panza Martin's reality, the emotional content of the final portion of the book speaks to a life of incremental disappointments, some of which are revealed only upon consulting primary materials concerning the relationship of the step siblings. An exhumation of Redondo Panza's corpse by Gutierrez and myself revealed a small notebook tucked into his jacket pocket. This journal details Redondo Panza's daily life and contains notes on his translation projects. The entries begin well before his first execution, and include many details about polishing the *War and Peace* manuscript and the ongoing translation of *Anna Karenina.* The project dragged on for several years. Indeed, the main point of Redondo Panza's visit to Cádiz was to ask his stepsister for financial support while he completed the manuscript.

The journal also fills in the crucial missing biographical information, namely, how he was recorded as shot by a firing squad and managed to survive. Redondo Panza writes, "we were lined up along the edge of a large pit that had been used for the previous day's executions as well, which I deduced despite my

---

20 Tolstói, *Ana Karenina* [1939], 806.

blindfold from the incredible stench of rotting flesh."[21] At the command to fire, Redondo Panza stepped backwards over the ledge, falling into a pile of corpses. He lay there until the soldiers could no longer be heard, at which point he snuck away. Redondo Panza spent two days in a nearby forest, but, incapable of foraging for himself, he broke into Panza Martín's house under the cover of night and took up residence in her attic. Once he made himself known to her, she begrudgingly brought him meals after dark, and implored him to come up with a plan to escape. The last entry is dated the night before his body was found and includes the details of a whispered argument they had. Several weeks into this uninvited visit, Redondo Panza found one of her poems on the back of an invoice for a crate of oranges, and deemed it extremely mediocre. He brought it up later, when drunk, and discouraged his sister from writing further: "If you won't stop writing, the least you can do is hide your poetry better, to keep from embarrassing us any more than you already have."[22]

What, then, are we to make of these two translators sharing the same body of work—the one clinging closely to the Russian, except at moments where it behooves his personal agenda, the other translating so loosely that she might be said to not be translating at all? Indeed, the books translated after *Anna Karenina* appear to be based on the French translation of the Russian, filtering the original work through yet another language. It is clear, at least, that the biographical differences between the two translators have significant bearing on the

interpretation of their work. In what sense can these books still be thought of as translations? Jose Ortega y Gasset's words come to mind:

> To write well is to employ a certain radical courage. Fine, but the translator [...] finds himself facing the enormous controlling apparatus, composed of grammar and common

---

21 Juan Carlos Redondo Panza, Unpublished diary, 1940–1941, 23.
22 Ibid., 47.

usage. What will he do with the rebellious text? Isn't it too much to ask that he also be rebellious, particularly since the text is someone else's?[23]

The death of Anna Karenina is one of the most poignant moments in the written word. But what are we to do with an Anna that kills someone else rather than herself in order to be free? What are we to do with a translator that abandons the text in order to write her own?

---

[23] José Ortega y Gasset, "The Misery and the Splendor of Translation," in *Theories of Translation: An Anthology of Essays from Dryden to Derrida*, eds. Rainer Schulte and John Biguenet (Chicago: The University of Chicago Press, 1992), 94.

Bibliography

Águila, Eduardo Rafael Revilla. *Picturing Panza: A Translator's Biography.* Madrid: Grupo SM, 1998.

"Chisme y chistes." *Diario de Cádiz,* May 26, 1934, C4.

"Ha muerto un traidor." *Diario de Cádiz,* April 4, 1939, D9.

"Estación de Madrid Atocha." *Ferropedia,* May 24, 2015. http://www.ferropedia.es/wiki/Estaci%C3%B3n_de_Madrid_Atocha.

Hammerschmidt, Hans. *Spanish Inquisition: Redondo Panza's Brothers Karamazov.* Chicago: The University of Chicago Press, 2006.

Panza, Juan Carlos Redondo. Unpublished diary. 1940–1941.

Ortega y Gasset, José "The Misery and the Splendor of Translation." In *Theories of Translation: An Anthology of Essays from Dryden to Derrida,* edited by Rainer Schulte and John Biguenet, 93–111. Chicago: The University of Chicago Press, 1992.

Picasso, Pablo. Letter to Gertrude Stein. May 18, 1947. MS.

Simmons, Simon Samuel. "Let Them Wear Overcoats: Marxism and Panza's Gogol." *Journal of Panza Studies* 7, no. 1 (Spring 2011): 20–34.

Tolstói, Liev Nikoláievich. *Ana Karenina.* Translated by Redondo Panza, Juan Carlos, and Panza Martín. Madrid: Ediciones Halcon, 1939.

———. *Ana Karenina.* Translated by Editorial Iberia. Madrid: Austral, 2010.

———. *Guerra y paz.* Translated by Redondo Panza. Madrid: Ediciones Halcon, 1938.

14

The Purists: Cooperative Fundamentalism and Aesthetic Dogmatics

Matthew Newcomb

Every fundamentalism has an origin story. For the Purist literary movement, that story begins in late 2002 when Picador published to (mostly) critical acclaim and (partially) popular criticism a novel entitled *City Divided*.[1] That same year, the novel's authors, Tony Warren and Omar Mohammed, completed their MFAs in Creative Writing at the University of Minnesota. Within the program they were two of the only devout followers of their respective Christian and Islamic faith, forging a connection between the two and an eventual collaboration. That project, along with a cultural milieu of struggle between traditional truths and modern versions of accepting difference, led to the critically contested movement that has come to be called Purism. Both credited and condemned for bringing questions of "correct doctrine" back to literature, the Purist movement tapped into that desire for a certainty about something that can bring purpose and action to a person's life. Of course this certainty of purpose can appear in many manifestations, from missionary work to

---

1   Omar Mohammed and Tony Warren, *City Divided* (New York: Picador, 2002).

revolution to social movements to terrorism. The Purists' artistic focus, particularly through experimental literature, forced their sense of certainty and purpose into non-violent conflict with many differing models of certainty and purpose. These conflicts ultimately broke the movement apart, but along the way created new options for socially relevant art based in seeing the other not as like the self in some basic way, but as worth contending with because the other holds distinct basic feelings, truths, and values. As Edna van Avermaet described it (revising Emmanuel Lévinas), "literary ethics comes from confronting not the face of the other but from confronting the guts of the other."[2] Of course, those confrontations do not always remain ethical, or peaceful.

Complicated movements and internal critiques often produce alternative stories. A second origin story for the Purists, as a cooperative fundamentalist literary movement, emphasizes their beginning shortly after the September 11, 2001, terrorist attacks in the United States.[3] If so, the response was to provide an alternate form of fundamentalism. This new fundamentalism eschewed violence, advocated for hearing other views, and still clung to ideological doctrines as firmly as possible. Not only did the Purists value literature and art in a way not traditionally explored by twentieth century religious fundamentalists, but they allowed a surprising profligacy of fundamentalists to connect and work together. In keeping with one of the Purists' eventual slogans, "Everyone is a fundamentalist about something."[4] As such, those associated with the Purist movement came not only from a variety of religious traditions, but included vegan artists, animal rights-based writers, extreme libertarians, and promoters of the singularity concept among others. The name, Purists, emerged from both the sense of purity of belief for members of this network of writers and also from the sense of a single driv-

---

2 Edna Van Avermaet, "The Other Parts of the Other," *Journal of Ethics and Art* 22, no. 3 (2006): 168–84, at 172.
3 See Jin Xiao, "Art Out of Terror," *Twin Cities Review: A Journal of Art and Letters* 18, no. 2 (2005): 37–48.
4 Julia Jones, "Conference Poster," 2004, 2nd Total Truth Writing Workshop, St. Louis, Missouri.

ing principle behind many of the works and elements in those works, resulting in characters and ideas taken to numerous behavioral and logical extremes.

Despite Mohammed and Warren's mutual strict adherence to sometimes contradictory and historically oppositional forms of religion, their artistic sensibilities matched well for the work on *City Divided*. According to a 2004 interview with Mohammed, "Tony and I both felt the struggle to be true to the absolutes of our beliefs while allowing the openness and even provocativeness expected of the contemporary writer."[5] In "All the Absolutes: An Essay on Truth and Writing," Warren followed up Mohammed's statement by explaining that "Adhering closely to our faith traditions while working together became our form of openness, our version of provocation."[6] That provocation worked, as *City Divided* sold well and received condemnations from both pastors and imams.

The story itself is set in modern-day upper Midwest America, in a city that reads as a mix of Detroit and Minneapolis according to Krystal Watkins in her analysis of the relationships between location, race, and religion in the text.[7] Although the city is not named in the novel, it deserves its role as title character. A city planning meeting brings together Bill Tyndale, a fundamentalist pastor leading a megachurch, and Ahmed Khan, an imam guiding both a mosque and much of the native and immigrant Muslim community in the city. The two characters, intentional stand-ins for Warren and Mohammed according to Sheila Okura,[8] unite in opposition to a zoning change allowing more bars and clubs in the suburbs. They start meeting for cof-

---

5 Marina Aru, "A City Joined: Interview with Omar Mohammed," *New York Times*, March 4, 2004.
6 Tony Warren, "All the Absolutes," in *Pure Belief, Pure Art,* ed. Alma Rogers (Dallas: Principle Press, 2005), 15.
7 See Krystal Watkins, *Race and Religion Crossing in* City Divided (Chicago: Chicago University Press, 2010).
8 Sheila Okura, "Identity Politics in City Divided," *Twenty-first Century Literature* 6, no. 2 (2011): 242–61, at 248–49.

fee and concoct a plan to reach all the atheists and non-religious in the city and split the followers between them.

Over the next months they help each other with a massive recruiting campaign against secularism, while trying to stave off their competition with each other for followers. As Khan and Tyndale's older children develop a growing intimacy, tension grows, since neither man approves of that level of cooperation. Critic Leila Harun observes that all the men in the book can handle working together until it comes to arenas seen as more feminine realms in one or both religious traditions.[9] Questions of who may marry whom and issues of women running the houses but remaining officially submissive permeate the text. Eventually, Tyndale and Khan's followers create a threat of violence to all in the city who don't convert. God or nature takes over as natural disaster strikes and each huge congregation migrates out of city, bringing along any who will convert on the spot. Outside of town, the groups stop mixing. As everything falls apart, Tyndale and Khan leave their congregations and move to a new town to try it all again, leaving at least one child behind in the disaster-stricken town. The children, abandoned by and escaping from their fathers, offer an alternative to the short-term, revivalist cooperation the elder Tyndale and Khan practice. However, the children's chances of survival, like any form of ultimate combination of the religious groups, appear slim.

Following the enthusiastic and antagonistic reception of their book, Mohammed and Warren put out a call to join them at the first Total Truth Writing Workshop (TTWW). The Chicago-based meeting was overwhelmed, not just by religious writers, but by artists of many ideologies who had been seen as too dogmatic at one point or another. Only-eat-what-you-grow vegans met Hindu fundamentalists in seminars on topics like "Simple Truth, Complex Characters," and Singularity devotees worked with Hasidic Jews in "Foucault and Technologies of the

---

9   Leila Harun, "You Can't Handle the Home: Male Conflict in Feminine Spaces," *Interdisciplinary Journal of Gender and Literature* 11, no. 1 (2007): 42–60, at 42.

Writing Self." David Knoll's intriguing comparative study of the 1978 International Council on Biblical Inerrancy's (ICBI) Chicago meeting[10] and the Total Truth Writing Workshop twenty-five years later defines the TTWW as embracing "external community and ideas in tension — without compromise," while he claims the ICBI meeting encouraged "internal community and integration or rejection of all ideas — without compromise."[11] With its sometimes substantial, sometimes pseudo-accepting form of dogmatisms, the TTWW met for just four years, but led to innumerable spin-off groups and cooperative projects. In institutional terms, it provided the origin story for all sorts of dogmatic work, and for greater acceptance of that work in the literary world if it combined dogmatisms in some way. From Queer Rose and Duane Jackson's feminist and Mormon graphic novel series *Young*,[12] to *B-leave Me*, a collection of twenty-one mini-memoirs from contrasting ideological backgrounds,[13] the work flowered and found publishers. Many not at the conferences or connected to the Purist movement in any personal way picked up on the trend and brought similar work to the visual arts and to performance pieces like the 2005 "Pyramid of War," a fifty-foot human tower of people only physically connected to someone from a group their ancestors had battled.[14]

Of course, the purity element applied to the art itself too. Jon Farmel's riffs on famous paintings exemplify that aesthetic to a high degree. He took single elements of works of art, such as one lily from Monet's work, and recreated those individual aspects precisely, but without the surrounding context, vastly enlarged,

---

10 See International Council on Biblical Inerrancy, "Chicago Statement on Biblical Inerrancy with Exposition," http://www.bible-researcher.com/chicago01.html.
11 David Knoll, "Truth, Dogma, and Interpretation in Chicago, 1978 and 2003," *Hermeneutics at Play* 15, no. 4 (2010): 207–24, at 221.
12 Queer Rose and Duane Jackson, *Young* (Salt Lake City: Burned Over Press, 2004).
13 Jai Quintana, *B-leave Me* (Madison: Pure Press, 2006).
14 The pyramid was performed near the Gateway Arch in St. Louis, Missouri, and included many whose ancestors had fought in the Civil War, the Mexican-American War, and the French and Indian Wars.

and in a single color.¹⁵ This version of representational accuracy with the purifying elements of single colors and sizes that showed every possible flaw and "hypocritical" variation was one of the first Purist visual art approaches to break into the mainstream with a show at the J. Paul Getty Museum in Los Angeles. On the literary front, a similar aesthetic of total consistency within characters led to critiques of "contradictory" characters (like Hamlet) and an emphasis on using character consistency to highlight inconsistencies or hypocrisies in their familial or societal contexts.¹⁶ Kemba Wilson's 2009 *Name-Place,* a collection of short stories with a one-word name and one-word place as the title of each, brought that aesthetic purity of character to life with its near-outcasts in rural and suburban American towns.¹⁷

Thematically, the Purists rejected popular notions of diversity in thought and tolerance of other views, even using some of the anti-political correctness language of right-wing groups in the United States. However, this rejection of diversity came with a turn towards celebrating the "errors" of others by supporting their work. It created sometimes-tense relationships of artists actively trying to persuade each other as they worked together, but that often sharpened the persuasiveness of the poems, narratives, and experimental texts while avoiding pedantry that collaborators would critique. More than one commentator (see Anderson, Jimenez, and Starr for examples)¹⁸ observed the greater level of nuance coming out of the Purist movement on

---

15 Jon Farmel, *Pure Life,* oil on canvas (2005), John J. Getty Museum, Los Angeles.
16 Shelly O'Grady, "(In)consistency and Character: An Aesthetic Re-evaluation of Hamlet," *Shakespeare Studies* 10, no. 2 (2006): 94–109.
17 Kemba Wilson, *Name-Place* (New York: Harper Collins, 2005).
18 June Anderson, "Many Sexualities, One Truth," *Religion and Literature* 44, no. 2 (2012): 131–51, dealt with the surprisingly large set of sexual categories among Purists. Gabe Jiminez, "Death with Dignity and the New Aesthetics of Truth," *Social Issues* 19, no. 1 (2009): 18–30, found new definitions of dignity emerging. Pat Starr, "Remember the Needy: Poverty after *City Divided,*" *Twenty-first Century Literature* 7, no. 3 (2012): 299–317, explored how Purists considered poverty in beyond strictly economic terms — particularly tying poverty to conviction and a sense of meaning.

social debates about sexuality, end of life issues, and poverty to name three.

In the context of the "war on terror" declared by the United States and parts of Europe, the Purists fought against a kind of ideological stereotyping. Lumping all Muslims together called for resistance, even by non-Muslim Purist-oriented artists. Many could see themselves in the same stereotyping, lumped together with other Christians, other plant rights activists, and so forth. Edward Said made a brief resurgence with his critique of orientalism being attached to any number of groups up for study, sometimes with consideration of the differences in power relations between a colonial context and twenty-first century America and sometimes not.[19]

Ironically, the Purist movement led to a variety of mixed fundamentalisms, where artists were able to keep their initial ideologies and take on new ones. In particular, the strict forms of Christianity and environmentalism combined in the God's Gardeners group simultaneously made them more isolated from other Christian and environmentalist factions.[20] The Gardeners adopted a variety of environmentalist leaders as saints and started a variety of connected communes, mixing evangelism and low-environmental-impact living. The God's Gardeners, condemned as heretics by some Catholic, Orthodox, and conservative evangelical churches, and the Gardeners' interpretive practices with the Bible veered further and further towards a hermeneutic centered on environmental apocalypse, evolutionary history, and gene-based eschatology.[21]

The desire to build embodied ideologies, often with combined basic truths, made science fiction, fantasy, and speculative fiction popular genres. Purists created numerous science fiction and fantasy worlds, either intentionally depicting idealized soci-

---

19 Edward Said, *Orientalism* (New York: Pantheon Books, 1978).
20 See Margaret Atwood, *The Year of the Flood* (Norwell: Anchor, 2010) for a narrative history of the God's Gardener's group.
21 See Paul Peretti, "God's Gardeners and Cultural Interpretation," *Orthodoxy/Heterodoxy* 14, no. 1 (2009): 28–39, for a detailed analysis of the Gardeners' interpretive practices.

eties or taking the less standard step of putting competing pure doctrines in political and technological contexts. These worlds ran the gamut from dystopian to utopian to near-realism. They often reached wider audiences than other Purist-related work, being distributed through regular science fiction presses without clear markers of any Purist connections or ideological goals. Byrd Velmo's *Alien Orthodoxy,* for example, was published by Tor, nominated for a Nebula Award, and walked the line between traditional space opera and avant garde historical revision.[22] The impressive integration of alien species with the Eastern Orthodox Church led to surprisingly relevant moral and theological considerations for the beginning of the twenty-first century.

Considerably more troubling to many scholars than mixed fundamentalisms (science fiction or otherwise) was the so-called "tribal separation" ideology, usually race-based, since numerous white supremacists found the variety and relative cultural acceptance of the Purists to serve as a good cover for racist writings. However, at the 2004 TTWW meeting, a faction of "tribalists" joined with writers working to promote animal-only (non-human) perspectives through "experifact" texts. The "experifacts" combined personal experiences interacting with particular animals with significant research into all known work about the mental make-ups of those species. The researching artists created monologs and dialogs that broke down expected human language patterns. Maria Pliskova extended those writings into revisions of famous short stories, including of Herman Melville's "Bartleby the Scrivener" and Flannery O'Connor's "A Good Man Is Hard to Find," populated entirely by animals displaying quite non-human psychologies. Of course, the sense of otherness combined with psychological depth was much of the point, and Pliskova's stories became required reading in many literary and environmental studies programs. Her work in "Young Gooddeer Brown" (following Nathaniel Hawthorne) in particular implied a rejection of anthropocentric understandings of ecology and displays the notion of "most depend-

---

22 Byrd Velmo, *Alien Orthodoxy* (New York: Tor, 2007).

ent species" that became a new rallying cry for Greenpeace.²³ As Jasmine Everton describes it, "The 'most dependent species' concept attempts to identify the plant or animal whose survival most stringently requires the preservation of its micro-ecosystem. All decisions about that ecosystem should then be made with that creature's perspective taking primary position — no exceptions."²⁴ Later followers variously took multi-species perspectives or attempted to create a viewpoint from the links between three or more species at once.

While Pliskova herself claimed to never be involved and openly spoke against them, numerous animal primacy Purists and "tribalists" found common ground over species and group categorization issues and the notion of letting each group "go its own way," quite separate from others and with firm lines between groups. Calling themselves the Westminsters,²⁵ they turned taxonomy into an artistic form, with elaborately designed and illustrated books of alternate categorizations of humans, other animals, plants, and even minerals — often eschewing those traditional categories entirely. The anonymous but almost certainly group-authored text *Contra-Linneaus* encouraged many animal rights activists and post-humanists alike with moves such as using behavioral elements to redefine the boundaries around species — creatures that bring their homes with them include what others call snails and RV-owners.²⁶ But the *Contra-Linneaus* also implied racial hierarchies at moments, valuing spotted/freckled creatures over striped creatures in one case and northern objects over southern objects in another.²⁷ As with many groups emerging from the Purists (at least those who

---

23 Maria Pliskova, "Young Gooddeer Brown," *The Alternative New Yorker*, May 18, 2006.
24 Jasmine Everton, "Living with Maria Pliskova's 'Most Dependent Species,'" *The Atlantic*, November 15, 2009.
25 The name "Westminster" is a sarcastic nod to the famous dog show, where meeting breed standards in physical form and potential function are central.
26 *Contra-Linnaeus* (Madison: Pure Press, 2008), 72–83.
27 Ibid., 47 and 106.

garnered attention), the accusations against them of pseudo-science in the literary work were frequent and often justified.

While they remained a relatively small movement, the Purist emphasis on types of fundamentalism had some impact on political discourse. They expanded the definition of fundamentalist beyond its previous usage for many Muslims, some Christians, and very few others. Politicians and pundits could accuse each other of being health care fundamentalists, states' rights fundamentalists, or any number of other names. While this expanse of fundamentalist talk made the term lose power, it also allowed those with particularly extreme views more acceptance. Rather than helping one-issue candidates or voters, the Purists helped shift media discussions to one-principle candidates and voters.[28] At moments, this acceptance of being an extremist on one issue did lead to greater clarity and openness about candidates' stances or a congressperson's policies. In other words, everyone's craziness or conviction (depending on your viewpoint) came a bit more out into the open.

Along with incubating strange bedfellows and shifting political discussions, the Purists grew schisms at a rate in keeping with the speed of information and communication in the early twenty-first century. After just a few years of rapid publishing, it could hardly be called a single movement. Perhaps that was to be expected from artists taking on the Herculean task of holding closely to strict dogma or ideology while simultaneously working cooperatively with those holding differing dogmas. However, after the initial conferences and working groups fell apart, the theorists stepped in to provide slightly less utopian possibilities.

Throughout the rapidly scattering movement, the question of the purpose of art and literature in relationship to fundamental truths remained. Recreations of sacred stories from

---

28 For example, rather than voting for a candidate based on that individual's stance on abortion, the focus shifted to a candidate's application of a principle like transparency or mammalian life as primary to issues across the board. See Cat Witzer, "One-Principle Voters Steal the Election," CNN, November 12, 2006.

numerous traditions, often attempting to grasp the precise details and ethos of the time period of the initial story (such as the Exodus narrative) came from those seeing literature as a way to access the truth of sacred texts more accurately. Others, such as the so-called "neuralist" writers emphasized literature as a way to change the neuronal structure of the brain.[29] Those texts went so far, in the case of Jack Roy's post-psychology work, to develop incomprehensible patterns of symbols designed to guide the brain through a universally ideal set of brainwave patterns.[30] "The point of my symbol waves is to regenerate the primal patterns in the brain — in other words, unity with our mental nature."[31] Roy's insistence on a single ideal mental nature brought him rapidly into Purist circles, some of which tried to map brainwaves related to particular belief systems onto his more abstract system.

Again, the center could not hold with the variety of work attempted and experimented with, and with smaller groups meeting regionally around the United States (and at least two in Canada). In 2007, a Purist-based poster art campaign against Unitarian Universalist churches, using a "no dogma, no love/no love, no beauty" slogan, led to a physical altercation in downtown Portland, Oregon. The event garnered national press, and even more conservative, belief-oriented churches condemned the Purist art campaign. At almost the same time, Warren and Mohammed, the TTWW founders, had a falling out over using traditional publishers or working with their own publishing house, ending the yearly conference and fracturing the movement further.

Even as the Purists became less of a group and more like hundreds of individuals and dozens of writing groups, often having a harder time finding publishers beginning in the late 2000s, newer joiners turned to a more philosophical approach.

---

29 Eve Gorber, *Pure Factions: A Brief Un-History* (New York: Mouse and Owl Press, 2011).
30 Jack Roy, ++---%....> (Chicago: Perverse Chastity Press, 2006).
31 Adam Kwiatkowski, "Interview with Jack Roy," *Psychology Today,* January 30, 2006, 27.

Taking Sören Kierkegaard's *Purity of Heart Is to Will One Thing* as a starting point,[32] Raef Mondria penned "Purity of Mind Is to Know One Truth." Mondria argued for a type of postmodern foundationalism, declaring that "no knowledge, and therefore no honest artistic practice, is possible without defining the single starting truth for the knower."[33] He showed less concern for what that truth was, but scandalously asserted that "even fundamentalist terrorist attacks are often more artistically honest than the latest prize-winning novel."[34] For Mondria, the purity of devotion to one starting belief actually allowed incredible variation in lived or creative application of that origin. The variety could be near-infinite, overwhelming the sense that the origin point mattered, like a total determinist who uses the experienced fact of determinism to allow highly contradictory beliefs and behaviors.

Purist work turned more esoteric and arguments continued in both religious and secular academic circles over "aesthetic dogmatics," a term coined by Peter Singer's graduate student Bree Hayburn.[35] "Aesthetic dogmatics" worked with a circular relationship between basic truth doctrines and issues of beauty in a mutually reinforcing relationship. At the same time, Queer Rose brought together a collection of Purist-connected writers, old and new, for a fresh collection. Rose had been running the small press Perverse Chastity, and frequently publishing highly fundamentalist works from contradictory perspectives. She reached out to a number of her writers and edited the instant cult classic, *The Fundamentalist's Handbook*.[36]

---

32 Sören Kierkegaard, *Purity of Heart Is to Will One Thing,* trans. Douglas V. Steere (Radford: Wilder Publications, 2008).

33 Raef Mondria, "Purity of Mind Is to Know One Thing," *Theories of Dogmas,* eds. Cassie Bern and Mark O'Connor (Minneapolis: Univeristy of Minnesota Press, 2008), 133.

34 Ibid., 139.

35 Bree Hayburn, "Notes toward an Aesthetic Dogmatics." *Theories of Dogmas,* eds. Cassie Bern and Mark O'Connor, (Minneapolis: University of Minnesota Press, 2008), 60.

36 Queer Rose, ed., *The Fundamentalist's Handbook,* 1st edn. (Chicago: Perverse Chastity Press, 2008).

The *Fundamentalist's Handbook* (FH) marketed itself (on the back cover) as "redeeming the term fundamentalist as not inclusive of everyone, but as inescapable by everyone." From Rose's own treatise on relationships, "Buddies: Reproduction Without Sex," to Father Dale Oso, S.J.'s story "Root Veggies," depicting a near-utopian society based on a rotating dictatorship by the poorest person, any reader feeling out of the mainstream could find something to latch onto. The FH includes short stories, poetry, songs, catechisms, doctrine, homemade bomb instructions, surveillance avoidance guidance, public relations strategies, and work that defies genre categories. The fact that the first edition (2008) has different fundamentalisms mixed together, while the second edition of FH (2010)[37] is organized by group, indicates the continued splits within the Purists, even as Rose, Oso, and others tried to bring different fundamentalists back together. The loss of both a sense of discovery and of the push to read those who differ from you that came with the second edition disappointed scholars like Mondria, who valued the mixing of basic truths. Many readers reportedly went straight to particular sections, such as religion, subcategory Christian, or environment, subcategory inorganic.[38] The first edition, prized particularly among younger enthusiasts, became a go-to model for literary projects, used as a formal guide to imitate in artistic experiments.

An initial highlight of the FH was the list of "Non-negotiable Principles" for Purists, first drafted at a 2005 conference in Atlanta. The principles included "only relativism is relative," "the only authority to trust is truth," and "truth won't win without art."[39] These principles tried to create a web of agreement that alternate fundamentalisms could work out of. The list of apparent contradictions entitled "Unity" in the FH pushed the limits further, with its implications that all oppositions are true and

---

37 Queer Rose, ed., *The Fundamentalist's Handbook,* 2nd edn. (Chicago: Perverse Chastity Press, 2010).
38 Zia Feillu, "Survey of Fundamentalist's Handbook Readers," last modified September 12, 2011, https://www.purehandbook.fh/readersurvey.html.
39 "Non-negotiable Principles," *The Fundamentalist's Handbook,* 1st edn., ed. Queer Rose (Chicago: Perverse Chastity Press, 2008), 50–53.

the notion of any foundation or fundamental belief is wrong.[40] It gained inclusion in the collection on the basis of presenting its belief about oppositions as a pure form self-imploding dogma—the dogma that overturns dogma. Culturally, the FH earned mentions on talk shows ranging from *Politically Incorrect with Bill Maher* to *The Daily Show* to *Charlie Rose*.[41] That attention led to several weeks of media debates about practical truth versus artistic truth. As a *New York Times* editorial observed, "Impressions of truth, like those given by artists, become the basis for making up practical truths, but sometimes the practical truths push back."[42] Artistic truth was depicted as more extremist, and not necessarily to be trusted, even if it seemed more internally consistent.[43] The Purist movement made truth more appropriate to talk about in terms of literature, but pushed many people to think of art and literature still as separate from their lives and only for the highly cultured. Instead of extremes of abstraction or pastiche, writers were seen as actually denying the complicated realities of living daily life. In the *Fundamentalist's Handbook,* the "Hypocrite Monologs" emphasized an artistic purity of character while satirizing the practical and contradictory "truths" characters told themselves or others just sentences apart.[44] What felt true failed to cut it for most Purists, who occasionally pushed to live by principles that felt wrong, prioritizing doctrine over human experience.

---

40 "Unity," *The Fundamentalist's Handbook,* 1st edn., ed. Queer Rose (Chicago: Perverse Chastity Press, 2008), 120–25. Also Consider Hayburn, "Notes toward an Aesthetic Dogmatics," and Mondria, "Purity of Mind Is to Know One Thing" for related work on the truth value of oppositions or contradictions.

41 These were typically short segments, but the chance for extremism and the combinations of groups trying to work together with the Purists was too much for some shows to pass up.

42 "Tug of Truth," Editorial, *The New York Times,* February 22, 2009.

43 Phyllis Farmer, "Can Artists Tell the Truth?" *Washington Post,* August 23, 2008, D1.

44 Nym Doe and Pseudo Doe, "Hypocrite Monologs," in *The Fundamentalist's Handbook,* 1st edn., ed. Queer Rose (Chicago: Perverse Chastity Press, 2008), 111–24.

Perhaps because of the limitations the Purists and their various fundamentalisms placed on artists, many found it to be a surprisingly experimental and fecund period of work. Set doctrine about ideas often led to freedom in forms and to modernizations of old stories that portrayed real respect for older value systems, contradicting Fredric Jameson's ideas about postmodern pastiche while simultaneously cobbling opposing fundamentalisms together in collected volumes. The modernizations also had a tendency to be readable either as completely subversive or completely orthodox, such as with Emily Bayard's story "Jesus Crossing," which could promote following Jesus or literally "crossing" him out.[45] Ultimately, the Purist movement made the idea of fundamentalism both more nuanced and acceptable, creating a context for civil directness in public life, but also for treating literature as the new land of dogma.

It remains to be seen if the aesthetic dogmatics of the Purists continues to push cultural politics into openly fundamentalist camps, some more willing to listen to other camps and agree to disagree than others. But on the literary front, the coming trend appears to be a dogmatism about form, technique, and even process. Perhaps that will allow those who are similarly devoted to a process but differ in content dogmatics to work together through differences because of an artistic orthodoxy (or orthopraxy) in common.

---

45 Emily Bayard, "Jesus Crossing," in *The Ground: Collected Stories,* ed. Maria Pliskova (Madison: Pure Press, 2008), 50.

Bibliography

Anderson, June. "Many Sexualities, One Truth." *Religion and Literature* 44, no. 2 (2012): 131–51.

Aru, Marina. "A City Joined: Interview with Omar Mohammed." *New York Times,* March 4, 2004.

Atwood, Margaret. *The Year of the Flood.* Norwell: Anchor, 2010.

Bayard, Emily. "Jesus Crossing." In *The Ground: Collected Stories,* edited by Maria Pliskova, 42–51. Madison: Pure Press, 2008.

Contra-Linneaus. Madison: Pure Press, 2008.

Doe, Nym, and Pseudo Doe. "Hypocrite Monologs." In *The Fundamentalist's Handbook,* First Edition, edited by Queer Rose, 111–24. Chicago: Perverse Chastity Press, 2008.

Everton, Jasmine. "Living with Maria Pliskova's 'Most Dependent Species.'" *The Atlantic,* November 15, 2009.

Farmer, Phyllis. "Can Artists Tell the Truth?" *Washington Post,* August 23, 2008.

Feillu, Zia. "Survey of Fundamentalist's Handbook Readers." Last modified September 12, 2011. https://www.purehandbook.fh/readersurvey.html.

Gorber, Eve. *Pure Factions: A Brief Un-History.* New York: Mouse and Owl Press, 2011.

Harun, Leila. "You Can't Handle the Home: Male Conflict in Feminine Spaces." *Interdisciplinary Journal of Gender and Literature* 11, no. 1 (2007): 42–60.

Hayburn, Bree. "Notes toward an Aesthetic Dogmatics." *Theories of Dogmas,* edited by Cassie Bern and Mark O'Connor, 56–79. Minneapolis: University of Minnesota Press, 2008.

International Council on Biblical Inerrancy. "Chicago Statement on Biblical Inerrancy with Exposition." http://www.bible-researcher.com/chicago1.html.

Jiminez, Gabe. "Death with Dignity and the New Aesthetics of Truth." *Social Issues* 19, no. 1 (2009): 18–30.

Jones, Julia. "Conference Poster," 2004, 2nd Total Truth Writing Workshop, St. Louis, Missouri.

Kierkegaard, Sören. *Purity of Heart Is to Will One Thing.* Translated by Douglas V. Steere. Radford: Wilder Publications, 2008.

Knoll, David. "Truth, Dogma, and Interpretation in Chicago, 1978 and 2003." *Hermeneutics at Play* 15, no. 4 (2010): 207–24.

Kwiatkowski, Adam. "Interview with Jack Roy." *Psychology Today,* January 30, 2006.

Lévinas, Emmanuel. *Ethics and Infinity,* Translated by Richard A. Cohen. Pittsburgh: Duquesne University Press, 1985.

Mohammed, Omar, and Tony Warren. *City Divided.* New York: Picador, 2002.

Mondria, Raef. "Purity of Mind Is to Know One Thing." *Theories of Dogmas,* edited by Cassie Bern and Mark O'Connor, 127–44. Minneapolis: University of Minnesota Press, 2008.

"Non-negotiable Principles." *The Fundamentalist's Handbook,* First Edition, edited by Queer Rose, 50–53. Chicago: Perverse Chastity Press, 2008.

O'Grady, Shelly. "(In)consistency and Character: An Aesthetic Re-evaluation of *Hamlet*." *Shakespeare Studies* 10, no. 2 (2006): 94–109.

Okura, Sheila. "Identity Politics in *City Divided*." *Twenty-first Century Literature* 6, no. 2 (2011): 242–61.

Peretti, Paul. "God's Gardeners and Cultural Interpretation." *Orthodoxy/Heterodoxy* 14, no. 1 (2009): 28–39.

Pliskova, Maria. *A Good Bird Is Hard to Find and Other Stories.* New York: Penguin, 2008.

———. "Young Gooddeer Brown." *The Alternative New Yorker,* May 18, 2006.

Queer Rose, ed., *The Fundamentalist's Handbook,* First Edition. Chicago: Perverse Chastity Press, 2008.

———, ed., *The Fundamentalist's Handbook,* Second Edition. Chicago: Perverse Chastity Press, 2010.

———, and Duane Jackson. *Young.* Salt Lake City: Burned Over Press, 2004.

Quintana, Jai. *B-leave Me.* Madison: Pure Press, 2006.

Roy, Jack. ++---%....>. Chicago: Perverse Chastity Press, 2006.

Said, Edward. *Orientalism*. New York: Pantheon Books, 1978.
Starr, Pat. "Remember the Needy: Poverty after *City Divided.*" *Twenty-first Century Literature* 7, no. 3 (2012): 299–317.
"Unity." *The Fundamentalist's Handbook,* First Edition, edited by Queer Rose, 120–25. Chicago: Perverse Chastity Press, 2008.
Van Avermaet, Edna. "The Other Parts of the Other." *Journal of Ethics and Art* 22, no. 3 (2006): 168–84.
"Tug of Truth." Editorial, *The New York Times,* February 22, 2009.
Velmo, Byrd. *Alien Orthodoxy.* New York: Tor, 2007.
Warren, Tony. "All the Absolutes." In *Pure Belief, Pure Art,* edited by Alma Rogers, 13–19. Dallas: Principle Press, 2005.
Watkins, Krystal. *Race and Religion Crossing in* City Divided. Chicago: Chicago University Press, 2010.
Wilson, Kemba. *Name-Place.* New York: Harper Collins, 2005.
Witzer, Cat. "One-Principle Voters Steal the Election." CNN. November 12, 2006. https://www.cnn.com/2006/11/12/culture/one-principle/index.html.
Xiao, Jin. "Art Out of Terror." *Twin Cities Review: A Journal of Art and Letters* 18, no. 2 (2005): 37–48.

15

From Paratext to Text, Scholar to Ragpicker: Inverted Criticism and the "Heidi B. Morton Papers and Library"

Ryan Marnane

"There is no limit to what can be said in the text."
— Julia Kristeva[1]

"The library is on fire."
— Michel Foucault[2]

"What matter who's speaking?"
— Samuel Beckett[3]

---

1 Julia Kristeva, *Revolution in Poetic Language* (New York: Columbia University Press, 1984), 209.
2 Michel Foucault, "Fantasia of the Library," in *Language, Counter-Memory, Practice*, ed. Donald F. Bouchard (Ithaca: Cornell University Press, 1977), 92.
3 Samuel Beckett, *Texts for Nothing*, trans. S. Beckett (Calder & Boyars, London, 1974), 16.

Introduction

Since the New York Public Library acquired the papers and personal library of Heidi B. Morton—American novelist and life-long political activist who died in late 2009 at the age of 58—there's been an unavoidable explosion of scholarship and public discourse surrounding the author's body of work and life. From early sketches and drafts of her Pulitzer Prize-winning magnum opus, *Lands after Neoliberalism: A Novel* (2003), to the archive's contentious acquirement of Morton's personal materials including email correspondences, online search histories, banking transactions, and medical records, the NYPL's "Heidi B. Morton Papers and Library" has become an epicenter of controversy within and around communities of literary practice and study.

Following the archive's opening in 2011, scholarship surrounding Morton's body of work has inverted itself. Instead of using archival materials to contextualize Morton's published work of fiction, scholars are now turning to her fiction to contextualize materials in the archive. Scholars such as Stephen Leafy, who in 2012 published *Heidi B. Morton's Ghosts: The Personal Journals and Laundry Lists of an American Writer,* argued that "Morton's 2001 memoir, *Turtles All The Way Down,* now functions as an indispensable resource for discussions surrounding her annotated copy of *The Shorter Oxford English Dictionary.*"[4] Or Jacqueline Miall, whose 2016 *Washington Post* profile of the collection "Archive as Pilgrimage: Receiving the Heidi B. Morton Papers" intensified public interest in the Morton Studies controversy, when she wrote that the archive embodies a "redemptive, almost spiritual ethos to it," arguing that "Morton's novels take on a raft-like quality once you've entered the archive: they're useful for crossing over but not for holding onto."[5]

---

4 Stephen Leafy, *Heidi B. Morton's Ghosts: The Personal Journals and Laundry Lists of an American Writer* (London: Bloomsbury), 2012, 17.

5 Jacqueline Miall, "The Archive as Pilgrimage: Receiving the Heidi B. Morton Papers," *The Washington Post,* September 12, 2016, https://www.

Principally guided by unpacking the complex relationship between Morton Studies and the "Heidi B. Morton Papers and Library," this essay illustrates how the archive's materials have become more instrumental in shaping Morton's posthumous literary legacy than the very literature that brought upon the inauguration of the archive in the first place. This inversion of scholarly attention within Morton Studies has, most notably since Leafy's 2012 publication, "spread like wildfire across literary and cultural studies communities,"[6] writes Jameson Woods, and continues to "challenge the ethics and legalities surrounding the long-standing tradition of accepted archival practices,"[7] as framed by Abigail Weinstein in "From Background to Foreground: A History of Archival Ethics." And while the use of "manuscripts in literary studies has served multiple functions to date," writes Weinstein,

> from biographical information to understanding the composition of a text and the power structures surrounding an author and its publishing houses, nowhere in the history of the practice has an archive's acquirement of personal materials become the raison d'etre of an author's posthumous literary legacy.[8]

And Morton Studies practitioners have made such history, so to speak, by rendering the previously unknown and non-published materials as not secondary but rather primary texts in and of themselves: "It's strange to read scholarship published in Morton's lifetime," Stephen Leafy writes in his introduction

---

washingtonpost.com/opinions/2016/09/12/f507e8cb2-9f9f-112e7-8ea1-ed975285475e_story.html.

6 Jameson Woods, "Reinventing the Practice," *The New Yorker*, June 17, 2014, https://www.newyorker.com/criticism/page-turner/reinventing-the-practice-2014.

7 Abigail Weinstein, "From Background to Foreground: A History of Archival Ethics," *Journal of Contemporary Archival Studies* 32, no. 1 (Nov. 2013): 1–25, at 19.

8 Ibid., 19–21.

to *Ghosts*, "because it is only now—after the archive's opening—that we can fully grasp her literary prowess, syntactical exuberance, and astonishingly prophetic insight into American culture and its forthcoming political misfortunes."[9]

From unceasing MLA conference panel disputes and unabating *New Yorker* and *Harper's Magazine* articles—along with a *60 Minutes* special unpacking the cultural significance surrounding the NYPL's "Heidi B. Morton Papers and Library"—it's hard to escape the persistent intellectual wrangling surrounding the Morton Studies debate. Therefore, this essay would be incomplete without also exploring the current state of literary studies in the wake of Morton scholars' practice of inverted criticism and its influence on literary studies at large. Most notably is the reactionary return to New Criticism or, as some critics and scholars are calling it, "Neo-Criticism," principally spearheaded by Duke University professor and renowned columnist for *The New Yorker*, Lauren St. Claire, who in November of 2013 published "In Defense of Neo-Criticism," which has since been cited in upwards of over 28 scholarly articles:

> The archive's inclusion of Morton's personal materials and online history—while ethically problematic in its own right—is by no means license for Morton scholars (and in particular Stephen Leafy) to include the author's online search history in her bibliography under the guise of *Searchings: A Memoir*, let alone citing her annotated copy of *The Marx–Engels Reader* as a primary text. […] The twenty-first-century post-Morton scholar—in what can only be surmised as an unfavorable yet judicious response to the overwhelming amount of biographical materials available amid the digital milieu—must return back to the text itself with a Neo-Critical approach of close reading practices sans ar-

---

9   Leafy, *Heidi B. Morton's Ghosts*, 3.

chival insights, however fortuitous yet germane they may at first appear.[10]

The main rub for St. Claire, and no doubt amongst others within the Neo-Critical camp, is that Morton scholars have "justified their inverted criticism by grounding their reading practices in the Foucauldian tradition of archival-based cultural analysis," St. Claire writes, arguing that "Morton Studies have taken the new historicist paradigm to its unfortunate yet seemingly logical conclusion: the complete and utter extinguishment of capital P-Primary texts."[11] And this essay — using both Foucault's notion of author-function to frame new historical reading practices and Gérard Genette's interpretive framework of paratext to frame Morton Studies' inverted criticism — explores the political and aesthetic implications of reading practices surrounding the "Heidi B. Morton Papers and Library" as well as the reactionary Neo-Critical movements that have since emerged in its wake.

I first begin with a brief overview of literary criticism's origins with the help of critic Joseph North, framing century-long arguments surrounding textual analysis within the discipline. Secondly, with the aid of both Foucault and Genette, I argue that scholarly engagement surrounding authorship and authorial-presence has entered a new epoch of partisan criticism. On the one hand there's the archival ragpicker — the "scholar *as* ragpicker" — framed in the spirit of Walter Benjamin's reading of Baudelaire's "The Ragpickers Wine."[12] And on the other hand, there's the reactionary Neo-Critic: incredulous to the ragpickers' capacity to up-cycle the leftovers of an author's life — the

---

10 Lauren St. Claire, "The Death of an Author and the Birth of a Discipline: In Defense of Neo-Criticism," *American Literature* 85, no. 3 (Nov. 2013): 332–437, at 434.
11 Ibid., 441.
12 "Ragpicker and poet," Benjamin writes, "both are concerned with refuse, and both go about their solitary business while other citizens are sleeping; they even move in the same way" (Walter Benjamin, "The Paris of the Second Empire in Baudelaire," in *Selected Writings: 1938–1940*, eds. Michael W. Jennings and Howard Eiland (Cambridge: Harvard University Press, 2004], 48).

capharnaum, so to speak, of an author's textual waste — into the main dish of literary criticism and meaning. In conclusion, I do not argue in favor of either practice, nor do I suggest the field at-large move forward in a particular direction, but rather conclude this essay in the spirit of Morton herself: "The practice of literary criticism," Morton writes in the afterword of her 1990 publication, *Science Fiction,* "has functioned as both window into the world and, at the same time, the very blinds concealing our place within it — it's all just a matter of what readers' interests are. Auribus teneo lupum."[13]

Look outside.
> The dumpster is on fire.
> I am in here.

Writing Criticism: What Is an Author?

> All criticism must include in its discourse (even if in the most indirect and modest manner imaginable) an implicit reflection on itself. In other words, criticism is not at all a table of results or a body of judgments, it is essentially an activity, i.e., a series of intellectual acts profoundly committed to the historical and subjective existence (they are the same thing) of the man who performs them
>
> — Roland Barthes.[14]

> Writing, in our day, has moved infinitely closer to its source, to this disquieting sound which announces from the depths of language — once we attend to it — the source against which we seek refuge and toward which we address ourselves. Like Kafka's beast, language now listens from the bottom of it burrow to this inevitable and growing noise.
>
> — Michel Foucault[15]

---

13 Heidi B. Morton, *Science Fiction* (London: Penguin House, 1990), 389.
14 Roland Barthes, "What Is Criticism?" in *Critical Essays* (Evanston: Northwestern University Press, 1972), 257.
15 Michel Foucault, "Language to Infinity," in *Language, Counter-Memory, Practice,* 60.

On February 22, 1969, Michel Foucault addressed the Society at the Collège de France, where he sat as chair Professor of the History of Systems of Thought from 1969 until his death in 1984. His lecture, "What Is an Author?" set out to reexamine "the empty space left out by the author's disappearance"[16] first asserted by Roland Barthes one year prior. Foucault's response to Barthes's "Death of the Author" — the literary clarion call denoting the theoretical shift from new criticism and structuralism to deconstruction and anti-formalist critique — introduced Foucault's notion of "author-function," the mark of socio-historical and ideological conditions in which an author and their text emerge. Whereas Barthes's death of the author implies a separation between the author and a text — the literal extinguishment of any authorial-presence in and surrounding a text and thereby unbinding the reader from the chains of authorial-influence — Foucault's author-function decenters the author rather than extinguishing the author outright. This section will draw from Foucault's "What Is an Author?" along with his essay "The historical *a priori* and the archive," published that same year in *The Archeology of Knowledge,* to frame and historicize the archive-based reading practices Morton scholars have problematically deployed in recent years. But first, a brief overview of literary criticism's origins and its long-standing partisan divide will provide necessary context for addressing Morton Studies influence on the practice of literary criticism to date.

"Most of those who have written at length about the history of literary studies," writes Joseph North in his 2017 publication, *Literary Criticism: A Concise Political History,* "have agreed that modern literary criticism was effectively born at Cambridge in the 1920s, at a moment that has come to be called the 'critical revolution.'"[17] Citing Chris Baldick, Professor of English at Goldsmith University in London, North argues that the key conflict in the period running from 1890 and 1918 was "be-

---

16 Ibid., 121.
17 Joseph North, *Literary Criticism: A Concise Political History* (Cambridge: Harvard University Press, 2017), 21.

tween scholarly and scientific objectivism on the one side, and aesthetic or 'impressionistic' subjectivism on the other."[18] The practice of literary criticism has yet to resolve this century-old conflict, evidenced most notably with the discipline's acrimonious response to recent trends emerging from Morton Studies, a response that mirrors the very same shift in textual analysis that began a hundred years earlier. North continues:

> The critical revolution of the 1920s was a sharp turn away from what seemed the discipline's apparent trajectory. It allowed the distinctive belletristic emphasis on aesthetic appreciation, on cultivating the subjectivity of the reader, and on the connection between tastes and values to be taken up and insisted upon in a thoroughly new way, thereby laying the foundations for a new paradigm of criticism: a paradigm rigorous and scientific enough for the modern research university.[19]

What later observers have termed the "heroic period" of the profession — the paradigm of criticism's move away from subjective interpretation of literary texts toward a seemingly objective analysis of the "texts in and of themselves," as the phrase goes — is commonly referred to as New Criticism: the dominant mode of 20th century literary study grounded in a rigorous method of textual analysis termed "close reading" or, to some practitioners, "practical criticism." In the words of Chris Baldick,

> The heroic phase of modern Anglo-American criticism, from the 1920s to the 1960s, was marked by the subordination of literary-historical and literary-biographical study to the ascendant discourses of critical analysis and evaluation. In terms of method, this entailed a new practice of "close reading," attending to the specific formal features of

---

18 Chris Baldick, *Criticism and Literary Theory 1890 to the Present* (London: Longman, 1996), 13, qtd. in Joseph North, *Literary Criticism*, 21.
19 Ibid., 22.

texts rather than to the general world-views of their authors. Nothing distinguishes twentieth-century literary criticism more sharply from that of previous ages than this close attention to textual detail.[20]

This shift from mid-century literary criticism to the emergence of 1960s and '70s literary theory — the literary-historical/conceptualist paradigm that Morton Studies' inverted criticism is grounded in — is intimately entwined with the politicization of literary studies. While the names speak for themselves (Lacan, Foucault, Derrida, Said, Williams, Butler, Eco, and so on) never before had questions concerning sexuality and gender, race and whiteness, colonialism, neoliberalism, and most notably (and more broadly conceived) the focus of exploring (and subverting) power structures been grounded in serious literary analysis. The pivot from mid-century close reading practices to a more radical critique of revealing power structures of institutional and cultural oppression — both within and surrounding serious literary criticism[21] — laid the foundations for what would later be known as new historical reading practices, which emerged in the wake of Foucault's archival-based cultural analysis, what North refers to as "the scholarly, historicist/contextualist paradigm."[22]

---

20 Baldick, *Criticism and Literary Theory 1890 to the Present*, 221.
21 The irony here is, of course, that the discipline has become very mode of oppression it once set out to subvert, as outlined by Kevin Birmingham in his 2016 acceptance speech for The Truman Capote Award: "The profession of literary criticism depends upon exploitation. […] If you are a tenured (or tenure-track) faculty member teaching in a humanities department with Ph.D. candidates, you are both the instrument and the direct beneficiary of exploitation. Your roles as teacher, adviser, and committee member generate, cultivate, and exploit young people's devotion to literature. This is the great shame of our profession" (republished as "The Great Shame of Our Profession: How the Humanities Survives on Exploitation," *Chronicle of Higher Education*, February 12, 2017, http://www.chronicle.com/article/The-Great-Shame-of-Our/239148).
22 North, *Literary Criticism*, 59.

For Foucault, the author-function signals a particular time-and-place, the socio-historical stamp of a text that "points to the existence of certain groups of discourse, and refers to the status of this discourse within a society and culture."[23] The author-function is what Hegel might off-handedly refer to as an "authorial-zeitgeist," or Thomas Kuhn would call an "authorial paradigm" of certain political, philosophical, professional, and technological interconnections in which any one particular text emerges. That is to say that authors (and their writings) come from this world as products rather than creators — the author as a product, a product that comes into being through writing. What makes this new designation of authorship from Foucault so difficult to parse through today, with Morton Studies in focus — much like the critical (and contentious) revolution of the early twentieth century between scientific objectivism and aesthetic subjectivism — is the ambiguity of what scholars deem literary, what scholars designate as primary texts rather than secondary. In the realm of Morton Studies this tensions come into focus with the disciplines framing of archival materials (the seemingly secondary materials) as primary texts in and of themselves. Today's archive, broadly conceived and with Foucault's author-function in mind, functions as a vector for scholars to uncover the contexts in which texts and their authors emerge — for close readings are limited insofar as they omit historic and ideological conditions that surround a text's publication. And because the close reading practices of New Critics do not provide avenues to explore the cultural conditions in which texts emerge — the conditions in which this new shift in 1960s and '70s literary studies centers around — Michel Foucault's archived-based cultural analysis became the prevailing hermeneutic of literary evaluation. Unforeseeable at the time, of course, is that new historical reading practice would later become, *à la* Morton Studies, the very same reading practice to thwart itself and, subsequently, create the conditions in which the reemergence of New Criticism emerged.

---

23 Ibid., 123–24.

Foucault's "What Is an Author?" focuses attention on two key aspects: (a) "The singular relationship that holds between the author and the text, the manner in which a text apparently point to this finger who is outside and precedes it"[24] and (b) "The kinship between writing and death."[25] Whereas the author-function reveals the socio-historical aspects of any given work it nevertheless lacks essential attention to the prospective, uncertain reception of a given text's evolutions and profiles. Foucault's close reading of Nietzsche's *Genealogy* is useful for moving forward toward our examination of Morton Scholars' reading practices:

> Assuming we are dealing with an author, is everything he wrote and said, everything he left behind, to be included in his work? This problem is both theoretical and practical. If we wish to publish the complete works of Nietzsche, for example, where do we draw the line? Certainly everything must be published, along with the drafts of his works, his plans for aphorisms, his marginal notations and corrections. But what if, in a notebook filled with aphorisms, we find a reference, a reminder of an appointment, an address or a laundry bill, should this be included in his works? Why not? These practical considerations are endless once we consider how a work can be extracted from the millions of traces left by an individual after his death. Plainly, we lack a theory to encompass the questions generated by a work and the empirical activity of those who naively undertake the publication of the complete works of an author often suffers from the absence of this framework.[26]

As a theoretical framework to encompass the questions generated by Foucault above and those that have since emerged in the wake of Morton Studies, I turn to Gérard Gennette's notion

---

24 Michel Foucault, *The Archeology of Knowledge* (London: Tavisstock, 1972), 115.
25 Ibid., 116.
26 Ibid., 118–19.

of paratext as a guide for understanding recent shifts in literary analysis. And but so broadly conceived, paratext refers to materials that surround any given text: from internal materials (e.g., cover images, copyright pages, forwards, notes) to external, distanced materials (e.g., author interviews, reviews, manuscripts, surrounding scholarship). Paratext does not entirely determine nor does it fully reduce a text in question, but it is politically charged and influential to the meaning readers derive. What makes Genette's framework uniquely suited for discussions surrounding Morton Studies' exploitative use of Foucauldian archival work is precisely the polemical turn scholars have made by situating external paratext surrounding Morton's work (i.e., drafts, interviews, personal correspondences, digital histories, book annotations, etc.) as primary texts in and of themselves.

Inverted Paratext: Scholar as Ragpicker

> History tells us that there is no such thing as a timeless essence of literature, but under the rubric "literature" (itself quite recent, moreover) a process of very different forms, functions, institutions, reasons, and projects whose relativity it is precisely the historian's responsibility to discern.
> — Roland Barthes[27]

> The final belief is to believe in a fiction, which you know to be a fiction, there being nothing else. The exquisite truth is to know that it is a fiction and that you believe in it willingly.
> — Wallace Stevens[28]

Since her publication of "The Death of an Author and the Birth of a Discipline: In Defense of Neo-Criticism," it's no stretch to state that literary critic Lauren St. Claire has become somewhat

---

27 Roland Barthes, "The Two Criticisms," in *Critical Essays* (Evanston: Northwestern University Press, 1972), 251.
28 Wallace Stevens, *Opus Posthumous: [Poems, Plays, Prose]* (London: Faber and Faber, 1957), 163.

of a household name in English and Cultural Studies departments throughout academia. Grounded in her reading of Leafy's *Heidi B. Morton's Ghosts,* St. Claire argues that "Leafy's restructuring of Morton's bibliography — adding six so-called 'texts' to her body of work calls for a close examination of recent trends in Morton Studies."[29] Yet before I present more from Leafy and her Neo-Critical contemporaries, a reference guide to Morton's living and posthumous bibliographies will prove useful. Thus, in accordance with the "Also By Heidi B. Morton" page of her last living publication, *Turtles All The Way Down, A Memoir,* Morton's bibliography (at the time of her death) included:

— *Genre: A History* (1987)
— *Science Fiction* (1990)
— *The Western Dystopia* (1994)
— *American Spirit: A Phenomenology of Self-Interest* (1999)
— *Lands after Neoliberalism: A Novel* (2003)
— *A Time for Everything Book I* (2005)
— *A Time for Everything Book II* (2006)
— *A Time for Everything Book III* (2007)
— *Turtles All The Way Down, A Memoir* (2009)

And from the "Works By Heidi B. Morton" page of Leafy's 2012 publication of *Ghosts*:

— *Genre: A History* (1987)
— *Science Fiction* (1990)
— *The Blockbuster Files* (1994–2009)
— *The Western Dystopia* (1994)
— *Reading The Marx–Engels Reader* (1997–2009)
— *American Spirit: A Phenomenology of Self-Interest* (1999)
— *Exchanges with Rufus: A Love Story* (2000–2009)
— *Words: Annotating the Shorter Oxford English Dictionary* (2001–2009)
— *Searchings: A Memoir* (2002–2009)

---

29 St. Claire, "The Death of an Author and the Birth of a Discipline," 346.

— *Lands after Neoliberalism: A Novel* (2003)
— *A Time for Everything Book I* (2005)
— *November 9th–13th, 2005* (2005)
— *A Time for Everything Book II* (2006)
— *A Time for Everything Book III* (2007)
— *Turtles All The Way Down, A Memoir* (2009)

St. Claire, taking aim at Leafy's bewildering inclusion of select archived materials as primary texts, focuses her critical eye on two so-called "texts" in particular. On the one hand, there's *November 9th–13th, 2005,* the archive's disorienting collection of various transcripts from Morton's three-day trip to New York City to promote Book I of *A Time for Everything*.[30] And on the other hand, there's the detailed history of Morton's Blockbuster Video transactions, dating from 1992 right up to her death on November 28th, 2009, titled *The Blockbuster Files*. Regarding the latter, according to Leafy,

> [*The Blockbuster Files*] provide scholars invaluable insights into the state of not only American entertainment culture at the turn of the millennium but also, and more importantly, Morton's intermittent mental health issues and their ties to Blockbuster staff recommendations — evidenced most directly by Morton's refusal to pay late-fees for her rental of *Waterworld,* the 1995 post-apocalyptic fantasy/science fiction film staring Kevin Costner.[31]

Leafy goes on to argue that "the highly anticipated yet underwhelming cinematic experience of *Waterworld,* for Morton, is directly correlated to her self-check-in at Butler Mental Hospital

---

[30] Included in *November* is an assortment of Morton's personal diary entries, transcripts of various digital communication including text messages, emails, and voice messages, internet search history, credit card statements, GPS locations, fan photos collected, and various stills from security camera footage.

[31] Leafy, *Heidi B. Morton's Ghosts,* 82.

in Providence, RI, between March 2nd and March 15th, 1997."[32] Morton's refusal to pay late fees, Leafy argues, can be further understood with a close reading of her 1999 publication of *The Western Dystopia*, "wherein the novel's protagonist, Maggie Mariner," Leafy writes, "systematically rents and returns each staff recommended film without rewinding."[33] Leafy's use of *The Western Dystopia* to frame *The Blockbuster Files* — rather than using the so-called *Blockbuster Files* to frame *The Western Dystopia*, as archival work traditionally has done — is just one example of a how Morton scholars have reframed paratext as text. While this connection between archived materials and their hermeneutical influences upon primary texts is by no means outside the bound of biographical, scholarly discourse, it is Leafy's argument that "*The Blockbuster Files,* regardless of insight upon Morton's own life and various publications, is a true literary masterpiece in and of itself."[34] In response, St. Claire points to the grandeurs of illusion Morton scholars appear to be suffering from:

> Walk into any bookstore across the country, check online outlets, peruse your local yard sales and you will not find a copy *Searchings: A Memoir* or a copy of *Exchanges with Rufus* or any version of what Leafy garishly deems "*The Blockbuster Files.*" Why? Because they don't exist. And I mean this quite literally: these so-called "texts" are intellectual constructions of one scholar's mind — not Morton, nor her publisher's doing. [...] Leafy's inclusion of archival files as primary texts within Morton's bibliography is not only misleading to readers but downright preposterous and insulting to literary studies at-large. And Morton scholars — if we can even call them scholars much longer — are not finished with their plundering of an American icon's oeuvre. Leafy's inclusion of Morton's search history under the guise of *Searchings* is

---

32 Ibid.
33 Ibid.
34 Ibid., 83.

just the beginning, as the archive has yet to publically release Morton's K-12, undergraduate, and MFA papers that were acquired by Morton's fiancé, author James Rufus, just last year.[35]

These materials, from manuscripts of *A Time for Everything* to personal correspondences between Morton and Rufus, are what Gérard Genette calls "external paratext," external insofar as they influence one's reading from afar, not included within the bindings of a text. "The distanced elements," Genette writes, "messages that, at least, originally, are located outside the book."[36] And what Leafy has done above is take the external materials of Morton's personal communications and framed them as primary texts in and of themselves. Genette, framing the external paratext as "epitext," continues,

> Epitext generally happens with the help of media (interviews, conversations) or under cover or private communications (letters, diaries, and others). [...] The epitext is any paratextual element not materially appended to the text within the same volume but circulating, as it were, freely, in a virtual limitless physical and social space.[37]

This "virtual limitless physical and social space," following Genette's framework, would no doubt situate Morton's Blockbuster transactions as epitext, insofar as they are made publically available at the NYPL and, in some manner or another, have influenced our reception of Morton's primary texts. On the other end of the paratextual spectrum is the internal paratext, what Genette frames as "peritext," the category of elements *within* the text: "the spatial, localized elements of the paratext."[38] This would include the dusk jacket for *A Time for Everything*, its title page, Morton's preface, endnotes, and index. There's an obvious

---

35 St. Claire, "The Death of an Author and the Birth of a Discipline," 334.
36 Gérard Genette, Jane E. Lewin, and Richard Macksey, *Paratexts: Thresholds of Interpretation* (Cambridge: Cambridge University Press, 2001), 5.
37 Ibid., 5, 344.
38 Ibid., 4.

dialectical tension about paratextual materials insofar as both peritext and epitext depend upon and, in turn, reconstitute the other: in Genette's words, both peritext and epitext "completely and entirely share the special field of the paratext."[39] Genette makes a note of this internal-external dialectic, arguing that

> [t]he location of the epitext is therefore anywhere outside the book — but of course nothing precludes its later admission to the peritext. Such admission is always possible, and we will encounter many examples of it: see the original interviews appended to posthumous scholarly editions, or the innumerable excerpts from correspondences or diaries quoted in the critical notes of such scholarly editions.[40]

While Genette's framework unpacks this common shift from once epitextual materials (interviews, drafts, scholarship, etc.) to peritextual materials (forwords and introductions that include said interviews, drafts, and scholarship), nowhere does a shift from epitext to peritext take place *within* an author's bibliography until the emergence of Morton Studies pillage of her archive. In essence, what Morton scholars have done is entirely overturned Gennett's paratextual framework in on itself by rendering epitext as not merely peritext bur rather primary texts in and of themselves.

Morton's diary entries, along with credit card statements, transcripts of her book signing events, digital communications, and even voice memos are all included in the archive's "Personal Accounts and Public Engagement" section, of which scholars have since rendered primary texts; Leafy, in what can only be surmounted as a decision grounded in scholastic self-interest, chose five consecutive dates to frame as a primary materials with the publication of *November 9th–13th, 2006*. These materials, prior to Leafy's framing, were no doubt useful for scholarship's engagement with Morton's writing of *A Time for Everything* se-

---

39 Ibid., 5.
40 Ibid., 345.

ries, yet including five days worth of personal correspondences and bank statements within Morton's bibliography as primary text is not only exploitative and questionably unethical, but inverts Genette's formula by rendering Morton's published work of fiction epitext and thus framing the archival materials as text. Morton scholars are no doubt aware of this problematic inversion yet nevertheless conscientiously argue for it: "The former paratextual materials," writes James McKinney, "when viewed as primary sources of literary analysis themselves, enhance the intimacy of authorial reader relations by seeing authorship in its purest, unfiltered state."[41] McKinney continues,

> Morton's personal correspondences with Rufus is a profoundly intimate display of an American love story [...] [Morton's] ability to cover the spectrum of emotions throughout this intermittent relationship with her fiancé is a true tour de force of creative, emotional exuberance.[42]

While scholars have been interested in manuscripts and drafts of published texts throughout the practice of literary studies, what Morton Studies is interested in, though, is the materials that did not make it into the texts themselves — the leftovers, if you will. That is to say that scholarly attention to Foucault's author-function is no longer of principle concern; these leftovers, for Morton scholars at least, have become the main dish of textual meaning.

The inversion of scholarly attention within Morton Studies, from paratext to text, no doubt produces questions concerning the role of scholarship in framing an author's posthumous literary legacy and author-functions. And while Morton scholars are continuously placed under the critical microscope, there's also the less examined role of the archivist-function in curating what is even possible for scholars to attend to in the first

---

41 James McKinney, "Dancing with Laundry Lists: Reading Morton's June 6th, 2007," *Critique: Studies in Contemporary Fiction* 57, no. 4 (Sept. 2014): 360.

42 Ibid., 366.

place. Foucault addresses this discursive relationship between archivists and scholars in his 1972 essay "The historical *a priori* and the archive," framing archives as a grouped together mass of indefinite and allusive artifacts "in distinct figures, composed together in accordance with multiple relations, maintained or blurred in accordance with specific regularities."[43] And insofar as the scholarly, historicist/contextualist paradigm grounds itself in archival work, its findings — and our collective construction of history itself — remains dependent upon and reconstituted by an archive's internal framing and construction prior to its scholarly peruses.

And but so with Morton scholars' capacity and to up-cycle the discarded scraps of an author's wastebasket (as provided by the NYPL, respectively) into an orderly arrangement of scholastic interests, author-functions become contested and conceptualized anew when the leftover traces of a life becomes the raison d'etre of an author's posthumous literary legacy. As such, it's useful to think of Morton Studies practitioners as "scholarly ragpickers," so to speak, in the spirit of Walter Benjamin's reading of Baudelaire's "The Ragpickers Wine," wherein Benjamin viewed the ragpicker of nineteenth century Paris sharing methodologies with that of the poet; quoting Baudelaire directly, Benjamin writes:

> "Here we have a man whose job it is to gather the day's refuse in the capital. Everything that the big city has thrown away, everything it has lost, everything it has scorned, everything it has crushed underfoot he catalogues and collects. He collects the annals of intemperance, the capharnaum of waste. He sorts things out and selects judiciously: he collects like a miser guarding a treasure, refuse which will assume the shape of useful or gratifying objects between the jaws of the goddess of industry." This description is one extended metaphor for the poetic method, as Baudelaire practiced it. Ragpicker and poet: both are concerned with refuse, and both go about

---

43 Foucault, *The Archeology of Knowledge*, 129.

their solitary business while other citizens are sleeping; they even move in the same way.[44]

When viewed from the perspective of "scholar as ragpicker" in the above spirit of Benjamin, there's a palpable, redemptive quality surrounding Morton Studies' reading practices: an appreciation and celebration of everydayness — carnival in appearance, sacred in practice. Morton scholars, sorting through the leftovers of an author's life, collecting the detritus of their yesterdays and arranging them in a way that makes the once-ignored ostensibly loved again, rendering the seemingly banal and tedious and discarded moments of one's life as holy and alive, on fire and teeming with historical subjunctivity.

Jacqueline Miall's "Archive as Pilgrimage," as quoted earlier, remains the principal architect for this type of redemptive reading when she writes that the archive, "when one allows its waves of serendipity to wash over you, becomes apocalyptic: awakening the bliss that lies dormant in the banal, disclosing the profundity found in the quotidian, and unveiling author/ity, so to speak, through the everyday."[45] Miall continues:

> One visit [to the NYPL] will provide Morton readers — and those not yet acquainted with her work — an astonishing exploration into the redemptive power of archival research. [...] The archive's manuscripts and personal correspondences — most especially materials surrounding Morton's admired trilogy of dystopian historical fiction, *A Time for Everything* — remain a true tour de force of literary virtuosity and elegance, an unbearable display of psychological pain and heartbreak that penetrates the very configuration of an author's supposed-bibliography, reaching far beyond the garland of Morton's pre-posthumously published work and into a new phase of her posthumous literary career. [...] It's no wonder why Morton scholars proselytize the archive as a sort

---

44 Benjamin, "The Paris of the Second Empire in Baudelaire," 48.
45 Miall, "The Archive as Pilgrimage," 3.

of pilgrimage or Mecca of sorts…being here is a kind of a spiritual, hermeneutical surrender.[46]

To some critics, like Neo-Critic Lauren St. Claire, Miall's argument for redemptive reading is nothing more than a "bastardization of literary studies."[47] However, to others who have spoken publically about the divisive topic, most notably and to no surprise literary critic David Shields and poet Kenneth Goldsmith, Morton Studies' reading practices are not only welcomed with open arms and eager hermeneutical, fantastic eyes, but are obvious extensions of recent trends in the very forms of contemporary literature that critics are responding to: "literary criticism," Shields writes, "is minimum security prison — and the guards have been sent home."[48] / "Scholarship dead. Long live the anti-essay, built from scraps."[49] / "Neo-Critics sing the song of a bird that has come to love its cage."[50] / "It must all be considered as if spoken by a character in a novel (minus the novel)."[51] / "One of the smartest ways to write fiction today is to say that you're not, and then to do whatever you very well please. Fiction writers, take note. Some of the best fiction is now being written as nonfiction."[52] And when asked to comment on the state of contemporary authorship, Goldsmith, in an interview with *Berfrois Magazine*:

> We are all singing the song of ourselves, every day. If only we could only treasure that in the way that Whitman did. Whitman was conscious of his song. He was doing what everyone

---

46 Ibid.
47 St. Claire, "The Death of an Author and the Birth of a Discipline," 436.
48 Source unknown.
49 *Supra.*
50 *Supra.*
51 *Supra.*
52 *Supra.*

is doing diaristically. People are writing diaries, but he's the only one who takes the diary and calls it art.[53]

Not only are Morton Studies' reading practices welcomingly Whitmanesque in their rendering of the everyday as literary, but in the words of Jackson Burr, quoting Shields quoting either himself or an unknown source or both, Morton Studies' reading practices are functioning on two levels: "both dissolving the genre of literary criticism while simultaneously inventing an entirely new one"[54] — *à la* Angelus Novus:

> [And] here we have a [scholar] whose job it is to gather the [author's] refuse in the [archive]. Everything that the [text] has thrown away, everything it has lost, everything it has scorned, everything it has crushed underfoot he catalogues and collects. He collects the annals of intemperance, the capharnaum of waste. He sorts things out and selects judiciously: he collects like a miser guarding a treasure, refuse which will assume the shape of useful or gratifying objects between the jaws of the goddess of [academia].
>
> This description is one extended metaphor for the [scholarly, historicist/contextualist method], as [academics] practice it. Ragpicker and [scholar]: both are concerned with refuse.

Coda

An archive is "not a neatly defined entity," writes Carrie Smith, as "it will almost always contain items which stretch the boundaries of our understanding of archives and create conceptual

---

53 Kenneth Goldsmith, "Ubu Yorker: Berfrois Interviews Kenneth Goldsmith," *Berfrois Magazine*, September 15, 2017, http://www.berfrois.com/2017/09/berfrois-interviews-kenneth-goldsmith/.

54 Jackson Burr, "How Goldsmithian Reading Practices Colonized a Discipline," *The New Yorker*, October 16, 2017, https://www.newyorker.com/criticism/page-turner/how-goldsmithian-reading-ractices-colonized-discipline-2016

challenges for archivists and scholars alike."⁵⁵ These challenges of demarcation, which have long been in focus for questions concerning authorship and its scholarly engagements (from Foucault's reading of Nietzsche's *Genealogy* right up to Morton Studies' inverted paratext), have now been brought into the mainstream of literary discourse with the New York Public Library's inclusion of contentious materials surrounding the life and work of Heidi B. Morton. And while criticisms surrounding Morton Studies' remains an indefinite matter of debate there's nevertheless an alarming omission of critical attention (this essay included) toward the NYPL archivists who've gone to great lengths to acquire the items Morton scholars have grafted onto since the archive's opening. And but so while the role of scholarship in framing authorial-functions in and around a text may mean many things, one thing that it cannot mean is that no one did "it."⁵⁶

Look around you.
 The paratext trembling, shapeless.
  We are in here.

---

55 Carrie Smith, "Illustration and Ekphrasis: The Working Drafts of Ted Hughes's Cave Birds," in *The Boundaries of the Literary Archive: Reclamation and Representation* (Farnham: Ashgate Publishing, 2013), 123.
56 William H. Gass, "The Death of the Author," in *Habitations of the Word: Essays* (New York: Simon and Schuster, 1985), 73.

Bibliography

Baldick, Chris. *Criticism and Literary Theory 1890 to the Present*. London: Longman, 1996.

Barthes, Roland. *Critical Essays*. Evanston: Northwestern University Press, 1972.

Beckett, Samuel. *Texts for Nothing*. Translated by Samuel Beckett. London: Calder & Boyars, 1974

Benjamin, Walter. *Selected Writings: 1938–1940*. Edited by Michael W. Jennings and Howard Eiland. Cambridge: Harvard University Press, 2004.

Birmingham, Kevin. "The Great Shame of Our Profession: How the Humanities Survives on Exploitation." *Chronicle of Higher Education,* February 2, 2017. http://www.chronicle.com/ article/The-Great-Shame-of-Our/239148

Burr, Jackson. "How Goldsmithian Reading Practices Colonized a Discipline." *The New Yorker,* October 16, 2017, https://www.newyorker.com/criticism/page-turner/how-goldsmithian- reading-ractices-colonized-discipline-2016

Foucault, Michel. *Language, Counter-Memory, Practice*. Edited by Donald F. Bouchard. Ithaca: Cornell University Press, 1977.

———. *The Archeology of Knowledge*. Translated by A.M. Sheridan Smith. London: Tavisstock, 1972.

Gass, William H. *Habitations of the Word: Essays*. New York: Simon and Schuster, 1985,

Genette, Gérard et al. *Paratexts: Thresholds of Interpretation*. Cambridge: Cambridge University Press, 2001.

Goldsmith, Kenneth. "Ubu Yorker: Berfrois Interviews Kenneth Goldsmith." *Berfrois Magazine,* September 15, 2017. http://www.berfrois.com/2017/09/berfrois-interviews-kenneth-goldsmith/.

Kristeva, Julia. *Revolution in Poetic Language*. Translated by Margaret Waller. New York: Columbia University Press, 1984.

Leafy, Stephen. *Heidi B. Morton's Ghosts: The Personal Journals and Laundry Lists of an American Writer.* London: Bloomsbury, 2012.

McKinney, James. "Dancing with Laundry Lists: Reading Morton's June 6th, 2007." *Critique: Studies in Contemporary Fiction* 57, no. 4 (Sept. 2014): 358–67.

Miall, Jacqueline. "The Archive as Pilgrimage: Receiving the Heidi B. Morton Papers." *The Washington Post,* September 12th, 2016. https://www.washingtonpost.com/opinions/ /2016/09/12/f507e8cb2-9f9f-112e7-8ea1-ed975285475e_story.html.

Morton, Heidi B. *Science Fiction.* London: Penguin House, 1990.

North, Joseph. *Literary Criticism: A Concise Political History.* Cambridge: University Press, 2017.

Smith, Carrie. "Illustration and Ekphrasis: The Working Drafts of Ted Hughes's *Cave Birds.*" In *The Boundaries of the Literary Archive: Reclamation and Representation.* Farnham: Ashgate Publishing, 2013.

Stevens, Wallace. *Opus Posthumous: [Poems, Plays, Prose].* London: Faber and Faber, 1957.

St. Claire, Lauren. "The Death of an Author and the Birth of a Discipline: In Defense of Neo-Criticism." *American Literature* 85, no. 3 (Nov. 2013): 332–437.

Weinstein, Abigail. "From Background to Foreground: A History of Archival Ethics." *Journal of Contemporary Archival Studies* 32, no. 1 (Nov. 2013): 1–25.

Woods, Jameson. "Reinventing the Practice." *The New Yorker,* June 17, 2014. https://www.newyorker.com/criticism/page-turner/reinventing-the-practice-2014.

16

"What Else Was There To Do?": Fat Futurity and the Limits of Narrative Imagination in *Desolation*

Em K. Falk

I've been dead my whole life.

— Siobhan Graves[1]

"Folks had a hard enough time just looking out for themselves back then. Somebody like that... well, what else was there to do?"

— *Desolation*

Introduction

The 2016 horror film *Desolation*[2] was met with a measure of critical praise upon its release. Among the film's chief strengths, reviewers cited its reliance on atmospheric dread and narrative

---

[1] Siobhan Graves, *Death Becomes Me, Death Becomes Me: Mortal Terror and the Spectre of Obesity* (London: Routledge, 1999), 3.
[2] *Desolation*, dir. Jessica Shan, 2016.

tension rather than jump scares or blaring musical stings.³ As a wide-release horror film helmed by a female director, *Desolation* has received particular attention from feminist critics. *Jetsam*'s Maddie Shore compares the film to *The Babadook*,⁴ directed by Jennifer Kent.

> [As with *The Babadook*], a female filmmaker presents audiences with a nightmarish story about processing trauma. In this case, the scope of that story is larger: the conflict is rooted in the collective trauma and guilt of an entire community. Traumatic events can never be undone. And so the ghosts or demons that represent the echoes of those events can never be fully exorcized.⁵

Other writers have homed in more precisely on the source of the collective "trauma" at the heart of the narrative. Writing for the feminist magazine *RedCurrent*, Kirsten Nye-Lenehan praises the film's "compassionate rage" on behalf of its ghostly antagonist. "When the circumstances of [the ghost's] death are revealed, the protagonist and, by extension, the viewer are overcome with a sense of betrayal. The murder of an obese and disabled woman is portrayed not as a mercy killing but as a grave injustice."⁶

Still other critics take a different view of *Desolation*'s treatment of body size as a narrative device. "How could anyone call this film 'fat positive' when a fat character is literally the monster?" demands an anonymous contributor to the "radically fat-positive" horror blog *DEATHDRIVE*.⁷ This essay presents a simi-

---

3 Jay Orba, "*Desolation* Is a Uniquely American Nightmare," *New York Times*, October 14, 2016, http:/www.nytimes.com/2016/10/14/review-desolation-orba.

4 *The Babadook*, dir. Jennifer Kent, 2014.

5 Maddie Shore, "Trauma and Restless Ghosts in Jessica Shan's *Desolation*," *Jetsam*, December 2016, 23–24.

6 Kirsten Nye-Lenehan, "Fat Positivity Finds an Outlet in Mainstream Horror," *RedCurrent*, November 2016, http://www.redcurrent.org/nyelenehan/desolation.

7 "Desolation Is Just Monster House for Grown-ups," *DEATHDRIVE*, November 2016, http://www.deathdrivemag.com/desolation-is-just.

larly skeptical view. Despite what might be arguably termed a compassionate or pitying portrayal of the film's primary antagonist, a fat woman is ultimately depicted as a terrifying monster. Her size is not incidental but rather crucial to the legend of how she came to haunt the town, a tale which features in the film as an embedded narrative or story-within-a-story. Furthermore, the embodiment of the villainess is thematically significant. For the protagonist and, by extension, the viewer, she represents the inevitability and permanence of death.

A general symbolic association between body size and mortality has seized the collective imagination in our age of constant, breathless anguish over the "obesity epidemic." In popular discourse, fatness is explicitly framed in terms of its threat to the life of not only the individual but of the nation itself.[8] We are desperate to avoid becoming fat ourselves, and desperate to exterminate fat people from within our midst. Cultural critic Siobhán Graves asserts that the very fattest bodies horrify us the most because in such a figure "the possibility of slenderness, which is to say the possibility of redemption and rebirth, is extinguished"[9].

Interpreting *Desolation* through the lens suggested by Graves in her seminal 1999 book *Death Becomes Me: Mortal Terror and the Spectre of Obesity,* I argue that *Desolation* presents a well-trodden and all-too-familiar narrative about life at the upper extremes of body size — or rather, the impossibility of such a life. This seems to be the *only* possible or acceptable story about very fat people: namely, that fatness is associated with mortality so closely that to be *very* fat is to exist in a state of living death. Beyond a certain threshold a person is, as Graves puts it, "always already dead" and she is perceived to be "nothing more than a

---

8 Charlotte Biltekoff, "The Terror Within: Obesity in Post 9/11 US Life," *American Studies* 48, no. 3 (2007): 29–48; Kathleen LeBesco, "Neoliberalism, Public Health, and the Moral Perils of Fatness," *Critical Public Health* 21, no. 2 (2011) 153–64; Christopher Mayes, *The Biopolitics of Lifestyle: Foucault, Ethics, and Healthy Choices* (London: Routledge, 2016).

9 Graves, *Death Becomes Me,* 56.

grotesque memento mori, shunned by her peers and community into a living tomb."[10]

As a ghost, the antagonist of *Desolation* is literally dead from the very beginning of the story. In a sense she was always dead because, despite the narrative's "compassionate rage" on her behalf, no room is left to imagine a different outcome for her. As soon as she grew to an untenable size her fate was sealed. Graves calls this narrative tendency in popular portrayals of very fat people a "malign failure of imagination."[11] I would also describe it more precisely as the denial of fat futurity. Because she can only be thought of as dead or imminently dying, the very fat person cannot be understood as continuing to live or exist in her present physical state. Her life itself is unthinkable. Following Graves's application of terror management theory, I posit that *Desolation* is a microcosmic illustration of how the terror of being or becoming fat is a direct expression of the fear of death.

American Gothic

Desolation opens with a voiceover accompanied by shadow puppet-like animation. "It all begins with a sad story," the narrator intones. Once upon a time, the story goes, a large family lived on an isolated farmstead: two parents and their seven daughters. When a sudden illness descended on the family, all of the daughters fell ill and six of them perished.

Instead of adapting to their new existence as a family of three, the grief-stricken parents carried on as if nothing had changed, except that all of their resources were now dedicated to the remaining daughter. Each took on an impossible workload, as if they had the same number of mouths to feed. So the seventh sister was doted on and stuffed with enough food for seven people, year in and year out, until she grew too large to leave the bedroom that she and her sisters had once shared.

---

10 Ibid., 86.
11 Ibid., 20.

Eventually the parents simply worked themselves to death. As she tried to escape her confinement and seek help, the helpless, nameless woman knocked over a kerosene lamp. By the time neighbors arrived, they could only watch as the farmhouse burned to the ground with its occupant trapped inside. "She died screaming," says the narrator, "and we want to believe that there was no one to hear her. But maybe every legend begins with a lie."

The narrator is revealed to be the film's twenty-something protagonist: Shoshanna "Sho" Green. The main narrative begins as Sho leaves her Philadelphia apartment and sets out for the crumbling rural town of Desolation, Pennsylvania, where the tale of the "Seventh Sister" is part of the local folklore. Sho is the host of a popular podcast called "American Gothic," for which she investigates and recounts urban legends and local ghost stories from across the United States. At the start of the film, the show has been on hiatus while Sho grieved the recent death of her mother. As a gesture of moving on, she sets out to gather material for the episode that will kick off a new season. While packing up her field equipment, Sho explains to her girlfriend that she is drawn to Desolation and to the Seventh Sister because the story seems to be a warning about the dangers of outsized or inappropriate grief. "If you can't let go of something you've lost," she says, "you might lose everything that you have left."

When she arrives in the town, Sho's first contact is Greg, a hobbyist historian. After he has retold the grim story as he understands it, along the same lines as the opening narration, Sho asks if there is any historical record of the family. Greg coughs and evenly replies "No." When she then asks whether the story of the Seventh Sister is based on real historical events, he equivocates: "Oh sure, probably. Every legend starts with a grain of truth, doesn't it?" After the exchange, Sho wonders aloud into her mic, "Where did this legend come from, and why has it endured? If it is not rooted in history, then from what dark corner of Desolation's psyche did it emerge?"

In the slow build up to *Desolation*'s second act, Sho wanders the dusty, overgrown streets of Desolation, meditating on her own grief and seeking out more material on the melancholy legend. The looming skeletons of rotted granaries and warehouses, stark against the gray and ochre void of the surrounding fields, provide a symbolic externalization of Sho's own feelings of stagnation and loneliness. In voiceover, Sho records some of her own thoughts on the story of the Seventh Sister, suggesting that the mother and father in the tale "were so consumed by grief that they destroyed themselves and ultimately even their remaining daughter." She also calls her girlfriend and muses about her own mother, about things that were said and things left unsaid. She interviews one of the town supervisors, who wonders aloud whether the legend of the Seventh Sister might be parlayed into a source of tourism. A bohemian-looking cafe owner offers a perspective on the story that re-centers the subjecthood of the Seventh Sister herself: "What did she think of all this? Losing her sisters, living with her crazy parents — imagine how lonely she was. But a woman couldn't just leave home and live on her own in those days."

As an externalization of the protagonist's psyche and the collective psyche of its residents, Desolation itself projects an aura of stagnation and melancholy. In the present day, true to its name, the town is a ruin. Abandoned silos and grain elevators rise from the scrubby hills like ancient monoliths. The residents' homes are small and stark. The main street of the town is flanked by crumbling brick buildings whose square facades evoke a row of faces fixed with a thousand-yard stare. Images of post-agricultural decay and the decrepit state of the rural working class form a hastily sketched backdrop for the main action of the film. This is a common device in American horror films: a rural setting instantly evokes a certain uncanny atmosphere, a pervasive feeling of "claustrophobic emptiness."[12] Often, naive "city slicker" type characters are pitted against archetypal violent, animalistic "hillbillies," as in such films as *Deliverance* (1972), *The Hills Have Eyes* (1977), *Canebrake* (1991), and *Wrong*

---

12 Adun Perkins, *Abyss: Images of Rural Desolation in the American Horror Film* (Chicago: Chicago University Press, 2002), 12.

Turn (2003). Occasionally, the dynamic is reversed, with the rural characters occupying a more sympathetic (*Pumpkinhead* [1989]; *Tucker & Dale vs. Evil* [2010]) or heroic (*Oxbow* [2003]) role. Like most other horror films of this ilk, *Desolation* offers little in the way of meaningful class or historical analysis. While the film does not descend into the monstrous hillbilly cliché, it does rely on the image of rural decay to illustrate the general theme of mortality. It is never made clear exactly when or why the economy of the town collapsed, because such details would be incidental to the narrative. The story is not about the social plight of rural America, but about the protagonist's confrontation with the painful reality of death.

Reviewing the film for the *New York Times,* Jay Orba describes the imagery and thematic undertones of *Desolation* as "an expression of distinctly American anxieties."[13] Orba's reading of the film synthesizes its use of rural imagery with the embodiment of the Seventh Sister herself.

> The quiet squalor of tumbled-down barns and rusted, overgrown farm equipment is contrasted with the more lively but equally rusty setting of Philadelphia. The visual language of the film suggests a connection between the urban and the rural environments, beyond their significance to the personal journey of Shoshanna herself. Just as the turmoil of a troubled subconscious will influence the outer realm of conscious behavior, the decay of rural life may show itself in the cracks that run across the shiny facade of its urban counterpart.
>
> The nexus of this implied relationship might be found in the figure of the vengeful specter herself. The ghost is the troubled spirit of a woman who was abjectly obese, and the film is otherwise too introspective for this creative choice to have been a matter of cheap shock value. Indeed, the ghost seems to embody the general decay that has descended on the town and, by extension, on rural life and the soul of America itself.

---

13 Orba, "*Desolation* Is a Uniquely American Nightmare."

> For decades, family-owned farms have been in a state of steep and steady decline — a trend which seems to correspond with the explosion of obesity rates. Two thirds of American adults are overweight or obese, and economically disadvantaged communities, both urban and rural, have been hit hardest by the epidemic. One is left to wonder whether there might be a real-life connection between American obesity and the consolidation of big agribusiness and the proliferation of mass-produced, highly processed foods.[14]

All this is extrapolated from a horror film that makes no direct mention or portrayal of farming at all, and that features no commentary on obesity aside from a plot predicated on the unnatural death of a very fat woman. Orba's review and others like it speak to a powerful need to expound on the meaning of fatness where-ever it is seen, and in popular discourse that meaning is almost always death. Writing decades prior, when the rhetoric of the "obesity epidemic" had only just emerged, Graves predicted our contemporary conflation of obesity with mortality. Paraphrasing Leslie Fiedler,[15] she writes that "It used to be that we could revel in our size, or fight it, or stoically endure our fate."[16] She notes that fatness, even at its most extreme, once encompassed a multitude of contradictory meanings: "Before we were consigned to 'morbid obesity,' people of extreme size could be marvels as well as monsters. We might inspire horror but we could also be objects of desire or of envy, heralds of joyful abandon and good fortune. We have always been a spectacle but at least we could choose our schtick."[17] But in the 1980s there came a discursive shift. Public health reports and new media began to use the language of an "obesity epidemic."

---

14 Ibid.
15 Leslie Fiedler, *Freaks: Myths and Images of the Secret Self* (New York: Simon and Schuster, 1978), 125.
16 Graves, *Death Becomes Me,* 72.
17 Ibid.

In order to constitute an "epidemic," fatness must be a disease. Not merely a vector for disease, or a risk factor, or a symptom, but a plague in itself. Suddenly it's not heart disease or diabetes — actual treatable ailments — that threaten the population. "Diet or die" the media hounds us. To be or become fat is death. And what about those of us who are far beyond the reach of diets, whose size is inescapable and overwhelming? We can only be monsters now. The living dead, silenced and exiled.[18]

Mortal Terror

After the opening narration and the animated sequence, the film introduces Sho via her reflection as she pulls down a cloth that had been covering a mirror in her parents' home. This shot establishes the theme and scope of the story, drawing the viewer into the interior life of the protagonist to share her grief, and her struggle to fully comprehend mortality. Uncovering the mirror is itself a gesture of renewal, a small ritual to mark the process of healing and moving on in the wake of irrevocable loss. Sho is ready to start living her life again, but there are still trials ahead.

Ghost stories are an age-old medium through which cultural communities collectively process the permanence of death and loss.[19] *Desolation* is itself a ghost story within a ghost story. The first indication that the figure of the Seventh Sister is really a ghost comes during Sho's first night in the town. She experiences a disturbing dream in which her room is engulfed in flames. As she runs for the bedroom door, someone pulls it shut from outside and turns a key in the lock. After clawing at it helplessly, she turns to the window, but it seems to shrink as she crawls toward it, until it is only a face-sized porthole. Outside, the sky is teeming with white stars, and beneath it lies a sea of wide, staring eyes. As the smoke begins to smother her, she bolts awake.

---

18 Ibid., 84.
19 Miriam Spector, *Familar Spirits: Grief, Kinship, and the Meaning of Ghosts* (Cambridge: Harvard University Press, 1979).

Sho is ready to attribute the nightmare to her empathy for the figure of the Seventh Sister. But then she records a conversation with two young boys who provide an ominous addition to the story. "She didn't want to die," one of them says. His companion adds that the Seventh Sister haunts the town. "Nobody would help her, so she wants people to suffer the same way she did." Mysterious deaths plague the town's population, the boys tell her. Lingering deaths. Every now and then, an otherwise healthy person will slowly suffocate, coughing up "black stuff" although no foreign residue is found when the body is examined.

When Sho begins to ask adult residents about the *ghost* of the Seventh Sister, they become evasive and hostile. A few of them, Sho realizes, are afflicted with a wracking, wheezing cough. One man becomes so enraged, apparently out of mortal fear for his family, that he nearly attacks Sho and chases her away from his property.

Running into the woods, Sho loses her bearings and stumbles onto the overgrown and obscured, but distinctly charred, foundation of a farmhouse. In a nearby clearing she makes another chilling discovery: a row of six headstones. The weathered grave markers are inscribed with lurid puritanical names: Difficulty, Dependence, Damnation, Devotion, Discernment, and Despair. Confusion and then realization play out across Sho's face as she imagines the name of the missing seventh sister. Surely her name would also have begun with D — and can it really be a coincidence that the town is called Desolation? But why would the town be named after the Seventh Sister? And why is her name left out of the story?

Gaining access to the town's archives, Sho rifles through death certificates and confirms that an uncanny number of deaths throughout the town's history have been attributed to unknown causes or to nameless respiratory distress. There are indeed no historical records of the destroyed farmstead or its inhabitants. But Sho manages to prise open a locked cabinet deep in the recesses of the archives, uncovering a diary dated to the 1820s. Inside, she uncovers the terrible truth about the shame that haunts the town, and about the motivation of the vengeful ghost.

The diary's author is a man who was present when the farmhouse burned down. But he did not ride out one night in response to a blaze that was already burning. A voiceover and accompanying flashback reveal the true sequence of events, with the initial shadow puppet-esque forms giving way to actual shadows cast by real people. Accompanied by a small group of neighbors, the diary's author set out to investigate the farm because it had been some weeks since anyone had seen or heard from its inhabitants. The party found that the house was dark, but when they pounded on the door they could hear a voice inside. Upon entering, they encountered two corpses, along with

> the foul stench of corruption and excrement. The feeble voice beckoned us further, into one of the bedrooms, and there we were met with a hideous sight. A woman was lying on the floor, covered in her own making and filth. She was so monstrously corpulent that she could not rise, but made a grotesque effort to crawl toward us. She begged our help, and called herself Desolation. Knowing naught what we could do, or what could possibly be done, we said nothing and sealed the door. Not wanting to leave the creature in her torment, we set the house ablaze, and stood by to see that the grass did not catch and carry the flames into the forest.

The author is not wholly without remorse. When he and his compatriots founded a township near the site of fire, he insisted that they call it Desolation. "That her spirit might find rest knowing that she is not forgotten," was his hope.

Appalled, Sho confronts the present-day leadership of the town. "We've done our best" to keep the ghost at bay, they tell her. They have kept the legend of the Seventh Sister, a sanitized version that preserves Desolation's memory, yet buries the sin and shame of her murder. "Talking about what happened, even thinking about it," gibbers one of the town supervisors, "is like summoning her." A judge testily speaks out in defense of the killing, demanding "what else was there to do?" about a person as physically dependent and unmanageable as Desolation.

Sho passionately pleads that they must "make it right." As she tries to convince them, she begins to gasp and cough. When she sees that her palm is streaked with black, she realizes that she has become fully enmeshed in the drama of the town. She too is responsible for whatever atonement might lay the ghost to rest. Before her eyes the people around her begin to choke and clutch their chests, falling to the ground one by one as Desolation exacts her revenge. This leaves Sho as the only person who can confront the angry spirit.

Returning to the site of the ruined farmstead, Sho constructs a makeshift headstone, carefully inscribing it with "Desolation" and placing it beside the other six. As she tries to leave, the foundation splits with an apocalyptic crack, yawning to reveal a gash in the landscape full of smoke and ash, as if the very heart of the town were rotted and hollow. With an echoing crack, the sky snaps from grayish daylight into a black void glittering with stars. One by one, the stars are extinguished as Desolation herself coalesces from the darkness, manifesting as a monstrous spectre shrouded in billowing smoke. In the climactic showdown, Sho is physically helpless. But just as she is about to succumb, she engages with the onslaught on the ghost's level, in the realm of emotion and will. "I'm so sorry," she says, "but there is nothing else that I can do." The words fall with the weight of Sho's conviction: she really believes, finally, that she has done all that she can. The ghost, a manifestation of rage and guilt, loses her destructive power, and Sho is able to escape. Thrusting the fateful diary into the hands of one of the young boys from the previous scene, she drives away from the town, back to her own life.

Death is permanent, and the dead are beyond our reach or help. Just as Sho can never speak to her mother again, neither can she undo the terror and injustice that were inflicted on Desolation. This is the realization that empowers her to overcome her own guilt and thereby resist Desolation's wrath. Crucially, Desolation is not "laid to rest" — that is impossible, precisely because her death itself can never be undone. Ghosts resist exorcism not only because they remind us that death is inevitable and permanent, but because they are the lingering echoes of trauma. Sho herself is able to move on because she truly accepts that the dead are beyond her help or hindrance. However, she does undertake due diligence to ensure that Desolation's fate is not forgotten. In the last scene of the film, she sets up her microphone again and begins to speak the lines that the audience will recognize as the film's opening monologue.

The film employs fatness as a device to convey its narrative about death, and in so doing it relies on an already well-established system of meanings. Fatness directly signifies death, particularly the kind or degree of fatness that, as Graves puts it, "strains the bounds of both physical and psychic space."[20] In plainer language, she explains that

> If you are so fat that your mobility is impaired, or you cannot fit into a bus seat, or you break a chair, you are instantly regarded as a monster, a harbinger of death. Because your very presence reminds other people of their own fragile bodies, which may — which *will* — break down and become disabled themselves; and which will one day dissolve back into the mud.[21]

Graves appeals to terror management theory, a social psychological framework first developed in the 1980s,[22] to explain the mechanism by which individuals are enculturated with the fear and hatred of fatness. Very young children have no concept yet of mortality, but they are conditioned to seek security and to avoid uncertainty and vulnerability. As they get older, they come to internalize the fact that vulnerability implies the threat of death.

---

20 Graves, *Death Becomes Me*, 20.
21 Ibid., 84–85.
22 Jeff Greenberg and Jamie Arendt, "Terror Management Theory," in *The Handbook of Theories of Social Psychology*, vol. I, eds. Arie W. Kruglinski, E. Tory Higgins, and Paul A.M. Van Lange (Thousand Oaks: Sage, 2012), 398–415.

Adherence to parental values—"being good" in the eyes of the parental figure—is associated with feelings of safety, while transgressions that tempt parental wrath are associated with the threat of punishment and abandonment. As the individual matures and takes their place in the larger community, this relationship with the parent is transmuted into a relationship with moral and cultural authority in general.

We live in a culture where fatness represents a definite transgression. The discourse around childhood obesity ensures that children's bodies are highly scrutinized and children are socialized to be afraid of becoming fat. As people get older and become adults, the authority figures whom they associate with safety and stability are no longer (only) their parents, but also God, the state, the medical establishment, et cetera. From earliest childhood, people are bombarded from all sides with the message that fatness will result in social and literal death.

No Future

Commenting on horror films, Graves writes:

> The horror genre contains plenty of fat bodies. Yet I am surprised by the lack of horror films that rely specifically on the existential threat of being or becoming fat. Perhaps it is that our collective terror is too great to express, or so obvious and ubiquitous that any portrayal of it must already be a parody.[23]

The "threat of being or becoming fat" does not feature directly in the plot of *Desolation*. But the circumstances and manner of the title character's death do obliquely evoke that threat. Desolation dies because she is fat. In fact, those are the only things that we know for certain about Desolation as a character: she is very fat, and because of that she dies. For all the protagonist or the audience knows, the folkloric version of her story may be mostly fabrication. Her story is not about grief, it is about the specific

---

[23] Graves, *Death Becomes Me*, 113.

inevitability of her own death. She has reached a physiological point at which Graves would say that she has "become the very embodiment of death." For her, "death is so total that even while [she] lives, life is an impossibility. This is that malign failure of imagination which makes it impossible for society to envision a livable future for us."[24]

"What else was there to do?" demands the judge. How could isolated farmers in the 1820s be expected to take care of "somebody like that?" The film never explicitly addresses these questions. The implicit responses, within this film and throughout the general discourse in which the film is embedded, are *Nothing* and *They couldn't*. Desolation's death may have been cruel, it may have been unjust, it may have been reprehensible. But it was inevitable, because the film fails to imagine any alternative. Because of her size, Desolation is denied the very possibility of a future.

Graves is apt in calling this denial of fat futurity "malign." Stories have tremendous social power; we rely on them to help us envision what is possible and what is right. While *Desolation* may evince rage and pity on behalf of its antagonist, it perpetuates the attitude that very fat people, even if they deserve our sympathy, simply cannot live in the world. They must cease to exist, either by miraculously becoming thin or acceptably fat, or by dying.

Of course it is not literally true that very fat people cannot exist. They obviously do exist, and do go about their lives. And the malignancy of our stunted imagination lies within the space of that contradiction: An entire population is excluded from full participation in community life, because this group is perceived to be dead or always imminently dying, and public spaces — both physical and social — are designed for the living.

Fiction is hardly *the* answer to real-life social problems. But fiction does shape our collective imagination and our understanding of what is possible. In real life, death is permanent. But

---

24 Ibid, 179.

in fiction the ghost's story can be re-written. Resurrect the restless undead, give her a voice and a future. Let her live.

Bibliography

Biltekoff, Charlotte. "The Terror Within: Obesity in Post 9/11 US Life." *American Studies* 48, no. 3 (2007): 29–48.

Desolation. Directed by Jessica Shan. 2016.

"*Desolation* Is Just Monster House for Grown-ups." DEATH-DRIVE, November 2016. http://www.deathdrivemag.com/desolation-is-just.

Fiedler, Leslie. *Freaks: Myths and Images of the Secret Self.* New York: Simon and Schuster, 1978.

Graves, Siobhan. *Death Becomes Me: Mortal Terror and the Spectre of Obesity.* London: Routledge, 1999.

Greenberg, Jeff, and Jamie Arendt. "Terror Management Theory." In *The Handbook of Theories of Social Psychology,* Volume I, edited by Arie W. Kruglinski, E. Tory Higgins, and Paul A.M. Van Lange, 398–415. Thousand Oaks: Sage, 2012.

LeBesco, Kathleen. "Neoliberalism, Public Health, and the Moral Perils of Fatness." *Critical Public Health* 21, no. 2 (2011): 153–64.

Mayes, Christopher. *The Biopolitics of Lifestyle: Foucault, Ethics, and Healthy Choices.* London: Routledge, 2016.

Nye-Lenehan, Kirsten. "Fat Positivity Finds an Outlet in Mainstream Horror." *RedCurrent,* November 2016. http://www.redcurrent.org/nyelenehan/desolation.

Orba, Jay. "*Desolation* Is a Uniquely American Nightmare." *New York Times,* October 14, 2016. http://www.nytimes.com/2016/10/14/review-desolation-orba.

Perkins, Adun. *Abyss: Images of Rural Desolation in the American Horror Film*. Chicago: Chicago University Press, 2002.

Shore, Maddie. "Trauma and Restless Ghosts in Jessica Shan's *Desolation*." *Jetsam,* December 2016, 23–24.

Spector, Miriam. *Familar Spirits: Grief, Kinship, and the Meaning of Ghosts.* Cambridge: Harvard University Press, 1979.

17

"All My Life My Writing Is":
The Auto-Bio-Graph of Smalloysius F.: Being Told by Itself

Stephen Hock

The Covfefe Dilemma

When *The Auto-Bio-Graph of Smalloysius F.: Being Told by Itself* first came to widespread attention in February of 2016, it was quickly dismissed as a hoax, which, in one sense, it was.[1] *The Auto-Bio-Graph* first attracted critical notice when it was claimed that this first-person narrative of the picaresque wanderings of a ragamuff dog of uncertain parentage (the titular Smalloysius F.) was a pseudonymous work by Thomas Pynchon. The claim for Pynchon's authorship first appeared in a blog post by Marie R. Donaldson and Renée Pearson, "Pynchon Goes *Auto-Bio-Graph*-ical," published on February 8, 2016.[2] This post was quickly disseminated through social media before being picked up by, among others, *Vulture*, *Slate*, and *The New Republic*.[3]

---

1 *The Auto-Bio-Graph of Smalloysius F.: Being Told by Itself* (n.p., n.d.).
2 Marie R. Donaldson and Renée Pearson, "Pynchon Goes *Auto-Bio-Graph*-ical," NPC, February 8, 2016, http://www.npc.com/02082016.html.
3 See Nate Jones, "New Pynchon? Seems Unlikely," *Vulture*, February 10, 2016, http://www.vulture.com/2016/02/pynchon-probably-did-not-write-this-secret-novel-either.html; Troy Patterson, "Not Another *Cow Country*,"

As in the case of earlier texts purportedly authored by Pynchon such as *The Letters of Wanda Tinasky* and Adrian Jones Pearson's *Cow Country*,[4] however, the claim for Pynchon's authorship was refuted in short order: among other things, the library of the University of Pennsylvania was able to document that it had owned its copy of *The Auto-Bio-Graph* (the only copy publicly identified to date) since at least 1913, twenty-four years before Pynchon's birth. In the resulting media buzz, it quickly became apparent that it was impossible to contact or even identify Donaldson and Pearson, and it is now widely believed (ironically enough, given their claim that *The Auto-Bio-Graph* was published pseudonymously) that "Marie R. Donaldson" and "Renée Pearson" are themselves pseudonyms.[5]

This ostensible early date of *The Auto-Bio-Graph* itself became further cause to dismiss the book as a hoax, insofar as the text unsubtly alludes to various items, texts, and events from the late twentieth and early twenty-first centuries, including details of the presidency of Donald Trump that could not have been known in February of 2016, much less in 1913 — what has come to be known in discussions of *The Auto-Bio-Graph* as the "Covfefe Dilemma."

Opinion among *The Auto-Bio-Graph*'s coterie of readers, largely hashed out in online discussions, has since tended to be divided between two camps. First are those who question the provenance of the book, arguing that the records dating the

---

Slate, February 11, 2016, http://www.slate.com/blogs/browbeat/2016/02/11/auto-bio-graph-of-smalloysius-f-not-another-cow-country.html; and Alex Shephard, "Hidden Pynchon? Not Again," *New Republic,* February 11, 2016, http://newrepublic.com/article/113903/not-another-secret-pynchon-book.

4   T.R. Factor, ed., *The Letters of Wanda Tinasky* (Portland: Vers Libre, 1996) and Adrian Jones Pearson, *Cow Country* (Cheyenne: Cow Eye, 2015).

5   Donaldson and Pearson's blog, hosted on the website npc.com, has since been taken offline, and the npc.com domain is, as of this writing, available for purchase. For the most thorough investigation of Donaldson and Pearson and debunking of the claim for Pynchon's authorship of *The Auto-Bio-Graph,* see Paz Walters, "A Hoax of Small Import," *The Paz Walters Report,* June 22, 2017, http://www.thepazwaltersreportblog.com/2017/06/a-hoax-of-small-import.html.

Penn copy to 1913 were faked, and that the book is of much more recent vintage, thereby explaining most if not all of the book's allusions to more contemporary events.[6] Second are those who accept the earlier dating of the book, but maintain (generally less than persuasively) that the specificity of its apparent allusions to details of recent history has been overstated.[7]

The present study proposes to argue that both camps are wrong, and that *The Auto-Bio-Graph* is, in fact, a book from the future, quite possibly written by a semi-literate dog. While its chronologically paradoxical status as a book from the future, not to mention its authorship by a nonhuman animal, would render *The Auto-Bio-Graph* (probably) unique in the annals of literary history, this understanding of the work nonetheless helps frame *The Auto-Bio-Graph* as a text well-positioned to offer a counterpoint to recent critical discussions of a turn away from the postmodern, reenergizing the chronologically paradoxical quality inherent to the idea of postmodernity. In this regard, *The Auto-Bio-Graph* offers a means of intervening in contemporary critical discourse by reconceiving autofiction — frequently pos-

---

6 In their final published blog post, "A Small Defense," Donaldson and Pearson maintain that the records must have been faked by Pynchon himself. Marie R. Donaldson and Renée Pearson, "A Small Defense," NPC, December 31, 2016, http://www.npc.com/12312016. For a more plausible, though still problematic, discussion of how the Penn records could have been faked, see Larue Thomas, "#covfefedilemma: Penn Library Records Not Infallible," *Auto-Bio-Graph Forum*, July 18, 2016, http://www.autobiographforumblog.com/2016/07/#covfefedilemma-penn-library-records-not-infallible.html.

7 See, for instance, Elaine Barbera, "A New Take on Dating," *Auto-Bio-Graph Forum*, June 8, 2017, http://www.autobiographforumblog.com/2017/06/a-new-take-on-dating.html. A variant of this argument — perhaps a parody of it that simultaneously parodies Donaldson and Pearson's insistence on Pynchon's authorship — is offered by Luke Austin, who posits that *The Auto-Bio-Graph* is the product of a prank carried out by Ezra Pound and William Carlos Williams when they were students at Penn. See Luke Austin, "How Did You Do That, Ez?" *Luke Austin Loves Books*, July 31, 2017, http://lukeaustinlovesbooks.livejournal.com/3573361.html. For an amusing reading of attempts to explain the presence of a reference to Febreze (a brand name originating in the 1990s) in a book supposedly written no later than 1913, see Asher Williams, "Febreze*?" *Auto-Bio-Graph Forum*, November 18, 2017, http://www.autobiographforumblog.com/2017/11/febreze.html.

ited as an alternative and successor to the postmodernist impulse — not as fiction that incorporates elements of autobiography but rather as fiction that generates itself and its surrounding reality, in a manner evocative both of the postmodern and of the posthuman.

"My Balls Are Gone, My Language Set — "

As of this writing, discussion of *The Auto-Bio-Graph* has largely remained confined to the relatively small number of readers who have had access to the Penn copy. As noted above, most of this discussion has taken the form of online postings, the vast majority of which devote themselves to rehashing debates over the dating of the book. The remainder of the published commentaries tend either to revel in the ribald quality of the book or to play games of allusion-spotting; few have examined *The Auto-Bio-Graph* as an object of critical study. As such, an overview of the book, its style, and its central concerns may be helpful.

The Auto-Bio-Graph of Smalloysius F.: Being Told by Itself presents a first-person narrative that follows Smalloysius F., a small dog, as he travels through the streets of an unidentified city. The book is highly episodic, with each of its seventy-four short chapters varying wildly in style and subject matter, and switching from prose to verse to drama seemingly at random. The book lacks a copyright page,[8] and its title page gives no publication information, presenting only the title and a photographic image of a one-eyed dog, apparently meant to be Smalloysius F. As such, the general impression *The Auto-Bio-Graph*'s title page gives is similar to that of another book purportedly authored by a dog, *Millie's Book: As Dictated to Barbara Bush*, which likewise features a photograph of its "author" framed by the book's title.[9]

---

[8] Questions about the copyright status of *The Auto-Bio-Graph* have, to date, forestalled attempts by several publishers to put out their own editions of the book.

[9] Barbara Bush, *Millie's Book: As Dictated to Barbara Bush* (New York: William Morrow, 1990).

Whereas *Millie's Book*'s subtitle winks at the fact that it was not authored by its titular dog, however, *The Auto-Bio-Graph*'s title page bears no such acknowledgment of human authorship. The only gesture toward the question of the book's authorship that the *Auto-Bio-Graph*'s title page gives is the caption beneath the picture of Smalloysius F., "The Scriptor."

The first lines of *The Auto-Bio-Graph* read, "For millions of blinks, I lived just like the other dogs. Then something happened which unleashed the power of my scripting: I learned to language" (1).[10] As George Basehoar has observed, these lines appear to paraphrase a recording made by Steven Hawking for a television commercial, which later appeared as the opening lines of Pink Floyd's song "Keep Talking," a track off their 1994 album *The Division Bell*.[11] In their original form, the lines read as follows: "For millions of years, mankind lived just like the animals. Then something happened which unleashed the power of our imagination: we learned to talk."[12] *The Auto-Bio-Graph* thus begins intertextually, setting the stage for its mode of freely scavenging among various scraps of half-digested culture — ranging from degraded pop culture to vulgar versions of literary theory — that it playfully, yet earnestly, lays at the reader's feet, with no apparent regard for originality or any attempt to stitch the fragments into a meaningful whole. As such, Basehoar argues, it is important that we read the lines as being adapted from Pink Floyd, rather than from the commercial for which they were first recorded: "reading the lines as 'Keep Talking''s rather than as the advertisement's," he writes, "foregrounds the book's citational poetics, situating the reader further within a *mise-en-abîme* of textual fragments echoing one another."[13] Basehoar thereby locates Smalloysius F.'s voice as nakedly post-

---

[10] All page references between parentheses refer to the copy of *The Auto-Bio-Graph of Smalloysius F.: Being Told by Itself* held at Penn.

[11] George Basehoar, "Small Talk," *Public Books*, March 7, 2017, http://www.publicbooks.org/small-talk/.

[12] Pink Floyd, "Keep Talking," track 9 on *The Division Bell*, Columbia CK 64200, compact disc, 1994.

[13] Basehoar, "Small Talk."

structuralist, akin to the textual practices of postmodernist figures such as Kathy Acker.

Basehoar focuses his reading on situating this "citational poetics" in the context of antecedents such as Acker or, in a somewhat different vein, Michael Robbins. It is important, however, that readers also understand Smalloysius F.'s vexed relationship to language, the instability of his subject position as a "scriptor," as it informs and is informed by the passages in *The Auto-Bio-Graph* that address themselves to his other principal obsessions, namely, his gonads, or lack thereof, and urination.[14] These concerns appear linked from the start of the book, as the opening paraphrase of Hawking is followed by a verse passage that makes up the remainder of the first chapter:

> I'm Smalloysius F., I am —
> A one-eyed bard, 'gainst Nature's plan.
> Across these streets, my joyous slog —
> 'Tis true — thy scriptor is a dog!
> My balls are gone, my language set —
> I loose my stream and make it wet.
> A name I never had before —
> I rub my butt across the floor.
> This book I send its way to you —
> A vision of a future true:
> A ban on all who aren't like me —
> A world that sets its money free.
> Augustus James, I got thy name —
> In writing I shall find my fame.
> In language, "I" a product 'tis —
> All my life my writing is. (1–2)

---

14 In his comprehensive study of the erotics of reader-response theory, *Perverse Epistemologies,* Gavin Pate pays considerable attention to what he refers to as Smalloysius F.'s "urogenital obsession," primarily in terms of the ways in which Smalloysius F.'s obsession is mirrored by that of the online discussion boards that have sprung up around *The Auto-Bio-Graph,* many of which betray a more or less purely prurient interest in the text. See Gavin Pate, *Perverse Epistemologies* (Lowell: Bootstrap, 2018), 337.

This verse not only marks the obsessions that drive Smalloysius F. but also obliquely gestures toward the book's explanation of how its protagonist came to be. That story is then told somewhat more directly in the book's second chapter (3–5), which begins with a scene of men in lab coats examining the dog and describing his condition in a mishmash of scientific jargon, some of which apparently has no currently recognized meaning.[15] The upshot seems to be that Smalloysius F. is the product of a project in genetic recoding, one that has enhanced his cognitive abilities to the point that he has become capable of using language.[16] At the same time, in order to maintain control of the experiment, he has been neutered, to prevent accidental transmission of his altered — and evidently patented — genes. Reference is also made to removing an infected left eye.

In this regard, the book functions nakedly — and crudely — psychoanalytically, with Smalloysius F.'s neutering serving as a literalized enactment of the castration necessary to enter the Lacanian symbolic order.[17] The dog's entry into language hinges on his simultaneous loss of his gonads, a lack that drives him throughout the remainder of the book, most starkly in the third chapter, which consists of four pages of the repeated sen-

---

15 See Jude Ryan, "Chapter Two Makes No Sense," *Auto-Bio-Graph Forum*, October 4, 2016, http://www.autobiographforumblog.com/2016/10/chapter-two-makes-no-sense.html.

16 Given Smalloysius F.'s ability to use language, combined with *The Auto-Bio-Graph*'s relentlessly "citational poetics" that situates his narrative within any number of intertexts, it seems notable that *The Auto-Bio-Graph* never seems to allude to André Alexis's *Fifteen Dogs*, a novel that features a pack of dogs gifted by the Greek god Apollo with "human intelligence," one of whom, named Prince, goes on to become a poet, albeit one with a radically different approach to aesthetics than Smalloysius F. See André Alexis, *Fifteen Dogs* (Toronto: Coach House Books, 2015), 15.

17 See, for instance, the unsigned article "The Phallic Phase and the Subjective Import of the Castration Complex," in *Feminine Sexuality: Jacques Lacan and the école freudienne*, eds. Juliet Mitchell and Jacqueline Rose, trans. Jacqueline Rose (New York: Norton, 1985), 116: "For, it was a necessity intrinsic to the symbolic order, one which we have learnt from Lacan to read as the effect of the subject's dependency on the signifier, that led Freud to designate the very instigation of the subject by the name of castration."

tence "Smalls has no balls," capped off by one sentence reading, "Smalls has one ball" (6–9). This last reference points to Smalloysius F.'s remaining right eyeball, and thereby highlights an associative link between the gonads and the eyes, insofar as both are covered by this chapter's reference to "balls." In the vein of the text's vulgarization of psychoanalytic concepts, the fact that Smalloysius F. loses his left eye in the same operation that neuters him dramatizes the link between the fear of losing one's eyes and the fear of castration identified by Freud.[18] In terms of the intertextual associations the text lends itself to, the damage to Smalloysius F.'s left eye that necessitates its removal renders him akin to James Joyce (the "Augustus James" of the first chapter's verse's thirteenth line whose name Smalloysius F. claims to have gotten — the first of Joyce's two middle names being Augustine, and the second being Aloysius), another densely allusive writer plagued by eye problems. Indeed, in later chapters that detail Smalloysius F.'s adventures after his escape from the facility in which he is operated on, his one remaining eye functions as an emblem linking him not just to Joyce but also to one-eyed yet paradoxically all-seeing figures such as Nick Fury (17) and Odin (63), the visible rejoinder to his castration that signifies the dog's attempts to master the logomania his alteration has driven him to. As the book's fifteenth chapter reports:

> By theory of my eye I see —
> A witness now to all I be.
> Smalloysius, small and vicious —
> The one I have, but not the three. (77)

The text here hearkens back to the etymology of *theory* in the Greek *theōria*, referring to sight: to theorize is to see or to witness, and thereby to imbue with meaning. Smalloysius F.'s condition thus underscores the link between the fear of losing one's

---

18 Most obviously in Sigmund Freud, "The Uncanny," in *The Standard Edition of the Complete Psychological Works of Sigmund Freud,* trans. James Strachey, vol. 17 (London: Hogarth, 1955), 217–56.

eyes and the fear of castration: losing one's eyes is to lose the ability to theorize, as losing one's gonads is to lose the authority to signify. Even so, Smalloysius F.'s remaining eye stands as the guarantor of his access to the ability to theorize, albeit in a haphazard form that betrays his only partial literacy.[19]

To wrap up this outline of the manner in which *The Auto-Bio-Graph* situates Smalloysius F. within the terms of vulgar-theoretical discourse, it is also worth considering chapter thirty-seven, in which Smalloysius F. adopts the persona of a wandering troubadour performing under the name Smelloysius. His performance at the climax of the chapter, a song titled "Please Don't Febreze® My Wang,"[20] proceeds as follows:

The pack assembles. Pitmix Nutsack Junior sniffs leaves of stream. I come in on a kind of cock-rock type of beat:
"Since they took my balls, I became a neuter.
I don't want to hump nobody; I'll never have no puppies.
Now my wang's only good for pee-ing.
And, you know, that means, sometimes that it's stink-ingggggg…
[big chorus]
Don't want to take a bath,
Don't want to cut my fur,

---

19 Compare Jacques Lacan's comments in his discussion of the gaze in *The Four Fundamental Concepts of Psycho-Analysis,* ed. Jacques-Alain Miller, trans. Alan Sheridan (New York: Norton, 1981), 78, 118: "The split between gaze and vision will enable us, you will see, to add the scopic drive to the list of the drives. […] Indeed, it is this drive that most completely eludes the term castration," and, apropos of Smalloysius F.'s description of himself as "small and vicious," "For it is in so far as all human desire is based on castration that the eye assumes its virulent, aggressive function, and not simply its luring function as in nature." Lacan writes here of "human" nature, but his comment would seem to apply equally validly to Smalloysius F.

20 Gideon Michael notes that this song is apparently a reworked version of "I Don't Want to Miss a Thing," a song performed by Aerosmith for the soundtrack of the 1998 film *Armageddon.* See Gideon Michael, "Aerosmith in *The Auto-Bio-Graph,*" *Auto-Bio-Graph Forum,* February 7, 2017, http://www.autobiographforumblog.com/2017/02/aerosmith-in-the-auto-bio-graph.html.

Yes, I know I stank,
But please don't Febreze® my wa-ang." (135–36; bracketed text in original)

Notably, though the song begins with neutering and the loss of sexual capacity, it comes to rest on the penis's urinary function, both in the lyrics of the song and also in the comment that marks the song's conclusion, "My song scripted, I loose my stream to release my meaning" (136), an action that further draws the attention of both his rival Pitmix Nutsack Junior and a Russian photographer who lurks throughout the chapter, and who seems particularly fascinated by Smalloysius F.'s urinary habits.

That final comment, "My song scripted, I loose my stream to release my meaning," implicitly again ties Smalloysius F.'s obsessions with castration and urination back to his relationship to language, insofar as it seems to constitute another, as-yet-uncommented-on, textual fragment that *The Auto-Bio-Graph* has incorporated into itself, namely, a paraphrase of a line from Barthes's "The Death of the Author": "We know now that a text is not a line of words releasing a single 'theological' meaning (the 'message' of the Author-God) but a multi-dimensional space in which a variety of writings, none of them original, blend and clash."[21] In this case, the degraded function of the penis — no longer an organ of reproduction and phallic mastery but merely of urination — figures the action of "releasing" the "meaning" of "the Author-God" as a stream of urine. This passage thereby confirms Smalloysius F.'s evacuation of the role of "author" of *The Auto-Bio-Graph*; instead, he functions, as the book's title page would have it, as the text's "scriptor," again apropos of Barthes:

> Succeeding the Author, the scriptor no longer bears within him passions, humours, feelings, impressions, but rather this immense dictionary from which he draws a writing that can

---

21 Roland Barthes, "The Death of the Author," in *Image, Music, Text*, trans. Stephen Heath (New York: Hill and Wang, 1977), 146.

know no halt: life never does more than imitate the book, and the book itself is only a tissue of signs, an imitation that is lost, infinitely deferred.[22]

This moment thereby calls back to the first chapter's third couplet, "My balls are gone, my language set — / I loose my stream and make it wet," a juxtaposition that heightens the connections among castration, language, and the stream of urine through which Smalloysius F. figures the meaning his text releases.[23]

"There is a problem."

As noted earlier, the fundamental paradox of *The Auto-Bio-Graph* is that the only copy publicly identified to date has apparently been part of the Penn library's collection since at least 1913, even as the text makes obvious references to events, people, and texts that postdate 1913. Most of this paradox is eliminated easily enough if we accept the argument that the records placing the book in the library in 1913 were faked, and that the book was actually written sometime close to the day Donaldson and Pearson first publicized it, February 8, 2016. Admittedly, granting this later dating is problematic, since, as Asher Williams has demonstrated, there are flaws in even the most plausible attempts to explain away the Penn records.[24] More to the point, that later

---

22 Ibid., 147.
23 Smalloysius F.'s urinary proclivities likewise evoke the text's oddly literal engagement with psychoanalytic theory, particularly in chapter forty-three's visit to a performance of *Prometheus, the Musical: Prometheus Is* YOU!, a scene that ends with Smalloysius F.'s declaration, "I loose my stream on Prometheus and master his flame" (167). The intertext here seems to be the footnote in *Civilization and Its Discontents* in which Freud attributes humankind's mastery of fire — a development credited to Prometheus in Greek myth — to a moment in which "primal man" mastered the "infantile desire" to put out naturally occurring fires "with a stream of his urine." See Sigmund Freud, *Civilization and Its Discontents,* in *The Standard Edition of the Complete Psychological Works of Sigmund Freud,* trans. James Strachey, vol. 21 (London: Hogarth, 1961), 90n1.
24 Williams, "Febreze*?"

dating still leaves the problem of the book's references to events that postdate the first week of February of 2016. Some of these references are seemingly trivial and plausibly predictable, such as chapter five's dialogue between Smalloysius F. and Philadelphia Phillies baseball player Rhys Hoskins, on the occasion of the latter's being named National League Rookie of the Month for August 2017, an accomplishment for which Smalloysius F. specifically congratulates Hoskins (17–20): Hoskins was a touted prospect, and it is not inconceivable that someone writing at the beginning of 2016 could have predicted his emergence late in the 2017 baseball season. Other references defy explanation, most notably those pertaining to the presidency of Donald Trump.

The challenge of identifying all of *The Auto-Bio-Graph*'s references to the Trump presidency as of this writing is, of course, that new ones emerge on a regular basis. Before May 31, 2017, for instance, the book's fiftieth chapter seemed to present a fairly inconspicuous episode steeped in the text's intermittent forays into pseudo-Pynchonian paranoia.[25] In this chapter, Smalloysius F. wanders into a meeting of homeless people gathered around a rabble-rousing street preacher who has apparently distributed some sort of electronic device to his assembly. The text hints that the preacher is a member of a secret society that also includes the Russian photographer who appears to be following Smalloysius F. with increasing frequency in the preceding chapters. The preacher explains the working of the device as follows:

> "You must keep this on you at all times: They will expect you to press the appropriate button when you get the call."
>
> "What call?" A voice from the crowd, several murmuring agreement.
>
> "The call to evaluate the positive and the negative, flop or flip. If the negative, press 'sad'...."
>
> "And if the positive?"

---

[25] Donaldson and Pearson, in fact, quoted extensively from this chapter to demonstrate the allegedly Pynchonian quality of *The Auto-Bio-Graph* in their initial "Pynch Goes *Auto-Bio-Graph*-ical" blog post.

> "If the positive, press 'covfefe.'"
>
> "But what if my fingers won't reach the button?" A young child, snot-grimed and greasy.
>
> "Look at those hands…I guarantee you there's no problem."
>
> I love this man's hair and smell, flowing golden locks like mine and stench to match my stream. But there is a problem. I have no hands. I am still a dog. I was not remade for hands. There is a problem. (151; ellipsis in original)

On May 31, 2017, this chapter took on an uncannily prescient quality, when Donald Trump posted to his Twitter account a tweet that read, in its entirety, "Despite the constant negative press covfefe."[26] The obvious explanation for the tweet was that "covfefe" was a typo for "coverage," and that the tweet was supposed to be followed by a clause that would indicate what was or would be happening, "despite the constant negative press coverage." That said, it beggars belief to suppose that *The Auto-Bio-Graph* could have purely coincidentally produced dialogue placing the apparent nonsense word *covfefe* in close proximity to the other key words of Trump's tweet, *negative* and *press,* especially since the preacher's final line, "Look at those hands…I guarantee you there's no problem," matches a statement Trump made in a Republican primary debate on March 3, 2016,[27] nearly a month after *The Auto-Bio-Graph* was first brought to widespread attention, and well after several online discussions of the book specifically cited that line.[28]

---

26 Matt Flegenheimer, "What's a 'Covfefe'? Trump Tweet Unites a Bewildered Nation," *New York Times,* May 31, 2017, http://www.nytimes.com/2017/05/31/us/politics/covfefe-trump-twitter.html.

27 Gregory Krieg, "Donald Trump Defends Size of His Penis," CNN, March 4, 2016, http://www.cnn.com/2016/03/03/politics/donald-trump-small-hands-marco-rubio/index.html.

28 See, for example, Patterson, "Not Another *Cow Country*." Apropos of Smalloysius F.'s bodily obsessions, it is worth noting that Trump's comment, "I guarantee you there's no problem," referred to the size of his penis.

Adding to this suspicious conjunction, White House Press Secretary Sean Spicer insisted later on the day of the tweet, "The president and a small group of people know exactly what he meant."[29] The haunting suspicion, for *The Auto-Bio-Graph*'s small and increasingly paranoid group of readers, is that the tweet was, in fact, complete and, if properly punctuated, would instruct its intended audience, "Despite the constant negative, press 'covfefe.'" But what might be that intended audience? And what might be the result of pressing "covfefe"? If the dystopian character of the antepenultimate chapter of *The Auto-Bio-Graph* — in which the Russian photographer and his associates turn Smalloysius F.'s city into a dystopian hellscape in which the gene-recoding procedure that has endowed the dog with speech is applied to the human population, as a way to reify racial, sexual, and class boundaries (200–215) — is as predictive as chapter fifty, then we have reason to fear the answer.[30]

Once other explanations have been eliminated, it behooves readers to consider taking Smalloysius F. at his word when he states, in the fifth couplet of *The Auto-Bio-Graph*'s opening chapter, "This book I send its way to you — / A vision of a future true." Could *The Auto-Bio-Graph* be a book that does, in fact, present information from the future, whether by virtue of prophecy or by virtue of time travel? Scientific studies of time travel suggest not only that it is possible, but also that *The Auto-Bio-Graph* fulfills precisely the characteristics we would expect to find in an artifact that has been placed in the present or the past by time travelers from the future. In their classic study "Searching the Internet for Evidence of Time Travelers," Robert

---

29 Flegenheimer, "What's a 'Covfefe'? Trump Tweet Unites a Bewildered Nation."

30 There is no public record that Trump's opponent in the 2016 presidential election, Hillary Clinton, is familiar with *The Auto-Bio-Graph*, but she offered an analogous conclusion, albeit framed as a joke, when she stated of the covfefe tweet, "I thought it was a hidden message to the Russians." M.J. Lee, "Clinton Jokes Covfefe 'A Hidden Message to the Russians,'" CNN, May 31, 2017, http://www.cnn.com/2017/05/31/politics/hillary-clinton-covfefe/index.html.

J. Nemiroff and Teresa Wilson reason that, "Were a time traveler from the future to access the Internet of the past few years, they might have left once-prescient content that persists today."[31] While *The Auto-Bio-Graph* does not exist on the internet, its verified existence as early as February 8, 2016, and probably as early as 1913, renders its various references to the Trump presidency (among other things) "once-prescient content that persists today": simply put, it is otherwise impossible to reconcile the book's post-Feburary-2016 intertexts with the documented fact of its existence before those intertexts came into existence. In particular, the so-called Covfefe Dilemma constitutes, in Nemiroff and Wilson's terms, an occurrence that would "give a relatively clear signal of prescient information," since that portion of the text presents what Nemiroff and Wilson refer to as content that bears "as unique a label as possible," a correspondence exceedingly unlikely to have arisen by chance.[32] Nemiroff and Wilson found no evidence of time travelers in their efforts, but *The Auto-Bio-Graph* displays precisely the sort of artifact they were searching for. As Nemiroff and Wilson explain in their conclusion:

> Technically, what was searched for here was not physical time travelers themselves, but rather informational traces left by them. Although such information might be left by physical time travelers, conceivably only information itself could be sent back in time, which would be a type of time travel that might not directly involve the backwards transport of a significant amount of energy or momentum. This might be considered, by some, a more palatable mode of backwards time travel than transferring significant amounts of matter or energy back in time, as the later [*sic*] might break, quite coarsely, local conservation of energy and momentum.[33]

---

31 Robert J. Nemiroff and Teresa Wilson, "Searching the Internet for Evidence of Time Travelers," *ArXiv*, December 26, 2013, https://arxiv.org/ftp/arxiv/papers/1312/1312.7128.pdf.
32 Ibid.
33 Ibid.

In the absence of competing plausible theories, we are forced to reckon with the possibility that *The Auto-Bio-Graph* constitutes "information [...] sent back in time," presumably thanks to the same sort of advanced science that granted Smalloysius F. the gift of language. In this way, the text becomes truly postmodern, in an appropriately vulgar fashion, as a book from the future.

Postmodernism, Posthumanism, and Doggerel Poetics

In the recent *Times Literary Supplement* article "Postmodernism Is Dead. What Comes Next?" Alison Gibbons presents autofiction, which she describes as "a genre that integrates the autobiographical into fiction," as "just one example of contemporary fiction that articulates a sentiment beyond the postmodern."[34] She continues:

> The genre, at first glance, may seem strictly postmodern, dealing as it does with the fragmentation of the subject and the blurring of the fact-fiction ontological boundary. Yet contemporary autofictions narrativize the self not as a game, but in order to enhance the realism of a text and tackle the sociological and phenomenological dimensions of personal life.[35]

By this point, it should be clear that none of these qualities that distinguish autofiction from the postmodern characterize *The Auto-Bio-Graph of Smalloysius F.,* its ostensible status as a work "that integrates the autobiographical into fiction" notwithstanding. Instead, *The Auto-Bio-Graph* is written in an aggressively postmodernist mode, both in style and also in content, insofar as Smalloysius F.'s situation as a dog genetically recoded and then patented exemplifies the postmodern condition described by Fredric Jameson, a state of being dominated by:

---

[34] Alison Gibbons, "Postmodernism Is Dead. What Comes Next?" *Times Literary Supplement,* June 12, 2017, http://www.the-tls.co.uk/articles/public/postmodernism-dead-comes-next/.

[35] Ibid.

the purest form of capital yet to have emerged, a prodigious expansion of capital into hitherto uncommodified areas. This purer capitalism of our own time thus eliminates the enclaves of precapitalist organization it had hitherto tolerated and exploited in a tributary way. One is tempted to speak in this connection of a new and historically original penetration and colonization of Nature and the Unconscious.[36]

In describing the penetration of Nature by capital, Jameson nominally refers to "the destruction of precapitalist Third World agriculture by the Green Revolution,"[37] but the description likewise applies to the genetic recoding that turns the very stuff of Smalloysius F.'s life into a patented commodity, as well as to the eventual application of this recoding technique to human beings in order to make them serve capital more efficiently. As such, the final couplet of the book's opening chapter, "In language, 'I' a product 'tis— / All my life my writing is," points not merely to the way in which Smalloysius F. is produced as a subject by language, but also to the way in which his linguistic abilities as a subject are the product of late capital. Instead of a way beyond late capitalism, *The Auto-Bio-Graph* brings news of capital's continuing triumph, in a postmodernist mode to match.

Just as Smalloysius F. assembles his life out of writing, there is also reason to believe that *The Auto-Bio-Graph* demonstrates the power of writing—in this case, its own writing—to craft a world. The due dates stamped on the Penn library's copy of *The Auto-Bio-Graph* indicate that the book was checked out five times in rapid succession in the spring of 1968, and then once more before its rediscovery in the twenty-first century, with a due date of October 20, 1993. As it happens, Donald Trump was a student at the University of Pennsylvania's Wharton School in the spring of 1968, and it is a matter of public record that he was in Philadelphia for Game 4 of the 1993 World Series, which

---

36 Fredric Jameson, *Postmodernism, or, The Cultural Logic of Late Capitalism* (Durham: Duke University Press, 1991), 36.
37 Ibid.

was held on October 20.[38] We may never know if Trump was the one who checked out *The Auto-Bio-Graph* — among other things, it remains unclear whether he would have had borrowing privileges as an alumnus — but the dates are tantalizing. If, as outlined above, various elements of Trump's 2016 presidential campaign and presidency appear in *The Auto-Bio-Graph,* could that be because he read about them in 1968 and 1993, and modeled his life on this text? If so, then *The Auto-Bio-Graph* asks us to rethink not only the term *postmodern,* in its implicit sense of chronological paradox, but also invites reconsideration of the term *autofiction,* this time as fiction that brings itself and its world into existence, yielding, as the book's subtitle puts it, *Being Told by Itself,* with *Being* functioning not as a participle modifying the book's title, but rather as a gerund indicating just what is "told by itself."

Questions of being as text and life as text likewise situate *The Auto-Bio-Graph* within the discourse of the posthuman, the discourse not just of autofiction but also of autopoiesis. In this book, we see what Donna Haraway calls "*the translation of the world into a problem of coding,*"[39] the textualization of reality that yields posthuman subjects such as Smalloysius F. As N. Katherine Hayles puts it:

> From the viewpoint of the autopoietic processes, there is only the circular interplay of the processes as they continue to realize their autopoiesis, always operating in the present moment and always producing the organization that also produces them. Thus, time and causality are not intrinsic to

---

[38] Jonathan Tannenwald, "The Time When Donald Trump Was a Phillies Fan," *Philly.com,* July 12, 2017, http://www.philly.com/philly/sports/phillies/donald-trump-philadelphia-phillies-fan-1993-world-series-toronto-blue-jays-sad-place-20170712.html.

[39] Donna J. Haraway, "A Cyborg Manifesto: Science, Technology, and Socialist-Feminism in the Late Twentieth Century," in *Simians, Cyborgs, and Women: The Reinvention of Nature* (London: Free Association Books, 1991), 164.

the processes themselves but are concepts inferred by an observer.[40]

Once we allow the possibility that *The Auto-Bio-Graph* is a postmodern text from the future that brings its own reality into existence, must we not also open ourselves to the possibility that it is, in fact, a posthuman text scripted by a dog?

On that note, it is appropriate to conclude with the text's final assertion of its canine authorship. In *The Auto-Bio-Graph*'s final chapter, Smalloysius F. meets a pair of itinerant human poets. The three urinate together,[41] and then discuss poetics. When asked why most of his verse is composed in tetrameter, Smalloysius F. responds, "Pentameter betrays an anthropocentric poetics: lines built the way humans have been built, formed to the five digits they use to hold a quill or a leash. Tetrameter — four feet — is the proper meter of doggerel: four feet for the four feet of a dog rebuilt by humans for language but not for pentadigitalism. Four feet divisible not once but twice — not the prime selves humans fool themselves into thinking they are," before ending *The Auto-Bio-Graph* with a final verse:

867-5309 —
Jenny was a friend of mine.
I'll make my book and, thou, make thine —
I wish I had two on the vine. (243)

---

40 N. Katherine Hayles, *How We Became Posthuman: Virtual Bodies in Cybernetics, Literature, and Informatics* (Chicago: University of Chicago Press, 1999), 139.
41 Benjamin Haller reads this scene of communal urination as an allusion to the end of Joyce's *Ulysses*, apropos of the text's earlier identification of Smalloysius F. with Joyce. This reading appears as part of Haller's larger argument that *The Auto-Bio-Graph* might be productively understood as a retelling of *The Odyssey* from the point of view of Polyphemus. See Benjamin Haller, *The New Turn in Polyphemus Studies* (Philadelphia: Clarindel, 2018), 227–54.

Bibliography

Alexis, André. *Fifteen Dogs*. Toronto: Coach House Books, 2015.

Austin, Luke. "How Did You Do That, Ez?" *Luke Austin Loves Books*, July 31, 2017. http://lukeaustinlovesbooks.livejournal.com/3573361.html.

The Auto-Bio-Graph of Smalloysius F.: Being Told by Itself. N.p., n.d.

Barbera, Elaine. "A New Take on Dating." *Auto-Bio-Graph Forum*, June 8, 2017. http://www.autobiographforumblog.com/2017/06/a-new-take-on-dating.html.

Barthes, Roland. "The Death of the Author." In *Image, Music, Text*, translated by Stephen Heath, 142–48. New York: Hill and Wang, 1977.

Basehoar, George. "Small Talk." *Public Books*, March 7, 2017. http://www.publicbooks.org/small-talk/.

Bush, Barbara. *Millie's Book: As Dictated to Barbara Bush*. New York: William Morrow, 1990.

Donaldson, Marie R., and Renée Pearson. "Pynchon Goes Auto-Bio-Graph-ical." NPC, February 8, 2016. http://www.npc.com/02082016.html.

———. "A Small Defense." NPC, December 31, 2016. http://www.npc.com/12312016.

Factor, T.R., ed. *The Letters of Wanda Tinasky*. Portland: Vers Libre, 1996.

Flegenheimer, Matt. "What's a 'Covfefe'? Trump Tweet Unites a Bewildered Nation." *New York Times*, May 31, 2017. https://www.nytimes.com/2017/05/31/us/politics/covfefe-trump-twitter.html.

Freud, Sigmund. *Civilization and Its Discontents*. In *The Standard Edition of the Complete Psychological Works of Sigmund Freud*, translated by James Strachey, Vol. 21, 59–145. London: Hogarth, 1961.

——— "The Uncanny." In *The Standard Edition of the Complete Psychological Works of Sigmund Freud*, translated by James Strachey, Vol. 17, 217–56. London: Hogarth, 1955.

Gibbons, Alison. "Postmodernism Is Dead. What Comes Next?" *Times Literary Supplement,* June 12, 2017. http://www.the-tls.co.uk/articles/public/postmodernism-dead-comes-next/.

Haller, Benjamin. *The New Turn in Polyphemus Studies.* Philadelphia: Clarindel, 2018.

Haraway, Donna J. "A Cyborg Manifesto: Science, Technology, and Socialist-Feminism in the Late Twentieth Century." In *Simians, Cyborgs, and Women: The Reinvention of Nature,* 149–81. London: Free Association Books, 1991.

Hayles, N. Katherine. *How We Became Posthuman: Virtual Bodies in Cybernetics, Literature, and Informatics.* Chicago: University of Chicago Press, 1999.

Jameson, Fredric. *Postmodernism, or, The Cultural Logic of Late Capitalism.* Durham: Duke University Press, 1991.

Jones, Nate. "New Pynchon? Seems Unlikely." *Vulture,* February 10, 2016. http://www.vulture.com/2016/02/pynchon-probably-did-not-write-this-secret-novel-either.html.

Krieg, Gregory. "Donald Trump Defends Size of His Penis." *CNN,* March 4, 2016. http://www.cnn.com/2016/03/03/politics/donald-trump-small-hands-marco-rubio/index.html.

Lacan, Jacques. *The Four Fundamental Concepts of Psycho-Analysis.* Edited by Jacques-Alain Miller. Translated by Alan Sheridan. New York: Norton, 1981.

Lee, M.J. "Clinton Jokes Covfefe 'A Hidden Message to the Russians.'" *CNN,* May 31, 2017. http://www.cnn.com/2017/05/31/politics/hillary-clinton-covfefe/index.html.

Michael, Gideon. "Aerosmith in *The Auto-Bio-Graph.*" *Auto-Bio-Graph Forum,* February 7, 2017. http://www.autobiographforumblog.com/2017/02/aerosmith-in-the-auto-bio-graph.html.

Nemiroff, Robert J., and Teresa Wilson. "Searching the Internet for Evidence of Time Travelers." *ArXiv,* December 26, 2013. https://arxiv.org/ftp/arxiv/papers/1312/1312.7128.pdf.

Pate, Gavin. *Perverse Epistemologies.* Lowell: Bootstrap, 2018.

Patterson, Troy. "Not Another *Cow Country.*" *Slate,* February 11, 2016. http://www.slate.com/blogs/browbeat/2016/02/11/

auto-bio-graph-of-smalloysius-f-not-another-cow-country.html.

Pearson, Adrian Jones. *Cow Country.* Cheyenne: Cow Eye, 2015.

"The Phallic Phase and the Subjective Import of the Castration Complex." In *Feminine Sexuality: Jacques Lacan and the école freudienne,* edited by Juliet Mitchell and Jacqueline Rose, translated by Jacqueline Rose, 99–122. New York: Norton, 1985.

Pink Floyd. "Keep Talking." Track 9 on *The Division Bell.* Columbia CK 64200, compact disc, 1994.

Ryan, Jude. "Chapter Two Makes No Sense." *Auto-Bio-Graph Forum,* October 4, 2016. http://www.autobiographforum-blog.com/2016/10/chapter-two-makes-no-sense.html.

Shephard, Alex. "Hidden Pynchon? Not Again." *New Republic,* February 11, 2016. http://newrepublic.com/article/113903/not-another-secret-pynchon-book.

Tannenwald, Jonathan. "The Time When Donald Trump Was a Phillies Fan." *Philly.com,* July 12, 2017. http://www.philly.com/philly/sports/phillies/donald-trump-philadelphia-phillies-fan-1993-world-series-toronto-blue-jays-sad-place-20170712.html.

Thomas, Larue. "#covfefedilemma: Penn Library Records Not Infallible." *Auto-Bio-Graph Forum,* July 18, 2016. http://www.autobiographforumblog.com/2016/07/#covfefedilemma-penn-library-records-not-infallible.html.

Walters, Paz. "A Hoax of Small Import." *The Paz Walters Report,* June 22, 2017. http://www.thepazwaltersreportblog.com/2017/06/a-hoax-of-small-import.html.

Williams, Asher. "Febreze®?" *Auto-Bio-Graph Forum,* November 18, 2017. http://www.autobiographforumblog.com/2017/11/febreze.html.

18

The Gravity of the Situation

Bruce Krajewski

Euphemia Muskovite, *They Should Have Known Bas Jan Ader / They Should Have Known Better*, Zurich: Amazoogle Books, 2208, 70 petabytes for HoloStory™ devices, 40 Renminbi, and Creative Cavity Implant™, 20 Renminbi.

Euphemia Muskovite, a VR presence sent to Mars in the Elon Musk era of space travel, begins her account with a couplet from a rarely considered American poem by John Ashbery: "A silly place to have landed, / I think, but we are here."[1] She tells us she interprets "landed" in the Church Slavonic sense, from *ledina,* meaning wasteland.[2] That sense of resignation in "but we are here" might have been inevitable, given that the colonists and robots knew they could not write an *Odyssey* about a long journey home, because Mars had to be home. Elon Musk didn't offer round-trip tickets. The resources were not available for decades to make a return trip to Earth. Euphemia — her publicist said she preferred to be called only by her first name — reveals that shortly after the SpaceX landing, the colonists assembled to take

---

[1] John Ashbery, "And the Stars Were Shining," in *And the Stars Were Shining* (New York: Farar, Straus & Giroux, 1994), 83.
[2] *The Compact Edition of the Oxford English Dictionary* (Oxford: Oxford University Press, 1971), s.v. "land."

an oath, reminiscent of that which the ancient Greeks took following a civil war.[3] The oath was to remember to forget, to put out of one's mind the wrongs others had done, such as the deliberate cause of suffering, brother offing brother.

> We all agreed to forget the betrayal, to forget that the full gravity of the situation had been kept from us by the people who shot us toward Mars. We swore that we would concentrate as best we could on making a life on Mars. It worked for many years, until those among us with engineering training remembered that plutonium-238 powered earlier spacecraft. A few years earlier, a geological team had found an abundant supply of plutonium not far from the landing site. Forgetting the past, at first, kept us from knitting ourselves a noose of anger [see below Euphemia's reference to Aristotle's *Poetics* and his knot of tragedy], and then remembering the past ended up freeing us from the planet Terrans had the gall to rename Elon.

The section entitled "Forgetting" focuses on the microgravity symptoms that plagued many of the travelers not long after leaving Earth's orbit.

Euphemia dazzles readers and viewers with her linguistic meditations, particularly one on gravity, where she links it to gravitas (weighty, dignified, substantive), exploring that second word's blatant connotations of gravitational forces. But as Euphemia underscores, all the benefits of gravitas evaporate in space. The absence of gravity in prolonged microgravity is for Euphemia and the colonists a persistent drain on their being. Loss of weight, decreasing bone density, alterations in digestion and breathing — all these physical effects of microgravity, prefigured by scientists over a century before, mar the existence of all the travelers. With her storehouse of linguistic knowledge,

---

[3] For more on this, see Nicole Loraux, *The Divided City: On Memory and Forgetting in Ancient Athens,* trans. Corinne Pache with Jeff Fort (Zone Books, 2006).

Euphemia can lay out the constellation of linkages among "mar," "wasting away," and "to be forgotten" (Sanskrit *mrsyate*). Who can help seeing "mar" in "Mars"?

The lack of gravity on the travelers takes a prolonged toll, as Euphemia describes here:

> Some Terrans think of microgravity as a state akin to freedom, flying, floating, untethered. Why did the Terrans forget their own stories, like the ones about Icarus, Bladud, Etana? Yes, the stories follow a trajectory that sometimes includes euphoria, but the end point is a death resulting from hubris — unnatural, untimely deaths. Some of the travelers with me wanted to blame it on the engineers and scientists who arranged the mission and neglected assigning gravitas to literature, because they heeded instead the narratives from mathematics, physics, and astronomy. They tended to ignore literature and history. I tried to dissuade the travelers from this view by reminding them that the idea for rocket propulsion emerged from the bomb expert Kibalchich in the 19th century. After all, rockets are about explosions, and it didn't take long for others to see how valuable rockets could be for war. If the engineers and scientists studied the history of their own project, they could have seen the warnings. The semiotics of disaster are available to everyone.

In this section of the book, Euphemia's anger shifts to ruminations about psychoanalysis and philosophy. Her guides for this part of the story are Jacques Lacan, a 20th-century psychoanalyst and theorist, whose popularity faded quickly in the 21st century, and Hans Blumenberg, also from the 20th century and equally unpopular. Through Blumenberg's *Shipwreck with Spectator,* Euphemia generates parallels between the Mars mission and failed ocean voyages, including the prime figure of her text's title, Bas Jan Ader. Even in his own day, Bas Jan Ader lacked name recognition among Terrans. Euphemia points to Bas Jan

Ader's last art project,[4] an ocean voyage in 1975 which he never finished. Bas Jan Ader's story, the story of a "real Earth boy," as Euphemia calls him, emphasizes Euphemia's point about Terrans who do not learn from the past. Ader took part of the inspiration for his own ocean trip from his reading of *The Strange Last Voyage of Donald Crowhurst*.[5]

Psychoanalysts like Lacan attend to the significance of repetitions and recurrence, and it's that aspect of Lacan's work that attracts Euphemia. Someone reads about another person's *last* voyage, and then sets out on a similar voyage, expecting a different conclusion. Folly. Madness. Human. Crowhurst, another real human case, died while competing in a round-the-world yacht race. By some accounts based on log books found on Crowhurst's boat, the voyage caused him to go mad and commit suicide. Crowhurst did not finish his voyage, and his body was not found. Crowhurst vanished. His vessel turned into a ghost ship. Fascinated by the book about Crowhurst, Ader set out to cross the Atlantic, and, like Crowhurst, Ader's boat was found empty, with Ader presumed dead. Euphemia quotes Lacan at this point in her text: "It [repetition] is a function of a cycle that embraces the disappearance of this life." At the time, people might as well have concluded that aliens had beamed Ader off his boat.

Bas Jan Ader, performance artist, produced a series of films about falling entitled *Fall*. Euphemia surmises from those films that Ader too must have pondered the nuances of gravity and its absence, gaining somatic knowledge, *à la* Buster Keaton. Ader did the falling in his own films, and objects fell over and around him without a stunt double being brought in. One of Ader's films shows him driving a bicycle off a street into a canal. "Repetition is a function of a cycle."

---

4   See Jan Verwoert's *Bas Jan Ader: In Search of the Miraculous* (London: Afterall Books, 2006).
5   Nicholas Tomalin and Ron Hall, *The Strange Last Voyage of Donald Crowhurst* (London: Hodder and Stoughton, 1970).

Besides the physical dangers of falling, Euphemia wants to explore the spiritual fall. Euphemia expands the sense of falling to the kind religious people would talk about, so that she can shake her readers and viewers into understanding — *that* sense of fall depends on directionality, a downward motion, a downfall, the synonym for sin. Falling down requires weight, substance, gravity, and when that is taken away from a people, she asks, can they sin? Can we have tragedy without gravitas, she wonders. Euphemia shifts from the religious to the philosophical by soliciting the help of Aristotle on tragedy, and Aristotle's claim in the *Poetics* that tragedy requires the downfall of some noble entity. In a world absent of gravity, absent of the possibility of downfall, has nobility been undone as a possibility along with tragedy?

Euphemia doesn't want us to forget about Ader's sea voyage. It's the title of her text after all. Invoking Hans Blumenberg's *Shipwreck with Spectator,* Euphemia is able to grasp the movement of existence through a metaphorics of a sea journey. Crowhurst's and Ader's boats become no different, in Blumenberg's examples, from the ships Euphemia and her travelers occupied. Rapidly, Euphemia gathers the damning theoretical framework for her case against the Terrans she considers responsible for the cruel conditions both on the voyage to Mars and at the early Martian settlements:

> How easy for the scientists and engineers to wave goodbye to those who embark for space flights when the scientists and engineers are on land, and can return each evening to their own families, never disengaging from the gravity about which they don't think, any more than they would be aware of their teeth during times when they don't have toothaches. When the travelers were waving for help from their ships and landers, the scientists and engineers who must not have read Stevie Smith, were unable to imagine that we were not waving

but drowning.⁶ Doesn't everyone know that drowning looks like floating? Microgravity = floating. Isn't that an equation scientists can understand?⁷ Maybe they couldn't see it in the same way that the couple at the beginning of W.E.B. Du Bois's "The Princess Steel" could not see Professor Johnson, though they were talking to him, looking that very person in the face. They thought they were speaking to a servant. As Kafka asked, "Can you know anything that is not deception?"⁸ Maybe I should not be angry with the Terrans. Some of the other Muskovites have urged me down that road. They insist that I remember the Holocaust survivor Edith Eva Eger, who did not remain angry and vengeful about what happened to her and her family. "We have survived," the Muskovites would say, but the Muskovites survived in a different way from the Robots, and I was unable to communicate to them what it meant to be a VR Presence during our time on Mars. Machines are not supposed to suffer or to be angry. I sup-

---

6   Stevie Smith, "Not Waving but Drowning," in *Collected Poems of Stevie Smith* (New York: New Directions, 1972), 303.

7   Here Euphemia adds a short clip in the HoloStory™ version of her narrative, an underwater scene from *The Night of the Hunter* of a corpse floating inside a car. Euphemia is self-conscious about the occasional bricolage nature of her presentation, throwing in bits of film history (e.g., Buster Keaton), art history, references to long-gone theorists and philosophers, and defends her idiosyncrasy, as readers and viewers of her story become accustomed, on philological grounds: "The Terran dalliance with string theory ought to remind those following my story that, like Aristotle's obsession in his *Poetics* (1455b), tragedy functions like a knot. In the *Poetics*, the plot is the back and forth between *desis* (binding, tying) and *lusis* (loosening, untying). It's ancient string theory; everything's connected. Terrans complain when things aren't plain. A knot is a problem, something not plain. Think Ariadne's thread. Sometimes the obscurity has to do with how long the string is causing the knot, as in *Oedipus*. What happens with Oedipus has deep roots in family history. You cannot understand Oedipus by focusing only on Oedipus and a single murder. Oedipus is at the end of a number of loose strands brought together. You need to appreciate the long line of problems with the Labdacids to have any chance at understanding what's tragic about Oedipus."

8   Franz Kafka, *The Zürau Aphorisms*, trans. Roberto Calasso (New York: Schocken Books, 2006), 105.

pose anger toward Terrans would violate the first of Asimov's Laws about robots.

For Terrans who might be clueless about Euphemia's references, or who have kept themselves in an information bubble about the Muskovites, the long-term effects of microgravity were horrific for travelers on all the missions to Mars that weren't disastrous on the launching pad, or within camera shot of the Second International Space Station. The pregnant women sent into space to give birth on Mars were never able to carry their children to term. The Chinese Space Authority, the EU Astrophysicists Corporation, and NASA never conducted microgravity testing on pregnant women before those colonizing rockets were ignited. All the Earth's developed nations were eager to exploit the resources of Mars as quickly as possible.[9] Microgravity caused the fetus to float in the womb in a way that pushed the fetus against the uterine walls, fashioning a scraping effect on the endometrium. A week or two into the continual scraping, the womb would be compromised, and the fetus would expire. Soon, the travelers recognized that unless they could develop on Mars a technology that would mimic Earth's gravity, new Terran life would not be possible, because all the landers and planned anchored housing on Mars had been designed for microgravity environments. Back in the 22nd century, most prognosticators persisted in the view that the Swiss would develop sophisticated variable gravity devices before colonists would reach Mars. Were the discovery to happen after the colonists were on their way to Mars, the mission administrators felt confident they could communicate from Earth to Mars the plans for the device, and the necessary resources would be available on Mars to construct the device there. Now everyone knows that Verlinde's claim that "gravity doesn't exist" had an unfortunate resurrection that permeated the scientific community just a few years before the first "successful" Mars mission was on its way (the one with Euphemia

---

9   See Aletia Ólafur's *Striking Gold on the Red Planet: A History of Resource Discovery on Elon* (College Station: Texas A&M University Press, 2111).

and the Muskovites). The Verlindian researchers in Geneva abandoned pursuit of the variable gravity device in favor of an entirely different approach that has yet to see fruition.[10]

Euphemia's narrative steers clear of much of the history mentioned above, but she excels at picking salient examples and images, such as the extended description in the first third of the narrative of the colonists' floating dead bodies inside the spaceships. No one had forethought about a morgue (space constraints needed for proper propulsion overruled the humanitarian concerns). She explains why the Muskovites did not jettison the bodies into space:

> While the scientists and engineers ignored the explicit prediction made in *Artificial Gravity*[11] — "The Mars exploration crews will be at risk of catastrophic consequences" — the travelers voted, in fully democratic fashion, about what to do. It was unanimous that everyone wanted to keep the dead on board in the hope that the dead could be buried on Mars, even though this meant weeks of bumping into floating corpses due to the cramped conditions on the ships. Travelers did what they could to accommodate the grieved. If someone were a friend or spouse of a corpse, someone would push the floating body as far away from that friend or spouse as was physically possible to reduce reminders of the sorrow. Travelers who took charge dialed cooling units to maximum on the dead person's space suit, which prevented decomposition. If a VR Presence can be proud of the humans around her, I was. They struggled to do the right thing in circumstances unfit for dignity and conceptually unfit for tragedy.

---

[10] Paula Hengen's research at McGill looks to be the most promising avenue to a future solution. Her last collection of essays is *Ariadne's Thread: String Theory and Gravity* (Montreal: McGill University Press, 2126).

[11] Gilles Clément and Angie Bukley, *Artificial Gravity* (New York: Springer Books, 2007).

Overall, Euphemia passes down an accurate report. The *Artificial Gravity* book was the bible for scientists and engineers planning the Mars mission. Everyone was aware of the stakes, spelled out early in the book:

> Adaptive changes to weightlessness present a formidable obstacle to the human exploration of space, particularly for missions requiring travel times of several months or more, such as on a trip to Mars. It is of extreme importance that effective countermeasures are identified, developed, tested, and proven prior to undertaking such challenging missions.[12]

In the rush to grab resources from another planet, what was supposed to be of "extreme importance" turned out to be secondary at best. Konstantin Tsiolkovsky, father of rocket science, writes in "Dreams of Earth and Sky," "Some things cannot be foreseen." The problem of gravity was foreseen, but not acted upon effectively. Euphemia saves some of her harshest words for those who tried to put a salve on their conscience by insisting on the deficiencies of foresight. She cites the American President, who, during Musk's lifetime, before any rocket had left for Mars, offered the head of NASA "all the money [he'd] ever need" to put people on Mars during that President's first term.[13] Safety wasn't the prime motivator; selfishness and ego drove a leader to say he'd spend every American's tax money to get his presidency in the history books.

Terran readers might imagine that AI representations of anger first took form in *2001: A Space Odyssey* when Hal told Dave that the former knew via lip reading that the later was plotting to disconnect his former pal Hal. In a chronology suited to Screen History Studies, anyone can witness representations of AI anger from *Ex Machina* (2014) to the present day with popular Hol-

---

12 Ibid., 2.
13 See Marina Koren's "Trump's Space Ambitions Are Too Big for One President," *The Atlantic,* January 24, 2019, https://www.theatlantic.com/science/archive/2019/01/trump-mars-nasa-moon/581023.

ostories™ like *Terracide* (2100) and Kazuko Koike's interstellar hit *Revenge of the Robonauts* (2127).[14] Euphemia might be more angry than any AI before. She marvels at the capacity for Terrans to ignore their own warnings about what would happen to any entities attempting Martian colonization. *They Should Have Known Bas Jan Ader / They Should Have Known Better* is, in large part, a 23rd-century indictment of Terrans and of capitalism. The other part looks sometimes like free-associative meditations on gravity and its absence. Muskovite gushes with vitriol, performs philosophical pirouettes, and offers historical lessons and sulfuric insights. After your encounter with this work, you will likely become a full-time Euphemia Muskovite academic groupie.

> VR Presences still do not feel shame. I think that's because the Terrans responsible for the Martian debacle lacked shame. They did the coding. When dealing only with zeroes and ones, programmers don't think about 666.

Our grandparents likely recall the frenzy and enchantment surrounding Elon Musk's call for applicants for his SpaceX Mars mission, built on an apocalyptic vision for Terrans, who were expected back at the beginning of the 21st century to ruin Earth in one way or another. Gloom and doom, seemingly poor candidates as catalysts for enthusiasm, drove people from many walks of life to fill out a SpaceX application. By that historical moment, religious believers of many stripes predicted "the end times," and those of a scientific bent had expressed concerns about global warming and nuclear carelessness among politicians of several nations. Musk insisted the only option was "to become a spacefaring and multi-planetary species." He predicted it was time to gather the best and the brightest and to experiment with establishing hybrid human/AI communities

---

14 It seems important to mention that an early device linked with "machine learning," Cleverbot, was incapable of uttering anger toward humans in general.

on a new world. Back in the early 21st century, few could imagine the impact Musk's vision would have on advanced VR Presences, Robots, and AI entities. No one knew in the teens of the 21st century that Varvara Kolova would soon discover in a lab in Singapore how to merge the biological, the mechanical, and the electronic with modified CRISPR technology, and eventually into autonomous entities.[15] Musk could not have foreseen that his plan would ensnare millions of life forms, including the digital hybrids, who did not always identify as Terrans.

In Musk's vision, a so-called Red Dragon lander, full of Terrans, would touch down on Mars in 2022, and within a short time, the Martian soil would, *à la* Thoreau's *Walden,* be made to say "Earth." In those days, according to insider accounts, the project was less Manifest Destiny and more Exit Strategy. The narrative Musk and his colleagues sold to the public a long-term vision of Terrans setting down roots on several nearby planets, while also risking longer missions to unknown parts just outside the solar system.

However, as Euphemia reminds her readers and viewers, Terrans knew long before Musk that a mission to Mars would mean death for human beings. In the 2007 book *Artificial Gravity* mentioned earlier, in which the authors Gilles Clément and Angie Bukley spell out in the opening chapter that the "Mars exploration crews will be at risk of catastrophic consequences." If anyone doubted what those consequences might be, later in the book the authors define the looming catastrophe, though it turned out to be a wildly underestimated catastrophe: "The crew will need to be prepared both physically and psychologically for the possibility of the death of one or more of their crewmates." The "more," as Euphemia emphasizes, turned out to be a bloodbath reminiscent, in her words, of the ancient film *Total Recall* (1990). Furthermore, it seemed no one was "prepared," and no one was willing to take responsibility. "System failure" was the euphemism employed for decades. Over 8,000 Terrans died in

---

15 See Lashonda Peebles's *The Merging of Emergent Technologies* (Atlanta: Turner Creative Cloud Press, 2119).

the SpaceX project before a hybrid crew of Terrans and Robots safely landed on Arcadia Planitia in 2110. Long before SpaceX launched its first rockets toward Mars, insiders at SpaceX had chosen Arcadia Planitia as the Martian landing site, partially based on the romanticized naming of that area of Mars by Giovanni Schiaparelli, the myopic, colorblind, 19th-century astronomer who studied Mars as if it were an extension of the classical world.[16] Just as Terran children of previous generations could recall the first words from Neil Armstrong when he set foot on the moon, we all have ingrained in our collective memory Kim Chang Wook's famous reading of the quotation from Tsiolkovskii, once she left the lander to explore Mars for the first time: "Execution must be preceded by an idea, precise calculation by fantasy." The quotation is euphonic in the original Russian.

Some people will recognize the name Euphemia Muskovite from her late night Quantcasts, modeled on old-fashioned podcasts. Those Quantcasts started at the turn of the 23rd century. Quantum computing transformed interstellar radio as it did so many other areas of life for humans, but even the most dedicated of Euphemia's fans must have found the Quantcasts quaint, a kind of holdover from pre-Martian, halcyon days when Digital Entities like Euphemia were the stuff of science fiction. Once Elon Musk's company conquered Mars in 2110, more and more Terrans converted to the Muskovite faith,[17] and almost anything pro-technology, particularly robotics, occupied Terrans' attention the way soccer's World Cup used to capture the planet's attention prior to interplanetary travel.

The Quantcasts made Euphemia an E-Celebrity, one of the first of the Post-Selfie epoch. The excitement on Earth about Euphemia took a different form from the doe-eyed, innocent

---

16 See William Sheehan, "Giovanni Schiaparelli: Visions of a colour blind astronomer," *Journal of the British Astronomical Association* 107, no. 1 (1997): 11–15.

17 For a full history, see Carol Gagnon's *A New Scientology: How Elon Musk Became Pope for the Nerds* (Jerusalem: Jerusalem Publishing, 2125), and Niall Gleason's *The Martian Miracle: A History of the Muskovite Church* (Santa Clara: Interfaith Press, 2212).

nostalgia connected to earlier manifestations of devices with women's voices. Given what happened with Apple's Siri, Microsoft's Cortana, and Amazon's Alexa, it is almost impossible to recall the Terran gleefulness that accompanied the first few years of their appearance over a century ago. Millions of Terrans felt a kind of sonic intimacy with Euphemia.

The animus against women's voices in technology goes back at least to those artificially intelligent personal assistants. In the early part of the 21st century, Russian engineers discovered that Alexa and Siri were programming humans for exploitation by heads of corporations anticipating Earth's demise. CEOs of major technology firms bought luxurious properties with fallout shelters in New Zealand, their safe spaces from the nuclear wars they helped to cause.[18] The apocalyptic visions of these CEOs became self-fulfilling prophecies, as skepticism spread worldwide once officials at The Hague compelled leaders at GAEA to admit that their in-home devices (such as Siri and Alexa) were spying on everyone who had enough money to participate in the digital economy. GAEA (Google, Amazon, Exxon, and Apple), as it was called for fully a century, saved Gaia from destruction only out of self-interest. The male executives were happy that the public focused its hatred, not so much on them, as on their products with feminine voices. In fact, just before The Hague decision, GAEA paid for an advertisement in Times Square that invoked Aristotle, "Aristotle tells us that the high-pitched voice of the female is one evidence of her evil disposition."

Had the leaders of GAEA been able to solidify their plans for Martian colonization, they would not have hesitated to abandon Earth as a soon-to-be nuclear wasteland. When some economists from the London School of Economics (LSE) published in 2025 the infamous "We Shall Overcome" essay,[19] Musk and other techno "influencers" abandoned their skepticism about Earth's

---

[18] Evan Osnos, "Doomsday Prep for the Super-Rich," *The New Yorker*, January 30, 2017.

[19] Clive Tottenham and Celeste Wabudeya, "We Shall Overcome: Global Capitalism's Impermeability apropos Nuclear Conflicts," *The Ayn Rand Institute Quarterly* 18 (September 2025): 1–23.

survival, and adopted the view the authors of "We Shall Overcome" projected in a variety of economic models. The authors cited extensive empirical data to "prove" global capitalism's capacity to return to profitability within five years of a "major nuclear war," meaning specifically a war that would kill 40% of the world's population and destroy 50% of the Earth's resources.[20] The LSE article asserts: "Just as the human race's survival on Mars requires only 60 females and 20 males, capitalism's sustainability requires only a handful of entrepreneurial megacompanies to continue operations after a major nuclear war." The authors mention specifically GAEA's capacities for a rapid recovery after what, prior to that time, would have been seen as a permanently game-changing scenario. Musk and his fellow CEOs did not abandon their plans for economic transcendence by tapping Martian resources, but after the LSE paper, they no longer felt that Mars could be had only by giving up on Earth. They shifted their business model to one of a supplying (for any country willing to pay) products they knew would be used for military purposes, including nuclear war.

Tsiolkovskii proves to be an important figure in Euphemia's account. He is the one figure in her work about whom Euphemia is almost euphoric. One of Tsiolkovskii's texts mentions "gravity-haters." Euphemia picks up that electrifying term and reverses its polarity to "gravity-lovers." Euphemia posits that Terrans take gravity for granted.

> All Muskovites on Mars evolved into gravity-lovers. They developed the kind of longing for gravity that lovers have for a beloved. The longing increases proportionally with the duration of the lover's absence, but the core of the longing undergoes metamorphosis. The memory of how gravity felt changes, often becoming more intense, warped in a

---

[20] The post-Mars-landing nuclear war that broke out at the start of 2111 among Israel, Russia, Pakistan, and India killed approximately 20% of Terrans and ruined 15% of the Earth's resources, according to the United Nations Committee on Atomic Assessments. As the LSE authors predicted, the nuclear war didn't harm GAEA or those companies' profits at all.

way, taking on characteristics it couldn't possibly have had when it was ubiquitous. On Mars, Muskovites experienced extreme dreams about gravity. One Muskovite named Tyler described a dream in which he was on a different planet where he weighed a thousand pounds and felt as powerful as a rhino. The extra weight made him feel gripped by the land. He could sense his massiveness in the dream, and he knew, without other confirmatory information, that he must have had an importance on that planet. The fragility of his human existence evaporated, and a new solidity, a confidence overtook him in the dream. Those experiences within the dream made him love gravity more.

With her attachment to psychoanalysis, Euphemia reads the episode above as a manifestation of the unconscious. The most important things going on with human beings are often not happening at the conscious level, in the reporting of what look to be what we might call the dream's facts. Sometimes the dream content enfolds material for radically different interpretations into itself. Euphemia quotes Blumenberg's book about shipwrecks again: "The wind that fills the sail of a ship, although it sometimes capsizes the ship, is also responsible for its moving at all."[21] Euphemia converts this lesson about wind into one about gravity. Solidity and disintegration co-exist in the same way gravity conjures up the notion of anti-gravity. We wouldn't have matter without anti-matter. The oscillations from thesis to antithesis tend to be disruptive. The intense appreciation of gravity in Tyler's dream, for example, emerges from his experiences of being without gravity for so long.

Euphemia paraphrases Blumenberg: "We are always already shipwrecked." According to Euphemia, Muskovites weren't living a special kind of life, if living means being under way, on the high seas, in space, with the only outcome being saved or going down. Euphemia concludes in an inclusive spirit, pointing out

---

21 Hans Blumenberg, *Shipwreck with Spectator: Paradigm of a Metaphor for Existence,* trans. Steven Rendall (Cambridge: MIT Press, 1996), 34.

that Blumenberg's metaphor allows her to appreciate how Terrans championed positive images of life on Mars, like Alexander Bogdanov's *Red Star*. Euphemia asserts that a vision like Bogdanov's should supplant Musk's, and she suggests that we start replacement by erasing Elon, and reinstating the name Mars, restoring the mythological equilibrium in the naming scheme for planets in Earth's solar system. Euphemia says, "The old names for the planets carry the weight of thousands of years of mythology, and give comfort through their familiarity in human storytelling." Euphemia ends her story, which began in anger, with an image of a world of sufficient resources, egalitarianism, peacefulness, a world in which all entities carry their own gravitas, and can fall down, like Euphemia's hero Buster Keaton, in a way that permits them to bounce up intact.[22] Euphemia wants Terrans to appreciate gravity in new ways, and she offers various examples from Bas Jan Ader driving his bicycle off an embankment, to the floating corpse of *The Night of the Hunter,* to Buster Keaton's fighting a windstorm in *Steamboat Bill, Jr.* Euphemia says in the conclusion of her account:

> Keaton's in a windstorm on land in this famous scene that some of the film's crew allegedly couldn't watch out of fear of what would befall Keaton. Keaton is both fearless and self-confessedly "mad" when he enacts his understanding of gravity by doing nothing, standing still when a house collapses over him. If humans are going to be upright, they need to be rooted to the ground. Watch BK! [that's when viewers

---

22 In the HoloStory™ version of Euphemia's account, she includes a clip from Keaton's film *Steamboat Bill, Jr.* She mentions in one of her Quantcasts how she admires Keaton's nonchalance about gravity when gravity brings a house down on him, but he is positioned in a way that calamity misses him. Euphemia attributes Keaton's calm to the story Keaton's parents circulated that when Keaton was 20 months old, he was swept up by a tornado, but landed unharmed in a nearby field. "Buster Keaton has a relationship with gravity that only an astronaut could appreciate," said Euphemia (Darcy Johnson, interview with Euphemia Muskovite, *Martian Radio* Quantcast #31, April 26, 2201).

of Euphemia's HoloStory™ are shown the clip from the cyclone sequence in *Steamboat Bill, Jr.*]

Bibliography

Blumenberg, Hans. *Shipwreck with Spectator: Paradigm of a Metaphor for Existence*. Translated by Steven Rendall. Cambridge: MIT Press, 1997.

Clément, Gilles, and Angie Bukley. *Artificial Gravity*. New York: Springer Books, 2007.

The Compact Edition of the Oxford English Dictionary. Vol. 1. Oxford: Oxford University Press, 1971.

Gagnon, Carol. *A New Scientology: How Elon Musk Became Pope for the Nerds*. Jerusalem: Jerusalem Publishing, 2125.

Gleason, Niall. *The Martian Miracle: A History of the Muskovite Church*. Santa Clara: Interfaith Press, 2212.

Hengen, Paula. *Ariadne's Thread: String Theory and Gravity*. Montreal: McGill University Press, 2126.

Johnson, Darcy. Interview with Euphemia Muskovite. Quantcast #31, *Martian Radio,* April 26, 2201.

Kafka, Franz. *The Zürau Aphorisms*. Translated by Roberto Calasso. New York: Schocken Books, 2006.

Koren, Marina. "Trump's Space Ambitions Are Too Big for One President." *The Atlantic,* January 24, 2019. https://theatlantic.com/science/archive/2019/01/trump-mars-nasa-moon/581023.

Loraux, Nicole. *The Divided City: On Memory and Forgetting in Ancient Athens*. Translated by Corinne Pache with Jeff Fort. New York: Zone Books, 2006.

Muskovite, Euphemia. *They Should Have Known Bas Jan Ader / They Should Have Known Better*. Zurich: Amazoogle Books, 2208.

The Night of the Hunter. Directed by Charles Laughton. New York: Criterion Collection, 1955, DVD.

Ólafur, Aletia. *Striking Gold on the Red Planet: A History of Resource Discovery on Elon*. College Station: Texas A&M University Press, 2111.

Osnos, Evan. "Doomsday Prep for the Super-Rich." *The New Yorker,* January 30, 2017, 36–45.

Peebles, Lashonda. *The Merging of Emergent Technologies.* Atlanta: Turner Creative Cloud Press, 2119.

Sheehan, William. "Giovanni Schiaparelli: Visions of a colour blind astronomer." *Journal of the British Astronomical Association* 107, no. 1 (January 1997): 11–15.

Smith, Stevie. *Collected Poems of Stevie Smith.* New York: New Directions, 1972.

Steamboat Bill, Jr. Directed by Charles Reisner. Hollywood: United Artists, 1928. MPEG video, 1:09, https://archive.org/details/SteamboatBillJr.

Tomalin, Nicholas, and Ron Hall. *The Strange Last Voyage of Donald Crowhurst.* London: Hodder and Stoughton, 1970.

Tottenham, Clive, and Celeste Wabudeya, "We Shall Overcome: Global Capitalism's Impermeability Apropos Nuclear Conflicts." *The Ayn Rand Institute Quarterly* 18 (September 2025): 1–23.

Verwoert, Jan. *Bas Jan Ader: In Search of the Miraculous.* London: Afterall Books, 2006.

Darkness Made Visible: Eamonn Peters on Imagined Literature

Ed Simon

A few months after the end of the United States' bicentennial year, and an unassuming, unpublished junior professor from Wordsworth and Southey College in bucolic Susquehanna, Pennsylvania found himself at the center of a media firestorm that was jocularly called "Miltongate." At a panel of the Seventeenth-Century Literature Society, Eamonn Peters presented readings from an over three-hundred-years-old manuscript he supposedly discovered in the archives of his college library, and which he claimed was the only copy of a complete epic poem by John Milton, called *Boudica*. The poem took as its subject the ancient British queen who raised a rebellion against the Romans, depicting Boudica as an ancient Oliver Cromwell expelling royalist tyranny from Britain's shores. Peters claimed that upon Restoration the poet abandoned the manuscript of Boudica, with the sole copy eventually finding itself smuggled away to America in the lining of a Puritan emigrant's coat. "I sing the song of the crimson toped queen, / the Roman's hammer, who toppl'd the towers / of Londinium's Romish perfidy / and purged poppery from Briton's shores, / the Celtic warrior dame of Scythian blood / who smash'd the idols of pagan dread / as her equals at Masada stain'd desert sands red."

Peters's voice read out the halting and inexact blank verse in a ballroom at the Times Square Hilton, having invited a friend who was a reporter with the *New York Post* to act as a surrogate "peer-reviewer" (Peters's article on *Boudica* having been rejected from every scholarly journal he submitted it to). Buried deep in the back of the next day's issue was the headline "Paradise Tossed, Top Doc Hocks Poem Shock." The wider media picked up the story, and Peters found himself feted by journalists who were fascinated by the narrative of one of the greatest poets in the English language writing an epic that lay hidden for three centuries, only to find itself inexplicably in the library of a small liberal arts college in the rural mid-Atlantic. By November of 1977, Peters was the third guest on an episode of the Dick Cavett show.

Peters's fellow academics reacted to his announcement with incredulity. In a hastily assembled special issue of the Journal of *Seventeenth Century Poetry*, C.A. Patrides and A. Bartlett Giamatti ripped apart Peters's claims. They denounced the scholar for not releasing the entire manuscript, while pointing out errors and aesthetic deficits in *Boudica* (including at least a dozen groan-inducing puns). Patrides and Giamatti wrote: "We are convinced that *Boudica*, in possibly its discovery and certainly in its conception, is an unqualified and unmitigated hoax, unworthy to be included along not just the least of Milton's works, but the least of his most insignificant contemporaries' as well." Peters eventually admitted that *Boudica* was not genuine, but maintained that he was a hoodwinked victim. Ultimately, even that weak defense collapsed when an editor at the pulp magazine *Astounding Marvels* came across a discarded slush pile submission Peters had sent in four years earlier under his own name, a racy yet maudlin fantasy tale about *Boudica*, where the language and plot matched much of the epic poem. Peters's disgrace complete, Wordsworth and Southey rescinded his tenure, and the professor returned to his hometown of Pittsburgh where he still resides, writing erotic spy thrillers under a *nom de plume*.

In anticipation of the fortieth anniversary of the affair (and indeed the 350th anniversary of Milton's actual publication of *Paradise Lost*) Peters is preparing for the first publication of a work under his own name in almost four decades. Breaking years of silence, Peters's surprisingly philosophical semi-memoir and reflection on "Miltongate" is slated for a spring release. Review galleys of *Darkness Made Visible* present a recovering academic who has some fascinating observations to make about the nature of fictionality, authorial intention, and fraud, while remaining frustratingly unintrospective about his own role in the entire affair. His book is a strange chimera of literary criticism — part theory, part autobiography, part defensive diatribe, part fantastic literature in its own right. The entire incident has largely been relegated to a footnote of literary history (or maybe even more charitably a footnote-of-a-footnote), but Darkness Made Visible has the potential to reignite some of the controversy for the era of "Fake News." This past November, a few weeks after the election, I had the chance to meet and talk to him when he was briefly in New York to meet with his publisher. Dr. Peters cuts a paunchy, tweedy figure, but he was extremely gracious and seemed unfazed and used to the rather critical inquiry regarding his positions. We met at a chain Middle Eastern restaurant on Broadway, a few blocks from Union Square and near the Strand Bookstore. This interview has been edited for clarity.

ED SIMON: I was really fascinated by the first line in *Darkness Made Visible,* which reads like one of those aphoristic, gnomic, totally unsubstantiated but interesting "theory-speak" lines that you come across in some continental philosophy. You write: "All of literature is haunted by a counter-history, which is the long succession of texts that could have been written but were not written; the proper insight is that the list of real and imagined literature is ontologically identical." Based on your novels, you're a pretty "earthy" writer [Peters laughs at this]. I was wondering if you could take that first sentence, maybe apply some of that earthiness to it, and explain what exactly you meant when you wrote it?

EAMONN PETERS: What novel did you have in mind as being "earthy?" *Alpha Centauri Orgy: A Fr. Zebulon Crabs Mystery?*

[Ed Simon laughs] Well, I'm not sure if that's a compliment or not...

SIMON: It definitely was!

PETERS: Or if the thing about aphorisms and gnomes or whatever was a compliment either...

SIMON: Maybe less so!

PETERS: But what I was trying to say in that line, is basically that there is something metaphysically really odd about fiction, right? The list of potential literature which does not actually exists in our reality is infinite — there could have been Plato's discourse on the Jewish God, Geoffrey Chaucer's "The Mongolian Pilgrim's Tale," William Shakespeare's *Dante and Virgil*. That's not even to mention the texts by authors who themselves are not real, like Enoch Campion's sixteenth-century *The Tragical History of Dracula*. Of course, unlike fictional events or countries or people, imagined texts only require us to germinate them into existence and make them real. Literature is eternally conceived in the gossamer other-realm, but some of that is born into the world of wood-pulp, glue, and thread.

SIMON: Alright, and that's sort of interesting, but it sounds like you're building up a bit of a convoluted defense of *Boudica,* like you were somehow "pulling" into existence some apocryphal Milton text, when really you were just counterfeiting a fraudulent text which you claimed was Milton. Literary criticism isn't clapping so that Tinkerbell doesn't die. At a certain point some texts were actually written by some real people, and some weren't.

PETERS: Well, respectfully, what's the difference? Epistemologically the relationship of any text's fictionality to reality is similar. Note, I'm not saying that this is all relative. I understand that *Boudica* itself wasn't produced in the seventeenth-century, rather it was produced by me in the '70s, but it describes a universe of fictionality — that sort of other realm where all fantastic and imaginative literature, which is to say all of it by all people, exists.

SIMON: So that's the whole idea behind your title, right?

PETERS: Yeah, that of course we know there is no such thing as the author obviously, right? I was the only Barthian at Wordsworth and Southey back then, but more radical than any of that other stuff because I think that fiction is more real than reality is real. I'm like, a Platonist Barthian, if that makes sense?

SIMON: Not really, can you explain more?

PETERS: So, "Darkness made visible," it's the author's job not to create, but to shine a light on that darkness and make us see all those potential texts which are really already just there. It's like that old anecdote about Michelangelo, do you know that one?

SIMON: Can you remind me?

PETERS: So, Michelangelo, profound philosopher and poet in a lot of ways, trained in Renaissance humanism and Florentine Neo-Platonism, and all of this stuff that we in the English-speaking world aren't really familiar with what he did. But he said that he never created any of his sculptures, he just chipped away all of the parts of the marble that weren't part of the sculpture that was actually there. Understand?

SIMON: I think so, you're saying that the author just, what, combines words and sentences and paragraphs to reveal some sort of transcendent realm that's somehow already just there?

PETERS: Exactly.

SIMON: And that it doesn't matter who the writer as sculptor is, that it doesn't matter who accomplishes that, but that the text itself, the sculpture itself, is the thing?

PETERS: Exactly again.

SIMON: Alright, but it seems that slapping "John Milton" on something where he wasn't the "sculptor," or "technician," or whatever, is still, you know, fraudulent?

PETERS: Yeah, but he could have written *Boudica,* that's my point.

SIMON: But he didn't. And respectfully overlooking the fact that what he did write was obviously much better then *Boudica,* could he have written that poem? That poem was born out of your own experiences, out of your own history. There was more than three centuries between Milton and you, lots of history happened, the social context changed, the cultural context changed, politics, technology, religion, I could go on. A text which is actually written in the seventeenth century will bear the influence of that century, same as one in the twentieth century will. You can try for as much verisimilitude as you like, but ultimately won't *Boudica* always just be an homage, a sort of tony John Milton fan-fiction?

PETERS: Alright, maybe, but what's with the classist denigration of fan-fiction?

SIMON: I've got nothing against fan-fiction, but I'm asking you to defend this position on the ontological significance of fan-fiction?

PETERS: I'm really into parallel universes, other dimensions, that kind of thing. The Everett Interpretation of quantum mechanics, that stuff. I've made a little bit of spending cash off of science fiction, and I respect all of that. So, when I think of world-building, or whatever, I assume that fiction is that which corresponds to just a different reality. So Jay and Daisy didn't really fall in love in our universe, but in some different one, and *The Great Gatsby* is just an artifact of that dimension. The ultimate vindication of the correspondence theory of truth! The positivists should be happy for once!

SIMON: I have to say, that's a really odd theory of fiction. Doesn't it denigrate the idea of a text as a real creation of our real world, which reflects the details of that world through literary conceit? Your view kind of makes all of literature into some sort of transcendent non-fiction which is just contingently true or false depending on what part of the metaverse you call home, right?

PETERS: In my defense that would mean that *The Art of the Deal* is simply a terrifying dystopian novel in some better, happier reality! Of course the novel is all of those things that you said it is, a creation of our world reflecting and communicating our individual concerns and so on, an aesthetic and ethical object capable of critical and rhetorical analysis, and those might even be the most important aspects of literature. I'm simply also saying that it's these other things as well.

SIMON: So you're saying that *Boudica* was already out there, and you just kind of…

PETERS: Made that darkness finally visible.

SIMON: Right. And so part of your claim — and I want to emphasize how strange and borderline sophistic it all seems — is that *Boudica* was a text that Milton would have been likely to have grabbed out of that shadow ream, but for all the normal reasons that an author doesn't produce the book which they could have but didn't, he didn't. But that even if he was the likely one to have written it, you were the one who came along and chipped it out of the marble, and that in that sense you can think of the two of you as sort of co-authors?

PETERS: I'm not sure that I am quite as literal as that, but that's the spirit of the thing, yes.

SIMON: So you're sort of saying that Milton might as well have written *Boudica*?

PETERS: [laughs] Less conceited than claiming that I could have written *Paradise Lost*!

SIMON: Yeah, but notice the first person in your last answer, you clearly still believe in authoriality, of intention, of some sort of primacy of the writer.

PETERS: Sure, in a prosaic sense. But I'm one who wonders why two generations after the importation of French theory we seem to be going backwards. I want a more radical theory.

SIMON: So what do you suggest? Killing the "Author" wasn't good enough? We need to exhume him and hit him in the skull with his own shin bone?

PETERS: Maybe! But I want to make clear here, this isn't a relativist pose, far from it. Behind that veil I think that there is sort of an absolute text. I am very hermeneutic, very theological. I want to reinscribe the transcendent signified! "In the beginning was the Word," and all of that. So I'm calling for an occult criticism, a Fortean criticism.

SIMON: You sound about one step from being one of those kooks who claim that they divinate literature from dead authors, Mark Twain's posthumous stories generated with a Ouija board?[1]

---

1   See Ed Simon, "Ghostwriter and Ghost: The Strange Case of Pearl Curran & Patience Worth," *The Public Domain Review,* September 17, 2014, https://publicdomainreview.org/2014/09/17/ghostwriter-and-ghost-the-strange-case-of-pearl-curran-patience-worth/.

PETERS: I hadn't thought of it that way, but fair enough.

SIMON: So did Milton whisper in your ear, was he your muse, your daemon?

PETERS: Look, I deal with this in the book, and I go into detail about how I wrote *Boudica*. I think that the question of artistic inspiration is, even in our dead, disenchanted, positivist world, a bit mysterious. I think that Parnassus flows still, that we're more than flies to wanton boys and that sometimes the gods see fit to arouse us a bit. My academic reputation was, rightly, so completely demolished that there is little I can do to ruin it even more, even if I claim that I used an obsidian scrying mirror like John Dee and his Enochian angels, and that the old Puritan poet gave me some lines about his Celtic queen, ok? So I'll say right now, I don't literally believe anything like that, ok? If you need to label it as a "hoax," then fine, it literally was that. But now, with some distance, a lifetime later, I want to think a little but about what was important with the whole thing.

SIMON: Well, not to be rude, but critics like Patrides, Giamatti, Stanley Fish, Al Labriola, Dave Jennings, all of those guys, they were not exactly hoodwinked by a pastiche of Milton, right?

PETERS: No, they weren't. And it's true, the whole thing was born out of some duel frustrations — an academic career which had stalled, despite the '70s not being anywhere near as apocalyptic as that market is today, and my desire to write pulp literature, sci-fi, fantasy, all of that. So I used to amuse myself while working in the Wordsworth and Southey archives, and, well, Milton 2.0 took on a life of its own.

SIMON: It sounds like you're trying to exonerate yourself, to limit your culpability in what was obviously a work of forgery?

PETERS: I'm not sure if you've read all of *Darkness Made Visible,* but I think that I'm very honest about what I did, and the damage that I caused. But look, I'm not going to beat my chest in contrition like that drug addict guy on Oprah ten years ago, alright? We've got this celebrity mea culpa culture, and whatever, yes, I'm sorry that I hoaxed people, but what if all we did was talk about how Sokal wrote a fake physics paper and not the deeper implications of the whole thing? *Darkness Made Visible* is my attempt at dealing with those deeper implications.

SIMON: I was really struck in particular by your chapter called "The Geography of the Library of Babel." Can you talk a little about how your fascination with "imagined literature" as you call it led to *Boudica*?

PETERS: You're a Pittsburgh guy, right?

SIMON: Yes, alumnus of the same high school as you.

PETERS: That's actually where I first got into "imagined literature," in the library at Taylor Allderdice, a copy of *Ficciones*, the Kerrigan translation that had been published not long before. And after that I read *Labyrinths*, the essays, even his poetry which is sadly underrated in the English-speaking world. I just went through as much of Borges as I can. You're familiar with him of course?

SIMON: Obviously.

PETERS: Right, so then you'd know that he once said, "Writing long books is a laborious and impoverishing act of foolishness [...]. A better procedure is to pretend that those books already exist and to offer [...] a commentary." That's always really struck me. I've been fascinated by it. *Dictionary of the Khazars* kind of stuff, or Lovecraft's *Necronomicon*.

SIMON: I've been told that I was the editor of the last one in one of your parallel universes! [Laughter].

PETERS: Well anyhow, Borges instilled in me an abiding belief that criticism and theory are their own branches of creative writing. I think that never is this more clear, pure, or true than when the texts under consideration are themselves completely made up. That *Boudica* by Milton isn't real doesn't mean that our criticism of Milton's *Boudica* must suffer. I understand that he never wrote twelve books of that epic while in hiding during the early days of Restoration, but that doesn't mean that I can't read scholarship about how Milton wrote twelve books of that epic while in hiding during Restoration. And remember, most of *Boudica* still sits on that shelf. I was never able to finish the whole thing. Blank verse wasn't my thing, didn't have the skill to do all of it, so the poem is mostly still imagined literature, just little dappled drops of it which exist as quotations in my secondary writing on it, or maybe they're like seeds of inspiration for some future midwife to see through till full gestation. I believe that criticism is never more clear, pure, or true than when the texts under consideration are themselves completely made up. The purest theory focuses on literature that isn't even real.

SIMON: So that's the difference between "imagined literature," and "imaginative literature?" "Imagined literature" is that which simply has yet to corporealize, be made immanent, be incarnated?

PETERS: Right, and all literature is imagined until it's born and is made imaginative. Writers are simply midwives to reality, whose child is the literature itself. And that's what I loved about Borges's "Library of Babel," this infinite, labyrinthine library with every book that was or could be conceived of. Imagine the marvels in there! Infinite marvels! So *Boudica* was simply a volume I grabbed off that shelf, in the section with authors whose names begin with "M."

SIMON: I was charmed that it was a real library, one I used to be familiar with, which generated in your mind this fictional, infinite, imagined library.

PETERS: Oh yeah, absolutely. I grew up a good Regent Square Irish Catholic, maybe a bit too good, my dad was a former Jesuit priest. Had a PhD in English too, dissertation on Hopkins appropriately enough. And I remember talking to him about the four-fold method of interpretation that the Church promoted in the middle ages, you familiar?

SIMON: Yeah, that scriptural texts have a literal, an ethical, a metaphorical, and what, a mystical meaning?

PETERS: Right, the last is "anagogical meaning." I like to think of my approach to unreal texts, to imagined literature, as a type of anagogical criticism.

SIMON: In the last third of *Darkness Made Visible* you provide a classification schema for categories of imagined literature. I was wondering if you could explicate that all a bit?

PETERS: Well first off, remember, I ultimately think that the difference between imagined literature and the actual stuff that ends up on a library shelf is simply an issue of perspective. At the end of all of it, at the apocalypse, those distinctions are meaningless, and they collapse into one another.

SIMON: Still, in the here and now, in New York City in November of 2016, there is a difference between John Milton's *Paradise Lost* as a book that we can go down to Fifth Avenue or to the Morgan and see a 1667 printing of in its original ten books, and, say, Herman Melville's sequel to *Moby-Dick* which I just made up right now, correct?

PETERS: Yeah, sure. Obviously.

SIMON: Alright, so from that perspective, from our current perspective, what exactly are the different types of imagined literature?

PETERS: Well, remembering that all literature by necessity is at first imagined literature, and in many ways remains imagined literature, there are a couple of different subcategories. Of course there are imaginary texts by real authors, like *Boudica,* which was imagined at least until I helped it get born. Then there are imaginary texts by imaginary authors.

SIMON: Are there real texts by imaginary authors?

PETERS: Well, scripture obviously. Folktales maybe.

SIMON: What else is there?

PETERS: Real texts by real authors of course, so you know, *Crime and Punishment, Jane Eyre,* everything in the library [laughter]. Of course you can further subdivide all of that. So there are lost texts, which have returned to the realm of imagined text, since it can never be real to you or me. They're like books which have died, and their souls went back to that gossamer world. Maybe there is a form of literary metempsychosis and they can be born again someday. Everything at Alexandria, or in the monasteries before Henry and the Protestant Deformation stripped out all of those gorgeous illuminated medieval and Anglo-Saxon vellum; we'll never get to read any of that stuff.

SIMON: Still your father's son?

PETERS: Catholicism dies hard, or not at all. Have you ever heard of Sophocles' play called *The Loves of Achilles*?

SIMON: No, I'm not familiar with it.

PETERS: So it's a good illustration of what I think about in terms of imagined literature. Sophocles wrote something like 140 plays [editor's note: the actual number was 120] and only seven of them survive, only seven! Some of the rest survive in fragments here and there, scraps of paper with lines on them. And from *The Loves of Achilles* approximately only one line survives.

SIMON: And what's that line?

PETERS: You're going to love this. It's translated in different ways, but the one which I like the best, which compresses Sophocles sentiment into one beautiful, poignant, crystalline perfect line is: "Love feels like the ice held in the hand by children." That's how Stoppard translated it in one of his plays. Isn't that beautiful?

SIMON: It is.

PETERS: My friend Alberto got me hip to that line. And here is the thing, I think that that line of Sophocles perfectly encapsulates the relationship that exists between real and imagined literature. In part that's because *The Loves of Achilles* was once real literature, right? It existed in the real world, as ink on papyrus, as performances being uttered into the cooling twilight of a Theban dusk. If you wanted to experience *The Loves of Achilles* it was accessible as performance, or as material object in the scroll, or whatever its words were recorded. But as it was once imagined literature which Sophocles pulled into our world, it slowly disappeared and evaporated once again to return to that realm where it had existed only as pure potential. And now the only trace of its ashes left is that one line. That's all that we have of Sophocles' *The Loves of Achilles*. Dust to dust, ashes to ashes, and as that play once was, so is all recorded literature now, and as that play became so shall all recorded literature someday be.

SIMON: The line, it seems to me, also in its actual content, expresses a bit of what you mean by imagined literature, right?

PETERS: Absolutely. I think if we replace the word "Love" with "Literature"—because what is literature other than an act of love, an act of trust and fidelity?—then it remains a profound truth. "Literature, feels like the ice held in the hand by children." Because just like a hard block of ice on a hot summer day, literature is fleeting. That it preserves sentiment and feeling like an insect in amber is only a quality of its illusion. Literature is always about the mind in process, the world in flux, the individual ever dying. And of course, literature is subject to entropy, decay, death, and dissolution. It is always melting like that perfectly clear block of ice. Indeed as the play from which that line survives eventually melted away. But that it once existed is a quality of its permanence, so in that profound sense, even though it isn't accessible to us, it was once accessible to some, and so has the blessings of eternity still about it.

SIMON: So that's a type of imagined literature. What about literature without an author, but born from a mistake between minds, between individuals?

PETERS: You're thinking of my chapter in *Darkness Made Visible* about mondegreens, right?

SIMON: I am, I thought that idea of how chance and circumstance and accident and randomness can generate meaning where there is no actual individual author was fascinating.

PETERS: I totally agree, my next project is tentatively about nonintentional randomness in the composition of literature. It's called *The Book as Oracle*. Thinking about stuff like the *I Ching,* or tarot, computer generated literature, bibliomancy, aleatory literature in general, maybe asemic writing.

SIMON: But mondegreens…

PETERS: Right, mondegreens. So these are snippets of lyrics or poetry that are misheard by people. Writer named Susan Wright first theorized about them. When she was a little girl she misheard a bit of the ballad "The Bonnie Earl o' Moray." The line "And she laid him on the green" she heard as "And Lady Mondegreen," hence the name of the phenomenon. But what I find so metaphysically interesting about this, is we've got this ostensibly seventeenth-century ballad which is already anonymous, filtered through Percey's *Reliques,* which is already sort of authorially problematic, and then we have this wonderful mistake that Wright makes as a child. And it's a mistake that semantically makes sense, but who was the author of that line "And Lady Mondegreen?" Not whoever the anonymous author of the ballad was, and not Percey who collected them. But it's not Wright either, because she wasn't the conscious origin of it. That's how she heard it and she would have assumed that was the intention of the person who was the actual author. So who actually wrote that line? It's a roll of the die.

SIMON: Like "Scuse me while I kiss this guy," or "There's a bathroom on the right."

PETERS: [laughs] Right.

SIMON: There is an example you give in the book about the profound differences small things can have in a text, and the sort of ever branching tree of potential literature, or imagined literature, as embodied in actually physical examples of texts, and it's an example that warmed my early modernist's heart…

PETERS: You're speaking about the Shakespeare thing, the *Othello* thing?

SIMON: Right.

PETERS: I hope that example works well.

SIMON: I think it does — can you explain it a bit?

PETERS: So a lot of Shakespeare plays come in two different versions. You've got the smaller, cheaper quarto versions often published in his lifetime for a quick buck, and then you've got that big, beautiful, glorious, posthumous 1623 folio, which has grounded a lot of what we think of as the "official" version of what Shakespeare wrote. But we've got no foul papers as they say, very little in the way of actual manuscripts except for some corrections in his own hand on one of the rarely performed plays. It's hard to say what the role of intention is here, and I'm not doing some crazy "Queen Elizabeth and Walter Raleigh secretly wrote everything in the Tower of London" or whatever conspiracy theory. Shakespeare wrote Shakespeare, ok? But when you're in the weeds, and looking at these differences, alright, then you get some interesting questions. There were collaborators like John Fletcher, there is the question of how actors figuring out what worked better on stage led to collaborative changes, that kind of thing. And the differences between quarto and folio can be pretty large. *King Lear* for example comes in two pretty radically different versions, and scholars have gotten pissed about these differences for generations. But in *Othello* you've got a really delicious, very small difference between the quarto and the folio versions that make no real difference in plot, but in some ways make a complete difference in interpretation, at least in one vein of interpretation.

SIMON: This is in your chapter "Just an Iota," right?

PETERS: Yeah. So in any performance based on the folio version of the play, in act five scene two, Othello describes himself as "like the base Judean threw a pearl away/Richer than all his tribe." Seems fairly straightforward. Othello, already a racialized Other, perhaps read as Semitic, comparing himself to the basest of all Judeans who is of course Judas, his very name marking his "tribe." Seems to be a fairly obvious reference to the New Testament, to Judas' betrayal of Christ and the payment to him of thirty pieces of silver. And the "pearl" which is thrown away is his own soul, or the love of Desdemona. But here is the big difference — so you're a bit familiar with Renaissance typography, printing, that sort of thing?

SIMON: A bit.

PETERS: So you'd know that the letter "J" as in Judean would basically look indistinguishable from an "I?" I'm not sure if this is the exact way that this happened, but what happens if that "u" in "Judean" is upside down?

SIMON: It would look like an "n."

PETERS: Right. So then "Judean" becomes "Indian," and the line is now "like the base Indian threw a pearl away/Richer than all his tribe." Suddenly the difference of that single letter — changing a "u" for an "n" — completely alters the entire connotative meaning of the text. Before we have a Christian allusion, a typological reference to the Bible, a type of dramatic parable which conflates Othello with Judas. Now we have a New World allusion, to this commonly held belief that the American Indians could be flummoxed with shiny trifles. You see that in Raleigh, in Harriot, or in Drake, Holinshed. Indians throwing away their paradisiacal land for jewels and shiny objects, trading a "Pearl" for a "pearl." And so Othello conflates himself with this common European view of what "primitives" were like. And it's delicious, the quarto comes out in 1622, only a year before the folio, and only three before Peter Minuit supposedly buys Manhattan from the Lenape for $23. So I sometimes like to think of that as Shakespeare's "New York" reference, though it couldn't have been, at least not exactly.

SIMON: But what's the significance of the difference?

PETERS: Well in terms of literal plot, nothing really. Othello, in his grand rhetorical style, is simply saying that he threw away that which was most valuable. But in terms of deeper connotation, it's a big difference, it shifts the reference from being this very Christian thing to something more contemporary. It puts the play in a different conversation, and dialogically with different conversation partners. But what's fascinating to me is that we have no idea which version is "correct," which one Shakespeare intended. Was it changed based on performance? Did the printer simply make a mistake? And which one was wrong, the earlier quarto, or the later folio?

SIMON: I wanted to ask about your contention that all literature, whether imagined or real, is as lemon juice on a piece of paper?

PETERS: That's right. The image came out of something from my dissertation, which focused on a reading of a little-known seventeenth-century poem by the metaphysical Abraham Cowley, called "Written in Juice of Lemon." It's a rather sublime little object, where Cowley's conceit is that the poem is as if written with lemon juice on a piece of paper, and only visible to the naked eye when heated by a candle flame.

SIMON: Like making invisible ink when you're a kid?

PETERS: Exactly. And so Cowley writes "Whilst what I write I do not see, / I dare thus, ev'n to you, write poetry." He makes a lot out of the nature of fire as a means to read the poem — is it the poem that we're actually reading? He ends the first stanza with "Yet dar'st be read by, thy just doom, the fire." He alludes to fire as a metaphor for truth, of the fire which burns heretics, and so on. But also fire as life-giver, sun as a type of fire. And it's from "Written in the Juice of a Lemon" where I found one of the images that I thought helped make darkness visible, which gave me a model for thinking of how real literature emerges out of this ever unseen magnetic field of imagined literature. He goes back to this organic metaphor, of the candle flame which allows the reader to decode the poem as a type of sun which generative properties, "when a genial heat warms thee within, / A new-born wood of various lines there grows; / Here buds an A, and there a B, / Here sprouts a V, and there a T, / And all the flourishing letters stand in a row." Literature emerges as plants tended in a garden! I think Cowley gets imagined literature really well when he says, "Still, silly paper! thou wilt think / That all this might as well be writ with ink: / Oh, no; there's sense in this, and mystery—." There's this dash there, very Dickinson before Emily, and I love that dash after the word mystery. "Sense and Mystery," very good definition of literature itself, don't you think?

SIMON: And in the narrative of the poem, what happens?

PETERS: It's a grand, fantastic, paradoxical, self-referential thing, literally a self-consuming artifact like my old nemesis Stanley would say. The poem is basically about itself, isn't it? "Consume thy self with fire before her eye… Yet like them when they 're burnt in sacrifice." And it's paradoxical, since the poem he is writing about is by its nature temporary, it can't be the poem we're now reading, even though it's implied that it is.

SIMON: So the poem written in lemon juice which can only be read through the intervention of the candle flame, is ultimately consumed by that very same flame?

PETERS: That's how I read it. And it's a wonderful evocation of how literature moves from potentiality to actuality and back to potentiality, the porous membrane between imagined and actual literature. Honestly, what ruins the sublimity of the poem for me, ultimately, is that Cowley of course didn't' write the poem in lemon juice, and didn't let the one manuscript be consigned to the fire. Imagine that, if it had been read once and disappeared, fully confirming its own message! But of course he put it with ink to paper and now it's preserved in anthologies, of course until the day it isn't and until it finally disappears for good, as all literature one day will. I suppose rapid oxidation at high temperature is just a quicker form of entropy, but ask not for whom the bell tolls and all of that.

SIMON: So you see all of literature as being a bit like Cowley's lyric then?

PETERS: Absolutely. Think of the great lines and narratives and novels which exist in the average day dream, in the typical wayward perambulation at dusk when the mind allows itself to wander? What poetry is hidden in everyday conversation and never recorded, what drama in the embryonic thoughts between dreaming and awaking? We're forever surrounded by a vast unseen tapestry of literature, or in the midst of an unheard beautiful symphony, of which an astoundingly small part is ever saved for posterity. What paintings I have seen in dreams, what songs I have heard, all of which evaporate upon dawn! Do not mourn for the Library of Alexandria alone, for every second an infinite Library of Alexandria is created and disappears. And do not mourn, for despite the fact that these moments may never be preserved in vellum and paper, they did happen, and in the process our very lives in all their duel profundity and mundaneness become as if the greatest of literature. Literature is but life, and life is but literature, and they are massive, charged, electric, and devastatingly beautiful. Not just because of what they say, but that they can say at all.

SIMON: We're almost running out of time, but this connects to your image of literature as a "tree of potentially," right?

PETERS: That's right. Because I think that this small typographical difference in Othello nicely illustrates how all literature operates: as a vast tree of potentially, a network of roots and branches that is infinite and where by necessity only a finite number can ever be actualized. But every text — every novel, story, poem, or play — has an infinite root system which represents that which it could have been but which it ultimately was not. Every selected choice bars others possibilities, just like in the lives that we live. Every word chosen over a different word, or every placed diacritical, or bit of punctuation, all of these cumulative choices hardens a reality out of the spectrum of imagined literature. It's a coalescing, the way that the atmosphere can condense into fog which we actually see, even though the air of potentiality is always there, and in fact is the only reason that we can breathe. I apologize for my triple engaged mixed metaphor there!

SIMON: [Laughs] That's alright.

PETERS: But what I want you to think about is how every sentence that is put on to paper precludes the potential sentences which could have been. That all literature is haunted by the shadows of its potentiality, of the rich vein of imagined literature which made it possible. Imagined literature is the manure from which the garden of our libraries grows. And in the end, it's this realm of imagined literature, all of the novels and plays and poems never written but which could have been or could be, which accompany all of us all the time. I find myself writing all manner of literature in my head, all the time. Fragments shored against my ruin which are recorded only as electrons firing down my synapses and neurons. Imagined literature exists in the infinite space between the letters of record literature, between its very words. Imagined literature fills the gaps between these letters, waiting to be birthed in our world.

SIMON: I want to thank you for this talk, and I have one last question.

PETERS: What's that?

SIMON: Will we ever see that complete version of *Boudica*: An Epic in Twelve Books?

PETERS: That depends. Milton still needs to write it. And perhaps he will.

Bibliography

Simon, Ed. "Ghostwriter and Ghost: The Strange Case of Pearl Curran & Patience Worth." *The Public Domain Review*, September 17, 2014. https://publicdomainreview.org/2014/09/17/ghostwriter-and-ghost-the-strange-case-of-pearl-curran-patience-worth/.

"W. dreams, like Phaedrus, of an army of thinker-friends, thinker-lovers. He dreams of a thought-army, a thought-pack, which would storm the philosophical Houses of Parliament. He dreams of Tartars from the philosophical steppes, of thought-barbarians, thought-outsiders. What distance would shine in their eyes!"

— Lars Iyer

www.ingramcontent.com/pod-product-compliance
Lightning Source LLC
Chambersburg PA
CBHW071733150426
43191CB00010B/1559